A. Bronson Feldman
Shakespeare, Marlowe, and Other Elizabethans

A. Bronson Feldman

Shakespeare, Marlowe, and Other Elizabethans

Editor:
Warren Hope

Laugwitz Verlag

To the Memory of John Thomas Looney

special issue no. 8 of NEUES SHAKE-SPEARE JOURNAL
All rights for this edition reserved by Verlag Uwe Laugwitz,
Matthias-Claudius-Weg 11B, 21244 Buchholz, Germany
www.laugwitz.com

ISBN 978-3-933077-62-2

Contents

Chapter 1–Who Is Shakespeare? What Is He?   6

Chapter 2–Shakespeare's Jester–Oxford's Servant   8

Chapter 3–Shakespeare Worship   16

Chapter 4–Kit Sly and the Unknown Lord   34

Chapter 5–The Making of William Shakespeare   56

Chapter 6–The March of Hamlet   81

Chapter 7–Othello's Obsessions   83

Chapter 8–Othello in Reality   100

Chapter 9–The Confessions of William Shakespeare   132

Chapter 10–The Marlowe Mystery   182

Chapter 11–A Preface to *Arden of Feversham*   269

Chapter 12–A Tyrant's Vein   284

Chapter 13–Thomas Watson, Dramatist   296

Appendix I–Oxford's Sole Acrostic   334

Appendix II–The Rape of Antwerp in a Tudor Play   335

Index   342

Chapter 1–Who is Shakespeare? What is He?

William Shakespeare is a pen-name, a *nom de guerre*, adopted by an English aristocrat who, for strong reasons hinted at in his *Sonnets*, concealed his identity as a dramatist behind the blank business face of William Shakspere of Stratford-on-Avon. The aristocrat–in the opinion of European and American researchers of high classical and scientific training–was Edward de Vere, Earl of Oxford (1550-1604). We know (from contemporary testimony of Harvey, Webbe, and Meres) that Oxford was the chief of Elizabethan courtier poets, and a dramatist of great merit, though none of his plays survive under his real name.

Oxford's lifelong interest in the stage expressed itself in patronage of several companies of players, including as I have proved elsewhere, the Lord Chamberlain's troupe to which Shakspere belonged and for whom Shakespeare wrote. De Vere's title of Lord Great Chamberlain of England probably suggested his taking the place of the Queen's Lord Chamberlain as director of her court theater, especially since the other Chamberlains were not deeply attracted by such work. He himself acted in at least one court masque. His biographer, B. Ward, has demonstrated the Earl's genius for masquerade, particularly his repute for wit and comedy, while showing that his life was actually tragic. He had to hide from royal fury, court disgrace, and creditors. But he also loved mystery and knew how to plot without getting caught. The story of his life provided the inspiration for Shakespeare's choice of plots for plays. On the basis of this fact Sigmund Freud seems to have decided that Oxford was Shakespeare.

Oxford began writing plays in 1576, after his return from travel in France, Germany, and Italy. He suddenly separated from his wife and wrote *The Comedy of Errors* to account for the divorce. [See Chapters 1 and 2 of Feldman's *Early Shakespeare*–W.H.] *Pericles* was his fantasy-contribution to their reunion, which did not last long or peacefully. [See Chapter 3 of *Early Shakespeare*–W.H.] He fell in love with Anne Vavasor (the Dark Lady of his *Sonnets*) and precipitated a feud which A. Feuillerat recognized as similar to the feud in *Romeo and Juliet*. Lord Burghley, his father-in-law (whom even orthodox scholarship identifies as the original of Polonius), reconciled him again to marriage, and tradition makes the event comparable to the scandal stuff in *All's Well That Ends Well* and *Measure for Measure*. *Hamlet* and *Othello* are even more autobiographical. *King Lear* is a dreamlike presentation of problems of Oxford and his three daughters and his two sons, one illegitimate. He wrote the tragedy in his last home, King's Place, within walking distance of the London playhouses he loved.

The dedication of *Venus and Adonis* indicates that the name of Shakespeare is an invention, as clearly as the pun-master who wrote it could tell the world. This explains the hyphen on the title pages of *Shake-speare's Sonnets* and the first quartos.

Courtier, soldier, scholar (and melancholiest of lovers), Edward de Vere was the first force in the Renaissance of the English theater. When he died in 1604 the theater declined, and the plays of Shakespeare that were staged were old (as Ben Jonson informs us). Not one of Shakespeare's works has been dated after 1604 except on flimsiest testimony. They all belong to the lifetime of Oxford, historically, artistically, psychologically.

Chapter 2–Shakespeare's Jester–Oxford's Servant

Robert Armin merited the tribute of Professor Baldwin of Illinois who called the philosophical clown "Shakespeare's Jester." (T. W. Baldwin, "Shakespeare's Jester," *Modern Language Notes*, XXXIX, December 1924). The character of Armin as revealed in his scarce scriptures and extolled by John Davies of Hereford in *The Scourge of Folly* (1610) appears to have been marked by fate for the roles of Touchstone, Cleopatra's Clown and King Lear's Fool. All lovers of Shakespeare are sure to love Robin Armin and sue to know him better. Every admirer of Edward de Vere will be delighted to learn that "Shakespeare's Jester" was also the avowed servant of the Earl of Oxford, whom Francis Meres in his *Wit's Treasury* (1598) named first of "The best for comedy among us."

The connexion between Oxford and Armin was discovered in a very rare quarto entitled *Quips Upon Questions*. Through the courtesy of Dr. Giles E. Dawson of the Folger Shakespeare Library I was able to study the copy of these *Quips* once owned by John Payne Collier.

Quips Upon Questions was reprinted in 1875 by Frederic Ouvry, with the name of John Singer on the title-page, because Ouvry had been convinced by the jocose J. P. Collier that Singer, the buffoon of the Lord Admiral's company, was "Clunnyco de Curtanio Snuffe." (Most of Joseph Knight's article on John Singer in the *Dictionary of National Biography*, XVIII, 312, is concerned with *Quips Upon Questions*. Knight observed, "The ascription of this work to Singer, probable enough from internal evidence, rests upon the unsupported authority of Collier." What internal evidence Knight had in mind remains enigmatic.) Collier believed that the Admiral's men were playing at the Curtain theater in 1600. It is now well known that they were performing in that year at the Rose and the Fortune. (Joseph Quincy Adams, *Shakespearian Playhouses*, Boston: Houghton, 1917, pp. 156-157). Equally well established is the identity of the Clown of the Curtain with Robert Armin. (Baldwin, *op. cit.*, p. 447.

QVIPS

VPON QVESTIONS,
OR,
A Clownes conceite on occasion offered.

bewraying a morrallised metamorphoses of changes
vpon interrogatories: shewing a litle wit, with
a great deale of will; or in deed, more
desirous to pleafe in it, then to
profite by it.

Clapt vp by a Clowne of the towne in this last restraint,
hauing litle elfe to doe, to make a litle vse of his
fickle Muse, and carelesse of carping.

By Clunnyco de Curtanio Snuffe.

Like as you list, read on and spare not,
Clownes iudge like Clownes, therefore I care not:
Or thus,
Floute me, Ile floute thee; it is my profefsion,
To iest at a Iester, in his transgrefsion.

Imprinted at London for *W. Ferbrand*, and are to
be fold at the figne of the Crowne ouer againft
the Mayden-head neare Yelqhall.
1 6 0 0.

E. K. Chambers, *The Elizabethan Stage*, Oxford: The Clarendon Press, 1923, II, 300). For "Clonnico de Curtanio Snuffe" appeared on the title-page of the popular treatise, *Foole Upon Foole, or Six Sortes of Sottes*, also published in 1600 by William Ferbrand, and this treatise is unquestionably the work of Armin, the jester of the Lord Chamberlain's company. (Alexander B. Grosart, editor, *The Works of Robert Armin, Actor*, London: privately printed, 1880, Part I).

When Professor Baldwin credited Armin with the writing of *Quips Upon Questions* he had not seen the book. He said that it "should be carefully examined for further biographic detail." (Baldwin, *op. cit.*, 447 n.) If he had scrutinised the 24 leaves of the volume he might have urged examination of it not only for facts of the life of Armin but for revelations of Tudor theatrical history. Sir Edmund Chambers surveyed the *Quips* and found a single detail which he thought worthy of inclusion in his biography of the comedian in *The Elizabethan Stage*: "The author serves a master at Hackney." (Chambers, *loc. cit.*) Unfortunately, Sir Edmund left the remark without commentary. Yet it held the clue to several major riddles that have perplexed historians of Shakespearean drama. The passage from which the item was derived occurs in Armin's mock-dedication of the *Quips* to "Sir Timothy Trunchion alias Bastinado," whose aid the humorist requires against victims of his wit who may be scheming to ambush him. Our Robin wanted the weapon particularly for Tuesday, 25 December 1599. (The date is determined by the reference to Friday in the mock-dedication as 28 December.) For "On Tuesday I take my Iorney (to waite on the right Honourable good Lord my Maister whom I serve) to Hackney." (*Quips Upon Questions*, Ouvry's edition, Alj.)

Since the Lord Chamberlain's players were in possession of the Globe before September 1599 (Adams, *op. cit.*, p. 85), Professor Baldwin surmised that Armin was showing his quality at the Curtain in December in the service of another Lord. William Brydges, Baron Chandos, is known to have employed Armin sometime between 21 February 1594, when he succeeded to the title, and 4 August 1600, when the Stationers registered the *Second Part of Tarleton's*

Jests which announced that Robin was exhilarating the Globe. (Armin's. prefatory letter to Gilbert Dugdale's *True Discourse_on the Poisoning of Thomas Caldwell*, 1604, appeals to Mary Chandos, Lord William's widow, to remember the actor's "service to your late deceased kind lord." In *Poole Upon Foole* Armin told how he and the "Lord Shandoyes players" had wandered in Worchestershire.) But Professor Baldwin's conjecture that Armin went in motley for Lord Chandos at the Curtain in 1599-1600 seems to contradict our present knowledge of that nobleman's actors. There is no testimony extant that they ever performed in London; all records of their exhibitions deal with provincial tours. (John Tucker Murray, *English Dramatic Companies*, London: Constable and Company, 1910, II, 32). Moreover, if Armin's master when the *Quips* were composed had been Lord Chandos, the jester would have journeyed to wait on him at Sudeley Castle, far from Hackney.

Sir Edmund Chambers maintained that the Curtain was occupied by the Lord Chamberlain's troupe in 1599. (Chambers, *op. cit.*, II, 403) His argument has not been disputed. When Guilpin's *Skialetheia* (S. R.–8 September 1598) reported the playing of Plautus and "the pathetic Spaniard" at the Rose and the Curtain, the two leading companies of London were the Admiral's and the Chamberlain's. Marston's *Scourge of Villainy* (1598) connected the popularity of *Romeo and Juliet*, a triumph of the Chamberlain's men, with "Curtain plaudities." The fact that the latter were active at the Globe in the autumn of 1599 does not exclude the likelihood of their use of the Curtain. Before they moved to the Globe they had possessed James Burbage's Theater, and strained its resources to a point where they were compelled to use the Curtain as an "easer." When Armin changed his nom de jeu to "Clonnico del Mondo Snuffe," in the 1605 edition of *Foole Upon Foole*, he clearly indicated that he played in the Chamberlain's dramas at the Globe the same roles that he capped and belled for them at the Curtain.

The nobleman whom Armin called "the right Honourable good Lord my Maister" could not have been George Carey, Baron Hunsdon, who is generally regarded as the patron of the Shakespeare troupe in 1599-1600. Hunsdon held the office of Lord Chamberlain of the Queen's Household from April 1597 to December 1602. (E. K. Chambers, "The Elizabethan Lords chamberlain," *Malone Society Collections*, London, 1911, I, 39. The chronology of the Queen's Chamberlains in the present essay is taken from the same model study, page 39.) During those years he lived in the Blackfriars precinct of London, never in the suburb of Hackney. As a resident of Blackfriars, in November, 1596, he signed a petition to the Privy Council against the design of James Burbage for the restoration of the theater which had once dazzled there under the direction of John Lyly and the Earl of Oxford. (Ashley H. Thorndike, *Shakespeare's Theater*, New York: The Macmillan Company, 1916, pp. 333-335.) Although Hunsdon was nominally in charge of the royal entertainments, there is nothing to prove that he was an encourager of the stage of Shakespeare. Nashe's dedication of *Christ's Tears over Jerusalem* (1594) to Hunsdon's daughter gives the impression that the house of Carey offered cold comfort to devotees of cakes, ale and comedies. Henry Carey, the first Lord Hunsdon, who had served Elizabeth as Chamberlain from June 1583 until July 1596, was friendlier to mummers. "He lacked most of the literary culture of his class," (Chambers, *The Elizabethan Stage*, IV, 316) but extended protection to the actors who wore his livery at the Cross Keys inn during October 1594 when the Puritan magnates of the city persecuted them. (Chambers, *The Elizabethan Stage*, IV, 316) Between 1578 and 1583 old Lord Henry did maintain a household in Hackney, at King's Place. But Robert Armin was then only a goldsmith's apprentice.

There was but one literary nobleman dwelling in Hackney when Armin was master of motley at the Curtain. Edward de Vere, Earl of Oxford, the Lord Great Chamberlain of England, transferred his home to King's Place, Hackney, from Stoke Newington in 1596. (B. M. Ward, *The Seventeenth Earl of Oxford*, London: John Murray, 1928, p. 319.) Seven years before, this courtier, poet and dramatist had fallen in disgrace with fortune and men's tongues as a result of political and extra-marital scandals. His fortune improved by marriage with the maid of honour Elizabeth Trentham, but he never dispelled the shadows on his name. The curious way in which Armin alluded to him in the *Quips*, evading mention of his master's title, was not unusual. In March 1603 Henry Clinton, Earl of Lincoln, spoke of him in the same circumlocutory way to Sir John Peyton, Lieutenant of the Tower. He told Peyton, according to a letter of the Lieutenant, he had been "invyted... by a great noble man to hacney, where he was extraordinarily fested, at the which he muche marvayled, for that ther was no great correspondence between them, this noble man having precedence of hym in rancke (where by he towlde me I myght knowe him, ther being onely but one of that qualytye dwellying there.") (*State Papers Domestic*, 1603, quoted by Norreys Jephson O'Conor, *Godes Peace and the Queenes*, Cambridge, Mass.: Harvard University Press, 1934, p. 106.)

In the decade 1580-1590 a company of mummers led by the mercurial Duttons had toured the provinces wearing the livery of the brilliant Earl of Oxford. All trace of the troupe disappeared in the next nine years. Then in 1600 the anonymous drama called *The Weakest Goeth to the Wall* was printed – "As it hath been sundry times plaid by the right honourable Earle of Oxenford, Lord Great Chamberlain of England his servants" (so runs the title-page of the play's earliest extant copy, dated 1618). The lost tragedy of *George Scanderberg* was registered by the Stationers in 1601 with a note that it had belonged to Oxford's men. (Chambers, *The Elizabethan Stage*, II, 102). Is it possible that Armin joined the Earl's players after leaving Lord Chandos's company and before entering the Lord Chamberlain's? In that case we would have to imagine our "Clonnico" with the Oxford troupe sharing the Curtain with the Chamberlain's men in 1599. The chronicles of the Elizabethan theater would indicate that the Earl's own actors never pretended to the grandeur of a house like the Curtain. A letter of the Privy Council of March 1602 addressed to the Lord Mayor of London, designates the tavern named "the Boar's Head as the place they have especially used and do best like of." (*Ibid.*, IV, 335). Not until they united with the Earl of Worcester's players in the spring of 1602, we are told, did they venture to exhibit their quality on a grand stage, such as the Rose. When they performed at the Rose they were called Worcester's men, and William Kempe, formerly of the Chamberlain's company, was the star comedian. Armin's name is not associated in extant documentation with the Worcester group, only with the Chandos and Chamberlain companies. And contemporary allusions mark none but the Lord Chamberlain's servants as the receivers of Curtain plaudits when Armin flourished there.

How could our man of motley have served at the same time the melancholy Earl in Hackney and the Lord Chamberlain at the Curtain? That is the question.

The best answer that occurs to me is that "Lord Chamberlain" meant the Earl of Oxford (who was Lord Great Chamberlain of England) almost everywhere except perhaps at Court. Moreover, it is evident that acting groups were not invariably known by one patron's title, and that special casts were occasionally assembled from different troupes to fill special engagements. The opposition of the Puritan administration governing the City of London to theatrical affairs generally would also account for these otherwise mystifying changes in company names and switches in professional personnel. One thing is absolutely certain: standardization in the recorded designations of the various Elizabethan acting groups cannot be taken for granted. For example, as Lord Chamberlain of the Royal Household, Lord Hunsdon is assumed to have had the task of satisfying Her Majesty's predilection for drama. But it has yet to be proved that either the first or second Lords Hunsdon organized the splendid cry of players who called themselves the "servants of the Lord Chamberlain." The company emerged to public light in 1594, to eclipse the Queen's own histrions; and Sir Edmund Chambers has declared that the interval of four or five years between the last available record of Lord Hunsdon's actors properly so called (at Maidstone in 1589-1590) and the emergence in 1594 "renders improbable any continuity" between the former band and the famous Chamberlain's group. (*Ibid.*, II, 193). The two Hunsdons as Chamberlains of the Royal Household ostensibly sponsored the company at Court. So did the aged Puritan, William Brooke, Lord Cobham, when he held the office of Her Majesty's Chamberlain after the first Hunsdon's death, from August 1596 to March 1597. Yet no scholar has depicted Cobham as a patron of the mummers who confused his martyred ancestor Oldcastle with Shakespeare's Falstaff in the mind of London. Both Cobham and the Hunsdon's must have heartily consented to the supervision of the company's personnel and productions by the histrionic Lord Chamberlain of England. Henry Carey's duties of military command on the Scottish border would not permit him much time for the rituals of Thalia and Thespis; his son George was severely ill during the final three years of the Tudor dynasty. The Earl of Oxford was thus the sole "Chamberlain" in the realm capable of directing the Shakespeare troupe.

The ambiguity of the title "Lord Chamberlain" was manifested in legal documents of the time. In a Chancery suit of claim by lease for the manor of Much Hormeade the estate was called "the inheritance of Edward de Vere, Earl of Oxford, lord chamberleyn." (*Calendar of Proceedings in Chancery in the Reign of Elizabeth*, vol. I, p. 185.) In the correspondence of Robert Cecil, Lord Cranborne, there are several allusions to the "Lord Chamberlain" which appear to signify his brother-in-law, Earl Edward. There is a letter of 1 July 1603 by Mrs. Hicks, perhaps the wife of Cecil's private secretary, pleading for help in collecting money owed by "my Lord Chamberlain." The main security for the debt of this Chamberlain was an assignment of property at Castle Hedingham in Essex, the birthplace of Oxford. (*Calendar of the Manuscripts of the Most Hon. the Marquis of Salisbury*, XV, 164. The significance of this item and the preceding one was first indicated by Charles Wisner Barrell in "Lord Oxford as Supervising Patron of Shakespeare's Theatrical Company, " *Shakespeare Fellowship Quarterly*, July 1944, V, 40.) When the mummers of Armin's company uttered the title of Lord Chamberlain they certainly meant the master in Hackney. *Touchstone* is the chief witness to the truth of this idea, with *Quips Upon Questions*. "Shakespeare's Jester" was Oxford's servant. So, indeed, was William himself.

Chapter 3–Shakespeare Worship

For three hundred years a religion centering in the popular image of William Shakespeare, Gent., of Stratford-on-Avon, Warwickshire, has enjoyed ever increasing fidelity. The existence of the cult was first publicly acknowledged by Ben Jonson (about 1630), who jealously observed that the actors of London adored the gentleman from Stratford despite the criticism of Jonson and his classical friends. To protect himself against the charge of envy, the critic vowed that he had loved the man Shakespeare and honored his memory, "this side idolatry, as much as any." We have too little knowledge of the forms taken by the idolatry at this time. A century had to pass before it emerged into national light, in full panoply of dogma, ritual, and shrine. Babcock's *Genesis of Shakespeare Idolatry* shows how it survived the rationalist period and triumphed over it. But there has yet been no investigation of Shakespeare worship as a variety of religious experience, as an enigma of psychology.

The primary rationalization used to account for the international devotion to the divinity of the Avon is that people everywhere deeply appreciate his services to drama and world art. This claim cannot be taken seriously. If the hundreds of thousands of people who travel annually to Stratford were actually lovers of Shakespeare's work, there would be a greater interest in the production of his plays in their communities. They would moreover manifest an almost equal passion for the literature of his companions in literature, the great dramatists of his own time and those of prior and sequent times. The fact is, the worshipers of Shakespeare care less for poetry than they do for the theatre. And the better educated among them seldom know more of his work than a handful of trite quotations, usually remembered out of context, and occasionally distorted in a grotesque way. It is no accident that most of the plays of Shakespeare's prime survive off the stage and are rarely read outside the experts' libraries. Few of his devotees have looked into his *Measure for Measure*, *Coriolanus*, *Timon of Athens* – to mention just three examples – with any desire to do more than look. We cannot help noticing that the upholders of the cult stalwartly resent any reminder of their ignorance. Ordinarily they will admit with cheer, as one Hunter did in a volume on the Tercentenary Festival of Shakespeare at Stratford, that their understanding of the writer is limited and superficial. They find a mysterious bliss in the ignorance, and many would echo Hunter's avowal: "But from what I do know of his works, I can say with all due reverence, blessed be God for Shakespeare." What they do know of his works never leads them to any examination of the question of the poet's attitude to God, piety and skepticism, which perplexes so many of the learned in his plays. When they bless God for Shakespeare they have something else than literature on their hands. Could it be the personality behind his plays that fascinates and humbles them?

Brown and Fearon (*This Shakespeare Industry*) think that the reason for Shakespeare's legion of religious followers lies in the fact that his name has been "dinned into the general ear as one of the best and noblest of Englishmen." This, of course, would not explain why the name rings sweetly to the ears of Germans, Russians, Irishmen, and other nationalities not reputed for reverence of Englishmen. Besides, the argument is simply untrue so far as England is concerned. The general ear of that country has been dinned for ages by legends of Shakespeare's ignobility and sins. Every biography of the god dwells on the tales of his deer-thieving and venereal adventures, reports how he persecuted debtors for pence, hoarded grain during time of famine, and schemed to get a coat of arms on false pretenses. Every revelation since the great researcher Halliwell-Phillipps uncovered the main facts of his life that we now possess has only served to intensify the uneasiness that all worshipers of Shakespeare feel in the study of his character. Certain scholars have openly confessed a feeling of gladness over their ignorance of his personality. The late Horace Furness, editor of the monumental Variorum edition of Shakespeare's works, referred to one evidence of academic nescience about the dramatist as "another happy instance of our utter ignorance of Shakespeare's mortal life." Most of the books alleged to be biographies of the Stratford idol are made up of laborious speculation, and not a few of them are mere fictions. Witness the portrayals of Shakespeare as a country schoolmaster, a rural tragedian, a nobleman's page, a law student, a soldier, etc. Not one of these pictures bears a single fact to support it. Mark Twain compared the lives of Shakespeare that he read to reconstructions of prehistoric monsters–a small quantity of bones and a huge fabrication of plaster, two or three paragraphs of authentic statement and heaps of pages of pure fantasy. Attempts to deduce the personality of the poet from his writings, such as Frank Harris made in his "Tragic Life-Story" of *The Man Shakespeare* and Georg Brandes in his larger but hardly more illuminating book on the Bard, have not won favor in the eyes of Shakespeare worshipers, whether erudite or not.

It appears that the upholders of the cult do not want to know the truth about their deity. Dearer to them than any fact of his earthly career is a vial of water from the Avon or a splinter from the mulberry tree he is said to have planted by his home. The waters of Stratford's river, according to Brown and Fearon, "are deemed so holy that American Shakespeareans will actually send for bottles of this magic fluid, believing it to be an elixir." As for the famous mulberry tree, Washington Irving declared that so many articles of furniture and relics have been manufactured from it that the tree "seems to have as extraordinary powers of self-multiplication as the wood of the true Cross."

In the reverence for relics like the Avon water-bottles and the mulberry commodities we recognize the signs of real religion, which abhors researches into the terrestrial activities of the individuals it adores. The spirit of it glows in the verses that O. W. Holmes wrote for the dedication of the fountain erected at Stratford in honor of Shakespeare by an American millionaire. In eighty-odd lines of rapture Holmes extolled "This holy fount, whose rills from heaven descend," and put its "baptismal dew" in the same class with "Horeb's rock the God of Israel clave!"

In the same spirit, but with less gravity, David Garrick hailed the Jubilee for "Avonian Willy, bard Divine," held at Stratford in 1769.

His friend James Boswell deplored the omission of theological exercises from that event. He "wished that prayers had been read or a short sermon preached. It would have consecrated our Jubilee," he said, "while gratefully addressing the supreme Father of all Spirits, from whom cometh every good and perfect gift." There was no regret over the failure to play any of Shakespeare's works at the festival. Garrick called the dramatist "the God of my Idolatry", but his piety did not prevent him from acting versions of the plays which Shakespeare would not have recognized. It was not the work that Garrick idolized. Nor was it the man. It was a spirit, a creature of his own imagination, the projection of his ego ideal. Because this ideal was essentially identical with the statue erected in the unconscious vanity of his fellow Englishmen, Garrick's god became the god of all men who shared the secret aspirations of the English. I say secret, for if the faithful were conscious of the aspirations that lead them to worship Shakespeare, they would not account for their religion by rationalizations.

It is the remoteness from reason that makes the prevalent attitude to Shakespeare one of piety, of faith. If the believers became aware of the real motives of their cult they might recoil in shame, disgust or horror, as Henry James suspected when he probed the Shakespeare myth in his little masterpiece "The Birthplace." The chief psychologist among American men of fiction once declared that he was "haunted by the conviction that the divine William is the biggest and most successful fraud ever practiced on a patient world." He expressed part of his sentiments about the divinity in "The Birthplace," while scrupulously refraining from taking the name of the dramatist in vain. The name Shakespeare never appears in his story, only pronouns of capital awe, like He and Him and His.

James also employed the phrase "the Presence" to indicate his story's central figure, its ghost. Nobody can mistake it; he defines the birthplace itself as a national shrine, revered by the hero, a librarian, as "the most sacred known to the steps of man, the early home of the supreme poet, the Mecca of the English-speaking race." These words practically echo the expression of the actor

Henry Irving at the dedication of the American memorial fountain in Stratford, where he asserted that "The simplest records of Stratford show that this is the Mecca of American pilgrims...." James depicted his librarian as a gentleman afflicted with a profound desire to know the human nature of Shakespeare, not content with adoration of his divinity. Appointed curator of the national shrine, he prowls its rooms by night, seeking some spiritual contact with the man whom his employers supposed had been born there. Like Delia Bacon, the American lady who roused the first big controversy over the question of the actual authorship of the Shakespeare poetry, James's hero hunts a ghost. The curator also goes nearly insane with questing for the personality behind the myth. He is bothered by the way his pilgrim customers regard the "Birthplace," ignorant of the bare facts about the building, and jealously shielding their ignorance against the light he ventures to give. The librarian soon realizes that not a single particle of proof exists to show that the building celebrated as the native house of Shakespeare was in truth his birthplace. He is aware that scholars have exhumed documents showing that the idol was probably born elsewhere. Nevertheless, he is paid, and admonished by his government paymasters, to teach the travelers to the British Mecca that here indeed the supreme dramatist of the race first opened his eyes on the world. The poor bookworm is duty-bound to display to the pilgrims the very room of the blessed event. "The Holy of Holies of the Birthplace," James records, "was the low, the sublime Chamber of Birth, sublime because, as the Americans usually said – unlike the natives they mostly found words – it was so pathetic." A good deal of the pathos consisted in the sheer emptiness of the chamber, James points out. For it remains empty, except for the alleged "Fact."

To satisfy the doubting Thomases among the pilgrims, the owners of the shrine had filled the building with a multitude of things more or less pertaining to the poet, mainly irrelevance and swindle. The librarian's soul is sickened by it all. "None of Them care tuppence about Him," he is confident. "The only thing they care about is this empty shell – or rather, for it isn't empty, the extraneous preposterous stuffing of it." But what was the secret of the shell? That is the question he tormented himself with on his nights of insomniac walking around the sacred place. What aroused the genuine religious emotion in the hosts of visitors who paid the admission price? What had inspired the "Princess of Stuart and Plantagenet blood, destined to wear an imperial crown," as the French ambassador Jusserand wrote, to fall on her knees at the threshold of the house?

According to James, or rather his librarian, "What they all most wanted was to feel that everything was 'just as it was,'" when the god was born, that is, lowly and poor. In short, the pilgrims were seeking a modern embodiment of the sacred manger of Bethlehem, and were moved by an impulse similar to the passion of the faithful at the so-called birthplace of Christ.

Why Shakespeare should be uplifted to a position next to Christ in the fantasy of the tourists at Stratford, James does not or cannot explain. He seems to be more concerned with the blasphemy implicit in the English Mecca. He can hardly hide his indignation over the intellectual oppression of his hero, the administrative demand that the curator tell his audience infantile religious lies. "They insisted on your committing yourself. It was the pound of flesh." The parallel James makes between the curator's wage-contract and Shylock's bond in *The Merchant of Venice* bears oblique testimony to the novelist's conviction that the Stratford idolatry was somehow an insult to Christianity.

Yet James, too, links Shakespeare with Christ, having in mind the artist himself, the genius, whose creations help to enlighten and liberate mankind from brutality and darkness. "There was somebody," a live man, who worked out the Shakespeare poems and plays, James makes his hero remark toward the end of the tale. "But They've killed Him." The philistines, the enemies of genius, the profiteers from superstition, crucified him. "And, dead as He is, They keep it up, They do it over again, They kill Him every day."

This interpretation of the myth by another great artist has naturally not appealed to the majority of critics and collegiate commentators on Shakespeare. Against the ironies of the artists who write about the Stratford cult, against Irving, Coleridge, Emerson, Mark Twain, Walt Whitman, Henry James, the uncreative raise an outcry for … facts. They seek to silence the iconoclasts by demanding facts. Meanwhile they continue sedulously circulating their folklore.

The genius of James, I believe, hit on the primary key to the comprehension of the Shakespeare creed, when he stressed the flagrantly commercial nature of the "Birthplace." It reminds one of the American fashion of lauding Christ as the world's supreme salesman or advertiser or *entrepreneur.* In precisely the same spirit biographers of Shakespeare glorify him as a gentleman of trade, a genius in finance. J. M. Robertson felt sure that the poet had "a personality which, of itself, if under no pressure of pecuniary need, would not be likely to give the world any serious sign of mental capacity whatever." Professor Hazelton Spencer, however, voiced the popular opinion, stating that in the soul of Shakespeare, in some uncanny manner, the pursuit of beauty and the pursuit of money were musically reconciled. Brandes had no doubt that the divine William lacked the generosity which the world commonly thinks an ingredient of great poets: "His was certainly not one of those artist-natures that are free-handed with money when they have it, and confer benefits with good-natured carelessness. He was a competent, energetic business man, who spared and saved in order to gain an independence...." Brandes saw not the least contradiction between the mind that created *The Merchant of Venice* and *Timon of Athens* and the mind that hounded Stratford artisans for petty debts. "The instinct of his soul," says Brandes, "which never suffered him to stop or pause, but forced him from one great intellectual achievement to another, restlessly onward from masterpiece to masterpiece – the fierce instinct, with its inevitable egoism, which led him in his youth to desert his family, in his maturity to amass property without any tenderness for his debtors, and *per fas et nefas* (by hook or by crook: Latin by B., English, F.) to attain his modest patent for gentility – this instinct enables him to understand and feel that passion for power which defies and tramples upon every scruple." In other words, Shakespeare learnt how to utter the souls of scoundrels, not by unconscious identification of his unconscious evil wishes with theirs, but by acting like a scoundrel himself. He could paint a Shylock vividly because he was a usurer, too.

This astonishing conception of the poet is also cherished by the "dialectical materialists" of Russia (for instance, A. Smirnov), who picture Shakespeare as a big bold bourgeois, naturally a revolutionary or progressive, who repulses Shylock only because the Jew carries usury too far. Smirnov thinks that Shakespeare preferred profit to interest. He has no patience with the old Marxist notion (defended by Franz Mehring) that the dramatist represented the young court nobility of his time, who were victimized by the mercantile and financial bourgeoisie. The "dialectical materialist," together with the individualist and idealist Brandes, and the whole host of bourgeois biographers of the Bard, form a chorus that salutes the god of Stratford as an oracle of capital. That is why Matthew Arnold, while criticizing his countrymen as a nation of shopkeepers, could yet applaud "the great English middle class, the kernel of the nation," for being "the class whose intelligent sympathy had upheld a Shakespeare."

What inspires the popular worship is not merely the hero's money; it is the fact of his success, the fact of his rise from virtual rags to riches, his incarnation of the dream of little business aiming to become big business. Just as the commercial possibilities transformed the local cult of the Avon into what Brown and Fearon correctly term a "cosmic industry," so the commercial character of the Stratford deity aided to promote him into a world-god. These two journalists, who laugh at the absurdities of the Birthplace, themselves take pride in praising Shakespeare as "a man of property, a shrewd investor, and fond of a bargain." One can almost hear the undertone of envy in their praise. After all, it is not every artist or creative writer who unites in his nature the faculty of giving "airy nothing" the reality of literary illusion, with the faculty for accumulating cash.

Brandes scoured the annals of world culture for other exemplars of this strange combination, and he could set by the side of his Shakespeare only the Danish dramatist Holberg, and Voltaire. But these authors were not born in poverty and conducted their business enterprises in the stock exchange or genteel finance. Shakespeare, if we are to trust the legend, carried on trade with plain malt and wool, peasant real-estate, and tenements, not to mention his sale of the surplus stone from the New Place he bought in Stratford, while conceiving and executing his fantasies of lordly luxurious life for the theatre. And he rose, according to the gospel of Stratford, to the posture of "a capitalist shareholder, a bill promoter, a tithe-farmer," as James Joyce succinctly puts it, as well as "a lord of language," from the misery of a butcher's and leatherworker's household, from a home whose father was twice fined for allowing piles of ordure to accumulate before its walls. I repeat, it is in the fable of that rise that we will discover the source of the Shakespeare religion.

Incidentally, we may note here that Hanns Sachs rejected Freud's belief that the Shakespeare of Stratford could not have been the Shakespeare of the dramas and sonnets, because the Brandes view seemed to Sachs in perfect accord with psychology. "To me," he says, "the small-town boy, whose father was fined for the dungheap at the door, seems still the most likely author of *The Tempest* and *Measure for Measure*." I do not intend to discuss here the century-old question of the authorship of Shakespeare. I mention Sachs's remark just to indicate the magnetism which the lowly idol of Stratford can exert for men of advanced critical powers.

The creed of the idol was stated, with typical terseness, by Alexander Pope, in these lines:

> Shakespeare (whom you, and every play-house bill,
> Style the divine, the matchless – what you will)
> For gain, not glory, wing'd his roving flight,
> And grew immortal in his own despite.

The avowal of the poet himself, in the Sonnets, that he wrote for immortality ("Not marble nor the gilded monuments / Of princes shall outlive this powerful rime") is rendered null and void in the face of the Stratford creed. As we have already remarked, the writings of Shakespeare mean far less to his mythologians than the legend of his social climb. Our task is to determine the hidden psychological motives for the cult of that climb.

Psychoanalysis gives us the tools capable of bringing to light these unconscious motives, which Henry James had gallantly groped for in his story of the "Birthplace." Without the theory of Freud I see no way of working out the method in what Garrick called his "madness about Shakespeare," the madness of the majority of writers about the Bard. If the economic motives I have outlined were enough to explain it, we would still have to explain the failure of millions to acknowledge the economic basis of their Shakespeare worship. Even the economic determinists offer other reasons for their adoration of him, reasons of esthetics and morality. But why should economic or ethical or esthetic ideals drop people to their knees? Freud's answer to this riddle may well be tested on the Shakespeare theology.

Like all theologies, the cult of the Bard derives its basic energy from the id, the wishing-well of the unconscious. Before people can worship Shakespeare they must have experienced several wishes which they do not have the courage to allow into consciousness. These desires are treated as wicked, as deadly to the ego or vanity or soul (as you like it). They are nothing less than urges to violate elementary canons of law and order. For instance, the general injunction to honor one's father and mother. The souls who have not felt a longing to dishonor at least one parent are extremely scarce, and William Shakespeare certainly did not belong to their company. He abandoned his parents in a time when they badly needed his wages and comfort, and, if ancient Stratford tradition may be trusted, he disgraced his family by robbing the estate of Sir Thomas Lucy. It is questionable whether they sanctioned his choice of Anne Hathaway as a wife, a woman eight years older than he, already pregnant, and engaged to wed William immediately after his betrothal to Anne Whately of Temple Grafton. One wonders whether the young man, raised amid filth and educated to a brutal trade, honored his father and mother at least with lip-loyalty.

We lack the faintest idea of what he endured in his id and conscience when he broke the divine commandment to obey one's procreants. But we can imagine how most of the people felt who heard about these early escapades of Stratford's "favorite son." Their own consciences, secretly aching from old guilty thoughts of their own parents, and cravings for "wild oats" and revolt, underwent a solace and unction in the belief that the great playwright had actually performed what they just wished. And he, the mutinous son, had grown wealthy and brought his father the formal honor of a patent of arms. Who could resist the fairy-tale quality of this narrative of the butcher's boy who ran away to London and got rich from the stage? It is a daydream of covetous and frustrated sons come true. The story binds the fancy with a stronger magic than the myth of Dick Whittington and his cat or the tale of Jack and the beanstalk. These appall the young mind with a horrible ogre, the hazard of death and the more concrete horror of hard work. In the case of Shakespeare the ultimate gold is reached by a road of pleasure, the simple expenditure of genius, an outpouring (in the Miltonic phrase) of wild native warbles in less than forty plays. It is generally agreed that he did not make any money out of the Sonnets, which were printed without his consent. He never attained a prominence as an actor that could account for his rapidly heaped wealth. So, if we exclude the possibility that he acquired it by experiments with larceny, we are forced to the conclusion that he made his fortune from the plays. Exactly how this was accomplished, none of the experts in his works can tell. The devotees do not care to find out.

Public opinion has never taken earnestly the excuses produced elaborately by Victorian scholarship for the sublime William's neglect of his wife in the first draft of his last will and testament. He left her, as we all know, his second-best bed with its furniture, and the bequest had to be written between the lines, like the legacies to his fellow-actors Burbage, Heming, arid Condell. Most of his admirers feel sure that Shakespeare's connubial life was by no means sweetness and sunshine. The thought does not induce sorrow in them. Indeed, it probably induces a deep unconscious joy. They like to think of the hero as not only getting rich quick but scoring innumerable victories as a lover: they seize with avidity on tales of his adultery in London: they revel in visions of the Dark Lady of the Sonnets entwining him in her gypsy serpentine arms. Violation of the statute against adultery lifts him to a certain secluded rank among the heroes of the daydreaming masses.

At the same time popular belief holds the idea that he remained true and pure in love of his mother. To Celts, Teutons, and Americans this idea is particularly dear, and in itself sufficient to exalt Shakespeare among the gods. They are fond of depicting Mary Arden as a woman from a loftier social station than his father. They see her as the source of his inspiration, encouraging his talents, grieving for his misfortunes, believing in his redemption and success. It is the sentiment of her character mystically conceived that endows the so-called Birthplace with its pathetic atmosphere. Perhaps the sheer fact that she was christened Mary aids in hallowing it. At any rate, the faith that Shakespeare lived in devotion to his mother yields us, I think, the core of his mystery – the Oedipus complex.

With the wretchedly small number of facts that we possess about the wonderful William, it might seem a hopeless job to demonstrate his possession of the Oedipus complex. Let us see: The pinnacle of his career, most readers would admit, was reached when he gained the privilege of writing "Gent." after his name, with the purchase of his coat of arms. The symbol of gentility that he chose came from the aristocratic Ardens of Warwickshire, a family which he obviously wished to think consanguineous with his mother. By adopting the Arden arms he would be elevating himself, in unconscious imagination, to the splendor his mother occupied in his mind. In psychoanalytic terms, his instinctual drives would be rising to overwhelm his superego, to release the tensions of reproach and hostility which are generated from that internal pattern of parental authority. Making himself an Arden in heraldry was equivalent therefore to an assertion of amorous desire for his mother, a distorted avowal of the incest wish. And by restoring her to prosperity he proved himself the real "husband" of her home, in the old English sense of the word. He carried out the responsibilities his father had handled so disastrously, and thus became in fact his mother's darling man. It is a consummation devoutly wished by all his worshipers in their own filial dreams, their family romances and tragicomedies. The faith that Shakespeare consummated it, in my opinion, forms the root of the Stratford idolatry. It is no accident that the favorite of all the love-stories that scholars and journalists have construed for Shakespeare is the one making him the mate of a second Mary, the aristocratic Fitton. In the unconscious, the "quick forge and working-house of thought" in his hierophants, the social climbing of the divine William signifies a mounting to Mary Arden's bed. Hence the peculiar rapture over the legend of his rise.

Next to the ecstasy of the incest wish in the Oedipus complex runs the inevitable agony of the wish to abolish the father. After our review of his conduct with respect or rather disrespect to the Fifth Commandment of the Jewish-Christian code, we do not require more proof that the hero suffered from repressed yearnings to kill his father. The desire must have been especially violent in the butcher's boy when the old man withdrew him from school and apprenticed him to his bloody craft. According to William's earliest biographer, John Aubrey, he used to enjoy delivering speeches when he killed a calf. In such eruptions of rhetoric the little killer doubtless vented his defiance of tyranny and exulted over his prowess with the knife. But he never came as close to parricide, in the mind's eyes of the Stratford religion, as he did to incest. In the religion he remains the prodigal son, who saves his father from ruin, and assists the old failure to a well-moneyed and peaceful death. The faithful of Christendom cannot endure a god who murders his father; they would rather have a god who murders his son. So it is impossible for Shakespeare to accomplish the parricidal wish in the unconscious of his priests, except by the circuitous process that Freud named "secular distortion."

The changes in family relations and social morality which compelled the transformation of Christianity from a religion whose Heavenly Father sacrifices His Son into a religion whose Heaven-born Son becomes one with the Father paved the road for a similar transformation of the Shakespeare piety. Let us recall that Stratford remembered him as flourishing in oratory over the slaughter of a calf, not a bull. By slaying the infant animal he could identify himself at heart with the butcher-father. Psychoanalysis has long been familiar with the process by which young intellects submit to castration, more precisely emasculation, in the face of the terrible father-image they carry in the super-ego. Young Shakespeare might have unconsciously mutilated himself in this way, symbolizing the sacrifice in his eloquence over helpless calves. Something of the sort appears to have happened in the minds of his priests. They express it by the ritual surrender of the desire to overthrow the father, by seeking a compromise, a celestial unity with him. James Joyce has portrayed the simultaneous self-humiliation and self-transfiguration with exquisite art in his novel *Ulysses*. Here he presents Shakespeare as the murdered King Hamlet and the King's son: "He is the ghost and the prince. He is all in all." Joyce identifies the Bard with God: "The playwright who wrote the folio of this world... the lord of things as they are, whom the most Roman of catholics call *dio boia*, hangman god, is doubtless all in all in all of us, ostler and butcher, and would be bawd and cuckold too but that in the economy of heaven, foretold by Hamlet, there are no more marriages...." The mystic union of Christ and Shakespeare is described by Joyce in ecstatic terms: "God, the sun, Shakespeare, a commercial traveler, having itself traversed in reality itself, becomes that self." Under the metaphysical words can be detected the agony of the infantile ego, struggling to reconcile with the father of its fantasy, against whom it has sinned in thought, with lust to kill, to dispossess. By now it is everywhere recognized that Joyce's *Ulysses* charms us primarily because of the emotion manifested in his art's working out of this conflict. The recognition that Shakespeare is adored for much the same reason will take a longer time than the Joyce discovery, for the spiritual conflict at the bottom of the Stratford theology is far more complex.

In the cult of Avonian Willy, as Henry James brilliantly demonstrated, "somebody," a creator – an intellectual father – is in truth killed. The real writer of the Shakespeare lyrics and dramas (whoever he was) has to die in order that the god of Stratford may live, and the culpable souls of his worshipers be appeased. It will be remembered that Boswell keenly regretted the omission from the Shakespeare Jubilee of 1769 of some religious ceremonies "gratefully addressing the supreme Father of all Spirits, from whom cometh every good and perfect gift." He meant, of course, the Author of the Universe. In the Shakespeare piety, however, our hero of Stratford stands next to Him. As James Montgomery said, when the pilgrims enter the Church of the Trinity in Stratford or the Birthplace, and "Tread the ground by genius often trod," they "feel a nature more akin to God." The romantic fervor of Alexandre Dumas cherished the notion that, next to God, Shakespeare created the most. The question for students of psychological determinism is not how seriously shall we take these extravagant remarks. It is: What do the remarks mean translated into the language of brain-work? In other words, what do they mean by the proximity of Shakespeare to God, the concept Shakespeare and the concept God? Henry James, I feel confident, has supplied us with the answer in his "Birthplace." He alludes to the "supreme Father of all Spirits" in the theatre of Shakespeare as an artist whom the greedy, lustful, conscience-stricken idealists of the Stratford shrine and its worldwide tributaries put to death each day. They kill him by refusal to listen to his art, by falsifying his message, by lying about his lifework, by stifling the vitality needed for the expansion of his creative influence – in particular poetry and drama. Over the imaginary dead body of this "father" rises the religion of the "son," his other self, the jack-of-all-trades and gentleman of various investments who is the William Shakespeare we are taught to venerate. Along with the Spirits of

Macbeth, Othello, Falstaff, and Malvolio, the poet gave birth to William Shakespeare, the hero of the biographies. And this "perfect gift" has been welcomed with an ardor surpassing the world's enthusiasm for all his other creations. For in the sublime William he incarnated the *beau ideal* of the bourgeoisie, the capitalist esthete, the usurer of genius, the manufacturer of masterpieces, and wizard of thrift. Out of the pauper and butcher's apprentice he evolved the man who could plot the enclosure of peasants' commons round Stratford and at the same time win golden opinions for verses like these (from *Julius Caesar*):

> By heaven, I had rather coin my heart,
> And drop my blood for drachmas, than to wring
> From the hard hands of peasants their vile trash
> By any indirection.

Critics have long complained that the patrician soul of the dramatist never stooped to earnest portraiture of burgesses, middle-class folk of the England of his day. There is nothing so hard to see as the object right in front of our eyes. The portrait of the artist as a young maltster and money-lender that Shakespeare drew from the raw material furnished by the runaway from Stratford has been sadly missed. Naturally, for the creator disappeared in his handiwork; the son became one with the father, merging with the maternal holy ghost that haunts the Birthplace.

The Stratford idolatry became a national religion in England after the so-called Glorious Revolution had entrenched the merchants and bankers as the ruling class. Shakespeare became a god of his country then, when the nation woke up to the fact that traders and brokers were claiming the title of "gentleman," as in the plays of Richard Steele, Richard Cumberland, and other mouth-pieces of plebeian glory and hope. The idle children of the parvenu money-nobility went to the playhouses and witnessed productions of Shakespeare, radically revised and "improved," embellished with happy endings, operatic effects, and more or less witty and pretty additions by other playwrights. For nearly two hundred years English taste and intelligence were satisfied by the atrocities surveyed by Hazelton Spencer in his funny volume *Shakespeare Improved*. Under the spell of this renovated, up-to-date Shakespeare, the public schools forced their infants to learn by rote such wisdom as Polonius's advice to Laertes on how to be safely selfish, and Iago's counsel on thrift. Against this god of British burgesses the poets and critics of the absolute monarchy in France exhausted their arsenal of sarcasm, championing their own idols of feudal classicism. La Harpe sneered that "Shakespeare is the poet of the plain people," in contrast with Racine whose tragedies are "the delicacies of instructed men." Voltaire denounced Shakespeare as a drunken ruffian, yet in his bourgeois heart he confessed to feeling a power beyond "culture" in the Englishman's dramas. He grieved David Garrick by his "unchristian attack upon Genius." The conviction that Shakespeare was untutored, uncultivated – a voice of experience without the discipline of books – "warbling his native woodnotes wild," as Milton affirmed – endeared him to the British ruling class and their emulators below. The young romantics of the early nineteenth century carried this view of the poet as a child of raw nature, a sweet singer of empiricism, to laughable extremes. They upheld him as a model of "unpremeditated art," inspiration incarnate, just as the actors in Ben Jonson's day had lauded Shakespeare as a nearly illiterate magician, excelling by his natural gifts the whole company of University wits. And so the cult spread, across national frontiers, on the wings of what may be named class narcissism.

Natural and historical science, in the middle of the century, created by the thinkers of evolution, compelled some fundamental changes in the study of Shakespeare. But they did not divert much traffic from the shrine at Stratford, because they lacked the strength to make the changes consistent and long-lasting. Thus scholars came to discern that no genius springs self-determinate from the mother, but grows up in certain fertile circumstances, within reach of culture, wealth and liberty. They gradually credited Shakespeare with an enormous lore of books, including volumes in languages that few Britons could have learnt. They ventured to argue that his patrician muse blossomed out in circles of the highest aristocracy, far from the Cheapside crowd, the market-places and artisans' shops. They abandoned the doctrine that he rose from a barbarous wildness to the peak of literature, and began filling the wildness with materials of a luxuriant civilization.

Then they collided with the cult. The cult depended for survival on the folk belief that the artist and the capitalist were two and yet one. Shakespearean research seemed to be gesturing to subdue the capitalist, to make the artist paramount. It could not be halted; but the masters of the "cathedral" managed to slow it down. The official doctors and editors of the Bard's labors restricted their analyses of his art to painstaking testimony that it existed above all for the "boxoffice," *ad majorem gloriam mammoni*. They returned, in brief, to the gospel of the Avon according to Pope, with improvements. In defense of it they turn with astounding effect on persons who would apply the methods and results of psychoanalysis to their Bard. Critics of the cult are simply and downrightly damned as heretics. The ecclesiastic word is used without any intent of humor; weapons habitual to inquisitions with secular arms are employed to back it up. But thereby hangs a tale outside our present concern, which is the examination of the Shakespeare orthodoxy in the light of Freud's dynamic or evolutionary psychology.

Chapter 4—Kit Sly and the Unknown Lord

And ask your own hearts, ask your own common-sense, to conceive the possibility of this man being – I say not, the drunken savage of that wretched scoliast [Voltaire], whom Frenchmen, to their shame, have honored before their elder and better worthies – but the anomalous, the wild, the irregular genius of our daily criticism!

What! are we to have miracles in sport? Or–I speak reverently–does God choose idiots by whom to convey divine truths to man?

Coleridge: "Poetry, the Drama, and Shakspere" (1818)

The Taming of the Shrew was left us in the folio of "Mr. William Shakespeares Comedies, Histories, & Tragedies. Published according to the True Originall Copies" in 1623, in a fantastically unfinished shape. Actually, the comedy of the courtship of Katherine Minola and her sister Bianca by the two entirely different lovers Lucentio the Florentine and Petruchio of Verona is a play within a play. But the play of which it is only a part appeared in print as a queer fragment, leaving one to wonder whether it was ever composed in ink. Experts on Tudor literature have suggested that, for some reason none of them can explain, the comedy was cut so as to leave forever in the dark what occurred to the drunken beggar Christopher Sly and the nameless Lord who picked him up at the beginning of the drama and turned him temporarily into a seeming nobleman. The puppets, so to speak, were left dangling by Shakespeare in the bedchamber gallery where he chose to stage before them the farce of Petruchio and his Kate. Only persons who question the current commercial theory of the play's authorship hold the opinion that the poet made it deliberately incomplete.

In the anonymous comedy called *The Taming of a Shrew*, printed in 1594, "Slie" is disposed of with the craft falling short of art for which Anthony Munday enjoyed a humble fame. The drunken

tinker and the merry men who stifle their laughter at his sudden up-
lift to aristocratic luxury and privilege, all enjoyed at their nameless
nobleman's expense, show up at intervals to remind us that the play
of Padua is no more than a sporting piece enacted for them in familiar England—in fact in the very shire of Warwick the dramatist is
supposed to come from. We see Slie at last, unable to keep awake
for a show that is practically a parody of Shakespeare's, drop off to
slumber during which they gently deprive him of his princely dress
and restore him to "his own apparel." They return him to the alehouse entrance where they found him and their master determined
to exalt him to gorgeousness, putting the beggar in his own bed.
Waked up by a tapster, with whom his creator had set him quarrel-
ing at the start of the farce, he reports (to our surprise) that he has
been delighting in an excellent dream—not the long literary boredom
you might have expected him to growl about. He claims that his
dream was a piece of precious learning, "how to tame a shrew"; he
will go right home to apply the lessons to his wife. The tapster ac-
companies him expressing desire to hear more of the educational
dream. In modern performances of the tale of Kit Sly the actors
always make sure to bring him back in dumb-show to the scene of
the strange Lord's experiment, and there they leave him alone.

If we are left darkling over the lucky tinker's adventure as the
greater poet gave it to us, it is because we lack the commonsense or
courage to trust the true vouch of our eyes and the stark evidence
of our ears. First we have to assume that if Shakespeare intended to
finish the fate of Sly he would have done so with the same dramatic
ingenuity and lyric agility that he settled the fate of Nick Bottom the
weaver in *A Midsummer Night's Dream* after the ambitious artisan had
experienced his interlude of glory in fairyland. Sly's luck would have
presented the master-artist with fewer problems than Bottom's
dream did. So if the master-artist decided to leave Sly in the illusory
splendor he deposited him in, it becomes the duty of all minds
friendly to Shakespeare to find out the purport of the caprice, usually called the induction to *The Taming of the Shrew.*

The induction opens with a dispute over broken ale glasses between a character called "Beggar" and the Hostess of a tavern in the English village of Wincot. The Beggar denounces her as a baggage because she insulted him, denounced him as a rogue. "The Slys are no rogues," he protests in a temper of alcoholic megalomania. "Look in the chronicles: we came in with Richard Conqueror." The blunder in history made by the funny drunkard is easily accounted for by a well known anecdote of the Elizabethan theatre. John Manningham, a law student fond of stage pomp and gossip, first recorded the anecdote in his diary on March 13, 1602. Since the Manningham manuscript has impressed a few scholars with what seems to be proof of an editor's intrusion, they have argued that the famous forger and expert on Tudor drama, John Payne Collier, was responsible for the whole tale, because he first called attention to the diary. None of these critics ever complained about the report of a production of *Twelfth Night* vividly given in the journal. I suspect that their objection to the anecdote sprang from outrage over its portrayal of the morals of their idol, Will Shakspere of Stratford on Avon. In any case, the anecdote might shed light on Kit Sly. Here it goes:

"Upon a time when Burbidge played Rich. 3. there was a Citizen greue soe farr in liking with him, that before shee went from the play shee appointed him to come that night unto hir by the name of Ri: the 3. Shakespeare overhearing their conclusion went before, was intertained, and at his game ere Burbidge came. Then message being brought that Rich. the 3rd. was at the dore, Shakespeare caused return to be made that William the Conqueror was before Rich. the 3. Shakespeare's name William."

Manningham did not have to add that Burbage's name was Richard, which doubles the poignancy of the joke. The law student was of course better acquainted with the stage star than with the jack of all theatric trades, Will Shakspere, whose Christian name he needed to remember in telling the joke. I take Sly's allusion to "Richard Conqueror" to signify that the man he represents arrived in the realm of the theatre at the same time that Dick Burbage ravished London hearts with his rare talent. Unluckily we do not know when Burbage won stardom, nor in what role.

The Beggar displays an unusual acquaintance with English theatre in many phrases that trip from his lip. From the stage he surely got the little Spanish he knows, like "pocas palabras," distorted naturally as you would expect. The expression "Sessa!" which he tosses after it, and has baffled inquirers for centuries, strikes me as Sly's pronunciation of the French *Ca Ca!* – a battlecry sounded so long in English ears – often as *Sa! Sa!* – Washington Irving felt sure of the effect on his public when he drew the French cavalier in his *Tales of a Traveller* (1825) "flourishing feebly his little court sword with a *ca-ca!*" All inquirers have discerned in the ludicrous allusion of Sly to Saint Jerome, "Go by, Saint Jeronimy!" an echo of the most popular of Elizabethan plays, *The Spanish Tragedy*. (Scarcely do they name this drama without adding that Thomas Kyd wrote it, tho the evidence of Kyd's authorship is hardly better than the proof that Moses wrote the Torah. In Chapter 13 I argue that Kyd only copied *The Spanish Tragedy* for the Earl of Derby's players, that the real writer was the brilliant scholar Thomas Watson, none of whose dramas has survived under his own name: I contend that Derby's actors first played it for the Queen on January 1, 1581, under the title "The Story of Hieronimo.") No theatric character was better known to Tudor crowds than the little Spanish hero, Jeronimo. Dick Burbage won his earliest glory, I guess, in this part.

Dick Burbage died in March 1619, and his brother Cuthbert informed government authority that Dick had been an actor for thirty -five years. That would date the beginning of his career in 1584 maybe or early in 1585.

On February 2, 1585, the last children of William Shakspere and his older wife, the former Anne Hathaway, were baptized at the church of Stratford on Avon. Soon after this six-years episcopally blessed event, a host of inquirers agree, William Shakspere departed more or less rapidly from his malodorous birthplace. According to the inquirers, the prime instigation for his departure came from Sir

Thomas Lucy, whom Will is alleged to have lampooned in rime as "lousy Lucy."

The playwright Nicholas Rowe described the affair in the first printed biography of Shakspere (1709). "He had, by a misfortune common enough to young fellows, fallen into ill company; and, amongst them, some that made a frequent practice of deer-stealing, engaged him with them more than once in robbing a park that belonged to Sir Thomas Lucy of Charlecote near Stratford. For this he was prosecuted by that gentleman, as he thought, somewhat too severely; and, in order to revenge that ill-usage, he made a ballad upon him, and though this, probably the first essay of his poetry, be lost, yet it is said to have been so very bitter that it redoubled the prosecution against him to that degree that he was obliged to leave his business and family in Warwickshire for some time and shelter himself in London." An independent witness, Archdeacon Richard Davies (who died in 1708) stated that the poor leather-dealer's son was "much given to all unluckiness in stealing venison and rabbits, particularly from Sir Thomas Lucy, who had him oft whipt, and sometimes imprisoned, and at last made him fly his native country to his great advancement."

James Halliwell-Phillipps observed that Lucy attended the Parliament that closed its final session on March 29, 1585 and put the knight in charge of a bill for the preservation of game. So when Sir Thomas came home and found his Charlecote warren preyed upon by poachers, his ardor for chasing and chastising juvenile delinquents like the butcher-boy Will Shakspere would not be dissuaded by the knowledge that Will was already a father of three babes. It is therefor plausible to date the flight of young Shakspere from his business and family a few days before the anniversary of his birth or rather baptism, which took place on April 23 or May 3, according to the New Style of calendar favored by Pope Gregory XIII in 1582, but rejected by England as Romanist until 1752.

If William of Stratford trudged to London early in April 1585 and "came in with Richard Conqueror," that would explain why the first theatrical company he connected with was the Lord Strange's servants, formerly the Earl of Derby's troop. (Lord Strange was Derby's son.) In the manuscript outline of the plot of *The Seven Deadly Sins*, which the actor Edward Alleyn preserved, we see that Richard Burbage acted the part of Tereus, the legendary villain of Philomela's rape, at the Curtain theatre about 1590, together with Lord Strange's splendid company. William Shakspere's name is not found in the manuscript, but experts contend that he could have played the part of Lidgate the bookman, who sits with Henry VI (probably played by John Heminges, a veteran of the troop) thru the four divisions of the plot.

We learn from the same manuscript that John Sincler was a member of the Lord Strange's men. His name, spelt Sinklo, is found in the First Folio text of *King Henry VI, Part Three* (Act III, scene 1): "Enter Sinklo and Humfrey, with Crossbows in their hands," it says where modern editors put "Enter two Keepers." In the ensuing dialog Sinklo is recorded twice, "Sink." five times and "Sin." once, speaking for the First Keeper. The 1600 quarto edition of *Henry IV, Part Two*, presents him in the role of Beadle arresting Doll Tearsheet: "Enter Sincklo and three or foure officers." The last record of his appearance on the stage came with *The Malcontent* by John Marston in 1604. In the induction of *The Taming of the Shrew* the name Sincklo appears alone among the actors, singled out for high praise for the ability in one role. Will Shakspere may have seen John Sincler and the rest of Strange's men when they came to Stratford on Avon in February 1578. Sometime in 1580, the Earl of Derby's actors received payment from the town council of Stratford, if not for a play, at least for going away and leaving the local illiterates in quiet–including Will Shakspere's father and mother, who signed instead of their names a rough drawing of glover's dividers or else a pious cross.

When the Hostess of the alehouse goes off to get a constable to punish the Beggar, he defies the "baggage": "I'll answer him by law." Strange as it may seem to hear a vagabond like Sly voicing confidence in the law, it will be quite comprehensible the moment we realize that he stands, as I have hinted, for the fugitive Will Shakspere.

After his successful evasion of Sir Thomas Lucy's prosecution, he learnt to become almost too fond of law courts and cases, particularly in prosecuting people for money they owed him. Sir Sidney Lee declared that he "inherited his father's love of litigation, and stood rigorously by his rights in all his business relations." (*A Life of William Shakespeare*; New York, Macmillan, 1916, p. 321.) The earliest evidence of his activity in London shows him as busy with his precious occupation of usury. In March 1600 William Shackspere sued John Clayton of Bedfordshire for seven pounds he had lent him in Cheapside in 1592. Professor Leslie Hotson went to the trouble of locating a William Shakespeare of Bedfordshire in order to demonstrate that Clayton's financier of eight years' patience could not have been Stratford on Avon's favorite son. (London *Times Literary Supplement*, 22 November 1930.)

Certainly the loan-leech could not have been the poet of *The Merchant of Venice* and *Timon of Athens*. But there is bare room for doubt that the financier was the same William Shakspere who hounded the Stratford apothecary in 1604 for petty debt and payment for pecks of malt. In 1609 the same amorist of money sued John Addenbroke for six pounds and, when Addenbroke left town, "avenged himself by proceeding against Thomas Horneby," a blacksmith who had offered the debtor's bail. (Lee, 322.) While waiting for the officer of justice, who never appears, Sly falls asleep.

The dramatist at this point instructed the actors of *The Shrew*, "Wind horns. Enter a *Lord* from hunting, with his *Train*." The nameless Lord spends a few happy speeches on the quality and value of his hounds, whom his voice caresses in pronouncing their names. Observing the Beggar on the ground he wonders if the fellow is dead, or drunk. A huntsman reports him alive and warm from ale. After an instant's reflection on the image of death presented by the slumbering stranger, the Lord suddenly announces: "Sirs, I will practice on this drunken man." His Lordship's whim is to waft the Beggar to a perfumed bed, adorn his tough fingers with rings, and have "brave attendants" bring him "A most delicious banquet by his bed." The purpose of the Lord's sport appears to be to discover if the Beggar would "forget himself" and believe he had undergone a metamorphosis into a baron. The Lord's intention is to test the potency of fancy or flattering dream.

The unknown Lord gives detailed instructions on the way to "manage well the jest." He desires to see it in his "fairest chamber," which he wants decorated "with all my wanton pictures." And the victim of his joke must have music when he wakes, "To make a dulcet and a heavenly sound." The waking rascal is to be told that "his lady mourns at his disease." For the cream of the jest will consist in persuading the rascal that he has been "lunatic."

> And when he says he is, say that he dreams,
> For he is nothing but a mighty Lord.

The Huntsmen promise, "we will play our part," and convince the Beggar, bright as his wits may be, "He is no less than what we say he is."

No sooner is Sly transported to the nobleman's bedchamber than trumpets sound, heralding, the Lord supposes, a noble guest for the inn. We learn however that the trumpets signal a company of actors, "That offer service to your Lordship." When they approach he greets them with the hospitality of Prince Hamlet and reveals a memory for histrionic ingenuity as keen as the Prince's. He welcomes their offer to perform for him "With all my heart," and points to one player as deserving of special applause for the artistry with which he once acted a farmer's eldest son.

> 'Twas where you woo'd the Gentlewoman so well:
> I have forgot your name: but sure that part
> Was aptly fitted, and naturally perform'd.

Where modern editions of the comedy name the next speaker Player, the Folio informs us it was *Sincklo*. "I think 'twas Soto that your honor means."

Promptly the Lord responds, "'Tis very true, thou didst it excellent." Then he tells them how their cunning could be useful in assisting him with a sport he is enjoying at the expense of a peculiar Lord, one of "odd behavior," and most curious culture,

For yet his honor never heard a play.

He warns them that in whatever drama they enact that night, they will have to play without even a smile. The players assure him they may be securely trusted for grave behavior before the mirthless Lord, and he gladly welcomes them to his Buttery: "Let them want nothing that my house affords." A buttery was the storeroom for butts of liquor or bottles mostly. When the players have gone for the refreshment, the whimsical Lord commands his page Bartholomew to be prepared to disguise as the drunkard's lady.

Bid him shed tears, as being over-joyed
To see her noble Lord restor'd to health,
Who for this seven years hath esteemed him
No better than a poor and loathsome beggar.

And so the unknown Lord goes off, eager to observe the entertainment, and how his men will control their laughter "When they do homage to this simple peasant."

If I am right in dating the cold weather and warm humor of this scene in the early spring of 1585, then the unknown Lord's reference to the passing of seven years since the transformation of Sly would date the writing of these lines in 1592. This was the year of that simple peasant, William Shakspere's metamorphosis into Shakespeare the arch-poet and dramatist. On March 3, 1592, Lord Strange's servants acted at the Rose theatre the historic tragedy Henry VI, a play noted as "new" by Philip Henslowe, owner of the Rose. The sensation produced by this play in fifteen performances still echoes in Thomas Nashe's pamphlet *Pierce Penniless*, licensed for printing on August 8, 1592. Nashe applauded mainly the war hero of the tragedy: "How would it have joyed brave Talbot (the terror of the French) to think that after he had lain two hundred years in his tomb, he would triumph again on the stage, and have his bones new embalmed with the tears of ten thousand spectators at least (at several times) who, in the tragedian that represents his person, imagine they behold him fresh bleeding!" Since the role of Talbot called for a star with big valor in a small body, capable of courage and cunning in dealing with strong women, I surmise that Richard Burbage triumphed in the earning of those thousands of tears.

On September 3, 1592, the poet Robert Greene perished "for want of comfort" on a bed given him by charity. Soon after his funeral a pamphlet came out, clandestinely edited by Henry Chettle, entitled *Greens Groatsworth of Wit, bought with a Million* of *Repentance*. It contained an appeal of the dying poet to Christopher Marlowe, Thomas Nashe, and George Peele, to quit writing plays for the players, because the greed of the latter would forsake men of literature in time of necessity and leave them to die in despair.

"Yes, trust them not; for there is an upstart Crow, beautified with our feathers, that with his Tigers heart wrapt in a Players hide supposes he is as well able to bum-bast out a blank verse as the best of you; and being an absolute Johannes Factotum, is, in his own conceit, the only Shake-scene in a country. O that I might intreat your rare wits to be imployed in more profitable courses and let those apes imitate your past excellence, and never more acquaint them with your admired inventions! I know the best husband of you all will never prove an usurer, and the kindest of them all will never prove a kind nurse; yet, whilst you may, seek you better masters, for it is pity men of such rare wits should be subject to the pleasures of such rude grooms."

Not only the pun "Shake-scene," but the parody of the verse from *Henry VI, Part Three* (Act I, Scene 4, line 137) identifies the target of Greene's mockery as the fellow from Stratford, who had recently emerged from crepuscular occupations, a John of various facilities, to the fitful fame of a speculator in heroic plays. But the experts are wrong who argue that Greene aimed a barb of envy at the author of

Henry VI. Every phrase of his bitterness ejaculates contempt, not for a rival playwright, but for an inferior usurer, a lender of shillings to playwrights who turned cruel shoulders when penury racked them. The reference to "rude grooms" reminds us of the stage tradition that the moneylender came to London, in Samuel Johnson's words, "a needy adventurer, and lived for a time by very mean employments." Johnson repeated the old story of William Davenant, who hinted to friends that his mother had known William Shakespeare as a lover, that the Stratford usurer had found his first work in the capital as a holder of horses outside a theatre. Perhaps he had also helped the grooms in the stable nearby kept by Richard Burbage's father.

The discovery of poor Sly by the nameless Lord conjures to my mind the testimony of Sir Richard Phillips, the sheriff of London who edited *The Monthly Magazine; or British Register*, about the way Will Shakspere was rescued from beggary. Phillips met descendants of Shakspere's sister, Joan Hart, and in 1818 copied an account that one of them gave him of how her brother crossed the threshold of success. This account has been left alone by practically all the biographers of the Stratford fraud:"Mr. J.M. Smith said, he had often heard his mother state that Shakspeare owed his rise in life, and his introduction to the theatre, to his accidentally holding the horse of a gentleman at the door of the theatre, on his first arriving in London. His appearance led to inquiry and subsequent patronage." (*The Monthly Magazine*, vol. xlv, no.1 1818; quoted in *Shakespeare Facts and Problems* by E.K. Chambers: Oxford, Clarendon Press, 1930; II, 199.)

If the Hart tradition is taken as true, we would be confronted with the entrancing task of surmise and inquiry concerning the gentleman who found William Shakspere so worthy of the stage and patronage. The servants of the empty shrine in Stratford-on-Avon maintain a silence on the subject of this savior gentleman that feels almost solid. The silence will thicken when the reasons are presented for identifying the gentleman with Edward de Vere, Earl of Oxford. (See Chapter 5.)

The Earl's own company of actors had toured Warwickshire in the autumn of 1584. Shakspere might have seen them on November 24, the day they played in Coventry.

On the road they also stopped for some hours in Stratford. On January 1 "John Symons and other his fellows" displayed for the Queen and her court "feats of activity and vaulting" instead of a drama, and thus provided the last record of Oxford's theatrical servants performing at the court. (Chambers, *The Elizabethan Stage*, 1923, iv, 161.)

A strange fact is recorded about the acrobat John Symons who received payment for the New Year's night show. At the time he was paid he belonged to the troop of actors in the service of Lord Strange, Richard Burbage's troop, and the one that Will Shakspere joined. January 1585 saw more undramatic employment of the Earl of Oxford's troop. His musicians came to Oxford University to get one pound for their melodious contribution to the tragedy of *Meleager* by William Gager, that Christ Church College revived to entertain the University chancellor, the Earl of Leycester, Oxford's oldest rival for the Queen's favor. Later the town of Oxford's *alma-mater*, Cambridge, paid 6 shillings, 8 pence to his musicians for unknown work. (F. S. Boas, *Shakespeare and the Universities*, 1923, 19.) These must be the same musicians that answer the summons of Sly's Lord:

Wilt thou have Music? Hark, Apollo plays,
And twenty caged nightingales do sing.

Curious transformations were taking place in the world of histrionics in the year we have selected for Will Shakspere's appearance at the capital. One student of the period seems to have been struck by a trend of the chief dramatic performers pointing to clandestine guidance from no less a hand than the literary Earl Edward's.

"Surprising as it may appear," says Arthur Acheson (*Shakespeare, Chapman, and Thomas More*, London 1931, 46-7) "the facts lead to the conclusion that, when Alleyn joined Burbage in 1585, taking with him men from Worcester's and Sheffield's companies, to form the

Admiral's company, he, with his brother John Alleyn, Robert Brown, and Richard Jones, combined the remainder, or part of the remainder of the two companies with Oxford's company; this amalgamation working under Oxford's title in summer at the Curtain, and probably at the Boar's Head in winter, until 1589, in which year Oxford's company disappears from all theatrical records, not appearing again for thirteen years, and then appearing united and performing with Worcester's men at the Curtain and the Boar's Head." These mysterious epiphanies of the Earl of Oxford's players become more luminous when we surmise their origin in the "large and beautiful house, with gardens of pleasure, bowling alleys and suchlike," that John Stowe admired so much in his *Survey of London* (1598)altho the capital called it Fisher's Folly after the merchant who spent a fortune building it. This building seems to have become the heart of the histrionic world when Edward de Vere purchased it. In 1585 four properties adjoining it were bought from the mother and stepfather of Edward and John Alleyn, and held in these actors' names (G. F. Warner, *Catalogue of the Manuscripts & Muniments of Alleyn's College of God's Gift at Dulwich*, 1881, 251,252.)

Oxford's Folly and the Alleyn messuages were in the parish of St Helen's church in Bishopsgate, a short walk from Norton Folgate where Christopher Marlowe was resident in the fall of 1589. Near him lived the poet whom I have credited with *The Spanish Tragedy*, his friend Thomas Watson. William Cornwallis, who occupied Oxford's Folly after the Earl left it in 1591, employed Watson as a family tutor, and once remarked that the scholar could "devise twenty fictions and knaveries in a play, which was his daily practice and his living." (*Athenaeum*, 23 August 1890, 256.)

In the fall of 1585 Christopher Marlowe acquired the degree of Bachelor of Arts from Corpus Christi College in Cambridge. Doubtless his epic-tempered mind had already worked out the metres of his tragedy *Dido, Queen of Carthage*, which the children of Her Majesty's Chapel acted. The Children performed under the direction of the Welsh wizard Henry Evans and the elegant wit John Lyly, the Earl of Oxford's secretary. During Christmas of 1584 the Earl's company of boy players, won to work in tune by Evans, delighted the Queen with a performance of the lost *History of Agamemnon and Ulysses*. Marlowe's first play may have been inspired by that tale of the Trojan war. I suppose John Lyly was then dwelling at Oxford's Folly. A short ride from the mansion reached the earliest playhouse in England, the Theatre, built by James Burbage in 1576 a few feet east of the Shoreditch road later called Curtain Road, after the theatre built nearby for rivalry as well as vacation relief to the Theatre. The Burbage family lived in the neighborhood, on Holywell Street where it met Hog Lane. Close to their home William Shakspere got his first London place to sleep.

"Soon after his arrival," says Sir Sidney Lee, "he found a home in the parish of St. Helen's, Bishopsgate, within easy reach of 'The Theatre' in Shoreditch. There he remained until 1596," when he crossed the Thames to the Liberty of the Clink, apparently to escape taxes on personal property valued by revenue agents at five pounds (Lee, 274.) Eleven years before, his personal property amounted precisely to the goods described by Sly as all he owned in the second scene of *The Taming of the Shrew*. The scene portrays what must have been the reaction of Will Shakspere to his first experience of Edward de Vere's mansion in Bishopsgate.

"Enter aloft the drunkard with attendants some with apparel, bason and ewer, & other appurtenances, & Lord.

Beggar. For Gods sake, a pot of small ale.

The servants amaze him with offerings of Spanish white wine, known in England as sack, conserves or candied fruits, and they inquire what raiment he will wear this day. He replies deliberately, for he is not a man to be overwhelmed by visions and metamorphoses:

"I am Christophero Sly, call not me Honour nor Lordship. I ne'r drank sack in my life; and if you give me any conserves, give me

conserves of Beef; n'er ask me what raiment I'l wear, for I have
no more doublets than backs: no more stockings than legs: nor
no more shoes than feet, nay sometimes more feet than shoes, or
such shoes as my toes look through the over-leather."

Shakespeare's insistence on our taking heed of the name Christopher Sly begins at the very opening of the comedy, where he intro-
duces the "Beggar and Hostess" and adds the Beggar's name. The
dramatist points out that the man whom Sly stands or rather lies for
was not merely a cunning hypocrite; he was selected by destiny for a
sacred function, carrying "Christ," his anointed Lord and savior, on
his back, so to speak. They are doomed forever to traverse history,
in this way, Shakespeare seems to murmur through the name. The
strong shoulders of the fellow from Stratford bear the blame as well
as the credit for the sins of the world embodied and enacted by his
master, the godling of the "Folly," the Theatre, and the Curtain.
The name Christopher compelled the attention of Edward de Vere
not only on meeting Christopher Marlowe, which I guess occurred
in 1585, but also in parting with Anthony Munday, who seems to
have left Oxford's service in 1585. Tony obtained admittance to the
Drapers guild, where they registered his address "By Cripplegate, a
Poet,"but did not explain how the poet, formerly an actor and
patcher of plays, had turned draper. His father, Christopher Munday, belonged to the guild. When De Vere created Christopher Sly
he must have recalled how he had chosen the son of Christopher
Munday to bear the modest repute of the poetry published under
the name of "Shepherd Tonie." The unknown author of *The Art of
English Poesie* (1589), the most exquisite work of literary criticism
written under the last of the Tudors, must have been reflecting on
the lyrics of Shepherd Tonie when he declared, "I know very many
notable gentlemen in the Court that have written very commenda-
bly and suppressed it again, or else suffered it to be published without their own names to it; as it were a discredit for a gentleman to
seem learned, and to show himself amorous of any good art." The
unknown critic did not leave us in the dark about whom he meant

above all: "And in her Majesty's time that now is are sprung up another crew of Courtly makers, Noblemen and Gentlemen of her Majesty's own servants, who have written excellently well as it would appear if their doings could be found out and made public with the rest, of which number is first that noble gentleman Edward Earl of Oxford." The courtier critic went so far as to nominate "the Earl of Oxford and Master Edwards of her Majesty's Chapel" as penmen who "deserve the highest prize" for their comedies and interludes. (*English Reprints*, ed. Arber, 1869, I, xxxi, 77.)

Unhappily the author of *The Art of English Poesie* would not bring himself to examine the motives of the English aristocracy in disgracing the arts, especially the art that finds words for feelings, and true names for deeds. All he could do was lament: "For as well Poets as Poesie are despised, and the name become of honourable infamous, subject to scorn and derision, and rather a reproach than a praise to any that useth it." A key to the same can perhaps be located in the old English word for poets employed by the critic himself–*makers*. It reeked in the nostrils of numerous British plutocrats with the stench of pleb labor, but lacked the justification for that odor, the profits, the *pecunia* which they had all been taught *non ole*t.

Nobody in Britain adhered more devoutly to the plutocrat creed than William Cecil, Lord Burghley. He warned his son Robert to beware of parting with lands for funds: "the gentlemen that sell an acre of land, sell an ounce of credit," Cecil proverberated. "For gentility is nothing but ancient riches," and riches in his economic faith meant primarily spacious dirt. He watched in horror while Edward de Vere disposed of estate after estate for what seemed to Cecil a song.

It is the sorrow of Oxford's father-in-law over the spendthrift, song-making stage-enchanted Earl that we hear the nameless Lord sporting with Kit Sly appeals to him to give up his posture as a beggar:

Heaven cease this idle humor in your Honor.
Oh that a mighty man of such descent,

Of such possessions, and so high esteem
Should be infused with so foul a spirit.

The drunkard's answer to that appeal, Sir Sidney Lee observed, "has a direct bearing on Shakespeare's biography, for the poet admits into it a number of literal references to Stratford" and the surrounding country. *"Beggar.* What, would you make me mad? Am not I Christopher Slie, old Slie's son of Burton-heath, by birth a peddler, by education a card-maker, by transmutation a Bear-herd, and now by present profession a Tinker? Ask Marrian Hacket the fat Alewife of Wincot, if she knows me not…."

Lee affirms that Burton-heath is Barton-on-the Heath, the home of Edmund Lambert and his wife, a sister of Will Shakspere's mother. In 1578 John Shakspere, Will's father, and Mary his mother, had lost by mortgage their property at the village of Wilmcote. Edmund Lambert loaned him forty pounds for the land. In 1580 John felt able to pay off the mortgage but his brother-in-law insisted on full payment for other sums owed him. Their law wrestling continued for years. The Shaksperes never recovered mother Mary's farm at Wilmcote.

About four miles from Stratford in the days of De Vere once lay a small portion of the parish of Quinton named Wincot, and in the parish register antiquarians have come across a number of Hackets, none of them named Marian nor Cicely, who is mentioned as Marian's maid later in the prelude. (Incidentally, the mention of Sly's friend John Naps of "Greece" seems to be a joke at the expense of Greet, a village in Gloucestershire, not far from Stratford.) These antiquarians proved beyond the shade of doubt that Shakespeare plainly designed a Stratford-on-Avon neighborhood for his prelude. But what for? Not a shadow of explanation ever crossed their pages on their allusions to their idol's native shire. Since they dare not even toy with the fancy that Christopher Sly could have been created in the image of their idol, the whole scene makes no sense to them. That is why one of the editors of The Shrew, after repeating the old story about the beggar that Duke Philip of Burgundy played a similar game with–a story that Shakespeare could have read in *De Rebus Burgundicis* by P. Heuterus, published in 1584– ventured the ridiculous proposition: "It is from the point of view of such a deluded beggar that we must see both the wooing of Kate and the wooing of Bianca." (Professor Irving Ribner, Introduction to *The Taming of the Shrew*, 1966, xiv.) Deluded academics of this kind should stick to the "theatre of the absurd" and leave Shakespeare to the old-fashioned rational. Practically all interpreters of Shakespeare's comedy have blinded themselves to the apparition which he presents in the second scene of its induction or prelude. It is not simply the presentment of a pauper and sot lying in the bed of a nobleman who has chosen to put the pauper in his own place, letting the rogue receive the homage and services owed his lordship. The nameless nobleman is thus enabled to turn comically on Christopher Sly a cataract of criticism which has been poured on his lordship's head. The English lord who could carry out a job like this "transmutation" of the tinker Sly is doomed to see it thru nearly alone. None of his peers, no cousin nor gentleman of his circle can be invited to enjoy it with him. For they have been dealt enough and surfeit of his lordship's caprices and tricks of laughter. "Oh, this it is that makes your Lady mourn," cries one of his men, pretending to deplore Sly's insistence on distinguishing his appearance from reality. "Hence comes it," adds the Lord, "that your kindred shuns your house, As beaten hence by your strange Lunacy." Then the Lord repeats what the Earl of Oxford must have heard innumerable times from his father-in-law, if not from his Countess Anne:

Oh Noble Lord, bethink thee of thy birth,
Call home thy ancient thoughts from banishment,
And banish hence these abject lowly dreams.

He and his servants proceed to chant a lullaby for Sly that finely defines the aristocratic recreations that Edward de Vere used to be ardent for, riding on richly adorned horses, hunting with his brave hounds, hawking with his sun-companioning haggards and tercels. But the poet lingers more lyrically on the recreations that parted Edward de Vere from the majority of aristocrats. The musical ear which made him a lifelong friend of William Byrd and John Farmer and the quire children of the Queens Chapel gets the tribute of the verses I quoted alluding to Apollo's lute and choral nocturnes or madrigals. The fascination that Ovid's *Metamorphoses* exerted on his mind, ever since the childhood hours when his uncle Arthur Golding engaged to translate it, gleams from the lines describing three classical pictures in the Lord's gallery. These paintings of the fatal passion of Adonis and Cytherea, Io and Zeus, Daphne and Apollo, may not have belonged to the Earl of Oxford. His singular friend Lord John Lumley, the foremost collector of plastic art as well as rare books and manuscripts in England, surely owned the originals. Among the treasures of Lumley listed after his death in 1609 was a "statuary" or portrait of Edward de Vere. In 1583, June 20, Oxford wrote to Burghley a letter for the sake of Lumley indicating how alone the poet stood at the summit of English society:

"I have been an earnest suitor unto your Lordship for my Lord Lumley, that it would please you for my sake to stand his good Lord and friend, which as I perceive your Lordship hath already very honorably performed…among all the rest of my blood, this only remains in account either of me or else of them, as your Lordship doth know very well, the rest having embraced further alliances to leave their nearer consanguinity….through your Lordship's favor, I shall be able to pleasure my friend and stand needless of others who have forsaken me." (B. M. Ward, *The Seventeenth Earl of Oxford*, 1928, pp. 245-246.) Oxford thanked Burghley in this letter for his "friendly usage and sticking by me in this time wherein I am hedged in with so many enemies." However, five years later (5 May 1587), Burghley confided to Sir Francis Walsingham:

"I was so vexed yesternight very late by some grievous sight of my poor daughter's affliction, whom her husband had in the afternoon so troubled with words of reproach of me to her…she spent all the evening in dolour and weeping. And though I did as much as

I could to comfort her with hope; yet she, being as she is great with child, and continually afflicted to behold the misery of her husband and of his children, to whom he will not leave a farthing of land... No enemy I have can envy me this match: for thereby neither honour nor land nor goods shall come to their children." (Ward, 285)

The memory of those tears of Countess Anne burns in Shakespeare's verses of extravagant praise of the nobleman's Lady:

> *Lord.* Thou art a Lord, and nothing but a Lord,
>   Thou hast a Lady far more Beautiful
>   Than any woman in this waning age.

The final phrase, "this waning age," informs us the verses were composed in the last decade of the XVIth century, maybe in the last year. For a few lines later, having apparently forgotten that he had confined the Lord's lunacy to a seven-years period, the dramatist has one of his attendants say, "These fifteen years you have been in a dream." If my interpretation of the scene is true, and what we have here is a sardonic dramatization of the changing of William Shakspere from beggar to occupant of a playful Lord's sleeping place, and that change began in 1585, then the last revision of the prelude was made in 1600. The last words of the Lord in the scene are "this waning age."

The page who acts his Lordship's wife comes in to sit by the side of Sly, eluding his amorous invitation with a reference to his recent "malady" which is afterward denoted as melancholy, of course, Shakespeare's disease. By this time the poet appears to have forgotten that he introduced the company of Players as men who "offer service to your Lordship." He brings a Messenger from them to announce,

> Your Honors Players, hearing your amendment,
> Are come to play a pleasant Comedy.

To the peasant Christopher's question, "Is not a Comontie a Christmas gambold, or a tumbling trick?" the "Lady" replies, "No, my good Lord, it is more pleasant stuff." He exclaims, "What, household stuff!" At once ready for what Hamlet calls "country matters," a phallic frolic, such as the Slys have sliced for weddings from the day that marriage was invented. His concept of comedy attained ruling-class respectability only in our own period. In Shakespeare's opinion, comedy is "a kind of history." The original title of his first play, the *Comedy of Errors,* remember, was a *History of Error. The Taming of the Shrew* is an imaginary history uniting the facts of Peregrine Bertie's wooing and wedding of Lady Mary Vere with the truth about Edward de Vere's and Anne Cecil's marital misery. [For a full discussion of the play, see Chapter 5–The Woman Tamer in Feldman's *Early Shakespeare–*W.H.]

I said that Shakespeare had apparently forgotten his dating of the nameless nobleman's madness and his relation with the players. Would it surprise you to learn that he had deliberately made these mistakes to force our scrutiny of the secret history of the Sly saga? For exactly the same reason he left the happy Christopher falling asleep over the story of Petruchio and his Kate, and never showed what happened to him. The poet's prophetic soul could not tell, what would be his next transmutation?

In 1600, when, in my surmise, the induction to our comedy was written, London was still laughing at the famous comedian Will Kemp's *Nine Days Wonder,* describing his dance of the year before from London to Norwich. Kempe had sold his share of stock in the Lord Chamberlain's company, Shakespeare's troop, apparently in bad temper on account of criticism aimed at his type of clowning, in the latest version of *Hamlet* (see Act III, Scene 2, Hamlet's third counsel to the Players). Kempe's dance to Norwich had music supplied by his tabor player, Tom Sly. The dramatist may have been thinking of Sly and the clown when he worked on the only induction he ever made for a play. Kempe made a funny blunder in dedicating his *Nine Days Wonder* to Anne Fitton, intending her sister Mary, as he showed by calling Anne a Maid of Honor to the Queen. Perhaps in remembrance of the comedian's error, and the odd fact that the Earl of Oxford's wife and William Shakspere's wife were both named Anne, and so was Oxford's dark mistress Vavasor–who was also counted among the Queen's Maids of Honor when she was only a Lady of her Majesty's Bedchamber–Christopher Sly suddenly swears "by Saint Anne" before he wishes, at the end of the first scene of *The Shrew*, that the "very excellent piece of work" should come to a quick close.

Postscript

Percy Allen first suggested the basic equations between Sly and Shakspere and Oxford and the hoax Lord in *The Life Story of Edward de Vere as "William Shakespeare"*; London, Cecil Palmer, 1932; 299-304.

Chapter 5–The Making of William Shakespeare

"I am…haunted by the conviction that the divine William is the biggest and most successful fraud ever practiced on a patient world. The more I turn him round and round the more he so affects me."

Henry James to Violet Hunt (1903)

When the question comes up, Who was the real writer of the books that go under the name of William Shakespeare? you often hear in answer the nonchalant dismissal, Who cares if Shakespeare wrote them or another man of the same name?–All that matters is that we have the plays. (His other poems are seldom mentioned in this context. Nor do the speakers usually say "his" plays; they seem to prefer the impersonal article to the pronoun.)

Listening to those nonchalant words, I have always been surprised to observe how warmly people can care for books and shows, and yet turn cold shoulders on every inquiry into the life, the flesh and blood, that created them. It appears that the mind of the maker and the ways by which he conceived these brain-children of his do not interest the public who applaud them. Researchers into the dark continent of Shakespeare's nervous universe have always known or sensed that they would be poorly rewarded by the world, that the outcome of their explorations in terms of popular opinion or earthly goods could be predicted in the poet's phrase, love's labors lost. The proper mentality for culling academic honors in the region of the Bard, as they call him, is exemplified by the Variorum editor, Howard Furness and the psychiatrist Weir Mitchell: "We personally agreed," reported the latter, "that we did not want to know any more about Shakespeare than we did at present, that on the whole it would be more agreeable to know nothing about him except his books."

They shared the suspicion of Charles Dickens that the world would be more tranquil if left in darkness about the biography of the maker of Othello and Macbeth. "It is a great comfort to my thinking," Dickens told the researcher William Sandys on June 13, 1847, "that so little is known concerning the poet. It is a fine mystery; and I tremble every day lest something should come out. If he had a Boswell, society wouldn't have respected his grave, but would calmly have had his skull in the Phrenological shop windows." In the days of Dickens, Phrenology promised to become the science of human nature that Psychoanalysis finally travailed with.

The explorers of Shakespeare's skullworks know that their labor is disturbing to a favorite Western worship and therefore they must expect to be treated like iconoclasts. For hidden beneath the carefree air of those who pretend indifference on the question of Shakespeare's personality, under the actual joy which is shown especially by college intellects in the lack of our knowledge about the dramatist's character and reality, there lies a fear that dispelling this ignorance would mean curtains for the peculiar bliss they get from his plays. They suspect that into the making of each of these masterpieces flowed a stream of suffering from the dramatist's mind which they have no desire to see reflected in their own sufficiently troubled heads. And the bliss of wonder about such things, the curiosity that Aristotle and Anatole France considered the beginning of wisdom, is repelled as childishness.

However, the intellectual comfort of the play-loving public will hardly do for a criterion in matters of justice and mental science. The question of William Shakespeare's identity is one that calls for honesty toward an unknown genius who did the world tremendous recreational good and provided psychology with some of its deepest insights into human nature. Also the question renders an acid test for the validity of psychological methods and principles. The science of human nature proves its truth by predicting human identity. One should be able, on the basis of the acts and products of a mysterious man, to tell what kind of human we would discover if we ever made his acquaintance. Long ago it was said of prophets or persons who claimed to be prophets, "By their fruits you shall know them." By their fruits, their material output, not their looks or their claims. Well, we have the fruits of the man who called himself Shakespeare but we still do not know him. Of course, the several-sided bodies of his fruits, their histrionic form, their masquerade, had been largely instrumental in preventing us from catching on to the personality concealed behind all these amazing masks. Yet which of us has not sensed the singular in his dramatic variety? Nobody would deny that only one supreme and lonesome soul could have produced this masquerade. There was nothing like it on the stage before, and nothing, except the plays of his pupils, comparable to it since.

Rare are the writers who convey the feeling of a voice and heart like Shakespeare, and we are telling the truth when we say while reading one of his works that we are reading *him*. Surely researchers familiar with his deeds in literature should have enough information to select this genius out of any crowd of contemporaries he chose to mingle with or with whom he was forced to consort.

Judging by his poetic fruits, the major critics of Shakespeare (from Goethe and Coleridge to Georg Brandes and Sigmund Freud) have generally affirmed that he was aristocratic in his art and taste, an extremely delicate voluptuary who scorned the mechanically toiling masses and adored ancient nobility, feudal chivalry and feudal merriment, idle loveliness and learning of all sorts but especially the exotic and occult. Immensely curious about people, in particular the shady folks, more or less mad, who lived beyond the borders of polite society and the law, he liked best of all to watch them and listen to them. His passion for the theatre was a dreamer's passion; tho it had an element of the histrionic in it, he was too selfconscious and secretive to perform well in actor's paint. He was gifted or crafty beyond belief in language and perfervidly fond of puns. By his wit, by his outpour of words alone, it must be possible to detect the true Shakespeare. If he kept silent, it was probably because he felt melancholy or simply contemplative, stocking his memory with dramatic material. And in his dealings with women, he was presumably an intellectual jester and duelist, struggling always in their presence to master an unreasoning, infantile fear. You can almost smell the dramatist's anxiety in the company of proud energetic ladies; they certainly excited him to demonic reactionary behavior, at distressful times to brutality. And among his minor distinctions, two of the more useful for the purpose of establishing the identity of the poet might be his love and lore of dogs and his strange animosity toward cats. But it is unlikely that we shall ever possess more reliable documents on these animal attitudes than the clear avowal of his books.

Against the verdict of the artist's chief critics (all artists too) stand the decisions of a legion of scholars headed by James Orchard Halliwell-Phillips, who never swerved from his faith that the dramatist was a stranger to chivalry and the conversation of lords and ladies, not an artist truly but a shop-keeping soul, "working under the domination of a commercial spirit."[1] Sir Sidney Lee upheld this view with the most successful biography of the idol of Stratford-on-Avon. He saw, instead of a solitary narcissic rover after beauty, an unassuming sociable fellow, one of "continuous industry" and "the shrewd capacity of a man of business." Lee believed that his hero "seemed unconscious of his marvelous superiority to his professional comrades...His literary attainments and successes were chiefly valued as serving the prosaic end of providing permanently for himself and his daughters."(Note the omission of his wife.)[2] Even more emphatic in maintaining that Shakespeare was just a profiteer of the pen was John M. Robertson, who prided himself on being a Freethinker. He described the deity of the theatre as one "not much cultured, not profound, not deeply passionate: not particularly reflective though copious in utterance; a personality which of itself, if under no pressure of pecuniary need, would not be likely to give the world any serious sign of mental capacity whatever."[3]

Now the striking contradiction between the portrait painted by the esthetic analysts and that etched by the more erudite but less empathetic authors can be resolved if we think of their pictures as descriptions of two different men.

The scholars have compiled for us a fairly accurate account of the gentleman from Stratford-on-Avon on whose robust burgess's head the greatness of Shakespeare has been located or rather thrust.

We have still to recognize the man who achieved that greatness and gave it up, with this resolution announced in a sonnet to one very dear to him:

> My name be buried where my body is,
> And live no more to shame nor me nor you.

Yes, the dramatist's conviction that he was disgraced and shamed beyond redemption may well be added to the list of characteristics by which we expect to identify him. He felt disgraced by the same fruits which eventually obtained for his art the gratitude of humanity everywhere. "I am sham'd," he told his beloved, "by that which I bring forth, And so should you, to love things nothing worth." In fact, one of his motives for hiding his identity was his desire to protect this beloved from the contempt and derision which society had inflicted on him for producing valueless fruits. The conscience of the poet could not bear that his work should appear under his true name. In his Sonnets he plainly expressed the sorrow and terror he felt on observing

> That every word doth almost tell my name,
> Showing their birth, and where they did proceed.

How did the artist manage to conceal the authorship of poems and plays so blazoned with individuality? By now you know the answer. He lured the world which had despised and rejected him into taking the jack-of-all-trades William Shakspere (so the gentleman from Stratford spelled his own name, according to his birth and death registers) for the true author, and so executed "the biggest and most successful fraud ever practiced on a patient world."

The secret writer lived to see poor Will luxuriously paid for his acquiescence in the comedy. It was not a very hard role young Shakspere was called on to perform. All he had to do was to bring a certain theatrical troop the plays of his master–carefully copied by professional secretaries (so that the first editors of the dramas marveled at the fact that they found scarcely a "blot" in their "original" manuscripts.) Let the actors and other playwrights think what they pleased about the source of his wares. He kept his mouth customarily shut but always in good humor, resided alone and eluded every sort of public light, particularly those of the stage and the state. Never mixing as an equal with companions in London, he made it plain that he considered his home to be Stratford, returned to his native town once a year, and as soon as possible (perhaps as early as 1604), made his permanent residence there. (His name appeared for the last time in a list of the King's players on April 9, 1604.) He must have also served in business between the shy poet and publishers. The fact that he was a provincial, the son of a butcher and leathercraftsman, and poorly educated, would not prevent him from winning the fame of a dramatist. For there would invariably be good bourgeois spirits to protest against the snobbery of skeptics, to repeat the old adage that poets were born, not made, and to boast that one of their own class, while lacking the learning of books, was yet divinely wise in the interpretation of the heart. Moreover, the chief impression he appears to have made on his contemporaries–judging by a majority of printed tributes and anecdotes–was the stamp of a humorist, a maker of jokes, often practical. If provoked he could make fun of his critics (there is Tudor testimony that he staged at least one obscene joke about Ben Jonson), but common sense preserved the secret of his fortune and thus guarded in blissful nescience the foundations of his future cult.[4]

With a little painstaking I think we can piece together the primary skein of the fabrication by which William Shakspere of Stratford underwent metamorphosis into William Shakespeare of the Globe theatre and global literature.

First we go back to the time when young Shakspere was still in Stratford, never dreaming of the transformation he would suffer in London. His earliest biographer, John Aubrey, around 1680, recorded the hometown tradition, heard from the parish clerk, that "when he was a boy he exercised his father's trade," slaughtering sheep and cattle mostly, skinning them and turning the hides into gloves and so on. There is no tradition of his ability as a butcher, but he seems to have been agile enough at the trade to attempt the stealing and killing of a buck deer belonging to a knight of the neighborhood. The knight hounded him for this: "he was obliged," writes a later biographer, Nicholas Rowe (1709), "to leave his business and family in Warwickshire and shelter himself in London." Rowe got his information from the actor Thomas Betterton who visited Stratford to collect memories of the town's most admired son. Another writer, equally dependable, reported that poor Will, for stealing venison and rabbits, was often whipped and sometimes jailed.[5] Perhaps history here unhappily repeated itself; perhaps the whipt Will's blood could not help answering the same imperious summons that moved Thomas Shakspere of Warwickshire in 1359 to abandon his few goods in flight from charges of felony. Both Will and Tom may have inherited genes like those that would not rest until William Shakspere, the first known Englishman of that name, went to be hanged for robbery in 1248. Kindred genes burnt with hard gemlike flames in Walter Shakspere who went to jail in Colchester Castle during the reign of Richard II, and John Shakespeare who entered Colchester prison for disturbing the King's peace in 1381. Who but a chip off such a block of churls would have become, as "William Shagspere" did, too early a father in 1582, shortly after the death of Anne Hathaway's father? Two friends of her father had to swear and sign a bond with the Bishop of Worcester that she and William Shagspere might be husband and wife with only one church announcement of their matrimony (English custom usually required three announcements). No record of their marriage has ever turned up. The date of the butcher-boy's flight is unknown; however, no historian has doubted that he was present at the baptism of his last children, the twins Hamnet and Judith, named after his artisan friends Hamnet and Judith Sadler, on February 2, 1585. Not yet twenty, the hunted poacher made his way to London and went in search of a way to earn his bread.

John Aubrey was told by an aged actor named William Beeston that Shakspere "had been in his younger years a schoolmaster in the country." This actor has been welcomed as an authority on the Shakespearean stage although he was only a child when Shakspere died, and could only have known what his father Christopher Beeston, who had once been a servant in Shakspere's company, the King's players, and other members of this troop had told him. Apparently, they told him very little, if we may judge by Aubrey's notes on his memories, and that little contains much wrong. Beeston also stated that the man who killed the dramatist Christopher Marlowe was none other than Ben Jonson. This preposterous claim does not affect the credulity of Shakspere's idolators when they come to the Beeston statement that he had been a country schoolmaster–not an assistant teacher, an usher, mind you, but a master. If the runaway butcher did try teaching school, he certainly found the work uncongenial. He gave it up to become a holder of horses in the metropolis.

Speaking of the credulity of Shakespere's worshipers reminds me how the analytic powers of Hanns Sachs were bent and twisted for the sake of the cult. So enraptured was he with the legend of the young man who fled " from the dunghill at the door for which his father was fined, and the half-enforced marriage with the pregnant peasant girl," to become the world's most famous penman, that he had enormous difficulty digesting the facts that interfered with the fantasy. In his essay on Shakespeare's *Tempest*, he made a source of John Lacy, a young colleague of the actor William Beeston, a colleague of Shakspere of Stratford, whom Lacy could never have known. Moreover, Sachs quoted a note of John Aubrey as a remark made by Lacy on the character of William Shakspere, though nobody can say for sure whom Aubrey had in mind when he wrote it; it was not included in the latter's biography of Shakspere. The note occurs near the references of Aubrey to old Beeston; John Lacy had told the biographer that Beeston might be able to provide information for his purpose. The note says cryptically: "The more to be admired q(uia) he was not a company keeper, lived in Shoreditch, wouldn't be debauched, and if invited to writ: he was in pain."[6] Sachs followed the editors who read "court" instead of "writ".[7]

A descendant of Shakspere's sister Joan Hart, whose family occupied for many years the so-called "Birthplace" of Shakspere in Stratford, and collected money from visitors to the shrine–toward the end of their stay they sold it to a butchery business–informed Sir Richard Phillips that "he had often heard his mother state that Shakspere owed his rise in life, and his introduction to the theatre, to his accidentally holding the horse of a gentleman at the door of the theatre, on his first arriving in London. His appearance led to inquiry and subsequent patronage."[8]

The Theatre was indeed the name of London's largest playhouse in those days. It had been built in 1576 by the actor and ex-carpenter James Burbage, in the disreputable district of Shoreditch beyond the government limits of London, and Burbage kept a livery stable in Smithfield nearby. Near the Theatre stood the Curtain, a playhouse in which Burbage was also financially interested; his actors used it when the Theatre required a change. Both stages were reached on horseback by men who had the means and the desire to see plays without walking the distance between Shoreditch and the city. Pursuing the path of least resistance would have naturally led the young fugitive from Stratford to the brothels, bear-baiting pits and theatres of Shoreditch and a job at Burbage's stable. This is the employment that Robert Greene probably had in view when he denounced "Shakescene" in his *Groatsworth of Wit* as a "rude groom".[9] Burbage himself had once worn the livery of the Earl of Leicester, and this company probably led the troops who performed at the Theatre. But there is no evidence to connect the name Shakespeare with Leicester's players. We have no exact knowledge of the troop to which Rowe alluded when he wrote that Shakespeare "was received into the company then in being at first in a very mean rank." If we only knew the name of the gentleman whose horse he held at the door of the theatre and to whom he owed his introduction to the theatre and his rise in life, we might be able to tell precisely the stages of his progress to wealth and immortality.

My guess is that the unknown gentleman was Edward de Vere, Earl of Oxford, the member of the English nobility most attracted to the theatre, himself a poet and writer of plays, plays which are said to be lost. Oxford patronized more than one company of actors. A troop in his service had visited Stratford-on-Avon around the end of November, 1584, and Will Shakspere may have been drawn to their shows. We do not know where Oxford's players performed when they stayed in London, nor do we know the names of their stars. In 1585 the Earl of Oxford resided at a mansion called the Folly next door to buildings owned by the brothers Edward and John Alleyn, both players in the Earl of Worcester's troop. In that year Edward Alleyn joined Burbage, taking with him men from Worcester's and Sheffield's companies, to form the Admiral's company; "he with his brother John Alleyn, Robert Brown, and Richard Jones, combined the remainder, or part of the remainder of the two companies with Oxford's company; this amalgamation working under Oxford's title in summer at the Curtain, and probably at the Boar's Head in winter...."[10] The Boar's Head was a tavern in the district of Eastcheap, a stroll from Oxford's house. I would nominate this company as the one to which William Shakspere was introduced by his mysterious patron. In support of this nomination I have only a fantasy to offer, but a fantasy which the severest of critics will find not too far from the facts.

I imagine poor William Shakspere standing at the door of one of the theatres in Shoreditch and Edward de Vere riding up to encounter him. The time of the meeting is not long after the baptism of Shakspere's twins, perhaps two months, shortly before his birthday in April, a day of unknown date. I like to think they met under "the uncertain glory of an April day." The unknown scribbler of *Vox Graculi or Jack Dawes Prognostication* (1623) tells us that April meant a kind of renascence to the English drama: "About this time new playes will be in more request than old, and if company come currant to the Bull and Curtaine, there will be more money gathered in one after-noone then will be given to Kingsland Spittle (Hospital) in a whole moneth; also, if, at this time, about the houres of foure or five it wax cloudy, and then raine downright, they shall sit dryer in the galleries then those who are the understanding men in the yard."

The runaway's miserable appearance, I imagine, drew the eye of the Earl and plucked at his heart strings with an appeal to some unconscious memory. Possibly the two had met before by the river Avon, since De Vere owned the manor of Bilton there, near the Forest of Arden, about nineteen miles northeast from Stratford. At all events, he would have come out of the theatre after the play in a meditative mood and, seeing the forlorn fellow holding his horse, obeyed the caprice to invite him to a tavern for his first decent meal in months.

On learning that his name was William, the Earl would have remembered how the poet Edmund Spenser had nicknamed him "Willie" in *The Shepherd's Calendar* (August 1580), portraying his agility in a duel of rimes.[11] The thought of Spenser surely carried in its wake the remembrance of Spenser's friend Gabriel Harvey, who also figures in *The Shepherd's Calendar*. In July, 1578, Harvey had officially welcomed Oxford to Cambridge University with a Latin ode celebrating his virtues and arts. In this poem the Earl was urged to give up his passion for writing poetry in order to devote himself to a nobleman's duty in arms. "I have seen many Latin verses of thine," Harvey declared, "yes, even more English verses are extant; thou hast drunk deep draughts not only of the Muses of France and Italy....O thou hero worthy of renown, throw away bloodless books, and writings that serve no useful purpose; now must the sword be brought into play, now is the time for thee to sharpen the spear and handle great engines of war....thine eyes flash fire, thy countenance shakes a spear."[12] The image of the shaken spear in Oxford's face was not so far-fetched as it may seem; when the earl was only Viscount Bulbec, in his boyhood, he had carried on his coat of arms the crest of a lion grasping a broken spear. This picture must have haunted him all his life as a prophecy of his failures in war and love. If these memorial associations ran through De Vere's mind on learning that his new acquaintance had a name sounding like Shakespear, think of how fatally intimate with the Stratford fellow he must have felt when he was told that Will's father was named John, the same as the poet's father, and that Will had been born in April too. As a matter of fact De Vere was born on April 12 (1550), according to the Julian calendar kept in England until 1752, when the calendar by Pope Gregory, adopted by continental Europe in the dramatist's lifetime, in 1582, finally gained official consent in his country. According to the Gregorian calendar, De Vere's birthday falls on April 23, the day which has been celebrated for centuries as the birthday of the poet Shakespeare, and which may have been the birthday of the poacher Shakspere. He was baptized on April 26 (that was the Old Style date) and English custom would commonly bring a baby to the font three days after birth.

April 23, you know, is the date recorded in the church of Shakspere's grave as the day of his death. Popular superstition could not resist the poetic justice of depicting his life as a perfect circle beginning and ending on the same April day. The curious Earl may have also seen significance in the fact that the stranger from Stratford had a mother named Mary, with one syllable or two in common with his own mother's name, Margery. Will did have a sister Margaret, and Oxford's only sibling was christened Mary.

I suppose the poet asked his new acquaintance if he was a kinsman of Matthew Shakespeare of London who married the playwright George Peele's sister Isabel. We have no way of answering this question today. The trade that Matthew pursued is unknown. In my conjecture he was the father of Edmund Shakespeare the player, who was buried in December 1607 at the age of 28 in the London theatrical district of Southwark. The fancy of biographers made this Edmund the younger brother of Will Shakspere, just because his name happened to be Edmund, but there is not a bit of proof that Shakspere's brother ever left Stratford. The player Edmund was born in 1579; Matthew Shakespeare married Isabel Peele, sister of a playwright and player, in 1569.

Of course the Earl of Oxford would be interested in the story of Shakespeare's "half-enforced" wedding with the pregnant peasant Anne Hathaway. The Earl's own wife was also named Anne, and when he married her the gossip of the city detected something compulsory in the affair. Lord St. John remarked in a letter, "The Earl of Oxenford hath gotten himself a wife, or at least, a wife hath caught him."[13]

In the summer following, Queen Elizabeth paid a visit to Warwickshire with her court and the Earl of Oxford had entertained her with a mock-battle between forts which he erected by the Avon. The butcher John Shakspere and his boy Will could have been among the crowds who witnessed the sport.

Few biographers doubt that Will was unhappy with his Anne, though not for the same reasons that the Earl was wretched with his Anne. Both abandoned their wives and came back to them but never with reconciled hearts. The stranger from Stratford and the merry madcap Earl of Oxford also had lawlessly loved two ladies named Anne. De Vere's dark wanton, Anne Vavasor, merits a volume devoted to her long and wonderful life. But we are absolutely without information concerning Anna Whately of Temple Grafton who, on November 27, 1582, enjoyed the brief felicity of a marriage license granted by the Bishop of Worcester to her and William Shakspere. The next day Anne Hathaway's father's friends delivered the bond to the bishop that made her a legitimate mother. I doubt whether the fact that Shakspere's first daughter was baptized Susannah (in May 1583) while Edward de Vere's last daughter was named Susan (in May 1587) is more than coincidence. But if I am right in surmising that the first version of *Hamlet* was written in the year 1584 (it made a strong tragic impression on the humorist Thomas Nashe which he indicated in a book of 1589), then the likeness between this dramatic portrait of the real Shakespeare and the name of Will Shakspere's only son must have struck the Earl of Oxford as another chord of destiny between him and the runaway Will.

In Thomas Nashe's comic pamphlet *Strange News*, published in 1593, there is an "Epistle Dedicatory" to an enigmatic poet whom he calls "Gentle Master William," the most prolific lyric writer of the period. Charles Wisner Barrell has demonstrated in detail that this William is none other than Edward de Vere.[14] Nashe affirms that the copious poet was not just a patron generous to scholars but a friend to beggars too.

"There cannot a thread-bare cloak sooner peep forth," says he, "but you strait press it to be an out-brother of your bounty." So my fantasy concludes with a scene in which De Vere is so moved by the spectacle and story of the vagabond from the Avon country, bearing so many trivial resemblances to his own life, that he makes him also an "outbrother"–more exactly, an outson–and afterward his stage agent and mask.

He got the young fellow a place in his company at the Curtain, where Shakespeare's plays are known to have been memorably performed and tried out his abilities in different functions and roles. Theatrical tradition, reported by Rowe, declares that the "top of his performance" as an actor was in the mummery of Hamlet's Ghost. He was far more successful in the commercial affairs of the theatre, apparently collecting a large stock of play-apparel which he rented or sold at whimsical prices, and doing the same with stage manuscripts.[15] He may have marched with the two hundred proud players, arrayed in silks, whom the spy Maliverny Catlin described in January 1587, parading the streets of London with the livery of Leicester, Oxford, the Lord Admiral, and other magnates.[16]

By May, 1592, he was prosperous enough to lend one John Clayton in Cheapside seven pounds, a loan for which "Willelmus Shackspere" applied legal ingenuity to get repaid eight years later. When he made the Cheapside loan he was already notorious as a usurer and stage manager, indeed, in Robert Greene's phrase, a Johanes Factotum. In *A Groatsworth of Wit* (August 1592) the dying Greene attempted a satire on him, singling out for particular sarcasm a new posture of this jack-of-all-trades, his claim that he was "as well able to bombast out a blanck verse as the best" of the current playwrights. "In his own conceit," wrote Greene, "the only Shakescene in a country." His claim was backed up by a procession of blank-verse comedies and tragedies which arrived on the stage with a speed that bewildered all observers who had no inkling of the secret of the Stratford sphinx.

One cannot say definitely when the noble poet "Willie" determined to add Shakespeare to his pseudonym. That name does not appear connected with drama before the summer of 1592. Names like it, however, had long been familiar to the Earl of Oxford in his experience with plays and players, an experience that began in childhood at home with the company maintained by his father. He remembered Master Shakelock who had produced entertainment on the stage at Trinity College, Cambridge, in 1562-63. He had probably seen William Shakshaft of Lancashire act in rustic buffooneries between 1581 and 1587. Seeking a pen name to hide his theatrical authorship, he would not have missed the precious pun in the syllables of Shake-spear. It was not merely a familiar country name. It had a heroic ring, warlike, suitable to a writer of epic history plays. And also it had a sardonic echo, reminding of the god Priapus, and therefore fit for a writer of farce. One can see him enjoying the image of the shaking spear, reminding him of the desperate lion on his boyhood crest, and suddenly recalling the horse in Holy Scriptures whom the poet *Job* describes as laughing at the shaking of the spear (xli,21). That laughing horse must have recalled the grinning horse-holder at the door of the theatre, the lad with the name that was almost Shakespear. Here was the logical, the comically perfect candidate for the role of purveyor to the players of the dramas that Edward de Vere composed but dared not display as his own to a world that would have made him a laughing-stock for staining his blue blood with venal ink. Even the word poet in that caste-conscious age had become a term of ridicule and shame.

Oxford was of course well acquainted with the Essays of Montaigne, and perhaps had copied in his tablets the warning of that author against nobles hazarding their honor by engaging in literature. Yet Montaigne believed that the Roman comedies that went under the name of Terence were really written by his patrons Scipio and Lelius. "Could the perfection of eloquence," he said," have added luster suitable to a great personage, certainly Scipio and Lelius had never resigned the honor of their comedies, with all the luxuriances and elegancies of the Latin tongue, to an African slave. For that the work was theirs, its beauty and excellence sufficiently declare; Terence himself confesses as much, and I should take it ill from any one that would dispossess me of that belief."[17]But such beauty and excellence, the French sage contended, were unworthy of an aristo-crat, whose life should rightly be spent in "justice and the science of government and conducting his people both in peace and war." Oxford once thought so too. But his misfortunes with the arts of government and war compelled him to wonder why he would not be conducting his people almost as worthily by writing and producing their most influential works of histrionic art. The dilemma calls to my mind the title of a lost book, licensed in September 1580, which may have been a satire on the poet Willie. Its title was "William Wit, Wit's Will, or Will's Wit; Choose You Whether."

So long as De Vere lived with the former Anne Cecil, daughter of Elizabeth's chief minister, and remained a courtier in attendance on the Queen, he seems to have been content with the disguise of pastoral Will. His wife died in June 1588. From then on, his activities were ever deeper shrouded in mystery. He married again in 1591, but his bride, Elizabeth Trentham, did not have the wealth to pay the government the eleven thousand pounds which Crown attorneys claimed the house of Vere owed. They reckoned all the claims of the Earl's creditors in 1591 as amounting to 22,000 pounds. I suspect he deepened his personal disgrace by accepting money from Will Shakspere himself, money derived from the sale of his plays, and Shakspere's shares in the company. After the Earl's marriage he retired from the royal court. The impact of this departure on English poetry was lamented by Edmund Spenser in his "Tears of the Muses" (1591) in a poem extolling "Willy" for his (vanished) comedies and regretting the prevalence of desperately risible plays by fellows of vulgar blood:

And he, the man whom Nature's self had made
To mock herself and Truth to imitate,
With kindly counter under mimic shade,
Our pleasant Willy, ah! Is dead of late....
But that same gentle spirit, from whose pen
Large streams of honey and sweet nectar flow,

Scorning the boldness of such base-born men
Which dare their follies forth so rashly throw,
 Doth rather choose to sit in idle cell
 Than so himself to mockery to sell.

The patrician Willy let Spenser think that he scorned to compete in comedy with playwrights of plebean birth. That is one reason why we find the erudite but tedious Francis Meres in 1598 listing as "the best for comedy amongst us" first, in order of rank, "Edward, Earl of Oxford," and after seven lesser dramatists–"Shakespeare." The Earl had once remarked in a juvenile poem that his appearance of idleness was deceiving. I am never "less idle, lo!:" he wrote, "Than when I am alone." In the cell of solitude deplored by Spenser he was occupied in creating the paramount comedy of his career, a masterpiece which deserves to be entitled the Divine Will because of its semblance to the creation of man as conceived at least by the authors of *Genesis*.

Into an erection of dirt the God of the Old Testament blew a soul partaking of His energy and eternity. Round the vulgar, grasping, crapulent creature William Shakspere the peerless poet wove a veil of illusion that made the whole world see in him, not Nicholas Bottom the weaver and volunteer player of all parts, but a man worthy to be kissed by Titania, the queen of elves.[18] "Lord, what fools these mortals be!"

Spenser's peculiar expression "dead of late" makes me think of the court rumor reported by Roland Whyte to Sir Robert Sidney in November 1591: "Some say my lord of Oxford is dead." [19] There is no plain daylight testimony of what the Earl was doing at this time. In March 1595 he sent his former father-in-law a hasty letter from Bishopsgate, where many actors made their homes. Will Shakspere was then a resident there, acquiring credit for the books of *Venus and Adonis* (1593) and *The Rape of Lucrece* (1594), which were the first to bear the signature of William Shakespeare, both dedicated to the Earl of Southampton with expressions of daring affection. Oxford had hoped to have Southampton as a son-in-law, in vain.

With the coming of James Stuart to the throne of England in 1603 Will Shakspere was promoted from membership in the Lord Chamberlain's company of actors to the King's own company. I will not repeat here the proof that the Lord Chamberlain whom he had served for all the years in which the troop held a monopoly of Shakespeare's plays was actually Edward de Vere, Lord Chamberlain of England.[20]

What I wish to point out is the startling fact that, no sooner had Shakspere been enrolled among the King's men than he seems to have prepared–in the prime of his life–for retirement from the theatre. His name appears for the last time on a list of the King's troop on April 9, 1604. Hamlet had just come from the press; the greater tragedies of Shakespeare were still to be printed. Yet this April was the month he chose or was commanded to quit the royal sport. There is no record of the date when he disposed of his shares in the Globe and the Blackfriars playhouse. The truth of the matter is that he had no more dramas of Shakespeare to purvey. Edward de Vere died, most likely of the plague, on June 24, 1604. Hence the peculiar dearth this year of dramas meriting royal eyes and ears. Sir Walter Cope described the famine in a letter of 1604 to Oxford's brother-in-law, Lord Cranborne. He tells how Richard Burbage, the chief actor of the age, had come to him, "and says there is no new play that the Queen has not seen; but they have revived an old one called *Love's Labour Lost*, which for wit and mirth will please her exceedingly. And this is appointed to be played tomorrow night at my Lord of Southampton's unless you send a writ to remove the *corpus cum causa* to your house in Strand."[21]

Early in 1605 an anonymous pamphlet called Ratsey's *Ghost* appeared, making fun of actors and moneylenders and country upstarts who had gotten quickly rich. The writer has his hero, Ratsey the highwayman, advise a provincial actor to go to London: "There thou shalt learn to be frugal (for players were never so thrifty as they are now about London) and to feed upon all men, to let none feed upon thee; to make thy hand a stranger to thy pocket, thy heart slow to perform thy tongue's promise: and when thou feelest thy purse well lined, buy thee some place or Lordship in the country, that growing weary of playing, thy money may there bring thee to dignity and reputation." "I have heard indeed," says the player, "of some that have gone to London very meanly and have come in time to be exceedingly wealthy." The portrayal fits our Shakspere closely if not comfortably. In May 1602 he obtained the deed that made him proprietor of New Place, the biggest house in his town. By sheer fraud he had obtained a gentleman's coat of arms, without waiting for the government to permit his claim to the heraldry. [22]

Strictly speaking, it was his father who made the claim, according to the documents of the case, but since the claim had never been made before the son had the funds sufficient to get the heralds' office to pay attention to a claim from the Shakspere family, it is agreed that the bold William was the first to propose it. Hanns Sachs permitted his own imagination to transcend the bounds of fact when he contended that old John Shakspere was elevated to a knighthood. [23]

The infernal Will died in April 1616 of a fever contracted, according to the Rev. John Ward, Vicar of Stratford in 1662, at a merry meeting where he drank too hard. As a local financier concerned in the gathering of church taxes, the tithes, he had the right to be buried in the Stratford church. No name was inscribed on his grave, only four lines of doggerel putting a curse on anyone who moved his bones. He left a will that said nothing about theatrical interests or manuscripts. Sometime before 1623 unknown admirers raised on the wall of the church a monument to his memory.

It was sketched by William Dugdale, forty years after Shakspere's death, and the sketch was printed in Dugdale's *Antiquities of Warwickshire*. It shows an old and thin-faced personage holding a sack, probably containing imaginary wool. One of the last legal acts of father John was a suing for payment for wool he had sold, and it seems that son William had taken over his wool trade. In the next century, the Rev. Joseph Greene had the bust taken down for repairs, and he arranged for the repairs which included "beautifying" the monument. The result was the falsehood which blandly stares from Stratford Church at the present hour, a figure writing on a cushion, with a Latin inscription comparing the idol to the philosopher Socrates and the epic poet Vergil, whom Shakspere did not resemble in the least and Shakespeare hardly at all.

By 1616 less than half of Shakespeare's plays had been sent to the press. In 1623 a group of lovers of his work went to prodigal expense for the publication of the first complete collection of the plays. Two old actors of his company accepted nominal responsibility for the venture while Ben Jonson apparently took charge of the composition of prefaces and advertising verse. His friend Leonard Digges made an allusion to the dramatist's "Stratford Monument" which he saw in fancy dissolving to dust leaving the one true monument for him, the book. From the publication of the first folio the pretense was flamboyantly maintained that the gentleman from Stratford was the author, yet nobody from his family or Stratford was invited to take part in the publication.

It came out with a dedication to William Herbert, Earl of Pembroke, and Philip his brother, the Earl of Montgomery. Here, for the first time, we are solemnly assured that the brothers Herbert had favored the dramatist in his lifetime with extraordinary good will. No document connects their names with Shakspere. William Herbert was at one time nearly engaged to marry Bridget de Vere, the daughter of the Earl of Oxford. The Earl of Montgomery did marry Oxford's third daughter, Susan. And both men must have had their hands in the solemn sport of fulfilling his literary testament. More active in the masquerade was surely Oxford's legitimate son Henry, who inherited his earldom. In 1624 Henry de Vere celebrated his freedom from twenty months in the Tower of London, where King James had imprisoned him for too much taking of political liberty at court and in parliament, by marrying the heiress Diana Cecil, granddaughter of Thomas, a brother-in-law of Edward de Vere. This wedding took place on New Year's day: we do not have information on the plays that were performed in its honor, but it would not surprise us to learn that one of them was Shakespeare's *A Midsummer Night's Dream*, which even academic orthodoxy believes was performed at the wedding of Earl Edward's eldest daughter, Elizabeth, to William Stanley, Earl of Derby. By preserving the fiction of William Shakespeare's personality these earls were not only carrying out the wish the poet proclaimed in his *Sonnets*. They were protecting the honor and fortune of the house of Vere.

The man who inherited the titles of both Pembroke and Montgomery also had a profound interest and considerable power in theatrical affairs. In 1635 Cuthbert Burbage and other shareholders in the Globe playhouse petitioned him concerning their property rights in the Globe, and in their paper had occasion to mention the former partner William Shakspere. Instead of referring to him as the writer of the most famous dramas performed at their theatre, and a gentleman well known to Pembroke and Montgomery, they simply spoke of him as a "man player" and a "deserving" fellow.

By the year 1638 there was hardly a man alive who could separate fact from fantasy in the tradition concerning Shakespeare. The memory of Edward de Vere's generosity to the stage still lingered in a few gray heads, and Richard Brome alluded to him in his comedy *The Antipodes*, praising the men who acted his play:

> These lads can act the Emperors' lives all over,
> And Shakespeare's Chronicled histories, to boot,
> And were that Caesar, or that English Earl
> That lov'd a Play and Player so well now living,
> I would not be out-vyed in my delights.

The Earl of Oxford had been buried in the suburban church of Hackney and his widow erected a modest monument on his grave, so modest that no account of it survives. Nor is it now in existence. Time executed his testament remorselessly.

However, in 1661 there was a street in London named Vere and a theatre struggled to make a livelihood there for a while. So far as contemporary historians were concerned, the most illuminating anecdote they could obtain about Oxford was a dirty joke recorded by John Aubrey–that De Vere had gone in youth on a tour of Europe because he had been suddenly humiliated before Queen Elizabeth; while bowing to her, Aubrey says, he abruptly farted; when he returned to her Majesty's court she greeted him with the words, "My Lord, I had forgot the fart." The joke bears the earmarks of the cleverness in calumny for which Henry Howard, Earl of Northampton, Oxford's lifelong enemy, is notorious. Another anecdote, repeated by antiquarians more often, was first recorded by Francis Osborne in *Traditional Memoirs of the Reigns of Queen Elizabeth and King James I*. Osborne said that Montgomery, De Vere's son-in-law, "left nothing to testify his manhood but a beard and children, by that daughter of the last great Earl of Oxford, whose lady was brought to his Bed under the notion of his Mistress, and from such a virtuous deceit she (De Vere's Susan) is said to proceed." In Thomas Wright's history of Essex it is Lord Burghley, Oxford's father-in-law, who devises the stratagem to put De Vere to bed with his wife Anne, believing that she was "another woman," and the product of this aping of adultery is a son. The source of this gossip, in my opinion, was the cunning Henry Howard, who certainly had witnessed court performances of *All's Well That Ends Well* and *Measure for Measure* and could not have resisted applying a piece of their plots to the slanders he circulated against De Vere.

Oxford had poor luck posthumously too. The ablest defender of his character was Sir George Buck, poet, historian, and Master of the Revels at the royal court. However, Buck died insane, and the book in which he championed Edward de Vere was not published as he had written it. His *History of the Life and Reign of Richard the Third* was printed after his death with the passage concerning Oxford left out.

The resurrection of the Earl's genius did not transpire until 1920, when a school-teacher bearing, as Ernest Jones observed, the "unfortunate" name of Looney offered the first argument that William Shakespeare the artist was in truth the poet and dramatist Edward de Vere. Dr. Jones considered the argument absurd and the adherence to Looney's cause of Freud himself a marvel of irrationality. He suggested that the theory charmed Freud because of his childhood fantasies about having a different and grander parentage. I agree that these infant romances formed the basis of Freud's attraction to the Looney logic, but I wonder at Dr. Jones's implicit contention that the fantasies affected Freud's powers of reason and analysis to the point of blindness to the faults and wrongs of Looney's argument. What exactly was wrong with it, Dr. Jones had neither the time nor the patience to tell in his biography of Freud. He did make space for ridiculing Looney's cause and committing some mistakes which are curious especially coming from a psychoanalyst with an avowed "impatience for sloppiness." Evidently no one ever troubled to call his attention to the distortions of literary history that mar his otherwise excellent monograph on *Hamlet*, in which he ignored the Oxford theory. In his life of Freud he soared to higher flights from fact.[24] We may overlook the reference to Looney's book, *Shakespeare Identified*, as being published by Duell, Sloan & Pearce in 1920, when it was published by Stokes. But what are we to make of the citation of "Volume II" of Looney's book, which had no second volume? Moreover, Dr. Jones asserted: "The hare that Looney started has by no means come to rest, and a bevy of earls have since appeared on the scene"–meaning as claimants to the Shakespeare crown. Dr. Jones mentions the Earls of Derby and Rutland. He is manifestly just as ignorant about the Derby and Rutland claims as he is about the Oxford theory. The appearance of Derby on the scene occurred in 1919, a year before the publication of Looney's work. Professor Abel Lefranc (member of the French academy) who introduced the Derby hypothesis, had no knowledge of the Oxford argument when he wrote and published *Sous le Masque de William Shakespeare*. And Celestin Demblon issued his evidence that *Lord Rutland est Shakespeare* in Paris in 1913. In addition Dr. Jones drags into his mockery of the Oxford theory an irrelevant reference to the ludicrous idea that Christopher Marlowe wrote the plays of Shakespeare, leaving the unwary reader with the impression that Looney and Freud supported an idea no less ludicrous. The fact that the Oxford hypothesis had also received support by Gerald H. Rendall, one of England's leading classical scholars, and Sir

Geoffrey Callender, the eminent naval historian, thawed no ice in the Jones opposition. These authorities, and Freud's plea that he should study the De Vere claim, could not sway him from loyalty to the Stratford cult.

As in the case of Hanns Sachs, Freud was dear to him but dearer forever was the id necessity to uphold the drab Stratford idolatry, with its aid and comfort for the family romance or fairy-tale of the son who climbs from rags to riches–a daydream belonging to a libidinal stage older than the filial-complex revery of the parentage legend.

I wonder whether Sachs or Jones would have comprehended Shakespeare better if they had seen the astonishingly acute guess that Walt Whitman made concerning his identity. In his tome *November Boughs* (1888) Whitman answered the question "What lurks behind Shakespeare's Historical Plays?" as follows:

"We all know how much *mythus* there is in the Shakespeare question as it stands to-day. Beneath a few foundations of proved facts are certainly engulf'd far more dim and elusive ones, of deepest importance–tantalizing and half suspected–suggesting explanations that one dare not put in plain statement. But coming at once to the point, the English historical plays are to me not only the most eminent as dramatic performances (my mature judgment confirming the impressions of my early years, that the distinctiveness and glory of the Poet reside not in his vaunted dramas of the passions, but those founded on the contests of English dynasties, and the French wars) but form, as we get it all, the chief in a complexity of puzzles. Conceiv'd out of the fullest heat and pulse of European feudalism–personifying in unparallel'd ways the mediaeval aristocracy, its towering spirit of ruthless and gigantic caste, with its own peculiar air and arrogance (no mere imitation)–only one of the 'wolfish earls' so plenteous in the plays themselves, or some born descendant and knower, might seem to be the true author of those amazing works–works in some respects greater than anything else in recorded literature."

Endnotes

1. Halliwell-Phillips, J.O. *Outlines of the Life of Shakespeare* (London, 1887) 102.
2. Lee, S. *A Life of William Shakespeare* (London, 1898) 278-9.
3. Roberston, J.M. *Shakespeare and Montaigne* (London, 1909, 2nd ed.) 147.
4. Feldman, A.B. "Shakespeare Worship" *Psychoanalysis* 2 (1953) 57-72. (See Chapter 3 in this book.)
5. Lee, op. cit. 27.
6. Chambers, E.K. *William Shakspeare: A Study of Facts and Problems* (Oxford, 1930)II, 252.
7. Sachs, H. *The Creative Unconscious* (Cambridge, 1951, 2nd ed.) 274.
8. Chambers, op. cit. II, 299.
9. Feldman, A.B. "Greene's Groatsworth of Wit," *Shakespeare Fellowship News-Letter* (London, April 1951) 6-7.
10. Acheson, A. *Shakespeare, Chapman, and Thomas More* (London 1931) 46.
11. Looney, J. T. *"Shakespeare" Identified* (London, 1920) 341-6.
12. Ward, B.M. *The Seventeenth Earl of Oxford* (London 1928) 157.
13. Calendar of Rutland Manuscripts: 28 July 1571 (I, 94)
14. Barrell, C.W. "New Milestone in Shakespearean Research," *Shakespeare Fellowship Quarterly*, V (1944) 49-66.
15. Brooks, A. *Will Shakspere and the Dyer's Hand* (New York 1943) 55-58.
16. Read, C. *Mr. Secretary Walsingham* (London 1925) III, 181.
17. Montaigne, *Essays*, tr. Cotton, ed. Hazlitt (New York, n.d.)I, xxxix.
18. Gui, W. C. "Bottom's Dream," *American Imago* 9 (1952) 251ff.
19. Calendar of Penshurst Manuscripts: 9 November 1595 (II, 184).
20. Feldman, A.B. "Shakespeare's Jester–Oxford's Servant," *Shakespeare Fellowship Quarterly*, viii (1947) 39-43. (See Chapter 2 in this book.)
21. *Shakespeare Allusion Book*, ed. Munro (London, Oxford University Press, 1932) I, 139.
22. Greenwood, G.G. *Is There A Shakespeare Problem?* (London, John Lane 1916) 254-5.
23. Sachs, H. *Freud–Master and Friend* (Harvard University Press 1945).
24. Jones, E. *Life and Work of Sigmund Freud,* (New York, Basic Books 1953) III, 429-430.

Chapter 6—The March of Hamlet

Among the multitudinous perplexities of Hamlet one mote has troubled my mind's eye with a challenge that always carries a secret assurance it would be child's play to extract it. That is the question: Why should the Prince of Denmark swear, in the midst of the crisis of his first encounter with his father's ghost, by the patron saint of Ireland? What brought St. Patrick into Shakespeare's thought at the time he wrote this scene? Several metaphysical explanations have been offered, buried in the Furness Variorum edition of the drama: they appeal to none, not even to their authors. The suggestion I have to make has the merit at least of suiting common sense and illuminating other features of the play.

It occurred to me while perusing the scene in question, and feeling on my skin the bitter cold of its air, yet conscious that the time was not far away when Ophelia would be bringing on the stage blossoms of early spring, that Hamlet swears by St. Patrick for the simple reason that the day on which he encountered the paternal ghost is none other than the 17th of March, St. Patrick's day. Shakespeare and his countrymen were accustomed to thinking of dates according to the calendar of their church. Birthdays, funerals, weddings, and other events of social contracts were always noted as falling on Pentecost, or Lammas-eve, or Whitsuntide and so on. The heathen system of reckoning time that commerce has since made habit was only beginning to make headway at the dawn of the seventeenth century. If Shakespeare happened to be writing the first act of Hamlet on the night of the 17th of March, the name St. Patrick must have been prompt to rise to his view when he wanted his hero to swear by some saint.

Hamlet's reference to the Irish evangelist helps us to understand why the memory of the murder of Julius Caesar kept turning up as Shakespeare composed his tragedy. In the first act we are reminded vividly of the trauma that afflicted Roman imagination on the Ides, the 15th of March. We are reminded again of that horror when

Hamlet and Polonius talk about the latter's acting of the role of Caesar when he was a university wit. It is the enactment of Caesar's assassination that Hamlet dwells on. The first apparition of his father seen by the midnight guards of Elsinore came two days before the time of the tragedy's opening scene. By our reckoning, that would put the phenomenon on March 15, the anniversary of Caesar's death.

An alchemy of history and myth peculiar to Shakespeare's own imagination must have joined the murdered Caesar and the slain King of Denmark in his thought.

Thinking of the play as composed in the month of March throws light on its allusions not only to weather and season but also to the "Lenten entertainment" Hamlet promises the players. It may even explain why Hamlet calls Polonius a "fish-monger." For if Shakespeare had William Cecil, Lord Burghley, in his mind's eye when he created Polonius—as many scholars are convinced he did—he would not have forgotten how enthusiastic Burghley became in every Lent for his program to stimulate English naval industry by promoting the fish trade. The dramatist's Lenten diet while writing his masterpiece would account sufficiently for its numerous references to exotic food and hunger, especially to caviar.

From *Shakespeare Newsletter*, December, 1963. For his full-length study of the play, see Bronson Feldman, *Hamlet Himself* (Bloomington: iUniverse.com, 2010).

Chapter 7—Othello's Obsessions

For three centuries Shakespeare's tragedy of the Moor of Venice has served as a lesson in jealousy. Mainly upheld as a warning to passionate husbands, the play's portrayal of the effects of jealousy received infinitely more attention than its picture of the causes. Except by the poet and metaphysician Samuel Coleridge and his disciples, the motives of the cruel husband were examined with the abrupt empirics of the law office, according to the letter of the text. Coleridge denied that jealousy afflicted Othello; to him the guilt of the Moor consisted of a kind of idolatry, a private religion of wife-worship. This conception attracted few thinkers on the drama. Outside the thin Coleridge current the tragedy is everywhere taken as a study in jealousy. As such I propose to examine it, with a view to testing the theories of Freudian science on this disease of marriage. Psychoanalysis will hardly find in literature a richer field for its verification than the drama which William Wordsworth called one of the "most pathetic of human compositions," and which Thomas Macaulay hailed as "perhaps the greatest work in the world."

At first glance Othello appears to be a man self-possessed, in whose mind reason—the ego—governs desire or the id. We see him calmly greeting the summons from the rulers of Venice, who call him on the midnight of his marriage to a council of War. Threatened by the swords of his bride's father's servants, and the insulting speeches of the father, the Moor behaves with all the dignity of a Renaissance soldier and gentleman. We are inclined to feel that he is not boasting when he speaks of his "perfect soul" (1.2), serenely confident not only of his fine Italian manners but also of his austerely Christian conscience. The Moorish general comes before us as a model of courtesy and grace, by contrast with whom Senator Brabantio, crying out against the son-in-law whom his daughter has selected, strikes us as a barbarian.

On second thought there seems to be a couple of wrong notes in the harmony of Othello's behavior on his wedding night. We cannot help wondering why he eloped with Desdemona without the formality of asking her father to consider his likelihood as a son-in-law. The act was an affront to a powerful citizen, and would look most treacherous coming from a black foreigner. Presumably he felt that Brabantio would reject him. But why should that deprive him of the nerve for confronting the old man? A hint of guiltiness lurks in Othello's leaving home on this fatal night in order to celebrate the marriage at the Sagittary inn, which makes it difficult for his employers of the Venetian senate to find him in time of need. Apparently only two subordinate officers, Michael Cassio, his lieutenant, and Iago, his ancient or ensign, are in on the secret of his change of lodging, it is portentous, and a thing of state, that Othello should act so irresponsibly. The disquiet in our respect of him which is thus provoked cannot be allayed by the public assurance he makes, in the meeting with the Senate, that "the young affects" are in him "defunct" (1.3). In the very scene of this assurance we learn that he confesses to heaven the Vices of his blood. But he would have instantly repelled the suggestion that one or another of these vices had led his "perfect soul" astray this night. None of the "young affects," he would have us believe, prompted him to take Desdemona secretly from her home, to wed her clandestinely, and then to bring her to a tavern for the rest of the night. His feeling for her, he insists, results from an intellectual sympathy, a union of minds, and remains subordinate to his intelligence—"My speculative, and offic'd instrument." Without sharing the humor of Iago, who is nothing if not critical, we are bound to inquire whether a factor of self-deception might not be discovered behind the aged soldier's protest?

Since the Moor was seven years old, he informs us, he has lived the military life, and maybe worse, having been a wanderer in savage countries, and at one time a slave. "A natural and prompt alacrity," he says, "I find in hardness." Equally natural, though well concealed, is his alacrity for a certain softness. We do not see this in the open until the tragedy is well on its way. In the first act there comes barely more than one passage which could be interpreted as a betrayal of his weakness. When his wife pleads with the senators to allow her to go with him to Cyprus, he first requests them to agree. The next moment, however, he states that he must leave her behind, in charge of Iago, who has to stay to get the Senate's final commands. The contradiction here points to an unrest in Othello's soul, an unrest that could spring only from the frailty of his resolution about Desdemona. The Duke of Venice had left the question of her voyaging with him to their private determination. It looks as though the Moor's first impulse was to sail with her by his side, and that an impulse of shame or some other feeling of error had made him adopt a more "virtuous" pose, in the Machiavellian sense of the word, virile, warlike. The act concludes before we can decide whether Othello's whole show of manliness is a masquerade or not. Certainly he performs the role of the sensible soldier with artistic skill.

The military life, we learn at the outset of the play, has failed to instill in the Moor's heart the commonplace prejudice of the veteran of battles against the fellows who learn the art of war from books. From this prejudice springs the initial driving force of the tragedy—Iago's rage over the election of Cassio as the general's second in command. The ancient could not endure the promotion to lieutenancy of a mere scholar-soldier, the "beauty" of whose daily life serves to accentuate his lack of various qualities found useful in the bestialities of the battlefield. Othello must have known that the lieutenancy was desirable to Iago, and that the ensign had courage and brains to fill the position with distinguished ability, no matter how corruptly. Three grandees of Venice urged the general to choose Iago for the job. "But he (as loving his own pride, and purposes)" (1.1) chooses the foreigner Michael Cassio.

It is more than the compassion of one alien for another that inspired the Moor to pick the Florentine for his lieutenant. Othello affectionately calls the younger man, in the first part of the play, by his first name. We are led to think that a friendship or love exists between them in the noblest tradition of Plato or Pico della Mirandola. Not even Iago suggests that their love is less. The friendship falls short of perfection, we discern from the fact that Cassio was kept in ignorance of his chief's marriage until Iago told him of it (1.2). But the reason for this imperfection remains in the dark.

When Cassio arrives in Cyprus (the island, by the way, anciently sacred to Venus) he prays for his master's safety and wishes him Godspeed to reunion with Desdemona: "Great Jove," the scholar prays, "Othello guard... That he may bless this bay with his tall ship, Make love's quick pants in Desdemona's arms," and revive the spirits of the island depressed by the menace of the Turks. The amorous allusions in the speech are obviously meant by the dramatist to be taken in humorous sense (2.1), despite Cassio's anxiety for Othello's welfare. Shakespeare conceived Cassio as a humanist of his own time, a classically educated Christian youth, familiar with Shakespeare's favorite poet, Ovid, and not unacquainted with Italian erotic poets like Aretino. The dramatist endowed Cassio with the religious convictions of a Calvinist (see his opinions on salvation in 2.3). Puritan theology does not prevent the young Florentine from sporting with prostitutes. Nevertheless, it is clear that Shakespeare intended no sensual sting in Cassio's references to Othello's desire for Desdemona. Before he pronounces them, we are told, Cassio "looks sadly," and prays for the safety of his chief. It is Shakespeare's erotic wit that we must blame (if blame we must) for the image of Othello's tall ship riding in the bay of Cyprus, which inevitably calls to mind the notorious simile in the *Sonnets* comparing the poet's dark lady to a bay where all men ride.

If the Moor's mind suffers from carnal imaginings, we are given no sign of them when he makes his appearance in Cyprus, going to greet his wife. In fact their encounter summons into his consciousness thoughts of carnal extinction, of death. He kisses her almost in pain, as if life could never hold a joy worth this single minute of their meeting after the businesslike parting in Venice and the storm that divided them at sea. She healthily looks forward to a future of connubial joys and mutual comfort, but her husband cannot shake off his melancholy mood. With relief the old soldier turns to his dear Michael to deliver orders for the martial government of the isle.

In the same scene we discover that Iago suffers not only from his lack of advancement but from suspicion that Cassio has seduced his wife. And not only Cassio, whom he mocks as "too severe a Moraller"—but Othello too! The accusation surprises us, convinced as we are of Iago's keen intelligence and knowledge of the nature of his superior officers. Coleridge found it incredible that the subtle Iago should believe his charge, and described his malignity as "motiveless," or evil cultivated for its own sake. Yet suppose we imagine Iago as wishing to believe the slanders. He surely wished to believe his slanderous remarks on womankind (2.1). He loves to let his intellect dwell on fancies of obscenity. It may be that he derived an obscure pleasure from the thought of Othello and Cassio occupying his place by Emilia's side. This pleasure is not unknown among husbands of homosexual bent. And images of sex are quite confused in Iago's mind. Note the ardor of his description of the way Cassio and Roderigo behaved before their alleged brawl: "Friend all, but now, even now! In quarter, and in terms like bride, and groom Divesting them for bed..." (2.3). The simile trips off Iago's tongue as he talks to Othello, knowing that the general has just come from a bridegroom's bed. Malice peeps from the speech. The intensity of Iago's hate for the Moor, which is the real propeller of the play, cannot be accounted for by the mere frustration of his wish for the lieutenant's place. Coleridge correctly branded that as a hollow excuse for hate. Yet Iago is unconscious of any other cause for his malignity toward the Moor, except the utterly irrational surmise that Othello has lain with his wife. The crazy suspicion indicates that the fascination which the general unconsciously exerts for him is rooted in sex. Indeed the intensity of his hate for Othello may be described as a fury of outraged love, a love which Iago's cynical, sex-detesting ego dared not confess to itself.

The indignation of Othello at the spectacle of Cassio fighting with Roderigo is superbly justified by the dramatist. After all, Cyprus lives under martial law, in fear of Turkish attack. This is no time for the lieutenant to drink healths to Othello and his wife, realizing how poorly his wits admit alcohol. So we hardly recognize a loss of ego-sovereignty in the general when he declares, "My blood begins my safer guides to rule" (2.3). The expression of his anger against "Michael" goes to a peculiar extreme in speech. The man responsible for the offense, he cries, "Though he had twinn'd with me, both at a birth, Shall lose me." We had no idea till now that Othello considered Cassio so close to him, so intimate in brotherly love. The offense deprives Cassio of his office. But it has no power to deprive him of Othello's love. "Cassio," the Moor declares, "I love thee, But never more be officer of mine." The avowal tells us plainly that the Moor's love for the Florentine is not spiritual in its nature, not the result of attraction to Cassio's virtues, his culture traits. It is unreasoning love, a feeling that Othello's conscience (superego) is constrained to acknowledge to all Cyprus in the sight of Michael's disgrace.

The third act opens with renewal of the revelation of Othello's love for the scholar-soldier. Iago's wife is shown assuring him, "But he (the general) protests he loves you And needs no other suitor but his likings To bring you in again" to military favor. In this act we hear that the two men have known each other long. We learn that Othello's faith in Cassio extended to the point where he could bring the young man with him when he came wooing Desdemona, and let him serve as messenger for their love. (This renders more enigmatic Shakespeare's failure to explain Cassio's ignorance of his general's marriage.) Listening to Emilia depict the general as ready to forgive Cassio his drunken outburst, and restore the severe "Moraller" to his rank, we are justified in feeling bewilderment at the sight of Othello's conduct on observing the poor fellow departing from Desdemona. A few dry words from Iago at his ear are sufficient to plant distrust in the Moor's mind, distrust of his friend and his wife.

Coleridge sternly averred that Othello is not a victim of jealousy. The masses, on the contrary, both enlightened and illiterate, have judged the Moor guilty of that disease. He himself asserts at the close of his life that he was not "easily jealous," but confesses that he could be worked up to an extreme perplexity in which he was capable of thinking his wife a whore. The third act of his tragedy makes it perfectly clear that the working up was by no means a lengthy affair.

After seeing the wretched Cassio leave Desdemona he confronts her with questions that signify nothing if not disrespect for her. She mentions the man who "languishes in your displeasure." "Who is't you mean?" he queries; "Went he hence now?" The ingenuous questions give away the secret of his strenuous manliness. Unpleasant as the idea is to him, Othello must admit that his "virtue" depends on his devotion to the girl Desdemona, whom he thus dishonestly attempts to catch in wicked thoughts of Cassio. "Perdition catch my soul," the Moor exclaims, "but I do love thee, and when I love thee not, Chaos is come again" (3.3). This is a far different song from the one he sang to the Venetian senate, vowing that love was permitted in his spirit a place inferior to his passion for soldiership. The prime business of his life, he had sincerely fancied before seeing Cassio's farewell to his wife, was war. But now we discover that with the loss of affection for Desdemona, "Othello's occupation's gone" (3.3). The chaos he speaks of is mental, a perplexity into which he falls from a stature of nobility and civilization, torturously attained, to the level of the "Anthropophagi" whom he had met in his wanderings.

The descent of Othello's soul to its peculiar hell begins from the moment when he suspects the lurking of some "horrible conceit" behind Iago's arid remarks on Cassio's relations with Desdemona. The horrible conception lurks, of course, in his own mind. Nothing has been done or said to taint the atmosphere with hideous thoughts, unless it was the girl's casual allusion to Michael's talks with her in the period of Othello's courtship. But the Moor shows no affect for her remark that Cassio, "so many a time," when she had spoken of Othello "dispraisingly," gallantly took his leader's part. The source of his "conceit" cannot be found in Desdemona's nor in Iago's words, nowhere but in the dark of Othello's unconscious, his id.

He describes Iago's mutters and blurts in terms that be is accustomed to apply to himself, as utterances working from a heart that "passion cannot rule." Hastily agreeing with the ancient that Cassio's "an honest man" he demands a statement of the vileness that Cassio and Desdemona have already committed in his fantasy: "Give thy worst of thoughts The worst of words." In short, Othello wants obscenity. Still clinging to his life-mask of self-deception be declaims, "Exchange me for a goat, When I shall turn the business of my soul" to the craze of a suspicious husband. "I'll see before I doubt." Already he doubts, seeing the sin in his mind's eye, lingering in thoughts of the treachery of his wife and his officer. He is even willing to believe that her feeling for him is a perversion— "Nature erring from itself..." This monstrous opinion of the love of white woman for black man doubtless has a history longer than the duration of the play. It must have been engendered in Othello's mind at the time that Desdemona disclosed her care for him, and been fiercely repressed. It was probably at the back of his mind when he resolved to elope with her, too prudent or afraid to face her father and invite his consent to their union. The speed with which the Moor's contempt for Desdemona manifests itself under the whip of jealousy indicates that his love for her was not very deep. The origin of his love, he told the Venetians, was in her "pity" for his misfortunes. Apparently he never forgave her pity. The ex-slave enjoyed the patrician girl's kind condescension but despised her for it. His egoistic resolve to cast her off once he has obtained proof of her falsehood goes to pieces under the impact of the passion that stirs his nature to its very bedrock. Prove her wanton, he says to Iago, and then — "Away at once with love or jealousy!" Yet he cannot relinquish his hate for her. Not only remembering how she seemed to shake and fear his looks when he wooed her, but thinking how Cassio could have betrayed his confidence and love. It is the latter thought that drives Othello mad.

In fantasy the Moor beholds his friend kissing Desdemona, and in fury asks Iago to present him with "ocular proof" of her whoredom. He indulges in visions of his wife yielding her body to "the general camp, Pioneers and all." All this before his conscience wakes up to the fact that Iago has not yet given him a reason for her disloyalty. Challenged for a reason, Iago responds with a story of how Michael Cassio made love in his sleep. He taunts Othello with a vivid picture of soldiers sleeping together, and his report of Cassio's alleged gestures and whispers enrages the Moor to the point where he feels capable of killing, not Cassio, but his wife! "I'll tear her all to pieces." Then Iago screws him to the sticking point of murder by telling him that he had seen Cassio wipe his beard with the strawberry-spotted handkerchief that Othello had given Desdemona as first gift. It is only when Cassio is mentioned in connexion with the handkerchief that we hear how obsessed Othello is by the thought of it. When Desdemona tried to bind his aching head with it and dropped it, the Moor had shown no profound concern. "Let it alone," he said, although (we learn from Emilia) he had conjured her "she should ever keep it." Having renounced Desdemona in his mind, however, he was probably not displeased to see her separated from the precious napkin which, as we later hear, his mother had preserved as a love-charm, sure to save her from the loathing of her husband. The thought of it stained with Cassio's dust and sweat convinces Othello that Iago's charges are all true and inspires him with a craving for blood, worthy of the Anthropophagi.

In the middle of this crucial scene (3.3) Othello tells Iago, "I am bound to thee forever," apparently out of gratitude for the ancient's loyalty. The scene concludes with Iago swearing, "I am your own forever." I have suggested that Iago's devotion to the Moor is the outcome of an unconscious lust. Possibly there is another reason for their sinister alliance, a reason springing from the unconscious tendency of Shakespeare's art in creating characters. Dr. Ludwig Jekels once argued (in *Imago*, V, 1918) that the poet frequently split his characters in two, converting them to separate *personae*, each of whom then appears not altogether comprehensible until combined again with the other. Macbeth and his Lady, according to Jekels, presented the dramatic poles of such a schism. I believe that Othello and Iago offer a more reliable proof of his theory. English ethics require that we give the devil his due. Shakespeare knew that Iago was not fundamentally to blame for the downfall of Othello.

In fact, we might describe the ancient as the Moor's evil *alter-ego*. When Iago observes the encounter of Cassio and Desdemona he utters a noncommittal sentence or two and repeats the questions his master flings at him. At once the Moor declares: "By heaven, he echoes me, As if there were some monster in his thought Too hideous to be shown" (3.3). There is no hint of a monster in Iago's words; the hideousness hides in Othello's own heart. He wishes to think as evilly of his wife as Iago does of Emilia. All the lechery in Othello's soul emerges on Iago's tongue. And the servility of the general's inner attitude to his white overlords appears naked in his officer, who is again and again branded as a "slave." There is actually more in common between Othello and Iago than there is between the Moor and the Florentine, Michael Cassio.

That Othello's jealousy is for love of Cassio cannot, of course, be demonstrated by overt testimony. Only psychoanalysis can supply the evidence. The Moor's unconscious hides his true feeling for the Florentine by a trick of ambiguity, compelling his ego to couple the love with his honorable sentiment for Desdemona. His superego allows him to think lecherously of Cassio under cover of righteous horror of his wife's alleged guilt. The fourth act starts with a riot of fantasy about Desdemona lying "naked in bed with her friend." Othello learns that the "friend" possesses his napkin—by ocular proof. There follows a rush of breathless punning, in Shakespeare's most personal glossophiliac vein, on the word "lie" mingled with images of the magic handkerchief. Othello burns to force a confession from Cassio, and then to hang him. The thought makes him tremble. He falls into a trance with inarticulate utterance: "Noses, ears, and lips; is't possible? Confess? Handkerchief? O devil!" On waking from the trance, which does not appear to be epileptic but simply hysterical, the Moor asks, "Did he confess it?" He goes on to goad himself into frenzy with imaginings of how Desdemona "pluckt him (Cassio) to my chamber," and of how he will punish the Florentine. "How shall I murder him, Iago?" he cries; yet finds himself unable to lay a finger on Cassio. Instead be revels in fancies of killing the youth through nine years, and throwing his nose to a dog. One need not be trained in clinical Vienna to discern in this nose-image a substitute for the castration-wish. Othello's mind swerves quickly away from the thought of hurting Cassio and pounces happily on images of revenge against his wife. To cuckold him, he thinks, was bad enough; to have done it with his officer was worse. Iago says so.

A letter arrives from the Venetian senate instructing the general to return, leaving the government of Cyprus to lieutenant Cassio. He does not inform the letter-bearer that Cassio is demoted. The sight of Desdemona rejoicing at the news of their going home maddens him into striking her. Not for one moment is he impressed by the fact that the summons will separate her from her alleged lover, nor the fact that she shows no sorrow for leaving the isle. "Cassio shall have my place:" that is the idea rankling him as he turns from her in loathing, and blurts out his contempt for her sex and Cassio's kind: "Goats and monkeys!"

In the following scene (4.2) we see the Moor questioning Emilia about his wife's behavior. Earlier in the play he had urged Iago to set Emilia to spy on her. Eagerly Othello puts all the blame for the alleged sin on Desdemona, charging her with aggression in lust. He treats Emilia as a procuress and his wife as a prostitute, and still pretends that his life is staked on faith in Desdemona:

> But there where I have garner'd up my heart,
> Where either I must live, or bear no life,
> The fountain from the which my current runs,
> Or else dries up: to be discarded thence....

He wishes that she had never been born. Then she would never have tempted Cassio and robbed him of the Florentine's love.

It should be obvious by now that Othello's love for Brabantio's daughter was a makeshift passion, the device of a mind in terror of a certain chaos to save itself. The chaos feared by the Moor can be defined as a madness resulting from a revelation of his inner lack of manliness. This fear of unvirility springs from a deeply repressed homosexual impulse, manifested by his passion for Cassio. It is Cassio's violation of his trust, in the drinking scene, that prepares the way for Othello's explicit avowal of distrust for his wife. Unconsciously, I dare say, the Moor had never felt devotion for Desdemona. He had ventured to love her because she had pitied him, he thought, he, the soldier of fortune and misfortune, the former slave. It was a matter of pride, his courtship—a proof of his mounting in the world to equality with the grandees whose military hireling he was. Moreover, by marrying Desdemona he felt that at last he was overcoming the influence of his life as a lonely alien, assuring himself a home in Christendom, in civilization, far from the horrors of his Moorish infancy, he must have experienced always in his heart the want of pity, as a foreign mercenary, who had lost the religion of his father and mother, and lived by serving at war the Christendom which aimed to destroy their world. His sentiment for Desdemona, therefore, may be explained as the affect of a defense-mechanism against the pull of his barbaric past, the return of the repressed. The magnetic spell of barbarism in Othello's id functioned indivisible from his craving for sodomy. His martial exterior deceives nobody outside the play; the essence of Othello is effeminate. Frank Harris long ago pointed out, in *The Man Shakespeare* (1909), that in "sincerest ecstasy" the Moor reveals "as much of the woman's nature as of the man's."

No deeper than his faith in Desdemona was Othello's conviction of the truth of Christianity. His obsession for his mother's Egyptian -magic handkerchief discloses a childhood attachment to African superstition. It shows us what Brabantio meant when he said that, if Othello had his way with Desdemona and Venice, "Bondslaves and pagans will our statesmen be" (1.2). It is the pagan in Shakespeare's hero which induces him at the hour of his wife's murder to make a comparison between the event and the crucifixion of Christ. The allusions to darkness covering the whole land and the opening of the earth are unmistakable. And the Moor likens himself to "the base Judean," doubtless Judas Iscariot, who "threw a pearl away Richer than all his tribe." It is no accident that when Othello finally thinks of killing himself, he remembers at the same time how he had rescued a Christian from a Turk by killing the "circumcised dog." He smites himself just as he had stabbed the infidel. As a son of Mauretania he, too, bore the mark of the Semite covenant with God; but there is not a word of this in the play. The terror of castration, nevertheless, runs through the entire work, from the first scene where Iago declares that, before he will let the world see "The native act and figure" of his heart, he will wear that organ upon his sleeve for birds to peck at, to the last "bloody period."

Othello's Moorish fatherland is linked in the unconscious not only with sex-terror but also with vision of an id-paradise. At least his creator seems to have thought of Africa as a wonderland of libido. In the second part of *King Henry IV* he presented the vagabond Pistol raving of the happiness of rapine that the coronation of his comrade Prince Hal may bring him and his underworld friends. "A foutra for the world," shouts Pistol, "and worldlings base! I speak of Africa and golden joys (5.3)." All students of Shakespeare know what Egypt signified to him, in contrast with the austerity of Rome. He pictured Cleopatra (the Greek dynast) as black from "Phoebus' amorous pinches." He pictured the soul of Othello similarly colored, like his visage, from the African sun and the "sensual sting." It is curious that, on the night when Othello plans to murder his wife in her bedchamber, Iago lies to Roderigo that the Moor is planning to take his wife to Mauretania (4.2). The bed of Desdemona may have seemed like Mauretania to the Moor, just as the bed of Shakespeare's Cressida was indeed an India. Also curious is the reference of Othello's wife, in the following scene, of a servant girl she once knew, named Barbara, whose lover "prov'd mad And did forsake her." Barbara's name reminds us pungently of Othello's mother-country. In the first scene of the drama Iago compares him to a "Barbary horse."

The Anthropophagi, "the Cannibals that each other eat," with tales of whom Othello had lured Desdemona from her household tasks (1.3), contributed to his mental heritage. Their appetite can be detected in his sadistic visions of torturing Cassio for years and chopping Desdemona into messes, messes like those King Lear imagines the Scythians made of their "generation" in order to devour them. To the bitter end, however, Othello's conscience guards him against the lust for blood. He exults over the wounded body of Cassio but never stops to see if he is actually killed (5.1). The Moor leaves the poor Florentine crying for help and strides off swearing to spot the bed of Desdemona with her blood. Once in her chamber his mind swings violently away from the thought of killing her so, and settles on the resolution to "sacrifice" her bloodlessly, by suffocation. A man so unmanned was bound to think more steadfastly of the killing of a helpless girl—his rival—than of the killing of a brave soldier like Cassio, his beloved Michael. And the cause of this "sacrifice," the cause not to be named to the "chaste starts"? So far as Othello has moral strength to admit his purpose aloud, it is this: "she must die, else she'll betray more men" (5.2). The honor, the virtue of men means more to him than the noblest of her woman's qualities. She demands that Cassio be sent for and questioned about the charge against them. The idea of confronting Cassio with it never seems to have occurred to the Moor, though Iago feared it would. Apparently the ex-slave lacked the courage to face his former love, his *beau ideal* of gentle yet militant youth, or to lift a hand against him, except from behind, by Iago's agency. To kill his ego's idol must have struck him as a sort of suicide.

The key to Othello's personality is the handkerchief his mother gave him on her deathbed. When he first tells Desdemona what it meant to him, he says that an Egyptian charmer gave it to his mother (3.4). At the end of the tragedy he tells a different tale. He says his father gave it to his mother (5.2). One may infer from this contradiction that the Moor thought reluctantly of his father, the man responsible for his circumcision, his rival for the mother's love. On the other hand, Othello reveled in the memory of his mother. His first gift to Desdemona, on whom he pinned his faith in all womanhood, was the napkin, "that recognizance and pledge of love," which his mother had sworn would safeguard the love of husband and wife, until it was lost, when the husband's passion would transform to loathing. The symbolism of the strawberry-spotted cloth remains a riddle. Perhaps it points to a savage assurance of chastity by the preservation of a cloth marked by hymen stains. At all events, for the Moor of Venice the gift of the napkin was a gesture signifying that he had exalted Desdemona to the place occupied by his mother in his soul. The gesture was a delusion. The Venetian girl could never take the Moorish woman's place. Othello lost his faith in the former, and the morality of her creed and class; he never lost his infant faith in his mother's magic, and belief in the law of his "tribe." When he heard that Cassio was wiping his beard with the thing, the Moor made up his mind definitely to murder... Desdemona, the rival of his mother. But he had already marked his bride for death when he declined to let her pick up the handkerchief when it fell from her hand as she was trying to tie it on his sick head. He thrust her off and it fell. In this act of alienation his ego's cultural ramparts against the id, his Italian code of honor and his Christian dignity broke down. The "erring barbarian" that Iago recognized in him (1.3), and the "cursed slave" he saw at last in himself (5.2) rose to the light and ran amok. But his fury contented itself with the stabbing of Cassio and the smothering of Desdemona, leaving the former to the cold efficiency of his officer while dedicating himself to the task of sweet hot vengeance on the girl. A man so spiritually chained to his mother was fated to find all other women inferior, selfish, and treacherous. But he dreaded the very thought of the loss of masculinity, just as be feared the memory of his father, and he strove to cover his profoundly wounded sex with the glory of the most manly life he knew, the soldier's splendor. It veneered his feminine nature as poorly as his boast of descent from royalty protected him from the shame of the slave. As soon as he adventured from the life of a chattel and a war-hireling to the life of an independent civilian, a lover and husband, he was lost. No Iago was necessary to ensnare his soul and body. When he demands "that demi-devil" to tell why he deluded him, Othello is once more deluding himself. Facing once more the representatives of Venice and Christendom, his ego assembles as best it can the fragments of his civilization, his character armor, and he pretends again "the noble nature Whom passion could not shake" (4.1). To the last he lies about himself: "For nought I did in hate, but all in honor" (5.2). He wishes to die with decorum, with his boots on, so to speak. Yet he dies dropping tears, "as fast as the Arabian trees Their med'cinable gum," in womanly relief, catharsis, while assuring his auditors solemnly that he is a man "unused to the melting mood."

The Freudian exposition of jealousy, its homosexual current, its castration complex and menace to masculinity, its paranoia tendency, is wealthily confirmed by the tragedy of *Othello*.

In closing this survey of *Othello* I would like to point out the beautiful revelation it contains of the economic element in jealousy, the passion for proprietorship:

> O curse of marriage!
> That we can call these delicate creatures ours,
> And not their appetites.   (3.3)

As we go to press the following paragraph comes to hand from a letter by the author to Theodor Reik:

Yesterday I finished reading for the first time your "Psychology of Sex Relations" (1945). Again I was deeply impressed by your outstanding powers as a naturalist of the soul, while I remained unconvinced by your criticism of Freud.... The book includes a chapter on jealousy, which announces a theory of Shakespeare's Othello surprisingly like the one I have evolved independently, and stated in an article, "Othello's Obsessions," which will come out in the *American Imago*. I refer to the conceptions of Othello's sense of inferiority as a former black slave, and his relation to Iago as ego to subdued self. My interpretation of the Moor is more in concord with the Freudian doctrine of jealousy, but so far as your analysis goes — with the exception of the remarks on race hate—it parallels my own. I cannot agree with your opinion that Othello was disdained by the Venetian nobility. Brabantio, the Duke, and other representatives of the nobility in the play, voice not only respect, but affection for him. In my judgment, the fact that the Moor had been a Moslem made a stronger impression on the Christians of Venice than his (mixed) race, though of course his color and previous condition of servitude affected them to profound alienation. But I do not want to argue about our differences. I want only to express my happiness in finding a psychologist of your stature arrived at the standpoint of my analysis years before I ripened my opinions for public print.

Chapter 8–Othello In Reality

In THE AMERICAN IMAGO of June 1952 I presented some observations on the psychology of Shakespeare's Othello without any reference to the biographic background of his tragedy. I should like now to offer a series of facts which, in my judgment, account for the creation of the Moor and give us some insight into the unconscious that generated the play. These facts come entirely from the records of the life of Edward de Vere, Earl of Oxford (1550-1604), the poet and dramatist who for various reasons, both merry and serious, chose to hide himself behind the mask of "William Shakespeare." (1)

A.

From boyhood Edward de Vere was convinced that his true role in the history of his country would be played in the profession of arms, in which many of the Earls of Oxford had excelled. He dreamed of performing military feats comparable to those of the famous generals and heroes in the books that he loved to read. When he was fourteen years old his uncle Arthur Golding dedicated to the boy *The Abridgement of the Histories of Trogus Pompeius,* and informed the literary world "how earnest a desire" the little Earl had to peruse "and communicate with others as well the histories of ancient times, and things done long ago, as also of the present estate of things in our days, and that not without a certain pregnancy of wit and ripeness of understanding." This interest in history, Golding wrote to his nephew, rejoiced the hearts of all men who felt "faithful affection to the honorable house of your ancestors," and stirred up "a great hope and expectation of such wisdom and experience in you in times to come, as is meet and beseeming for so noble a race." He urged the young nobleman to follow the examples of Greek princes who shone not only as soldiers but also as scholars in the arts of peace.

At the age of nineteen Oxford wrote a letter to his guardian William Cecil, Lord Burghley, pleading for a chance to serve Queen Elizabeth and England in a campaign then being fought on the Scotch border. He reminded Cecil how often he had importuned him for permission to go abroad in order to study the art of war at first hand. "You have given me your good word," wrote De Vere, "to have me see the wars and services in strange and foreign places." (2) His desire, you see, was not simply for the experience of an English gentleman in arms but for contact with battle in exotic theatres of war.

He wrote this letter in November 1569. In the following March Elizabeth gave her consent for Oxford to join the Earl of Sussex and Lord Hunsdon in the north, where he witnessed the besieging of castles and burning of villages and perhaps a cavalry skirmish or two. The campaign was primarily one of terror against the Roman Catholics of the border shires who had taken part in an armed uprising to overthrow her Majesty's church. We have no testimony on the part De Vere played in the expedition. Presumably it was restricted to making a handsome figure on horseback by the side of the commander, his friend Sussex.

The rebels of the north had expected to receive assistance from the army of Spain which was then hard at work crushing Calvinist insurrection in the Netherlands. The Duke of Alva, the Spanish commander, would have been glad to send them aid, but their rebellion failed to spread and Elizabeth's generals swiftly quelled it. She decreed the extirpation of the Catholic insurgents with the systematic cruelty shown by the masters of Spain when they "purged" their country of the Moors. A correspondent of Lord Burghley alludes to the Catholic warriors as *our Moors in England.*" (3)

Young Oxford apparently enjoyed his first experience of war. He asked the Queen to let him volunteer for the Huguenots, the army of Calvinism in France, who were engaged in civil war with the government of Catherine de Medici. Elizabeth absolutely refused. She could not tolerate the idea of one of her subjects, a nobleman at that, fighting for rebels against a lawful sovereign. The Earl persevered in requests for service in the royal army or navy. The Queen was amused. She could not imagine so little and literary a young man, especially one who at times appeared startlingly girlish, managing an important job in her armed forces. Her mildly derisive attitude and Burghley's stolid objection to the martial aspirations of Oxford infuriated him to the point of tears but he would not give them up.

He married Anne Cecil, Burghley's daughter, in December 1571, hopeful that now his Lordship would assist him in proving his right to a post of honor in the state. It should be noted that he did not marry for political calculations only. She attracted him by her personal charms. Like Desdemona "she was half the wooer." Lord St. John bears witness, in a letter to the Earl of Rutland on July 28, 1571: "The Earl of Oxford hath gotten him a wife—or at the least a wife hath caught him." (4)

De Vere soon learnt that he could not use his father-in-law to advance his military career. When the Duke of Norfolk, son of De Vere's aunt Frances, was condemned to death for allegedly plotting to wed Queen Mary of Scotland and lift himself to the lordship of a Catholic Britain, all the Earl's eloquence failed to move Cecil to one word of mercy for his kinsman. The Queen wished to be clement, but Burghley's arguments scared her into signing the Duke's death warrant. He was beheaded in June 1572. Oxford was unable to raise his voice in indignation toward his father-in-law, whose own voice had a potency like Brabantio's, "as double as the Duke's." The Earl's anger found vent in browbeating and upbraiding Countess Anne, making her life so miserable that her mother was stirred into wishing he would die. (5)

He renewed his application for a royal license to travel, in vain. Companionship of soldiers, the fireworks of his war games—imitations of artillery, tournaments, hunting, hawking, and books—particularly volumes of history and geography—helped him to forget his troubles. Thomas Twyne's *Breviary of Britain* (1573), dedicated to De Vere, remarks on the "singular delight" he obtained from books on foreign countries and bygone events. (Out of such literature came the stuff of Othello's tales of his travels in "antres vast and deserts idle." From its maps Shakespeare derived his picture of the "men whose heads Do grow beneath their shoulders.")

In the summer of 1574 Earl Edward suddenly ran away from home and sailed to Belgium. The rumor ran that he intended to join the English Catholics in Brabant, the fugitives from the revolt of 1569. His real aim seems to have been the satisfaction of a desire to watch the ablest soldiers in Europe, Mondragon, Davila, Valdes, and their fellow officers at their business of breaking revolt in the Low Countries. Elizabeth commanded him to return and he obeyed. One upshot of this fortnight's escapade was a bit of bragging and fantastical lies quite in the style of Othello. He told some drinking companions in London that he had been appointed lieutenant general of the Spanish army in Flanders and led some valorous fighting at bridgeheads as well as a brilliant siege. (6)

Her Majesty finally granted the unhappy dreamer permission to travel for a year. He reached Italy in the spring of 1575, carrying letters of recommendation from King Henri III of France and the Venetian ambassador in Paris. He hoped to do more than amuse himself in Venice. As he wrote to Burghley, the Venetians expected a naval attack by the Turks "on the coasts of Italy or elsewhere." He looked forward to a glorious fight: "If I may I will see the service." If the Turkish fleet would not test the mettle of the Venetians this year—"then perhaps I bestow two or three months to see Constantinople, and some part of Greece." (7) Italy remained at peace during his journey. Lord Burghley was impatient for his homecoming, having a strong dislike of the Papist peninsula. He declined to use his influence to continue the Earl's travel license for another year. After a view of the Carnival at Venice, Oxford returned to England, arriving in April 1576.

He refused, however, to live any more with his wife or to see the daughter she had borne in his absence. He asserted that the child was not his own, and permitted scandalous gossip about the Countess to spread in the royal court. Not a particle of evidence exists to prove that she was ever tempted to stick on her husband's brow the horns of cuckoldry. "She hath always used herself," Cecil wrote to the Queen on April 23, "honestly, chastely, and lovingly towards him. And now upon expectation of his coming so filled with joy thereof, so desirous to see the day of his arrival approach, as in my judgment no young lover rooted or sotted in love of any person could more excessively show the same, with all comely tokens: and when, at his arrival, some doubts were cast of his acceptance of her, true innocency seemed to make her so bold as she never cast any care of things past, but wholly reposed herself with assurance to be well used of him. And with that confidence, and importunity made to me, she went to him, and there missed of her expectation." (8).

The source of the falsehoods about Oxford's wife remains obscure. Lord Henry Howard, the Duke of Norfolk's brother, has been blamed for poisoning the Earl's mind against her. No doubt, Howard did much to stimulate his cousin's malice toward Anne and her father. Oxford is said to have branded Lord Harry "the worst villain that lived in this earth." The Iago of this tragedy, in my opinion, was not a nobleman but a commoner, a soldier of fortune, young, clever, resourceful and treacherous, just like Othello's ensign. The real Iago, I think, was a scoundrel named Rowland York.

"This York," says the antiquarian Camden, "was a Londoner, a man of a loose and dissolute behaviour, and desperately audacious, famous in his time amongst the common hucksters and swaggerers, as being the first that, to the great admiration of many at his boldness, first brought into England that bold and dangerous way of foining with the rapier in dwelling, whereas the English till that time used to fight with long swords and bucklers, striking with the edge, and thought it no part of a man, either to foin or strike beneath the girdle." (9)

He first appears in documents of state a volunteer among the "Moors," the Catholic insurgents of the north. "He is but a child," writes a correspondent of the Earl of Warwick, "and seems very sorry for this fact," his impetuous enrollment in the ranks of treason. The "child" was pardoned, partly for the sake of his brother Edward who served the Earl of Leicester, Warwick's brother. In the spring of 1572 Rowland volunteered to march with the Protestant champion Sir Humphrey Gilbert, and a company of Englishmen in want of employment, in the army of the Dutch revolution against Spain. Lieutenant York distinguished himself for courage and cunning in their encounters with the Spaniards. The poet George Gascoigne, who was with him in the Netherlands, published a little book about their adventures which contains a hint of a voluptuous bargain they once made with some nuns: "Young Rowland York may tell it better than I." In January 1574 the gallant Rowland emerges in the records of Lord Burghley as a companion of the Earl of Oxford, involved in certain shadowy dealings with a secret agent of Spain. About this time Lady Oxford submitted to her father some "Notes by an Ill-Used Wife," which declare that she was kept out of her husband's chamber during two meals "...by York and others within." (10)

Two years later we find York in the company of the Earl at Dover, and so intimate with him that when De Vere went up the Thames to London on April 20 he landed alone with York and spent two or three days in mysterious privacy at the adventurer's house. Here Oxford produced his cluster of pretexts for divorcing Countess Anne without the annoyance of legal formalities. (11)

The main thing we learn from his argument is that he detested his wife for her subservience to her father. Still he did not dare to come out openly against the power of the house of Cecil. He pursued his solitary way in politics, struggling to stay faithful to the patriotism of his ancestors while cultivating the cosmopolitanism of a lover of Renaissance Italy and France.

Toward the end of 1578, still dreaming of a career in arms, he accepted the dedication of the *Defense of Military Profession* by Geofrey Gates, a native of his own shire of Essex and a veteran of the Calvinist crusade in the Low Countries.

B.

During the Christmas holidays of 1578, when the royal court was wondering with Sir Philip Sidney

Whether the Turkish new moon minded be
To fill his horns this year on Christian coast?

Oxford suddenly disrupted the peace of the court by breaking off
his ties with the Roman Catholic faction. He declared that Lord
Henry Howard and Charles Arundel, who had been drinking comrades for years, were enemies of England, in the service of the Jesuits. The Howard circle retaliated with a volley of fascinating accusations, several of which may serve to illustrate Othello.

Charles Arundel testified that De Vere's word was not to be
trusted in anything because "he hath perjured himself a hundred
times and damned himself to the pit of hell." For examples of the
Earl's powers as a liar Arundel recounted the yarn about Oxford's
alleged adventures in the Spanish army, and next called attention to
his claim that while in Italy he had commanded the troops of the
Pope, with such valor and discretion that he prevented a civil war.
(12)

"His third lie," Arundel continued, "which hath some affinity to
the other lie, is of certain excellent orations he made, as namely to
the state of Venice, at Padua, at Bologna, and divers other places in
Italy ... being reputed for his eloquence another Cicero, and for his
conduct a Caesar."

Othello's speech to the state of Venice proves what Shakespeare
might have accomplished in a senate with his pen. His tongue, I believe, would only have wagged him into trouble. In the records of
the Earl of Oxford's attendance in the House of Lords there is no
sign that he ever tried for the glory of an orator.

Othello is accused of being a "practicer of arts inhibited" (1.3).
Oxford was charged by Arundel with practicing black magic, of
conjuring together with some friends of the Chapel Royal, to raise
the Prince of Darkness out of hell.

At this point I would like to digress a moment to speak of Brabantio's guess that the Moor had practiced on his daughter with
"drugs or minerals that weaken motion." The phrase reminds me of
a service that De Vere did to science. He was one of the earliest

Englishmen to encourage the doctors and apothecaries who upheld Paracelsus's theory of chemistry in medicine.

To return to the Moor: He is shown to be a man capable of scheming and conniving at assassination. Lord Henry Howard and Arundel charged Earl Edward with precisely the same crime. Several times, they affirmed, he proposed ways and means to kill the Earl of Leicester and other politically potent men whom he hated because he could not compete with them. He practiced, Arundel wrote, "with a man of his own, that now serves in Ireland, to kill Ralegh whenever he goes to any skirmish." Howard reported a device the Earl toyed with to have Christopher Hatton, the Queen's Vice-Chamberlain, killed "one night upon a brawl," perhaps a brawl like the one engineered by Iago on the night of Roderigo's murder. Another of Oxford's schemes, said Howard, was a "practice" with *Rowland York* for the destruction of Francis Walsingham, the secretary of the Queen's Council. Even more significant for the analysis of *Othello* is Howard's testimony of De Vere's hatred for Sir Philip Sidney, whose personality, I shall later try to prove, Shakespeare consciously reviewed in drawing the portrait of Michael Cassio. According to Howard, De Vere conceived a "practice to murder Sidney in his bed and to escape by barge, with a caliver ready for the purpose." No day ever passed, Arundel swore, "without practice to draw blood among his own friends. ... He set myself upon (Francis) Southwell, my Lord Howard upon me." If we may believe these hostile witnesses, the Earl's temperament reeked with "butcherly bloodiness." Even if we take their testimony as nothing but reflections of his dramatic fantasy, it cannot be denied that the fastidious Oxford did get pleasure from occasional visions of bloodshed. He was not only capable of crying like Othello for "Blood! blood! blood!" He could also imagine himself drinking the blood of his enemies. He was entranced by the Anthropophagi, especially by the account of them he read in the chapter on Cannibals in Montaigne's *Essays* published in 1582. Othello thinks of chopping his wife into messes, like the barbarous Scythian, or he who, in the words of *King Lear*,

    makes his generation messes
To gorge his appetite.

The oral vehemence, the repressed cannibalism, of the author
makes itself felt in these outbursts of his protagonists. The Earl of
Oxford indicated the force of his own oral libido in a statement he
made to Charles Arundel, the oldest of the Earl's recorded memories. He remembered having been curious in his infancy to know
what blood tasted like, and he obtained some drops for his tongue.
A favorite oath of his was "by the blood of God."

    The ferocity of Othello's beloved Cassio while intoxicated recalls
another charge against Oxford: "In his drunken fits he is no man
but a beast, dispossessed of all modesty, temperance and reason,
and roars as one possessed with a wicked spirit."

    Violations of the sex code of Elizabethan England would natu-
rally be given a prominent place in the Howard-Arundel indictment.
In view of the strong homosexual tendency we have discerned in
the connexion of Othello and Iago and the posture of the Moor
toward Cassio, we are not surprised to learn that De Vere was
charged with homosexual vice. The indictment offers lurid details to
prove him guilty of sodomy. No other violation of contemporary
sex law is given such attention in the recital of the Earl's antagonists.

    When Oxford confronted the Queen with his denunciation of
the Howard ring he discovered that he had no witness to back him
up. He "found himself the sole witness and lone accuser," wrote the
ambassador of France. "He has lost credit and honor, and has been
abandoned by all his friends and all the ladies." The ambassador
wondered if he did not belong to "the Spanish faction." (13)

    Then in March 1581 Anne Vavasor, an unmarried kinswoman of
Charles Arundel, had the bad luck to give birth to a son in the
Court. She vowed that Edward de Vere was the father. The Queen
in fury commanded the Earl to be locked up in the Tower of London. Anne Vavasor occupied another cell there. De Vere's wife
poured Christian coals of fire on his head by writing to him of her

undying love, and asking what he would have her do to recover his good will. He was set free in June but forbidden to show his face at Court. Elizabeth ordered him to stay in his house until she reached a decision in the case of Howard and Arundel, who were under political arrest. They both had powerful friends in the confidence of her Majesty, and obtained their freedom by the summer of 1583.

In November Francis Walsingham's secret agents learnt that Arundel was implicated in the Throckmorton plot to murder the Queen. He fled to Paris, and spent the rest of his years in the pay of Madrid. The proof of his treason helped to restore Oxford to royal favor, but Elizabeth could not forgive his sarcasms against her which Arundel had revealed.

Early in December 1581 Oxford wrote a response to his Countess's many pleas for renewal of their life together. His letter has not been preserved. On December 12 she answered it as follows: "My very good Lord, I most heartily thank you for your letter, and am most sorry to perceive how you are unquieted with the uncertainty of the world, whereof I myself am not without some taste. But seeing you will me to assure myself of anything that I may as your wife challenge of you, I will the more patient abide the adversity which otherwise I fear, and—if God would so permit it and that it might be good for you—I would bear the greater part of your adverse fortune, and make it my comfort to bear part with you. As for my father, I do assure you, whatsoever hath been reported of him, I know no man can wish better to you than he doth, and yet the practices in Court I fear do seek to make contrary shows. ... Good my Lord, assure yourself it is you whom only I love and fear, and so am desirous above all the world to please you, wishing that I might hear oftener from you until better fortune will have us meet together." (14) Her husband pitied her. He wanted to be kind. At Christmas time he consented to her going with him to the holiday revels of the Court.

Still he could not bring himself to say goodbye to the mother of his first and only son. His devotion to Anne Vavasor led to disaster in March 1582. He fought a duel with his mistress's uncle, Thomas

Knyvet, the Keeper of Westminster Palace, a man whom Queen Elizabeth warmly favored. Both were wounded in the fight but Oxford more dangerously. The sorrow of his father-in-law and the tears of his Countess could not prevail with the Queen to end De Vere's disgrace. "He hath been punished," Burghley declared, "so far, or further, than any like crime hath been, first by her Majesty and then by the drab's friend in revenge, to the peril of his life." (15)

By the begging of Cecil and the advice of Walter Ralegh, Elizabeth was at last persuaded to restore the poor Earl to the Court. On June 1, 1583, he "came to her presence, and after some bitter words and speeches, in the end, all sins are forgiven." (16)

His efforts to vindicate the stand he had taken against Lord Howard and Charles Arundel now bore fruit he had famished for. Royal detectives explored Lord Henry's relations with Mary, Queen of Scots, while he was placed in the custody of a stern Protestant. In December 1583 Arundel sailed from England to escape prosecution for his role in the Throckmorton conspiracy to set Mary on Elizabeth's throne.

One of Arundel's first enterprises in exile was the notorious book known as *Leicester's Commonwealth*, which historians treated for centuries as a Jesuit work. It came out in Italian under the title Flores Calvinistiei. The French edition, issued in the autumn of 1584, Discours de la Vie Abominable de Comte de Lecestre, accuses the Queen of England's favorite of making it his duty as well as pleasure to sow rancor between the lords of the realm and their wives. The book blames him for the anguish that Oxford caused Burghley's daughter to suffer, all part of a plot, it says, "to satisfy an inveterate hate" Lord Leicester bears to the Lord Treasurer. (17)

This statement will not seem altogether groundless if I am right in assuming that Rowland York was the most active in secret to inflame De Vere permanently against his wife. York's brother Edward was a member of Leicester's retinue; and when Leicester went to the Netherlands to head the English troops there he elected young Rowland to an important command. We know that this Earl enjoyed various devices for the discomfiture of Oxford, not the least of which was the poem by Gabriel Harvey called "The Mirror of Tuscanism" (1580), which satirized De Vere's passion for foreign culture. Harvey took pride in styling himself "Leicester's man." From the hostility between the two Earls sprang the much discussed quarrel of Oxford and Philip Sidney, Leicester's nephew, in August 1579. That dispute, I will soon endeavor to show, left traces in the imagery of *Othello*.

Charles Arundel's tract also slanders Anne Vavasor. It states that Leicester offered her a large bribe to be his paramour: "No mean bait to one that used traffic in such merchandise; she being but the leavings of another man before him, whereof my Lord is nothing squeamish, for satisfying of his lust, but can be content (as they say) to gather up crumbs when he is hungry, even in the very laundry itself, or other places of baser quality." When Philip Sidney wrote his loud but feeble reply to *Leicester's Commonwealth* he said nothing in defense of Anne Vavasor.

In the year of this pamphlet's publication two books appeared that contributed to the making of two of the greatest plays of the age. The second edition of Philip Lonicer's *Chronicorum Tureicorum* was printed in 1584 bound together with Giovanni Contarini's history of the war between Turkey and Venice. Christopher Marlowe used the volume in writing *The Jew of Malta*, a tragedy with grand echoes of Shakespeare's *Merchant of Venice*. The greater poet may have used Contarini in getting ready for his *Moor of Venice*. I believe that he read Gabriel Chappuys' French translation of Giraldi Cinthio's *Hecatommithi* (1565), from which the plot of *Othello* is ultimately derived. Shakespeare had enough acquaintance with Italian to read Cinthio as well as Berni's *Orlando Innamorata* and Ariosto's *Orlando Furioso*. The former poem has at least one line that sounded in the deeps of the dramatist's memory while he composed *Othello*: "Me qual che ruba la reputazione" (compare Cassio's outburst on reputation—2.3—and Iago's speech on the filching of good name—3.3. Ariosto certainly inspired Othello's lines on the sibyl who sewed his fatal handkerchief in "prophetic fury" (3.4). *Orlando*

Furioso tells of a lady who produced a gift with "furor profetico"; the phrase is not to be found in the Elizabethan translation of the poem (by Sir John Harington, 1591). With Chappuys' translation of Cinthio in 1584 the dramatist's unconscious began combining the elements of *Othello*. (18)

The manuscript Lute Book of Thomas Tallis, musician of the Chapel Royal, is dated 1584. In it can be seen the song of "Willow," which Desdemona says she heard from her mother's maid Barbara (4.3).

C.

In March 1585 John Sturmius, the outstanding Protestant educator in Germany, wrote to Queen Elizabeth urging to intervene in the war of Spain and the Netherlands. He spoke of the new German technics of cavalry and nominated the Earl of Oxford, whom he had met in 1575, first in his list of potential leaders in the new method of warfare. "If the German discipline were set up by someone in single companies," said Sturmius, "the explanations and undertaking of this art and faculty would be easy. And if all the horsemen would obey some one faithful and zealous personage, such as the Earl of Oxford, the Earl of Leicester, or Philip Sidney, it might be more convenient, speedy and fitting to entrust this matter to him." Elizabeth was unwilling to try the new discipline and stubbornly refused to stake her kingdom in battle with the empire of Spain. (19)

The Spaniards' siege of Antwerp, the commercial capital of the Western world, raised the English demand for intervention to fever temperature. Hundreds of men in the southern shires enlisted for service under the Dutch flag.

In June 1585, while King Philip was discussing with Pope Sixtus V a project for invading England, twelve deputies from Holland arrived in London and fell on their knees before the Queen, to plead the necessity for her sovereignty in their land. Her Council insisted that help must be sent to Antwerp but she refused to debate the propriety of her heading a vulgar revolution.

On June 25 the Earl of Oxford eagerly applied to Burghley for assistance in obtaining an army command. Specifically he needed money to keep up appearances at Court until her Majesty would give him the coveted appointment: "For, being now almost at a point to taste that good which her Majesty shall determine, yet am I as one that hath long besieged a fort and not able to compass the end or reap the fruit of his travail, being forced to levy his siege for want of munition." (29) One of his expenses in this season appears to have been the cost of a painting of himself bearing arms. This painting, after a remarkable transformation, many years later, came into the possession of English royalty as the Hampton Court portrait of *William Shakespeare*. (21)

On August 10, 1585 Elizabeth at last agreed to send five thousand auxiliaries to the Netherlands, a thousand of whom would form cavalry. Their wages were to be repaid by the Dutch five years after the conclusion of peace. As security for the debt she took the cities of Flushing and Brill and the castle of Rammekins. The States-General of Holland admitted to membership whatever general she appointed for the auxiliary troops. Unhappily these arrived too late to save Antwerp from falling into King Philip's hands.

"About 2000 Englishmen have gone to Zeeland," Bernardino de Mendoza reported to Philip from Paris. They were headed by Colonel John Norris; "and 4000 more were to follow. The latter force is being raised, and it is said that the leader of it would be the Earl of Oxford." On August 28 the Earl's guard landed at Flushing. The next night, Mendoza wrote, Oxford himself departed for Zeeland "by the Queen's orders." So it seemed as if his heart's desire for military life was finally to be gratified. The Dutch government, on September 3, prepared for a review of the English soldiers at the Hague, and gave instructions for the victualling of Oxford and his retinue, John Norris, and other chief officers of the newcomers. (22)

On September 1 the Earl of Leicester lamented to his friend Francis Walsingham the desperate condition of the Low Countries.

He acknowledged his willingness to accept command of the English auxiliaries, but thought "the other nobleman named" was far above him. The Queen, alas, was still sore on account of his clandestine marriage to Lettice, Countess of Essex. "I see not her Majesty disposed to use the service of the Earl of Leicester," Walsingham grieved in a letter of September 5. (23) Though Leicester had spent his life at Court and had no more experience of warfare than Oxford had, he was determined to have the leadership of the new army. All his political force was exerted to gain the privilege. Yet for a long while Elizabeth kept his hopes dim. His nephew Sidney, who had set his heart on obtaining the governorship of Flushing, despaired. The young knight lost his head with his habitual rapidity and left London on false pretense in order to hurry down to the seaport where Sir Francis Drake was getting ready to sail to the West Indies. Recalled to the Court on September 21, he endured a royal tirade and received the consolation of his uncle.

By September 19 the spies of King Philip in England were sure that Leicester would be made chief of the expedition. He arranged to travel in magnificence, swearing absolute fulfillment of the Queen's instructions for a defensive war. She desired a swift peace, and her Lord Treasurer was anxious about the effect of the fighting on England's cloth trade with the Spanish Netherlands. Cecil was probably glad to see a politician like Leicester take command of the army rather than his hotspur son-in-law. Sidney obtained the governorship he coveted, and Leicester's stepson, the nineteen-year-old Robert Devereux, Earl of Essex, was elected General of the Horse. Burghley got his son Thomas the command of the city of Brill.

The Dutch leaders were certainly happy to see these champions of church reformation at the head of the English troops. It is questionable whether they trusted the renegade Catholic, Oxford. He strutted and fretted for six weeks in the wings, so to speak, of the theatre of war. Then suddenly he was summoned home. He obeyed the mandate. The tears of the lonely Countess Anne, now nursing her third daughter, amid sorrowing over her husband's unquenchable passion for Anne Vavasor, doubtless helped to call him back.

On October 14 Leicester was told that the Earl of Oxford had sent his money, apparel, venison and wine by ship to England. The ship was captured on the same day by Spaniards off Dunkirk. They found a letter from Burghley on board, announcing the choice of De Vere as General of the English Horse. A week later William Davison wrote from Flushing: "My lord of Oxenford is returning this night into England, upon what humor I know not." (24) The next day Elizabeth signed the Earl of Leicester's commission as her Lieutenant General, and on December 8 his fleet was on its way to Holland. With him went Oxford's first cousin, Francis Vere, a young man already a veteran.

In the beginning of June 1586 Leicester wrote to Secretary Walsingham urging him to send Rowland York over, "whom I have written for." He wanted Rowland for a captain of infantry. (25)

D.

Earl Edward went back to his spendthrift activities among players, playwrights, and the other "lewd friends" who, according to his father-in-law, swayed him by their sycophancy. He occupied a luxurious mansion named Fisher's Folly, after the rich merchant who built it in the theatrical district of Bishopsgate. Next door was a dwelling of the brothers Edward and John Alleyn, who earned their bread on the stage, in the Earl of Worcester's company. In such an atmosphere his Lordship so far forgot his profession of arms as to talk at times like an actor. The martial Othello also drops into histrionic figures of speech.

> Were it my cue to fight, I should have known it
> Without a prompter. (1.2)

Othello's outcry, "Arise, black vengeance, from the hollow hell!" (3.3) suggests the spectacle of Revenge personified (as in the famous *Spanish Tragedy*) rising from a stage trapdoor over the cellar familiar to sixteenth century actors as "the hell."

Ned Alleyn soon became one of the most admired tragedians of the period, attaining his greatest popularity in the dramas of Christopher Marlowe. The name of Shakespeare does not appear in contemporary records in connexion with Allen, yet he seems to have performed in a few of Shakespeare's plays before they became the exclusive property of the Lord Chamberlain's company. A dateless inventory of Alleyn's costumes, which alludes to *Pericles* and *Romeo,* mentions a "Blue damask coat for the Moor in Venice." (26) I assume that this play was an early version of our *Moor of Venice.* We have yet to determine when it was written.

In the spring of 1586 De Vere found himself in financial straits as never before. He had sold his lands with the prodigality of Roderigo, and was so poor that Burghley had to feed and clothe his children. The annual grant of one thousand pounds that the Queen gave the Earl by privy seal on June 26 was probably not intended for his personal expense. In fact it came from secret service funds. Francis Walsingham himself spoke to her Majesty in favor of this grant to Oxford, but for what purpose none can tell.

In July 1586 the Earl heard good news that must have given him a twinge of envy. Sidney handed over half the troops under his command at Flushing to Peregrine Bertie, Lord Willoughby, De Vere's brother-in-law, whom Sir Philip described as "my very friend, and indeed a valiant and frank gentleman, and fit for that place." Bertie's soldiership soon gained the respect of the Spaniards, and an old ballad of the war celebrates him as a fellow unafraid of all the devils in hell. We know that the Earl of Oxford once hated him and tried to prevent his sister Mary from marrying him, going so far as to threaten her lover's life. We have good reason to believe that he produced a travesty of their wedding in *The Taming of the Shrew.* It is conceivable, therefore, that the poet was thinking of his brother-in-law when he wrote the solitary allusion to Othello's brother (3.4). Iago says,

> I have seen the cannon
> When it hath blown his ranks into the air,

And, like the devil, from his very arm
Puff'd his own brother—

and yet the Moor did not become angry. The peculiar calm thus described makes me think of how Oxford must have felt when he
contemplated the chance of Lord Willoughby's death, in 1586.

In August the exciting story arrived of a quarrel between the
Dutch Count Hohenlohe and Edward Norris, a brother of Colonel
John, which ended with the drunken Count cutting open Norris's
forehead with a goblet and rushing at him with a knife. Sir Philip
Sidney ran between and with the aid of other soldiers present
pushed Hohenlohe out of the room. Leicester strove to make peace
in vain. (Compare the brawl in *Othello*, 2.3)

Late in September came the tragic news of the wounding of Sid-
ney. He had rushed with a boldness uncalled for into the battle of
Zutphen, a Spanish bullet pierced his thigh. He died on October 17.
This event certainly affected Oxford profoundly.

He had known the knight well, ever since the days of 1569 when
Philip came wooing Anne Cecil, whose wits were then secretly occupied with the dream of becoming the Countess of Oxford. After
the Earl's return from Italy the rivalry between him and Sidney assumed a threefold form. They opposed each other as clandestine
Catholic against avowed Calvinist, partisan of alliance with France
against partisan of alliance with the German princes, and thirdly as
defender of romantic culture against upholder of strict classicism. It
is possible that George Whetstone had their feud in view when he
wrote his elegy on the death of Sidney:

The French he saw and at their follies smiled;
   He seldom did their gauds in garments wear.
In Italy his youth was not beguiled;
   By virtue, he their vices did forbear.
Of this byspeech he ever more did care,
   An Englishman that is Italianate
   Doth lightly prove a Devil incarnate.

> In German plain his humour best did please;
> They loved him much, he honored them as far.

In the course of the two poets' antagonism over the question of solidarity with France occurred the tennis court quarrel about which Sidney's admirers have made so many pages. What happened, briefly, was this—according to our sole witness, Fulke Greville, the follower of Sir Philip. (27) Sidney was enjoying a game of tennis in September 1579, in the presence of some French aristocrats, when Oxford came into the court and proposed to join in the play. Philip at first ignored him, then used words of righteous reproach. The Earl became angry and ordered him and his party to leave the field. Sidney would not submit and his reply provoked the Earl into calling him a puppy. He repeated the epithet. "That is a lie!" Sidney answered and strode off to prepare for a duel. His Lordship would not fight him. The Queen lectured Sidney on the duties of gentry to nobility, and attempts were made to patch up a peace. "For my part," Sidney declared to Sir Christopher Hatton, "I think tying up makes some things seem fiercer than they would be." Apparently his ego kept kindling over the dog metaphor of Oxford. In Sidney's novel *Arcadia* he echoed his letter to Hatton: "See whether any cage can please a bird, or whether a dog grow not fierce with tying." He denounced Oxford as a coward and still the Earl refused to cross blades with him. A peace was eventually achieved, perhaps even friendship. For in January 1581, after De Vere's break with the Roman Catholic faction, he and Sir Philip united to accept a tournament challenge by Philip Howard, Earl of Arundel.

Two similes in *Othello* indicate that the dramatist never forgave Sidney for the tennis court affront. Both apply to Michael Cassio, the spitting image of Sidney, the canine insult Oxford had flung at him. With two cups of wine, Iago remarks,

> He'll be as full of quarrel and offense
> As my young mistress' dog.

Later Iago states that Othello had punished Cassio "as one would beat his offenseless dog to affright an imperious lion" (2.3). What else but wounded narcissism associated the figure of the Florentine puritan with the picture of a puppy twice?

The "imperious lion" in the dispute of 1579 was the Earl of Leicester, the main adversary of union with France.

Let us review the points of resemblance between Sidney and Cassio. Both men were soldiers who had learnt the trade from books. Both showed a kind of gentle beauty in their lives that made them objects of admiration. Cassio too is a devout Calvinist: he preaches the doctrine of predestination of the saved and the damned; and he is "too severe a moraller." He is quick-tempered, rash, and nearly inarticulate in rage, precisely like Philip, who once threatened his father's secretary with a dagger for interfering with his mail. It is difficult to imagine Sidney having a romance with a courtesan like Bianca. But he did make love to Penelope Devereux, a lady never reputed for puritanism, who cheerfully had children by the Earl of Devonshire before she married him. We have already noted the fact that Philip had been a wooer of Oxford's "Desdemona." He knew the ill-fated Anne from boyhood and must have often heard the orphan De Vere enchant her away from household tasks with his stories and boasts. "Brabantio" Burghley liked Philip's personality better, but could not resist the glitter of a marriage contract between the Cecils and the Veres. We have observed in the Howard-Arundel accusations how De Vere's jealousy of Sidney led him to fantasy in which the Earl murdered his rival in his bedchamber. The homoerotic significance of this vision confirms our analysis of Othello's relations with Cassio.

The name Michael Cassio, incidentally, remains an enigma to me. Shakespeare invented it along with the names of all the characters in *Othello* with the single exception of Desdemona, the one person named in Cinthio's novel. When I inspect the word Cassio again the idea obtrudes itself that we have here a distorted anagram for *Essex*, who took Oxford's place as General of the Horse, like Cassio supplanting Othello in the government of Cyprus. All that "Michael" suggests to me is a picture of a militant angel.

The dramatist 's compassion for Sidney must have been somatically strengthened by his feelings about Sir Philip's leg injury. He too had been made lame for life. At the beginning of March 1582, the reader will recall, "My Lord of Oxford fought with Master (Thomas) Knyvet about the quarrel of Bessie Bavisar (i.e. Anne Vavasor) and was hurt." (2S) Shakespeare's Sonnets clearly indicate the result:

I, made lame by fortune's dearest spite (XXXVII).
Speak of my lameness, and straight will I halt. (LXXXIX.)

Here I would like to mark a coincidence. In the lore of medieval medicine each part of the human body lived under the influence of a zodiac sign, that of the archer Sagittarius being dominant over the thigh, which would be bled by believing doctors when the astrological configuration was favorable. (29) In view of this fact, it is strange that Shakespeare should have chosen the name Sagittary for the inn to which Othello takes his bride on the night of their elopement, as if in anticipation of Cassio's fate.

In contrast to the angelic Cassio stands the diabolic Iago, whom I have identified as the professional warrior Rowland York. The sound of "Iago" suggests the fellow's name, pronounced without the usual stress on what Shakespeare termed "the dog's letter." In Iago's first dialog with Othello he speaks of someone who had insulted the Moor and regrets that he did not fulfill a wish to "yerk" him under the ribs. The verb alone calls up the memory of York, not only phonetically but by its reminder of the sword-thrust "under the girdle" that history alleges he introduced in England.

The name of Othello's ensign is Spanish, though Shakespeare gives us no other evidence of his villain's nationality. At the close of the tragedy he is branded a "Spartan dog." One might venture to translate this as *Spanish* dog. The justification would be that Rowland York did join the Spaniards and ended his life in their camp. On January 19, 1587 he avowed himself a contrite Catholic and betrayed for Spanish silver the fortress of Zutphen which Leicester had put in his charge. Not long after, he died of an obscure disease.

Iago's nationality forms a peculiar link between him and the Moor. The traditional enmity of Spaniards and Moors manifests itself in the play as a reaction to envy and unconscious love. But the villain, though he bears the name of the patron saint of Spain, is by no means representative of the people. Like Othello he is an "extravagant and wheeling stranger, of here and everywhere." We find him again in Shakespeare's *Cymbeline*, masquerading as the Italian Iachimo, and contriving similar evil between husband and wife, haunting the heroine's bedroom. It will be recalled that the Londoner York first appears in historic records as a fighter for the "Moors" of Northumberland and Westmoreland. He was but a child then. He was just a boy when the Earl of Oxford chose to stay with him rather than return to his wife. The child in the Earl discovered a kindred soul in Rowland, one that rejoiced like himself in the mischief of interrupting the marital pleasure of his lord (*the primal scene*).

It was not difficult for Oxford to imagine himself a Moor. He was accustomed to hearing Queen Elizabeth call him her *Turk*. This nickname appears to have been designed for fun with the Gaelic word *torc*, meaning boar. The Earls of Oxford carried the emblem of a wild boar on their coats of arms, and courtiers who disliked Edward de Vere referred to him as "the Boar." (30) These nicknames hint that he was considered an untamed animal, a pagan, and an outcast. Something of the sort is what Hamlet means when he speaks of his destiny "turning Turk" (3.2).

In the person of the Moor of Venice our poet displayed how despised and rejected he felt, cut off from his own kind. He felt unmanned, deep in his mental core shorn of his sex. The menace of castration which he had depicted hanging over himself in the person of the *Merchant of Venice* materialized in the loss of his generalship. "Othello's occupation's gone." He felt betrayed, like Christ, a savior deprived of his single chance to save.

The Biblical imagery that pervades *Othello* shows us more than a longing for Christian salvation. It shows the ego of the writer daring to lift itself to divinity. He refers to his hero in language the God of the Old Testament employed in identifying Himself. When Moses inquired about the name of the Lord, He replied: "I am that I am." On October 30, 1583, Edward de Vere used the sacred phrase for himself in a letter to his father-in-law protesting an effort to control his private business: "I pray, my Lord, leave that course, for I mean not to be your ward nor your child. I serve her Majesty, and *I am that I am*, and by alliance near to your lordship, but free." (31) The same words are uttered by the poet in the Sonnets:

> I am that I am, and they that level
> At my abuses reckon up their own.

As for Othello, "he is that he is," remarks Iago (4.1), doubtless in remembrance of what he had affirmed about his own nature "I am not what I am" (1.1).

Othello compares himself to Judas Iscariot, "who threw a pearl away richer than all his tribe." He partakes of both Christ and Iscariot, taking on his soul a double guilt, just as Jesus took on himself the sins of the world and Judas the sin of betraying the Lamb of God to the sacrifice. The literary likeness between the crucifixion of Christ and the murder of Desdemona has been noted in my psychoanalysis of Othello.

An unknown critic of the 18th century observed that Shakespeare, in writing the murder scene and the verse, "It is the cause, it is the cause, my soul," seems to have had in his mind's eye the following lines from the prophet Jeremiah (V): "They are waxen fat, they shine: yea, they overpass the deeds of the wicked: they judge not the cause, the cause of the fatherless.... Shall I not visit for these things? saith the Lord: shall not my soul be avenged on such a nation as this?" Among the things mentioned as requiring heavenly vengeance are adultery and "harlots' houses." (32) The cause of the fatherless was particularly dear to Oxford, because he lost his revered father at the age of twelve. Soon after, his uncle Arthur Golding had to repel from his name the stigma of bastardy. The Queen herself, De Vere told Charles Arundel, had called him bastard, "for which cause he would never love her."

The dark lady whom he glorified in his poems and plays seems to have been illegitimate. The apparition of Anne Vavasor enters *Othello* distorted in the character of Bianca, the prostitute who becomes devoted to Cassio in the week between his arrival in Cyprus and his fall from Othello's love. Bianca's presence in the scene where Cassio's leg is nearly cut in two aids us in identifying her. The middle syllable of her name conveys the name Anne. Bianca itself means white, which makes me think of Shakespeare's description of his mistress "Rosaline" in *Love's Labors Lost*:

> A whitely wanton with a velvet brow,
> With two pitch-balls stuck in her face for eyes.

Rosaline, by the way, is denounced by her lover Biron — for no rational dramatic motive — for committing fornication.

Jealousy on account of this Anne composed a large part of the emotion that inspired the writing of *Othello*. In 1587 she seems to have turned her eyes with serious affection on old Sir Henry Lee, a gentleman of the Leicester faction who carried his fifty-seven years with a light heart and a graceful body, long exercised in tournaments. She became Lee's mistress. She bore him, too, a son. A couplet in *Othello*, one of a set delivered by Iago against women in general, sounds as though aimed with particular malice at her:

> If she be black, and thereto have a wit,
> She'll find a white that shall her blackness fit.

The sadism aroused in De Vere by her desertion had an outlet in sarcasms and orations delivered at the head of his wife, on the perennial theme of her father's failure to advance the son-in-law's interests. On May 5, 1587 Cecil wrote to Walsingham for assistance in getting the Earl some land he had been petitioning for. "I was so vexed yesternight very late," Cecil confided, "by some grievous sight of my poor daughter's affliction, whom her husband had in the afternoon so troubled with words of reproach of me to her—as though I had no care of him as I had to please others... she spent all the evening in dolour and weeping. And though I did as much as I could to comfort her with hope, yet she, being as she is great with child, and continually afflicted to behold the misery of her husband and of his children, to whom he will not leave a farthing of land.... No enemy I have can envy me this match; for thereby neither honour nor land nor goods shall come to their children." He complained that while he paid the bills for sustenance of the Earl's three daughters, he received no gratitude: "If their father was of that good nature as to be thankful for the same I would be less grieved with the burden." (33)

Lord Burghley wished Walsingham to direct the legal process for the profitable outcome of Oxford's plea — "For anything directed by me is sure of his lewd friends, who still rule him by flatteries." We are sorry that none of these friends was named. It might have helped to clarify the biography of several of the outstanding authors and actors of the period. We know that Oxford's own company of players was active at this time, for a spy of Walsingham's reported these men as setting up bills of plays every day in the week.

The versatile Robert Greene must have been one of the Earl's "lewd friends." In dedicating his *Card of Fancy* (1584) to Oxford, Greene flattered him with allusions to Alexander and Caesar, and added: "Your Honour being a worthy favourer and fosterer of learning hath forced many through your excellent virtue to offer the first-fruits of their study at the shrine of your Lordship's courtesy."

Greene and an anonymous contemporary play furnish my sole proof — and very frail proof it is — that *Othello* was originally written prior to the spring of 1587. On June 11 of that year Greene's *Farewell to Folly* was entered in the Stationers' Company register. In this trivial book he made fun of a comedy named *Fair Em, The Miller's Daughter of Manchester*, performed by the servants of Lord Strange. Now, nobody takes seriously the old claim that William Shakespeare wrote *Fair Em*. Whoever composed it was a humorist friendly to Shakespeare. The play contains one statement which a few scholars regard as a clear allusion to *Othello*: "I cannot, madam, tell a loving tale or court my mistress with famous discourses." If the Moor's love-making to Desdemona was famous when *Fair Em* was staged, their tragedy must have been acted a long while before the licensing of *Greene's Farewell to Folly*. I feel sure that Shakespeare's first draft of *Othello* was made not long after October 21, 1585, when he left the Low Countries to return to London and idleness and melancholy. Appropriate to this time are the speeches of Desdemona and her Moor in Act 4, Scene 2:

> Alas, the heavy clay!—Why do you weep?
> Am I the motive of these tears, my lord?
> If haply you my father do suspect
> An instrument of this your calling back,
> Lay not your blame on me; if you have lost him,
> Why, I have lost him too.
> —Had it pleas'd heaven
> To try me with affliction, had he rain'd
> All kinds of sores and shames on my bare head,
> Steep'd me in poverty to the very lips,
> Given to captivity me and my utmost hopes,
> I should have found in some part of my soul
> A drop of patience; but alas! to make me
> The fixed figure for the time of scorn
> To point his slow and moving finger at ....

In passing I should like to invite a glance at this passage in Greene's *Farewell to Folly* concerning the secret poets of the day. He speaks of "Theological poets, which, for their calling and gravity being loth to have any profane pamphlets pass under their hand, get some other Batillus to set his name to their verses. Thus is the ass made proud by this underhand brokery. And he that cannot write true English without the help of clerks or parish churches will needs make himself the father of interludes." Interludes is an old term for plays. The special target of Greene's irony was a playwright who dared to quote sacred scripture for mere romantic purposes, precisely like the author of *Othello*.

If Lord Strange's servants were the first actors of the tragedy, Edward Alleyn probably obtained his blue coat for the main role when his company temporarily united with Strange's men about the winter of 1588-89. This was the season when England rang bells and kindled bonfires for joy over the wrecking of the Spanish Armada, when Englishmen would have been lifted to highest ecstasy by the lines:

> News, lads! our wars are done.
> The desperate tempest hath so bang'd the Turks
> That their designment halts; a noble ship of Venice
> Hath seen a grievous wrack and suffrance
> On most part of their fleet. (2.1)

The Earl of Oxford had a minor role in the famous encounter of England and Spain at sea in July 1588. He purchased and equipped a ship for the fight, but somehow missed the decisive battle, and had to go looking for action on land. The Earl of Leicester, who commanded the English land forces, offered him the control of the port of Harwich, but Oxford would not accept it. To him it meant more idleness, more ignominy. He preferred to retire from the theatre of war.

According to the anonymous writer of *The Art of English Poesy* (registered in November 1588) De Vere occupied himself secretly with literature. Nobles and gentlemen of the Queen's own servants, says this author, "have written excellently well, as it would appear if their doings could be found out and made public with the rest, of which number is first that noble gentleman, Edward Earl of Oxford."

He may have been moved to revise *The Moor of Venice* at this time because of the guilt he must have felt after the untimely death of his wife on June 5, 1588. She was buried with gloomy pomp in Westminster Abbey, and he did not attend the funeral. He may have been overcome by sorrow and shame.

The playwright George Peele, in November 1590, borrowed a notion from *Othello* for his "Polyhymnia", a poem in honor of Sir Henry Lee's "farewell to arms." The Moor's comment on the hand of Desdemona (3.4) had deeply impressed Peele.

A liberal hand; the hearts of old gave hands,
But our new heraldry is hands not hearts.

The younger poet echoed it:

A liberal Hand, badge of nobility,
A Heart that in his mistress' honour vows
To task his hand in witness of his heart.

The year 1590 is even more noteworthy for the publication of the Dutchman Edward Daunce's *Brief Discourse on the Spanish State*, a polemic with a vivid reference to the theme of *Othello*:

"All other creatures and even beasts spare those of their own family; but the family of the Othmani and the Spaniards alone are distinguished by this; that they will kill even their own children and their chaste wives." (35)

The Othmani or Ottomans were the ruling dynasty of Turkey. It has been conjectured that Shakespeare made his protagonist's name from the first syllable of theirs. I think it most likely that he invented the Moor's name by wit-work with the old French word *otelle*, which means a kind of *spear*.

The second syllable hints to the ear of hell, to whose pit Charles Arundel asserted De Vere had damned himself. Most Christians of the time were persuaded that the children of Islam as well as Israel worshipt the lord of hell. For Shakespeare the infernal region had its earthly equivalent in the genital zone of woman:

But to the girdle do the gods inherit,
Beneath is all the fiends':

There's hell, there's darkness, there is the sulphurous pit.
(King Lear, IV vi)

Perdition caught the poet's soul indeed when he lost faith in and spurned the women of his life, his mother, his wife, and his mistress.

In his mind's flight from female sexuality he looked for refuge in Platonic love, playing the warlike yet tender father to beautiful and athletic boys. When this idealist relation dissolved to pederasty he recoiled into hatred of all humanity, in which love still glistened but almost exclusively in oral channels. From these there was no escape but starvation. Narcissism saved him from that doom.

E.

Ferdinando Stanley, Lord Strange, died in April 1594 and his younger brother, William, inherited his immense fortune and the earldom of Derby. Three weeks later Ferdinando's widow wrote to Sir Robert Cecil of a "motion of marriage" between Earl William and Cecil's niece, Elizabeth Vere. "I wish her a better husband," said the widow. (35) Lord Burghley and Oxford gave their consent to the wedding and it took place on January 26, 1594, with "solemnity and triumph" graced by the Queen and her court. In the opinion of numerous scholars, the Lord Chamberlain's servants (formerly Lord Strange's men) acted *A Midsummer Night's Dream* on this occasion.

Young Stanley was a studious yet hotblooded son-in-law. Oxford liked him and enjoyed staying at his house. He visited his daughter and Derby in September 1596, and probably discussed the progress of the war in the Low Countries, where Cousin Francis Vere, already knighted, was making a splendid reputation. Some months before, Francis had sent an appeal to Earl Edward to send over his servant Edward Hammon, a "theorician" of the art of war. Francis's brother Horace was there too, distinguishing himself for tranquility of head in the fiercest cavalry charges. The conversations of the two earls on arms and arts were meat and drink to the elder one.

He was deeply distressed in the summer of 1597 when Lady Elizabeth's coquetry with the Earl of Essex—his rival of 1575—provoked her husband to a frenzy of jealousy. She fell sick under the tongue-lash of Derby; he locked her away in a country mansion. Her father's pleading helped to bring Stanley to his senses and her back to the metropolis. (36)

A performance of *Othello* may have contributed to the reconciliation. In 1598 Ben Jonson explored the comic possibilities of the tragedy in his play *Every Man in His Humor*. The learned have paid imperfect attention to this comedy's striking mimicries of Shakespeare. The husband Kitely is afflicted by the suspicion of cuckoldry. "My head aches extremely on a sudden," he complains, and Dame Kitely puts her hand on his forehead and cries out (2.2). Afterward he wonders, "What meant I to marry?" (3.3) This trifling variant of Othello's "Why did I marry?" is followed shortly by a comment like the Moor's on the suspected wife's hand—"how hot it is" (4.6). Even a detail like Othello's sarcasm, "Put up your bright swords or the dew will rust them," has its parallel in Jonson's play in Kitely's command, "Put up your weapons" (4.1). Finally, Iago's counsel on money is imitated in Old Knowell's speech beginning "Get money" (2.2). The Lord Chamberlain's men performed *Every Man in His Humor*, and Will Shakspere of Stratford is alleged to have acted Old Knowell.

Othello became for the British public a lesson in jealousy. Judging by the facts set forth here, I conclude that the play is Shakespeare's apology for having failed as a statesman, a leader in war. He had tried to convince himself and others that he was one whose nature "passion could not shake" (4.1). "Fear not my government," his hero says (3.3). His government, however, on the battlefield as in domestic perplexity, was not to be relied on, and the poet knew it. Sensuality unmasked the despot in him. Even while he pleads—Not guilty! My downfall was Iago's fault. I am "one that lov'd not wisely but too well"—he condemns himself with the desire for immortality in hell, in the "steep-down gulfs of liquid fire" that symbolize his insatiable lust. He conjures devils to whip him away from the celestial sight of Desdemona (Anne Cecil) in the same breath that he deplores her frigidity: "Cold, cold, my girl! Even like thy chastity." Unconsciously he made his choice—damnation with Anne Vavasor rather than salvation with Anne Cecil. For the sake of this torturous and cryptic love he renounced the traditional occupation of his ancestors and in *Othello* wrote his farewell to arms.

NOTES

1   See "The Confessions of William Shakespeare," THE AMERICAN IMAGO, vol. 10, Summer 1953 [found in Chapter 9 of this book]. J. Thomas Looney, *'Shakespeare' Identified* (London, 1920).
2   Lansdowne Manuscripts (British Museum) 11, folio 121.
3   Calendar of State Papers Domestic (Elizabeth) Addenda: xvii, 5.
4   B. M. Ward, *The Seventeenth Earl of Oxford* (London, 1928) 61.
5   Calendar of Salisbury Mss. 29 April 1576.
6   State Papers Domestic (Elizabeth) Mss. CLI, 45.
7   Ward, op. cit. 102.
8   Ibid. 119.
9   William Camden, *The History of the most Renowned and Victorious Princess Elizabeth* (London, 1675) 397.
10 Calendar of State Papers Domestic, Add. xv, 107. George Gascoigne, *A Hundred Sundry Flowers*, ed. Prouty (1942) 194. Calendar of Salisbury Mss. II, 63, XIV, 19.
11 Salisbury Calendar, II, 131, 144.
12 The quotations from Arundel and Howard are from the unpublished State Papers Domestic, CLI, 44, 45, 46, 49, 51, 57.
13 British Public Record Office: Transcripts from Paris: 28, ff. 304-306, D e p e - sche 304, by Mauvissiere de Castelnau; copy in *Philip Howard, First Earl of Arundel*, ed. Pollen and MacMahon (Catholic Record Society, 1919) 29.
14 Ward, op. cit 226.
15 Harris Nicolas, *Life and Times of Sir Christopher Hatton* (1847) 321.
16 Ward, 233.
17 Pollen and MacMahon, op. cit. 58, 66. For the succeeding quotation about Anne Vavasor, see Frank J. Burgoyne, ed. *History of Queen Elizabeth* (1904) 49.
18 Two other books that probably went into the making of *The Moor of Venice* are Andrew Cambine's *Empire of the House of Ottomans*,—which was printed in 1562 in the same volume as John Shute's *Commentaries... of the Wars of the Turk against George Scanderbeg Prince of Epiro*,—and Peter Bizarus's *History of the War*

between the Venetians and the Holy League against the Turks, for the Isle of Cyprus.
This work was translated into French by Belleforest (1573), the same scholar
who gave Shakespeare the story of Hamlet. "The History of George Scanderbeg" is the name of a lost play acted by the Earl of Oxford's players and published in 1601.

19 Calendar of State Papers Foreign (1583-1584) 406.

20 Ward, 251.

21 Mr. Charles Wisner Barrel, editor of the 1949 edition of Looney's *Shakespeare
Identified*, discovered the original of the Hampton Court painting by X-ray and
infra-red photography.

22 Calendar of State Papers Spanish (1580-1586) 545, F. ten Raa and F. De Bas,
Het Staatsche Leger, cited by Ward, 252.

23 Calendar of State Papers Domestic (1585) clxxxii, 6. Cal. S. P. Foreign (1585)
xx, p. 8.

24 Thomas Wright, *Queen Elizabeth and Her Times* (1838) II, 266. Calendar of
State Papers Foreign (1585) 104.

25 *Correspondence of Robert Dudley, Earl of Leycester*, ed. Bruce (1844) 304.

26 J. P. Collier, *Memoirs of Edward Alleyn* (1841) 20.

27 Greville, *Life of the Renowned Sir Philip Sidney*, ed. Smith (1907) 63. Cf. Ward,
166. Whetstone's elegy is quoted from Thomas C. Izard, *George Whetstone*
(1942) 253.

28 Ms. Diary of Rev. Richard Madox, quoted by Ward, 227.

29 See Otto Rank, *Art and Artist* (1932) 114.

30 *Shakespeare Fellowship News-Letter* (London, March 1947) 5. Calendar of State
Papers Dom. (1572) XCII, 16.

31 Lansdowne Mss. 42, no. 39.

32 We are indebted for the association of Jeremiah and Shakespeare to the research of Walter Whiter, whose *Specimen of a Commentary on Shakspeare* (London, 1794), based on John Locke's doctrine of the connexion of ideas, should
be familiar to all students of the forerunners of Freud.

33 Ward, 285.

34 Quoted by Lilian Winstanley, *Othello: The Tragedy of Italy* (1924) 150.

35 Salisbury Calendar, IV, 527.

36 Ibid. VII, 333, 392. On August 20, 1597 Derby announced, "If anyone can
say that I know my wife to be dishonest of her body or that I can justly prove
it by myself or anyone else, I challenge him the combat of life." The three
witnesses to this statement are "W. Burghley, Howard, Ro. Cecil." It would be
curious if this Howard turned out to be the same Lord Harry who intrigued
against Oxford and Lady Derby's mother in 1576.

Chapter 9–The Confessions
of William Shakespeare

1

"Shakespeare," says Hanns Sachs in the reminiscences of his many years of collaboration with the founder of psychoanalysis (*Freud: Master and Friend*, 1945, p. 108), "was the most frequent topic of our discussions when they turned to literature. Freud's remarks about the Oedipus complex in Hamlet had fallen on fertile ground... Somewhat later Freud turned his attention to other plays: to *Richard III* and *Macbeth* in 'Some Character-types Encountered in Psychoanalysis,' and to *The Merchant of Venice* in 'The Motive of the Choice of the Caskets.' Several of his disciples, myself among them, followed his example and found rich analytic pasture in Shakespeare's plays. In our discussions he made me notice how [Shakespeare, although a master in displaying or concealing his technique of motivation at will, is not, like Ibsen, mechanically conscientious about it. He throws logic and consequence to the winds and courts contradictions if they suit the emotional situation.] ... Freud later gave credence to the story that the author of Shakespeare's work was a scion of the old and noble line of De Vere. He lent me the book which presented and defended this new hypothesis (*'Shakespeare' Identified in Edward de Vere, the Seventeenth Earl of Oxford*, by J. Thomas Looney), but I remained unconvinced. To me the small-town boy, whose father was fined for the dungheap at the door, seems still the most likely author of *The Tempest* and *Measure for Measure*."

The last remark of Sachs appears to be a sort of retort to Freud's remark in *Civilization and Its Discontents* (1930, p. 55): "We do not think highly of the cultural level of an English country town in the time of Shakespeare when we read that there was a tall dungheap in front of his father's house in Stratford."

In the numerous commentaries and notes on Shakespeare written by psychoanalysts this passage from Sachs is the only one that mentions the conviction of Freud on the question of Shakespeare authorship. A curious silence prevails on the matter in the literature which professes to interpret drama and poetic genius in the light of Freud's discoveries and doctrines. Sometimes the silence takes on the air of an almost morbid resistance. For example, in the first English printing of his *Autobiographical Study* (New York. 1927. p. 130) we find the declaration: "I no longer believe that William Shakespeare the actor from Stratford was the author of the works that have been ascribed to him. Since reading *Shakespeare Identified*, by J. T. Looney, I am almost convinced that the assumed name conceals the personality of Edward de Vere, Earl of Oxford." In the second English version of *An Autobiographical Study* (London, 1935) we are surprised to find that this avowal has been suppressed. It was made in earnest to correct a wrong impression that Freud had given the readers of *The Interpretation of Dreams* and the original edition of his self-chronicle (1925). When he issued these two works he had trusted the judgment of Georg Brandes that *Hamlet* was composed soon after the death of the dramatist's father—in 1601. On discovering that there was no reliable proof for Brandes's assertion Freud added the note to his autobiography warning his disciples and students that he had lost confidence in the traditional accounts of the dramatist's life. Now something happened between the two translations of 1927 and 1935 to induce him to withdraw this challenge to the upholders of the Stratford-on-Avon cult. In its place, as a footnote on the erroneous statement of the text concerning the occasion of the writing of *Hamlet*, now stood the innocuous words: "I have particular reasons for no longer wishing to lay any emphasis upon this point."

Why the particular reasons could be indicated in the American version of 1927 and had to be banished from the British version, we may surmise from the fact, that the editor of the latter, Ernest Jones, failed to make any allusion to Freud's new hypothesis on the poet's personality in the different editions of his own essay on *Hamlet*. Jones persisted in repeating the guesswork of orthodoxy on the provenance of the play, guesswork which is dear—and profitable—to the British shrine at Stratford. To the sponsors of that shrine (lucidly etched by Henry James in his story "The Birthplace") a tribute to the analytic talent of J. Thomas Looney would ring as heresy and sacrilege. Coming from Freud, it might provoke them to retaliation anger against the disciples of psychoanalysis within their economic reach, doubtless to the detriment of British psychiatry. It was to be expected that the prudence of Ernest Jones, the dean of English analysts, would act to cut out the offensive declaration in favor of Edward de Vere. The Earl of Oxford is not simply a "claimant" to the crown of Shakespeare, you understand. He was a poet and playwright who enjoyed hurting the feelings of high and mighty respectable Britons, and his reputation in his native country is prodigiously bad. To have presented the founder of psychoanalysis as a champion of the Oxford claim to Shakespeare's honors meant risking the smirch of bohemia on the medical psychologists who had toiled so hard to "naturalize" the Freudian theories in Britain. It meant perhaps a resurgence of the kind of obloquy that medicine men flung on Dr. John Elliotson when he introduced hypnotism to English hospitals.

After Freud's death his *Outline of Psychoanalysis* came out in German (1940) with a footnote renewing his offensive against the Stratford cult. As translated by James Strachey in 1949 this footnote runs: "The name 'William Shakespeare' is most probably a pseudonym behind which there lies concealed a great unknown. Edward de Vere, Earl of Oxford, a man who has been regarded as the author of Shakespeare's works, lost a beloved and admired father while he was still a boy, and completely repudiated his mother, who contracted a new marriage soon after her husband's death" (p. 96). This pronouncement was greeted by the disciples of Freud with a silence that would have been deadly if it had not been so ridiculous. It is indeed edifying to observe the most voluble followers of the great critic of human nature presenting a spectacle of what he called "the aversion to learning anything new so characteristic of the scientist." (Cf. *The Basic Writings of Sigmund Freud*, in the Modern Library edition, p. 186.) They continued to pay homage to the Shylock of Stratford.

It is certainly true, as Henry James affirmed (in "The Birth-place"), that the real William Shakespeare covered his tracks as no other human being has ever done. At the same time he was bound to suffer the doom of all humanity and betray himself, unconsciously, in every gesture and word. None of the titanic masks under which he strove so artfully to hide himself (Hamlet, Macbeth, Othello, Lear, etc.) proves invulnerable to the analytic art of Freud. Psycho-analysis promises one fine day to make the dramatist as familiar to us as any poor mortal may be. When that day arrives we will stand wonderstruck before the fact that nearly four hundred years were necessary to solve the mystery of the world's biggest "jig-maker".

Since the publication of *Shakespeare Identified* in 1920 the disciples of Looney have assembled a mass of testimony in support of his theory which is sufficient to explain every major problem of the Shakespeare poems and dramas. The facts and arguments mar-shalled in *The Seventeenth Earl of Oxford* by B. M. Ward (1928), *Hidden Allusions in Shakespeare's Plays* by Eva Turner Clark (1931), *The Life Story of Edward de Vere as "William Shakespeare"* by Percy Allen (1932), and *Personal Clues in Shakespeare Poems and Sonnets* by Gerald H. Rendall (1934)—to name only four important books in defense of the new hypothesis—have gone unanswered by the official ora-cles of the Stratford fidelity, except where they have seen fit to have some fun with mistakes of the Oxfordians. It is an ancient habit of the oracles to strain at gnats and swallow camels, as Mark Twain long ago pointed out. (Cf. *Is Shakespeare Dead?*) I myself have under-gone the muteness treatment after publishing evidence that Edward de Vere was the Lord Chamberlain who directed the company of actors for whom William Shakespeare worked. [See Chapter 2—W.H.] To the historical proof that the name "Shakespeare" (often spelled in his time with a hyphen) is a pen name, a nom de guerre, I now propose to add the proof of psychoanalysis, along the lines suggested by Freud.

I intend to restrict myself to the examination of the writings of Shakespeare which are formally, on the surface, autobiographical. By limiting ourselves only to the work in which he speaks in his own person we can hope to avoid the accusation that we are projecting or reading into his lines whatever we wish. We shall deal with the man himself so far as his ego dared to show its nature in candor. Consequently we shall not touch on any of his plays, nor the two long narratives about *Venus* and *Lucrece*. The boundaries of our research are set by the signature of William Shakespeare in the dedications of these tales, and the first person singular of his Sonnets. In the interpretation of these I shall assume that the author means exactly what he says, unless there is formidable, factual evidence to the contrary. This assumption is demanded by the principle of economy in science, which prohibits the multiplication of hypotheses. Shakespeare stated the principle long before scientists became conscious of it: "More matter, with less art" (*Hamlet*, 2.2).

Shakespeare's fidelity to his art, poetry, was religious, obsessional. To his way of thinking it marked his election as one of "God's spies," born to hold mirrors up to nature in order to reveal her darkest secrets. At work on his priest-like task he felt remote and superior to the rest of the race, and disdained its popular interests. ("Lord, what fools these mortals be!") When the first of his works to carry his name, *Venus and Adonis*, came from the press it flaunted as a motto an arrogant couplet from Ovid—his favorite poet—verses that may be translated this way:

Let the vulgar admire the vile; for me, may tawny Apollo
Minister brimful cups from the Muses fountain, Castalia.

In the spirit of aristocracy burning from these words he chose Henry Wriothesley, Earl of Southampton, as the man most worthy of the dedication of his poem. The Earl was turning twenty, and already famous for his love of Italianate literature as well as his personal beauty. Perhaps Shakespeare designed the *Venus and Adonis* to gratify the sensual imagination of the young nobleman and to warn him against the dangers of extreme self-love (narcissism). Philip Stringer's adulation of the young Earl, in Latin verse written in 1592, made the warning necessary. Delicately Shakespeare reminded

Southampton of his social duty, expressing the wish that the content of the youth's heart might always answer his wish "and the world's hopeful expectation." We have not the smallest testimony concerning the effect of the poem or its dedication on the Earl at whom it was aimed.

There is absolutely no evidence that William Shakespeare of Stratford-on-Avon was acquainted with Henry Wriothesley. The sole link between them is the bare name at the close of the dedication to *Venus and Adonis*.

The dedication opens and concludes, with an air of affected humility, the pride of a poet showing off a brain-child to a world hard to convince of the merits of poetry. If Southampton seemed pleased with the trifle now presented to him—a toy of nearly twelve hundred verses—Shakespeare vowed he would "take advantage of all idle hours," till he had honored the young Earl with "some graver labour."

"But if the first heir of my invention prove deformed, I shall be sorry it had so noble a god-father, and never after ear so barren a land, for fear it yield me still so bad a harvest."

These few words have probably provoked more commentary than all the rest of the book. Many scholars have taken them as an avowal that the *Venus* was the first product of Shake-speare's pen, even a product of his adolescence in Stratford. Nothing had come from his hand in book-form prior to the publication of this poem (registered with the London Stationers on April 18, 1593). It appeared reasonable to suppose that "the first heir of my invention" meant this was his first book. The explanation left many students dissatisfied and uneasy. They could not imagine Shakespeare treating so contemptuously such plays as *The Comedy of Errors*, *The Taming of the Shrew*, *The Two Gentlemen of Verona*, *Henry VI*, *Titus Andronicus*, and *Romeo and Juliet*, all of which are dated with expert confidence before April 1593. They preferred to hunt for another explanation of the mystifying phrase. So far their scourings for a better interpretation have been in vain. They would have us believe that the poet was cunning past man's thought.

There is general agreement that the passage was intended to be witty, and a few researchers acquainted with the dramatist's methods have seen in it a ripe example of his most chronic wit-work, paronomasia. Suppose we view the phrase in question as a pun. We are then confronted with a joke about sex in rather queer taste. The "first heir" emerges with the double meaning of (a) the earliest brain -child of the poet's "invention," and (b) the earliest heir or male child to spring from his virility (invention being Latin for coming-in, i.e. sexual intercourse). If this interpretation is true we should expect to find that the poet had dedicated his son and heir to the Earl of Southampton—"so noble a godfather." We are not surprised therefore to find the defenders of Stratford tradition resisting the suggestion of a pun in the foreword to *Venus and Adonis*. The sole boy born to their idol was the twin Hamnet, baptised in February 1585, who was buried in Stratford in August 1596. He could not be the first heir of the poet's ingenuity. Moreover, the reference to Southampton as a godfather implies that Shakespeare's son was actually named after Henry Wriothesley. The friends of the Looney theory are gratified to announce that the sole heir of the Earl of Oxford was in truth named Henry. And he was born on February 24, 1593, and christened on March 31, a little more than a fortnight before the entry of *Venus and Adonis* in the ledger of the Stationers Company. His baptism took place in the church of Stoke Newington, within walking distance of the Theatre and the Curtain, two playhouses of fame in the life of Shakespeare. In June the Lord Chamberlain's men performed on a stage in Stoke Newington, acting *Hamlet* and *The Taming of a Shrew*. This was the company to which William Shakespeare belonged for most of his theatrical life. The Lord Chamberlain, as I have attempted to prove in detail elsewhere ("Shakespeare's Jester—Oxford's Servant," *Shakespeare Fellowship Quarterly*, Autumn 1947 and Chapter 2 of this book.), was very likely Edward de Vere himself, the Lord Great Chamberlain of England. The April in which *Venus and Adonis* went to press must have been a merry month for the Earl of Oxford. Not only could he rejoice in the son his second wife had given him—solace for his conceit of masculinity, the mettle daunted three times by his first wife, who left him at death with three remarkable daughters. The Earl could also rejoice in the friendship and affection of the handsome Southampton, who had been engaged to marry his eldest daughter, the strong-tempered Lady Elizabeth. The engagement was arranged by Oxford's father-in-law, Lord Burghley, whose ambition for his grandchildren craved their union with the bluest and wealthiest blood in the kingdom. Southampton apparently did not enter the contract with Lady Vere wholeheartedly, and according to the Jesuit Father Henry Garnett succeeded in breaking their engagement in 1594 to the astonishing tune of 5000 pounds. The rupture did not spoil the relations of Oxford and Southampton. The latter remained to his death a staunch and intimate friend of Oxford's heir. Unfortunately we are still in the dark as to the nature of the bonds between the father and Henry Wriothesley. But the curious fact that Oxford's heir was the first Vere in twenty generations to be named Henry furnishes food for thought on the matter.

Edward de Vere had some reasons to fear that his son might prove deformed. His own body, while celebrated for its athletic graces in youth, had always been pathetically short. In 1581, when he was thirty years old, Oxford had been reviled by Lord Henry Howard for certain "botches and deformities of his misshapen life." In the spring of 1582 he fought a duel with Sir Thomas Knyvet on account of a girl of the Queen's Chamber, Anne Vavasor. The duel ended with Oxford wounded dangerously, "to the peril of his life," Lord Burghley said. The scar of this event may have impressed the Earl with the idea that he was doomed to be deformed. It is noteworthy that in the spring of 1583 a son was born to him who died shortly after his birth. The psychic wound inflicted by this event would inevitably excite his castration complex, which would induce retaliation on the mother. We know how miserable he made his Countess Anne. The birth of his second boy surely revived the memory of the loss of his first, and waking the old grief would stir up unconscious cruel thoughts of his new wife. He stood ready to blame her for the possible deformity of his heir, and secretly vowed, in the abysmal gloom of his ego, if the child turned out crooked, never again to "ear so barren a land." It is a fact that the Earl and his Countess Elizabeth lived together for eleven years after the birth of Henry and had no more children.

On May 9, 1594, *The Rape of Lucrece* was registered for publication, and for the second time the name of William Shakespeare was blazoned in print, and, as in the *Venus and Adonis*, not on the title-page but at the end of the dedication. For the second and last time Shakespeare dedicated a book of his, once again to the Earl of Southampton. This time his dedication, while sustaining the pretense of "untutored" poetry, sounded notes of sincerity that make the wit and charm of the foreword to the *Venus* seem mere trickery. The foreword to the *Lucrece* rings with an avowal of infinite love:

What I have done is yours; what I have to do is yours; being part in all I have, devoted yours.

The passion of these words has long been recognized as homoerotic, a breath of the libido of Plato's Greece and the Italy of Leonardo da Vinci, Aretino, and Bazzi alias Sodoma. But the avowal has not been taken seriously by most inquirers in the life of Shakespeare. They have not looked at the works of Shakespeare produced after May 1594 in the light of his declaration that they would all be "devoted" to Southampton, from a love "without end."

We catch several glimpses of this love in action in a contemporary satire entitled *Willobie his Avisa* (1594). From this pamphlet we learn that Henry Willobie (also called H. W.) was a London youth fond of Italian and Spanish fashions, who fell hotly in love with a lady named Avisa, and pining in secret grief for her confessed his desire to "his familiar friend W. S., who not long before had tried the courtesy of the like passion, and was now newly recovered of the like infection." Scholars have long been convinced that these initials stand for Henry Wriothesley and William Shakespeare. The theatrical imagery used in describing their relations clearly identifies W. S. We know of no H. W. in Shakespeare's life who could be termed, in 1594, his familiar friend, except the Earl of Southampton. True, the companionship of the two men is depicted in the poem as far closer and warmer than one would expect between the jack of all trades from Stratford and the aristocrat. But there is no sound reason for identifying W. S. with the man from Stratford. The satire plainly alludes to W. S. as "the old player." Objective testimony informs us that the career of Shakespeare of Stratford as a player had barely begun when *Willobie* was composed. He was just thirty years old at the time, hardly an age for a vigorous businessman to be branded an old gamester. And he would never have dared to address the Earl of Southampton as "friend Harry," like W. S. does so cheerfully. The Earl of Oxford, on the other hand, fits the part of the old player perfectly. He was forty-four years old when Willobie came out, and there was no gentleman in England so deeply learned in the ways of the stage. In his youth he had been something of an actor himself. A mass of respectable evidence has been gathered to prove that he was the target of the satire (Pauline K. Angell, in the *Publications of the Modern Language Association*, 1937). Whoever wrote *Willobie his Avisa* possessed the secret of the Earl of Oxford's dramatic career, and incidentally could parody with amazing cleverness the Earl's own erotic poetry.

In August 1593 John Danter, the printer of *Romeo and Juliet*, issued posthumous sonnets by Thomas Watson in a book named *The Tears of Fancy*. The final poem happens to be a sonnet which is also attributed (in the contemporary Rawlinson Manuscripts) to Edward de Vere. Today it is impossible to prove the true authorship. For our purposes it does not matter; it is enough to know that the name of Oxford could be connected, around the year 1593, with a sonnet of love. This was the time when Shakespeare's love sonnets were circulating among his private friends, sonnets that were above all devoted to his "friend Harry," the Earl of Southampton.

Before proceeding with our analysis of the Sonnets, I would like to point out that the man behind the mask of William Shakespeare was known to at least one other clever poet beside the author of *Willobie his Avisa*. In January 1593 the English Rabelais, Thomas Nashe, published his *Strange News of the Intercepting Certain Letters*, with a deliberately bewildering comic dedication, "To the most co-

pious Carminist (meaning song-maker—F.) of our time, and famous
persecutor of Priscian (i.e. breaker of grammar rules—F.), his very
friend Master Apis Lapis," also hailed as "Gentle Master William."
Authorities in Tudor literature have utterly failed to elicit the identity of this William, and none ever made an effort to elucidate the
cryptic dedication. That William was a nickname of Edward de
Vere, has in my opinion been conclusively proved by Charles Wisner Barrell in his study of Nashe's remarks (in the *Shakespeare Fellowship Quarterly*, October 1944). Independently of Barrell, in England,
Gerald Phillips suggested that the Earl of Oxford was the object of
Nashe's humor. In *Shakespeare identified* Looney had already presented a strong argument for thinking that the poet Edmund
Spenser held Oxford in mind when he lamented (in *The Tears of the
Muses*, 1591) the departure from the comic stage of a dramatist
whom he called "Our pleasant Willy." The Earl seems to have assumed the name in disguising himself as a poet in the pastoral vein.
We know that he wrote copious poetry. The Cambridge University
writer Gabriel Harvey, in 1578, applauded him for great excellence
in letters: "I have seen many Latin verses of thine," Harvey said:
"Yes, even more English verses are extant." Unfortunately erudition
has so far exhumed scarcely more than twenty of his poems, mostly
juvenile things. We are even unluckier with regard to the dramatic
writings of Oxford. Elizabethan learning extolled him as an author
of interludes and comedies, but none of his plays survives, at least
not under his own name. It is worthy of mention that Gabriel Harvey, in the work of 1578 already quoted, had praised Oxford for his
prowess in tournaments and asserted that his countenance seemed
to shake a spear! As Viscount Bulbeck he carried a crest with a lion
shaking a broken spear. This picture, Harvey's rhapsodic metaphor,
and perhaps an irresistible impulse to *double entendre*, seeing in the
spear a symbol of sex-war, could easily have prompted De Vere to
adopt the pen-name of William Shakespeare for his dramas of war
and love. I conjecture that he adopted the name on encountering
the runaway from Stratford at the theatre where the latter earned a
living as caretaker of horses. Oxford, I have no doubt, was respon-

sible for poor William Shakespeare's admission to actors' circles, and employed him probably as the agent for bringing forward his own plays. It is possible that the two had met before, during one of the Earl's visits to his estate at Bilton on the Avon, a short distance from Stratford. The discovery of a sharpwitted and businesslike fellow actually named William Shakespeare must have struck the Earl of Oxford as a gift of the gods, for he needed somebody to represent his interests in the theatre directly, to avoid the vulgar scandal and commercial taint that were sure to afflict any nobleman who took an open part in the vagabonds' game of the stage. To the extent that he was able to tell the story, in verse, he told it in the Sonnets of Shakespeare.

Shake-speares Sonnets: that is what they were called when they first came from the press in 1609, five years after the Earl of Oxford's death. The publisher was one Thomas Thorpe, a man of low reputation in the book trade. Thorpe took the liberty of dedicating *Shake -speares Sonnets* to a friend named Mr. W. H., "the only begetter of these ensuing Sonnets." Disciples of Looney have demonstrated that Mr. W. H. was none other than William Hall, who doubtless obtained the poems by stealth. In 1606 Hall acted as "begetter" of a theological booklet entitled "A Fourfold Meditation," which is now understood to be the work of Philip Howard, the Roman Catholic Earl of Arundel, who had died in 1595, a martyr prisoner in the Tower of London. The *Meditation* came from the press of George Eld, the same man who printed *Shake-speares Sonnets*. The former also bore the initials W. H., and the only "begetter" admitted that they were "conveyed by a mere accident" to his hands. It is conceivable that the accident was connected with the felony that Rose Jones was suspected of committing against Oxford's widow in 1606. She and her husband would have been deeply interested in a book by the Earl of Arundel, who had known Oxford intimately in the years when the latter was a convert to the Catholic faith. The two Earls were related by blood: Arundel's father was the son of an aunt of Edward de Vere. When we learn that William Hall belonged to the parish of Hackney, where De Vere and his widow lived, our suspicion of the source of Hall's lucky accident turns nearly to conviction.

The *Meditation* was dedicated by the publisher to one Mathew Saunders, to whom "W. H. wisheth, with long life, a prosperous achievement of his good desires." The words remind us acutely of Thomas Thorpe's dedication of the Sonnets to W. H. "To the only begetter of these ensuing Sonnets," Thorpe wrote, in lurid capital letters. "Mr. W. H. all happiness, and that eternity promised by our ever-living Poet, wisheth the well-wishing adventurer in setting forth." The adventurer is Thorpe of course, hopefully setting forth a volume which he anticipated would net him a delectable profit. In the "all" that follows the initial H we can detect a typical Elizabethan pun. The reason for the special wishes of felicity and immortality was uncovered by Colonel B. R. Ward in *The Mystery of Mr. W. H.* (1923), a triumph of Oxfordian research. Ward found in the parish register of Hackney a record of the marriage of William Hall, on August 4, 1608, nine months before the appearance of the Sonnets. Very likely they were set forth on the occasion of the birth of this "only begetter" 's first child: He would have cordially appreciated the application to himself of the theme of "Our ever-living Poet" in the first nineteen Sonnets, the promise of eternity through wedlock and offspring. The expression "ever-living" is unquestionably a euphemism for *defunct*. Shakespeare used it in *Henry VI* (Part I, 4.3) in reference to the dead King Henry the Fifth, "That ever-living man of memory." Hall and Thorpe must have been aware that the poet was dead. The "accident" that conveyed his private poems into Hall's hands probably occurred while the Countess Elizabeth de Vere was sadly occupied with departure from King's Place, the house in Hackney where her playwright husband spent his last years and died. She sold King's Place in 1609.

2

We may take the word of Shakespeare that the Sonnets, being part in all he had devoted to the Earl of Southampton, were mainly designed for the pleasure of the youth who was engaged to marry the Earl of Oxford's eldest daughter. Southampton was reluctant to enter the bonds of matrimony, and Shakespeare lectured him on their necessity and redeeming features in *Venus and Adonis*:

> Torches are made to light, jewels to wear,
> Dainties to taste, fresh beauty for the use,
> Herbs for their smell, and sappy plants to bear;
> Things growing to themselves are growth's abuse:
> Seeds spring from seeds, and beauty breedeth beauty;
> Thou wast begot; to get it is thy duty.

The opening of the Sonnet-sequence executes tuneful variations on this teleological theme, together with promises of immortality and the gratification of egoism through the reproduction of the beloved self. The narcissic megalomania of parents was never stated before or after with such voluble candor. The beautiful young man to whom these poems are addressed is censured again and again for narcissism in peril of sterility:

> But thou, contracted to thine own bright eyes,
> Feed'st thy light's flame with self-substantial fuel,
> Making a famine where abundance lies,
> Thyself thy foe, to thy sweet self too cruel.

Shakespeare was quite familiar with the disease, having suffered all his life from its delicious poison. When he spoke of Narcissus in his tale of Adonis it was with the poignancy of self-revelation:

> Narcissus so himself himself forsook,
> And died to kiss his shadow in the brook.

The voice of the disease may be heard lucidly in a letter the Earl of Oxford wrote to his father-in-law in 1576, while traveling in Italy far from his wife. He wrote requesting the sale of some of his lands, against Burghley's advice: "I have no help but of mine own," De Vere said, "and mine is made to serve me and myself, not mine" (*The Seventeenth Earl of Oxford*, by B. M. Ward, 110). A few month later he warned Burghley—the most powerful politician in England—that he would not discommode himself to please his wife or her father: "for always I have, and I will still prefer mine own content before others" (*Oxford*, 126). We shall see to what lengths—in imagination—the egoism of Oxford could go, in harmony with the narcissism of "Will Shakespeare."

In the first Sonnet I hear sounded in consonance with the narcissism theme a motive of nearly equal power in the mind of the poet, the motive of identification of Southampton with himself. The theme does not appear on the surface of the Sonnet, and persons who are not convinced by the Looney-Freud hypothesis will not see it. I refer to the lines extolling the poet's beloved friend as

> now the world's fresh ornament
> And only herald to the gaudy spring.

Southampton's birthday fell on October 6, and I suppose that Shakespeare designed the epithet as a compliment to beauty that could make winter seem a swift interlude before the season of the rose. (The italics of the word *Rose* in the Sonnets have led some scholars to the fancy that the word implies a complimentary pun on Wriothesley, which could be pronounced as if it were Rosily.) But the phrase "herald to the gaudy spring" fits Oxford better than Southampton, since the former was born on the threshold of the English spring, on April 12, 1550. The epithet is therefore interpretable as an unconscious memory of the poet's own brilliant youth, when he was a royal ward (like Southampton), in the care of Lord Burghley (like Southampton), and the observed of all observers, like his young love. The poet recalls the beauty of Southampton's mother as she was when they were both young at Court:

> Thou art thy mother's glass and she in thee
> Calls back the lovely April of her prime. (Sonnet III)

The choice of April to represent the flowering time of beauty cannot be an accident. In recollecting the April of his own prime while contemplating Southampton's good looks, Shakespeare may have been conscious of a wish, to be the lad's father. The desire probably acted as the preconscious form of the deeper identification concept.

Parenthetically we may note here that in Sonnet III we get the application of agricultural imagery to the womb and sexual intercourse, just as we get it in the dedication to *Venus and Adonis*.

The second Sonnet, it appears to me, sets the chronological mood of the beginning of the sequence. It warns the poet's love of the ravages that "forty winters" will perform on his brow and body. Naturally, orthodox investigators have not found any particular significance in the selection of the number forty to stand for old age. The favorite son of Stratford, as we have already remarked, was only thirty when the "first heir" of Shakespeare's "invention" was a year old. Edward de Vere, on the other hand, was then forty-four.

In the tenth Sonnet we come across the first avowal of affection between the poet and his young friend: "Make thee another self, for love of me," Shakespeare exclaims. In Sonnet XIII he appeals to him frankly as "Dear my love." At the same time he reminds the beloved that he is fatherless, and comes of a fine house in danger of decay.

Sonnet XIV, modestly claiming for the poet a certain skill in astronomy, declares that in the eyes of the beloved he beholds two stars that predict "Truth and beauty shall together thrive," if the young man weds as Shakespeare wished he would. If not the poet prognosticated: "Thy end is Truth's and Beauty's doom and date." Truth here can only mean the kindred whose alliance with the beauty of Wriothesley is keenly desired by the writer. There can be no doubt as to the family meant if we accept the viewpoint of a non-Oxfordian such as J. A. Fort, that "the sequence of sonnets on the subject of marriage begin when Southampton was 'contracted' to Lady Elizabeth Vere" (*A Time-Scheme for Shakespeare's Sonnets*, 1929, 23). The name Vere was frequently punned upon by Elizabethans because of its likeness to the Latin for "true." The motto of the house of Vere punned on the name: *Vero nihil verius* (Nothing truer than truth). Editors have weakened the force of the paronomasia in the Sonnets by removing the capital T from Truth.

Shakespeare's plea for Beauty's marriage with Truth in order to make his dear youth a father after his own heart concluded with Sonnet XVII. After this the sequence alters directly to one of love-making, and the theme of identification sounds ever more clearly. "My glass shall not persuade me I am old," the poet affirms, so long as his love remains youthfully fair. When time's furrows are driven across his hero's face, however, he expects to die.

> For all that beauty that doth cover thee
> Is but the seemly raiment of my heart. (XXII)

How could Shakespeare's flesh survive, he wonders, when South-ampton's carnal brightness is gone? The homoerotic nature of their attachment emerges plainly in the announcement at the close of this poem: "Thou gav'st me thine (heart), not to give back again." It was written, I think, toward the end of 1594, after the younger Earl renounced his contract with Lady Elizabeth Vere.

The eighteenth Sonnet assures the beloved youth that he will attain immortality even if he does not have children by "Truth." Shakespeare's "eternal lines" will gain him eternity. Some critics have judged this boast of the poet's transcendence over death, and the passages in other Sonnets just like it, as mere conventional echoes of the classics, which promised the preservation through time of the names of all those who befriended the bards. On the contrary, I judge these passages to be a childlike declaration of the poet's megalomania. He hated the very thought of death, especially since he felt that he would die before the brand of "vulgar scandal" and public disgrace on his name and household could be erased. Having failed to achieve the immortality of "public honour and proud titles" by services more masculine he revived the fantasy of omnipotence which he shared with all infants in his infancy, and assured himself that he would obtain immortality by the road of incantation, poetry, which was rather disdained by men of affairs and state in his day. The Earl of Southampton would consequently become immortal too: "My love shall in my verse live ever young" (XIX). In the strained meter of the adverb "ever" Oxfordian ears detect a play on the name E. Vere. If they are right we have here another instance of the imaginary identification between the great writer and his boyish love.

Their homoerotic relation is clarified in Sonnet XX, which humorously complains that there can be no sexual intercourse between Shakespeare and the "Master-Mistress" of his passion, because Nature has thwarted the former's irrepressible lust by her addition to the beloved's beauty of the mark of the male. "She prickt thee out for women's pleasure," Shakespeare asserts, and the obscenity should suffice to end all speculation concerning his homosexuality. Charges of pederasty were brought against Oxford in 1581 by his enemy, Lord Henry Howard, but there is no evidence that he ventured beyond a poet's uncontrollable fancy of inverse love. It is possible that Shakespeare experimented with male-love, but in general, we may be sure, his neurosis (which Freud diagnosed in *The Interpretation of Dreams* as hysteric—cf. the Modern Library edition of his Basic Writings, 310) would subdue the perversion. One sign of the dramatist's neurosis often manifested in the Sonnets is insomnia. But he dares not give us a clear glance at the thoughts that will not let him sleep.

We know that Shakespeare suffered from misfortunes of which history has left us unmistakable traces in the life of Edward de Vere. The Earl of Oxford had never succeeded in gaining the confidence of his Queen, and her prime minister, the Lord Treasurer Burghley. His efforts to get military and naval glory ended in frustration, and never received the public attention that Lord Henry Howard's accusations of treason brought him. Calumny stuck to his name from the time of his birth, when the imputation of bastardy was made against him. The money necessary to combat such slanders in the courts of public opinion he spent in pursuit of his pleasures, among professional authors and actors, and similar people of ill repute. In the summer of 1594 Oxford wrote to his former father-in-law pleading for legal aid in the improvement of his fortune. He promised Burghley that he had resolved "not to neglect, as heretofore," the chances to amend his estate (Ward, *Oxford*, 312). Out of royal favor, the Earl lived in the suburbs of London, Stoke Newington or Hackney, and became practically a stranger to the Court which he once dazzled with his talents. In the light of this fact alone does the Sonnet make sense, in which Shakespeare tells Southampton that he cannot associate with him in public and show affection freely,

> Till whatsoever star that guides my moving
> Points on me graciously with fair aspect,
> And puts apparel on my tatter'd loving,
> To show me worthy of thy sweet respect. (XXVI)

Oxfordian analysis finds more than a banal astrologic reference in the line about the poet's star. The Earl's coat of arms carried a solitary silver star, which legend said blazed there in memory of a miracle to which a star had guided an ancestor's troops during the first Crusade (Ward, 4). The poet Andrew Marvell may have been thinking of this myth when he composed his celebration of the union of the Fairfax family and "starry Vere".

Shakespeare confesses in Sonnet XXIX that he lives despised by Fortune and the eyes of men, in "outcast state". In the next poem we learn that his mind dwells on "old woes," and occasionally cries "For precious friends hid in death's dateless night." Like Othello (5.2) he claims that his eyes are unaccustomed to tears. Nevertheless he seems to have a multitude of aged griefs to weep over, above all, "love's long since cancel'd woe." He has outlived so many friends (XXXI). The love he once gave many now belongs to one alone, the Earl Henry. (From this avowal we must conclude that the feeling of Shakespeare for his wife was no sacred passion.) "Thou," he cries to Southampton, "hast all the all of me." The outcry repeats the idea of the dedication to *Lucrece*. Southampton apparently did not esteem the possession as highly as Shakespeare did. The young man even preferred the poetry of artists younger than his friend, elaborate stylists like George Chapman, whom I take to be the rival writer so elegantly derided in the Sonnets.

The following Sonnets indicate that Shakespeare and his love sometimes met at the latter's reequest, and *Willobie his Avisa* informs us how well known their intimacy was. The tale of *Willobie* about the love of H. W. for a woman whom W. S. had tried vainly to conquer is not unlike the story that these Sonnets tell. They allude to a sin the poet's dear friend has committed, a "sensual fault," involving someone whom Shakespeare regarded as belonging to him. The hint of rivalry in love is unmistakable. The poet forgives the "sweet thief" who has robbed him of the woman in question, but their friendship is now bereft of all its glamor and idealism. Shakespeare's quickness in adopting the Christ posture was not simply histrionic. No doubt he was deeply disappointed to learn that Southampton cared more for a mere female than he did for the sublime Will. But he was afraid to lose the voluptuous Wriothesley. He stood ready to meet the younger lover on any terms he might whimsically select, realizing that their companionship could do the youth shame (XXXVI). This self-denial and sacrifice was ascetic as well as practical. The poet's profound masochism relished his isolation from mankind, which he portrayed in drama after drama with all the wormwood enmity of an English Timon, a misanthrope with a special bias against women.

In Sonnet XXXVII we are presented with the vivid image of the dramatist as "a decrepit father . . . made lame by fortune's dearest spite." He rejoices to think that by his love he may catch part of the splendor that is Southampton's from beauty, birth, wealth and wit. Enjoying that young brightness he simultaneously enjoys the illusion that he is no longer "lame, poor, nor despis'd." It is impossible to take this self-portrayal seriously and believe in the Stratford story, or the allegations made on the authorship question for Francis Bacon, William Stanley, Roger Manners, and the other luminaries of Tudor times who have been placed in opposition to the Looney-Freud hypothesis. Only the Earl of Oxford could be said to have been lame, poor, and despised at the time this poem was written. I have already spoken of the wound that Sir Thomas Knyvet inflicted on the Earl in 1582 in a duel over the fatal lady Anne Vavasor. I have mentioned his financial straits, after having sold 56 properties in land between 1572 and 1592. As for his being despised, it will be enough to quote Sir Walter Ralegh's remark to Lord Burghley when the latter, in May 1583, appealed for the knight's assistance in regaining the Queen's favor for the scapegrace Earl. "I am content," Ralegh wrote, "for your sake, to lay the serpent before the fire, as much as in me lieth; that, having recovered strength, myself may be most in danger of his poison and sting." (Ward, 244.) Ralegh was thinking of De Vere's vitriolic wit. Whatever the reason for their hostility, the fact remains that the Earl had more enemies at Court, and in the city and country, than he had friends. According to the Sonnets, indeed, he had but one friend left (in 1594), Henry Wriothesley. And even he did not hesitate to steal the poet's girl.

Writing of Oxford's sale of his lands reminds me that he was particularly lavish in 1576 when he travelled to Italy. In my opinion, Shakespeare had the Italian tour in mind when he declared (in XXXIII) that he had seen many a glorious sunrise over mountains. And he must have been thinking of the ruin of his birthplace, Castle Hedingham in Essex, when he writes of having seen "sometime lofty towers" torn down. In December 1591 the Earl alienated the house of his ancestors to his three daughters and former father-in-law. In the same Sonnet which evokes the memory of ancient towers (LXIV) the poet remembers having watched the sea devouring the shore and the earth recover space from the sea. The thoughts of lofty towers and the sea were naturally linked in Oxford's mind because he had spent his boyhood within seven miles of the North Sea, and once occupied a family home at Wivenhoe by the sea, in a house famed for towers that served as sea-marks. Here the Earl pursued the interests which he named his "country Muses" (Ward, 89).

Sonnet XL reiterates the dramatist's appeal to Southampton not to become his foe on account of the woman they both coveted: "I do forgive thy robbery, gentle thief," Shakespeare repeats, darting after the honey of his charity the sting of irony at Southampton's "Lascivious grace." Not even the beloved Earl could feel free from the poet's poison, when the impulse to sarcasm swayed him. But Shakespeare refused to suppress the impulse when his rival took the liberty of making love to the woman in the poet's own seat. The allusion to Shakespeare's "seat" in Sonnet XLI has gone too long without comment from admirers of the Stratford myth. We would like to hear their opinions on which of Shakespeare's residences his noble friend employed.

In the forty-second Sonnet the theme of identification is openly stated, with a brutal and subtle confession of the perverse pleasure which the dramatist derived from the treachery of his two loves:

> But here's the joy: my friend and I are one;
> Sweet flattery! then she loves but me alone.

The repressed homosexuality of Shakespeare becomes painfully manifest here. It is obvious that his imagination rioted in fantasies of the woman yielding herself to the man in whom he saw the mirror of his own youth. Unknown to his infinitely clever ego was the fantasy beneath these thoughts, the fantasy of taking the woman's place. That she possessed the "master-mistress" of his passion, he admits, was the chief cause of his sorrow. He could get joy out of it only by fancying himself sharing her joy. The identification with this mysterious woman was, I have no doubt, deeper than Shakespeare's identification with the noble youth. In the former I find the central factor in the poet's neurosis. She stood in his mind's eye for the unconscious image of his mother, for whose lost love he suffered all his life. The proof of this unfortunately cannot be offered in a study of the Sonnets by themselves. The plays provide most of my evidence. I have taken one, a farce apparently far removed from the theme of incest, *The Comedy of Errors*, and demonstrated by means of a detailed analysis of the whole play that Shakespeare's chief sorrow came from the loss of his mother's love—after he had introjected her to his heart of hearts. [See A. Bronson Feldman, *Early Shake-speare*—W.H.] But he struggled until his death to convince himself that he did not need her, nor anybody like her. Spurning her entire sex he searched for love among men and lads, but narcissism of the intensest type made him turn away from all but the few whom he could consider reflexions of himself. When these failed him he retreated with happiness to the gentlemen and ladies of the empire of his dreams, modelled unconsciously after the members of his unholy family.

It has been surmised that the books by Shakespeare of which he speaks in Sonnet XXIII were groups of his poems. The idea has presented itself to me that they may have been his published plays. The opening simile of the Sonnet, comparing himself to "an unperfect actor on the stage," shows that he was thinking of the theater critically when his books came to mind. Very likely he was thinking of his plays again when he composed Sonnet XLVIII. Here he writes of "jewels" he owns which his beloved considers "trifles". The jewels of a poor artist are his masterpieces; only works of art would have been viewed as trifles by persons not artists belonging to the master-workman's circle. Shakespeare speaks with pride of the care with which he took his way, a phrase signifying a decision that marked a major change in his life. The lines that follow, concerning the locking of his jewels "under truest bars," indicate that the decision had to do with his career as a writer. It must have been the resolution to conceal Edward de Vere behind the mask of William Shakespeare. His friend's failure to esteem his poetical works should not surprise us, not after perusal of the eighth Sonnet which informs us that music which gives the poet happiness offends the beloved; he does not listen to it gladly. Southampton, in short, was one of those men whom *The Merchant of Venice* warns against (5.1) because they are "not moved with concord of sweet sounds." Such men, the drama declares, are fit for treasons. It would be interesting to know if the warning was written with Southampton in view, or his fiery friend, the Earl of Essex, whose insurrection in 1601 nearly cost Henry Wriothesley his head. We know that Southampton was extremely fond of the theater, but there is no evidence in his correspondence that he cared for its products in literature. Plays were just pastimes for him. His empiric intellect wanted nothing more than amusement from the "millions of strange shadows" which his theatrical friend beheld when he thought of their love. In the description of Adonis, Shakespeare remarks (LIII), he finds a counterfeit of his friend. The remark furnishes a clue to the meaning of *Venus and Adonis*. Shakespeare also beholds his beloved Earl when Helen of Troy is pictured. Personally I see the Earl of Southampton portrayed in Shakespeare's comedy of the Trojan war as the prince Patroclus, the beloved comrade of Achilles.

Sonnet LV takes off for a moment the poet's mask of humility, drops the pretense of his phrases about "untutored lines," "my slight Muse," "poor rude" verse. In an ecstasy of egoism he tells Southampton that no royal monument will outlast "this powerful rime" which he creates. The unpoetic youth probably smiled at the promise that his praise and memory would live in Shakespeare's verse till doomsday. Maecenas certainly took Horace more seriously. The English genius's affirmation of his own greatness rings tragically to us because we realize how deeply he suffered from the necessity of hiding his identity. De Vere had to keep the world from discovering that he was England's supreme dramatist, for the discovery would have meant his damnation as a nobleman. The stains of a playwright's ink on his hands held up before the House of Lords would have made his family the laughingstock of the kingdom. He felt that he had disgraced the house of Vere enough. Hiding himself was not too hard, since the actor in him loved to play at masquerades. But he fretted and fumed behind the veil, and the libido of his exhibitionism beat imperiously against it. The temptation to betray himself to the world's eyes can be sensed in virtually all his plays.

It was the compulsion for concealing himself, for keeping his connexion with Southampton a secret, rather than sheer passion that made Shakespeare describe himself as the young man's slave (LVII, LVIII). The poet felt that he lived as in a prison ("outcast state"). He had to restrain his vanity when Southampton put it through capricious ordeals in arranging their meetings. Morally the word "slave" has no more significance in this context than the word "vassal" (LVIII), which the poet had already employed in Sonnet XXVI. The younger man never exerted on the artist's imagination the effect that Shakespeare's self-love, with its attendant self-chastisement, could always contrive. No, says the poet (LXI), it is not the spirit of Southampton that troubles his sleep with shadows resembling the youth. It is "Mine own true love that doth my rest defeat." Shakespeare almost touched here the core of his neurosis. He apprehended that there was something in his own spirit, his ego, that while inspiring passionate love managed to "pry" into his deeds –"To find out shames and idle hours in me." The essential parent-hood of the conscience was never delineated more potently. If only the poet had possessed the pitiless self-probing strength to deter-mine the sex of that "true love" whose vigilance broke his sleep! In learning precisely whose mental slave Shakespeare was, we would immensely advance our knowledge of human bondage in general.

The truth finally breaks out, in the sole form Shakespeare could recognize it:

> Sin of self-love possesseth all mine eye
> And all my soul and all my every part;
> And for this sin there is no remedy,
> It is so grounded inward in my heart. (LXII)

Few writers have been so infantlike frank. Shakespeare proclaims that he is convinced, "no face so gracious is as mine, No shape so true, no truth of such account." (It will be observed that "truth" is fetched into the verse to represent all the other qualities claimed by the poet distinct from the physical. "No truth of such account" is nearly a paraphrase of *Vero nihil verius*, Oxford's motto.) Megaloma-nia could scarcely reveal itself more nakedly: "I all other in all worths surmount." When Shakespeare looks in a mirror and sees himself "Beated and chopt with tann'd antiquity," he realizes that

his self-adoration is a sin. He does not say it is wrong, in the unre-
ligious sense. Even the ravages of the years on his countenance
were beautiful in his eyes. Perhaps he felt that by these wounds he
was exalted closer to Christ, with whom he sympathized in most
peculiar fashion, as the use of the symbol of the cross throughout
these poems and the plays will testify. Like Christ Shakespeare was
willing to lose the whole world if that was the price for conserving
his own soul. What the dramatist failed to understand was the way
his soul was divided against itself. He was keenly aware of the civil
war within his mind but had at best ephemeral perceptions of the
character of the combatants. He could say sincerely that Southampton was "all the better part of me" (XXXIX) and in the next breath
condemn him, from the star-chamber of his arrogant ego, as a lascivious thief and traitor. The better part of the poet thus condemned his bad part. Always he sang of himself.

People who praised Southampton's external charms, according
to Sonnet LXIX, talked differently about his mind and deeds. The
churls then hinted that his "fair flower" (the Rose) grew too close to
rank weeds. Bridget Manners, who was invited to contemplate matrimony with him in 1594, objected that he was fantastical and "so
easily carried away." In outbursts of rage, frequently over straws in
which he saw his honor at stake, he would risk bloodshed, at least
tear his adversary's hair. His loving critic had done far worse in his
youth. De Vere killed a servant in his father-in-law's house when he
was seventeen; the inquest jury refrained from curiosity about the
"accident." After deserting his wife in 1576 he committed adultery,
and Anne Vavasor contended that he was the true father of the boy
she bore in the Queen's palace in March 1581. Lord Henry Howard
and Charles Arundel drew up an indictment against Oxford, including so many crimes and rumors of crimes that you might conclude,
if you gave them credence, De Vere was the archfiend of the age.
Shakespeare might attempt to answer, "Slander's mark was ever yet
the fair" (LXX), but mankind is bound to believe that where there is
so much smoke there must be some sparks. Slander, at any rate,
made the unlucky Southampton dearer to Oxford. Incidentally,

from the couplet—"Thou hast past by the ambush of young days, Either not assail'd, or victor being charg'd," I would guess that Sonnet LXX was composed before the Court started whispering, in 1595, that Southampton was treating Elizabeth Vernon with "too much familiarity."

Because of the infamies which had accumulated on his reputation Shakespeare determined that his "poor name" should not be remembered by his friend (LXXI). To prevent the telling of "some virtuous lie" on his behalf, when the future would demand to know what merit in him had earned anyone's love, the poet resolved:

> My name be buried where my body is,
> And live no more to shame nor me nor you.
> For I am sham'd by that which I bring forth,
> And so should you, to love things nothing worth. (LXXII)

Once more we are confronted with the public opinion of Shakespeare's productions, the "trifles" he privately considered jewels. This time we have the conception of his poetical works not simply as playthings, unworthy of an aristocrat's earnest handiwork, but as the objects that compel the poet to inter his name. Could we be told in plainer English that William Shakespeare is actually a nom de guerre, a weapon in the struggle for survival of the artist in Earl Edward de Vere?

The dramatist feels at liberty to speak so plainly for the reason that he feels himself approaching the verge of death (LXXIII). We have the word of the learned Francis Meres (in *Palladis Tamia*, 1598) that the sonnets circulated only among Shakespeare's private friends. It appears that these were mostly artists who respected his anxiety to hold the world ignorant of his identity. They had all experienced his bounty in the days of his youthful affluence. I doubt whether any member of his class except Southampton was acquainted with "William Shakespeare", though Oxford's wife, and Anne Vavasor, may have known that he wrote plays for the common stages. None of those he trusted, however, was so discreet as the fugitive from Stratford, who became one of the leading grain-speculators and money-lenders in his home town. And no finer comedy came out of the times than the legend that this rough-hewn gentleman was the nonpareil poet of the Earl of Oxford's *invention*. The comedy struck Oxford himself as worthy of two scenes in his plays, the Induction to *The Taming of the Shrew* and the dialogue between Touchstone and William in *As You Like It*. Possibly it also inspired the dream of Nick Bottom in the *Midsummer Night's Dream*. There were occasions when the dramatist feared that he would be found out, on account of the singular power of his literary method. He wrote an entire Sonnet on the matter (LXXVI;

> Why write I still all one, ever the same,
> And keep invention in a noted weed,
> That every word doth almost tell my name,
> Showing their birth, and where they did proceed!

The sudden shift of accent in the word "ever" marks the author's signature. One reason for the sameness of his style, he declares, is: "all my best is dressing old words new." This can only refer to his practice of rewriting the dramas of his youth. Orthodox erudition long ago depicted Shakespeare as commencing his career with theatrical tailoring, the revising, patching, and interpolating of poetry in other men's plays. This grotesque notion of the way his genius went to work was necessary to support the Stratford fantasy. Academic inquiry is now leaning to a chronology of the plays which is sure to upset the Stratford cart, one which furnishes ammunition for the Looney-Freud theory. When one professor envisions *Romeo and Juliet* as an old play in 1592, and another sees *Hamlet* on Shakespeare's stage in 1588, the dawn of victory cannot be far off for the Oxfordians, who date the commencement of Shakespeare's dramatic career in 1576, when "The History of Error" was prepared for the Queen's stage, the play that became *The Comedy of Errors*.

The style of Shakespeare (defined by Thomas Nashe as Chaucerisrn) seemed so antiquated when the Sonnets were made, by contrast with the "new-found methods and compounds strange" of Chapman, Jonson, and Marston, that young Southampton, always looking for novelty, neglected the old player-Earl for the sake of his competitors. Their parade of erudition, their metaphysical flights, and tireless experiments with language, in short, their Art, attracted Southampton more than the homely-looking style of Shakespeare, which he defended as "natural". In mockery of his rivals he instructed Wriothesley: "thou art all my art, and dost advance As High as learning my rude ignorance" (LXXVIII). In other words, love prompted him to write, not the craving for fame, nor any of the other motives that drove Chapman and the rest to pen-toil. The wonder is that anyone should have taken Shakespeare's mock-modesty for the real thing. Even the ingenious John Milton—who shared all the academic defects of the rivals—condescended to chatter about Shakespeare as if he were a warbler of "native wood-notes wild." The greater artist put his finger on the main fault of the Chapmans and Miltons in a single clause: "What strained touches Rhetoric can lend" (LXXXII). Shakespeare did alter his verse toward the close of his life, but he insisted that his art stayed ever subservient to nature, to truth:

> Thou truly fair wert truly sympathiz'd
> In true plain words, by thy true-telling friend.

His "tongue-tied Muse," he says, goes on her way regardless of the fashions in literature (LXXXV). The epithet points to the Sonnet (LXVI) in which Elizabethan culture is denounced because of its hatred of free speech: "art made tongue-tied by authority."

Southampton's absences made his lover miserable, but Shakespeare loved his melancholy too. Nothing could part him from it. One of the boyish lyrics of the Earl of Oxford succinctly describes the favorite posture of Shakespeare:

> I am not as I seem to be,
> For when I smile I am not glad;
> A thrall, although you count me free,

I, most in mirth, most pensive sad.

These lines were written many years before the disasters of Oxford's life, though not long after the death of his father and his mother. It is safe to say that, with the exception of these two deaths, he was responsible for practically all the misfortunes that happened to him. He could not resist danger if it lured him with the right baits of sex and politics. I am inclined to believe that he unconsciously left himself open to the blade of Sir Thomas Knyvet which, in March 1582, nearly put a period to his romance and tragedy. In the seventy-fourth Sonnet he grieves over his fate, seeing his corpse descend to the grave, "The coward conquest of a wretch's knife." Yet he was not altogether woeful over the wound; there lingered about it an erotic pulse. "Speak of my lameness, and I straight will halt," he tells the beloved Wriothesley (LXXXIX).

Thou canst not, love, disgrace me half so ill,
To set a form upon desired change,
As I'll myself disgrace.

The grimace of the paranoiac shows itself under this extreme humility, which tempts the sadism of the loved one. "Hate me when thou wilt," Shakespeare cries: "Now, while the world is bent my deeds to cross" (XC). In 1594 Oxford was gnawing his heart in chagrin over his failure to obtain a royal monopoly of the imports of oils, wools, and fruits, from which he hoped to restore his family's wealth. He also applied in vain for the stewardship of the Queen's Forest of Essex. Next he strove to convince her Majesty that he could administer profitably the tin mines belonging to the Crown. In March 1595 he begged Lord Burghley:
"have a feeling of mine unfortunate estate, which, although it be far unfit to endure delays, yet has consumed four or five years in a flattering hope of idle words." (Calendar of the Cecil Manuscripts, V, 149.) Such were the "petty griefs" that Shakespeare endured when he expected Southampton to desert him.

When the poet estimated the value of Wriothesley's love to him he measured in terms of perishing aristocraèy:

Thy love is better than high birth to me,
Richer than wealth, prouder than garments' cost,
Of more delight than hawks or horses be. (XCI)

The allusion to garments, and the line about clothing "newfangled ill" which precedes it, are significant in view of the constant pleasure that the Earl of Oxford got from clothes. When he was sixteen his garments cost about a thousand pounds a year (Ward, 31), and when he was thirty-one his passion for apparel seems to have brought on him public ridicule (same, 189, 193). The satirist harped on his effeminacy: "No words but valorous, no works but womanish only ..." when Gabriel Harvey wrote that he was well aware of De Vere's prowess as a duelist on horseback. Unhappily he never had a chance to show what he could accomplish on the battlefield or in war at sea, although he pleaded with the Queen for service in her army or navy. He remained a soldier in imagination, like his melancholy Prince of Denmark.

Shakespeare may have been thinking of another soldier-hero of his, Othello, when he wrote Sonnets XCII and XCIII. He fancies himself in these poems "Like a deceived husband," who asks only that he be kept in ignorance of his cuckoldry: "Thou mayst be false, and yet I know it not." Since the poet makes no mention of his other love, the sinister lady travestied as Avisa, I conjecture that his jealousy at this time sprang from the notoriety of Southampton's affair with Elizabeth Vernon. To the year 1595 has also been ascribed Thomas Nashe's "Choice of Valentines," a piece of pornography boldly dedicated to Southampton. Its prelude removes beyond question the meaning of the symbol rose so often introduced in the Sonnets. Nashe hails the Earl as the "fairest bud the red rose ever bare." One glance at the obscene poem suffices to inform us why Shakespeare warns his hero of the canker that threatens his "fragrant rose,"—"the beauty of thy budding name" (XCV).

For a long time (if we judge by Sonnet XCVII and its two sequels, whole seasons) the poet absented himself from Southampton. It has been conjectured that Shakespeare produced these poems on returning from the provincial tours of the Lord Chamberlain's players. But the poems clearly state that their author was away from London in April, when the playhouses were flourishing. My own belief is that Oxford produced them after visits to the stannaries, the tin mines in Wales, about which he wrote Burghley industriously in April 1595 and March 1596. In the summer of 1596 De Vere spent some days in unknown rural surroundings, and his letter to Sir Robert Cecil of September 6 alluding to the journey is reminiscent of Sonnet XLVIII. It will be remembered that the poem begins, "How careful was I when I took my way, Each trifle under truest bars to thrust." The letter begins thus: "The writing which I have is in the country, for I had such care thereof as I carried it with me in a little desk." By this time the beloved Wriothesley had come to understand the lone loveliness of Shakespeare's poetry. The gulf between it and work like that of Nashe, Barnabe Barnes, Gervase Markham, each of whom dedicated books to Southampton, and fabrications like those of George Chapman, was recognized by contemporary critics, and Southampton himself was too well cultivated, too exquisite in sensuality, not to feel the glory Shakespeare gave him. He probably coveted more poems than the dramatist could produce, and resented the energy which the latter expended on his "trifles". This, I suppose, was the reason for Sonnet C, in which the poet gravely rebukes his Muse for long silence concerning him "that doth thy lays esteem." Shakespeare challenges her to reply if she has been using up her strength on "some worthless song," or "Darkening thy power to lend base subjects light." He finds various sugary excuses for not composing more about his "fair friend," and assures him that three years have made no perceptible changes in his charms. This assurance (CIV), it has been plausibly argued, was delivered late in the summer of 1595. The poet insists that he never swerves from the single theme of his lifework:

Since all alike my songs and praises be
To one, of one, still such, and ever so.

The year 1595 saw the completion of another sequence of love sonnets, by Edmund Spenser, a poet cordially acquainted with Edward
de Vere (who has been identified as the Willie of Spenser's *Shepherd's Calendar* and *The Tears of the Muses*). Spenser's *Amoretti* had a
happy ending, and were crowned with his wedding. He then turned
with fresh energy to the task of preparing the six books of his *Faery
Queen* for the press. He travelled from Ireland to London in 1595 to
arrange for their publication. I have no doubt that Shakespeare had
an opportunity to read the epic in manuscript. The first three books
came from the press in 1590 with a series of dedicatory sonnets,
including one to the Earl of Oxford, whom Spenser informed,

th' antique glory of thine ancestry
Under a shady veil is therein writ,
And eke thine own long living memory.

Sonnet CVI has been judged by several scholars a tribute to the
Faery Queen. Indirectly it thanks Spenser for the "antique glory" by
applauding his "antique pen".

The dramatist returns to the topic of his jewel-cutting for the
pork-pated multitude in the hundred-and-tenth Sonnet. As if in response to a criticism of Southampton for not confining his genius
to the lyric and epic, Shakespeare tells the "sweet boy" what the
drama means to him. After admitting that he has made himself "a
motley to the view,"

Gor'd mine own thoughts, sold cheap what is most dear,
Made old offences of affections new,

and even flirted with untruth on the stage, he affirms,

These blenches gave my heart another youth.

By straying from his proper path as a nobleman and turning his precious dreams into theatric commodities, Oxford renewed the blisses as well as the sorrows of his young manhood. Indeed he preserved by his playmaking the spirit of his boyhood, so that in the whiteness of his age he still looked on life with the sanguine temper, the buoyancy of King Lear. Apparently Earl Edward accepted money for his dramas. He blames "The guilty goddess," Fortune, for not providing a better reward for his labor "Than public means which public manners breeds" (CXI), meaning the theater, which classical philosophy regarded as an expositor and censor of public manners. Shakespeare deplores the fact that his life-work puts on his good name the brand of a business which Englishmen associated with prostitution. By long practice with "motley," his nature almost appeared to be "subdu'd To what it works in, like the dyer's hand." The effect of composing stage blank-verse for years shines from the correspondence of the Earl of Oxford. In 1600, submitting application to his brother-in-law Robert Cecil for the Governorship of Jersey, he spontaneously broke into the characteristic rhythms of Shakespeare: "Although my bad success in former suits to her Majesty have given me cause to bury my hopes in the deep abyss and bottom of despair...." (Ward, 333). The poet appealed to Southampton to pity his doom, and let him go ahead with his dramaturgy.

Toward the end of 1595 Southampton quit the courtier's life and attempted to establish a reputation as a soldier. He schemed with his friend, Elizabeth Vernon's cousin, Essex, for an English expedition to rescue the port of Calais from the Spaniards who menaced and finally captured it in April 1596. In May the two Earls sailed to Spain for a retaliatory attack on the port of Cadiz. With them sailed the brothers Francis and Horace Vere, Oxford's first cousins, two of the most famous fighting men of the period. They set fire to Cadiz and returned to England, rather disappointed with their voyage. In the following July, Essex and Southampton launched an expedition to the Azores, hoping to strike a grand blow at that flank of the Spanish empire. This voyage accomplished little, and after Southampton came home he went to travel on the continent, hardly knowing what to do with his exuberant virility. In 1598 he took a modest position in the group that accompanied Sir Robert Cecil on an embassy to France. In Paris the restless Earl learnt that his beloved Vernon was pregnant. He raced to London, listened to her entreaties, and clandestinely married her. When the Queen found out that the younger Elizabeth, her Maid of Honor, was a mother, she furiously commanded Southampton locked up in Fleet prison. All this time it is unlikely that he maintained his romantic relation with the Earl of Oxford. I agree with those researchers who sense a breach of years between Sonnet CVI (on the *Faery Queen*, published in 1596) and CVII, which refers to the death of Queen Elizabeth ("The mortal moon hath her eclipse endur'd") in March 1603. CXVI, which preaches in the manner of Plato about ideal love, may have been composed in honor of Southampton's marriage, in August 1598. In the same month William Cecil, Lord Burghley, died. This patriarch of statesmen acted as a father to Oxford from the time he was twelve until the month of his own death. On him the Earl fastened the enmity of his oedipus complex, and transformed his real father into a demigod replete with virtues. Several times Oxford tried to rebel against Burghley's authority, but each rebellion left him weaker than before. He vented his impotent fury on his wife, Burghley's daughter, who rained tears over nearly all the years of their married life. "No enemy I have," wrote Burghley in May 1587, "can envy me this match; for thereby neither honour nor land nor goods shall come to their children." The father-in-law took charge of the feeding and educating of De Vere's three daughters, but the Earl did not exhibit gratitude. "If their father," said the Lord Treasurer of England, "was of that good nature as to be thankful for the same, I would be less grieved with the burden." (Ward, 285.) An excellent picture of their mental relations can be seen in the tragedy of Polonius and his Ophelia. Perfectly respectable scholarship has long been accustomed to pointing out the features of William Cecil in the ancient politician who would not have Hamlet for a son-in-law. In the first quarto of *Hamlet* (1603) Polonius is called Corambis—a palpable hit at Cecil's motto: *Cor unum, via una.* And the likeness between Cecil's maxims and the excessively admired advice of Polonius to his son (1.3) is pure parody. (Cf. Martin Hume, *The Great Lord Burghley*, 25.) The passing of this paternal figure and the secret nuptials of Southampton must have made Oxford feel half-abandoned and half-emancipated.

After a brief sojourn in Fleet jail Southampton was released, without hope of redeeming his fame while Queen Elizabeth lived. He wanted to go with Essex to quell insurrection in Ireland, in March 1599, and Essex appointed his friend a commander of cavalry. Her Majesty refused to let him serve so. When Essex came home with a treaty of peace from the rebel Tyrone, she raged at him for not pursuing the Irish with fire and sword. Her indignation had ample wind to beat Southampton's head again for supporting Essex's policy. The two Earls nursed their hatred of her government until it flared into armed revolt, in February 1601. The outcome of their desperate folly was the beheading of Essex and the imprisonment of Southampton in the Tower of London. The Earl of Oxford was summoned out of retirement in order to serve with the lords who tried the rebel earls. What he felt while he listened to Francis Bacon exhaust an arsenal of law to get the death penalty for his dear friends, none can tell. Oxford had to sign the unanimous decision of the lords for the execution of Essex. His eloquence surely helped to save Southampton's head. One of the first acts of King James, on corning to the throne of England, was to release poor Wriothesley from the Tower. It is reasonable to assume that Shakespeare celebrated this event, in Sonnet CVII, which greets his true love, "Suppos'd as forfeit to a confin'd doom." It is also reasonable to explain CXXV, which presents the poet bearing "the canopy" in a procession of state, as a memorial to the coronation of James on July 25, 1603. The Lord Great Chamberlain of England took first place among the peers in the ceremony, and afterward enjoyed a short exaltation by his Majesty's appointment to the Privy Council. The Lord Chamberlain's actors were chosen to be the King's own troupe. Oxford was too old to become intoxicated by his new pomp. Besides the Court still swarmed with men whom he bewildered, who feared his irony, and hated his pride. His enemy Lord Henry Howard was also elected to the Privy Council, where be soon exerted influence to punish Ben Jonson for his tragedy *Sejanus*, which was alleged to be a tribute to Essex and a satire on Howard. Shakespeare's company acted *Sejanus* and continued to pay scant attention to Court warnings against their introduction of political disputes into plays.

The denunciation of the "suborn'd informer" at the end of Sonnet CXXV has not yet been explained. I would like to suggest that it is Shakespeare's expression of contempt for Henry Fiennes, Earl of Lincoln, who in September 1603 sent information to the Privy Council concerning plots against the Crown. Lincoln urged a state investigation of "those speeches of the Earl of Oxford" that hinted of a conspiracy to place the house of Hastings on the throne instead of the Stuarts. Sir John Peyton, Lieutenant of the Tower, dismissed Lincoln's accusations when he heard of the alleged conspiracy in Hackney. He knew the Earl of Oxford: "I knew him," he wrote, "to be so weak in body, in friends, in ability, and all other means to raise any combustion in the state, as I never feared any danger to proceed from so feeble a foundation." (Cf. Norreys O'Connor, *Godes Peace and the Queenes*, 1934, 104, 107.) Presumably Oxford believed that Lincoln was suborned or incited to play informer against him, by a Howard or a Ralegh.

The song beginning "O thou, my lovely boy"—it is a song rather than a sonnet—CXXVI concludes the sequence of poems devoted to the Earl of Southampton. For the last time Shakespeare glorifies him as a youth apparently free from the common human wear and tear of time. At the same time he warns the "boy" that "Nature, sovereign mistress over wrack," is still to be feared, for the day of her reckoning and his beauty's ruin cannot be escaped. When we recall that Nature personified is but an image of the mother kept in the unconscious as a goddess, we recognize in these lines an utterance of the poet's terror of his mother, a woman whom he could not think of without thinking of death. Psychoanalytic students familiar with the studies of *Hamlet* by Ernest Jones and Fredrick Wertham need no introduction to this dual dread of the dramatist. They can comprehend it this side theory by perusing the letter that the Countess Margery de Vere, Edward's mother, wrote in April 1562, to cast off her shoulders the burden of the boy's financial perplexities. She informed Lord Burghley that his late father had kept "most secret" from her the sources and distribution of his wealth. Now that Earl John was dead she wished to be exempt from the cares of his estate. "I had rather leave up the whole doings thereof," she says, "to my son," who had just passed his twelfth birthday. Let "my son, " she told Burghley, "who is under your charge," have all "the honour or gain (if any be)" from her husband's last will and testament. There is not a breath of affection or concern for the lad in the letter. And not long after the widowed Countess married Charles Tyrrell, a member of the Queen's bodyguard. They resided at Castle Hedingham, Edward's birthplace, while the orphan underwent the pedagogy of Lord Burghley, his guardian, in the capital city. (Ward, 22.) Shakespeare's plays contain many a portrait of mother Margery, the "sovereign mistress over wrack" in his psyche.

I cannot leave the Southampton sequence without a backward glance at four sonnets of peculiar force and importance. The eighty-seventh marks a breaking point, an estrangement between Shakespeare and his boy-love. To me it is a work of humor, bitter humor. Goodby, the poet says: "thou art too dear for my possessing, And like enough thou know'st thy estimate." The poem perhaps taught Southampton a lesson in evaluation of his friends. As we have seen, he came to appreciate the artistry of Shakespeare at least in lyric; and he may have come to see his stature in drama in those months of 1599 when he spent so much time at the theaters, and later when he corresponded with his wife about the affairs of Falstaff. (*The Shakspere Allusion Book*, 1932, I, 88.) The occasion of the sonnet seems to have been provoked by jealousy, the outrage of Shakespeare over his friend's enthusiasm for a rival bard. Oxford had experienced a similar jealousy in the days when Sir Philip Sidney competed with him in poetry. The most popular product of their rivalry was a series of songs inspired by Oxford's poem, "Were I a

King." (See *The Poems of Edward de Vere*, ed. Looney, 38.) John Mundy set this poem to music in his *Tenor*, printed in 1594, about the time when the Farewell sonnet was made. The old wish to be a king ran with fresh vigor in Shakespeare's mind as he wrote the final couplet of his Sonnet:

> Thus have I had thee, as a dream doth flatter,
> In sleep a king, but waking, no such matter.

On the surface the couplet seems to say that the poet possessed Southampton in the same way a dreamer may possess a kingdom. Below the surface, psychoanalytically interpreted, the lines suggest that the beloved in the dream is a hidden queen. The "master-mistress" of Shakespeare's passion consequently emerges as a surrogate for the "sovereign mistress" of his soul, his mother, whom he unconsciously conceived as a queen with a penis. The meaning of the couplet becomes clearer when we set beside it the speech of Romeo about his last dream (5.1):

> If I may trust the flattering truth of sleep,
> My dreams presage some joyful news at hand…
> I dreamt my lady came and found me dead;—
> Strange dream, that gives a dead man leave to think,—
> And breath'd such life with kisses in my lips,
> That I reviv'd, and was an emperor.

Sonnet CXIX is actually a sequel to the one before it. That poem apologizes for unfaithfulness to Southampton. The poet endeavors to explain why he turned away from his friend to make love to a woman undescribed. Sick of the young man's sweetness, Shakespeare went in search of a medicine of "bitter sauces" to purge him before he lost his taste for Southampton's friendship. He found his relief in a siren who poured tears into his heart and raised his temperature to the pitch of madness. He recovered, and went back to his beloved boy, proud of having discovered "That better is by evil still made better." His philosophy assigned a reason for this in his epic comedy King *Henry V* (4.1): "There is some soul of goodness in things evil." Let us leave to theologians the question whether violation of the Almighty's canon against adultery is here justified. The question for us is, what kind of woman drew Shakespeare from loyalty to his wife and his friend? Was she the same whom his friend had stolen from him at the outset of their friendship? The poet gives the impression of reference to Sonnet XXXV (dealing with grief for Southampton's "sensual fault") in CXX, which asks forgiveness for having betrayed Wriothesley for the sake of the siren.

> For if you were by my unkindness shaken,
> As I by yours, you've pass'd a hell of time.

Whether we consider it philosophy or foolishness, none will question the sincerity of the dramatist's self-defense. There is anguish in it. Hedonism has scarcely shown itself so hideous and honest as in Sonnet CXXI. "'Tis better to be vile than vile esteem'd..." The poem is in fact an excoriation of the society that measures virtue by face-value. Shakespeare exposes the economic ethics of his world, which judges a pleasure just though vile, if one can get away with it respectably. Once more he adopts the Christ posture to accuse people of hypocrisy who pretend to abhor adultery while leering or smirking at his "sportive blood". Immediately after this he adopts the Hamlet pose:

> Or on my frailties why are frailer spies,
> Which in their wills count bad what I think good?

Shakespeare will not submit to the claim of any woman or human to juridic or moral superiority. Believing himself fashioned in the image of the Almighty, he denies the right of any mortal to score his sins.

> No, I am that I am, and they that level
> At my abuses reckon up their own.

In the whole range of Elizabethan literature, not one passage has been noted to equal the almost blasphemous audacity of Shakespeare's "I am that I am." On the fringe of that literature there is one document whose writer proclaims himself in the words of The Word, as named in *Exodus* (3:14). On October 30, 1584, Edward de Vere wrote to his father-in-law protesting against high-handed intervention in his affairs: "But I pray, my Lord, leave that course, for I mean not to be your ward nor your child. I serve her Majesty, and I am that I am." (Ward, 247.) Could there be two brains in England with the tranquil megalomania to write the Biblical phrase so confident of righteousness? In Oxford and "Shakespeare" alone do we see this colossal narcissism displaying itself in concord with its opposite, the self-effacement which Ernest Jones found as the chief characteristic of what he termed the God complex. (*Essays in Applied Psychoanalysis*, 1923, 208.) No other Englishmen exhibited such delight in their inaccessibility, in surrounding their lives with mystery, in playing the Lord. Fortunately for Oxford-Shakespeare there was enough of the vulgar voyeur in him to countervail the celestial exhibitionist. The feudal-reactionary trend of his mind failed to overcome his fierce curiosity about the revolutions capital and labor were making in his world. He was not afflicted severely with the habit which Jones calls one of the most distressing traits of the God syndrome, namely, "the attitude of disinclination toward the acceptance of new knowledge." In 1599 Dr. George Baker dedicated to the Earl *The Practice of the New and Old Physic,* one of the pioneer books of Paracelsan chemistry in medicine. Oxford also befriended and employed as his secretary Nicholas Hill, the man who might well be styled the father of atomic theory in English science. And the passion for "the histories of ancient times, and things done long ago, as also of the present estate of things in our days," which his uncle Arthur Golding observed in him at fourteen (Ward, 24), burnt as bright as ever in him at fifty-four. After all, he did not conceive of himself as the Divine Father but simply as the Prodigal Son.

3

After the Southampton sequence come the poems far-famed as the "Dark Lady" Sonnets. They are not, strictly speaking, a sequence; they do not tell a story, nor develop a concatenation of thoughts. In comparison with the polished and intricate rimes that precede them they sound like explosions. One could liken them to dream-work stript of the secondary elaboration, though they are liberally sprinkled with wit and here and there show off a superficial ratiocination. In the prior series anxiety manifested itself and prevailed in separate poems. In the "Dark Lady" series anxiety is everywhere dominant.

The opening Sonnet of the series (CXXVII) may be reckoned a defiance of the color vogue favored by Queen Elizabeth herself. Under her red-headed Majesty beauty was publicly styled a monopoly of the fair in hue. Dark-haired ladies put on blond and auburn wigs—"Fairing the foul with Art's false borrow'd face," they painted their skins to suit the imperial style. But Shakespeare's mistress, he announces, by the fascination of her black brows and eyes is transforming the fashion. Of course he exaggerates; but if we discount the poetic flamboyancy, there remains the fact that his mistress was a woman of some eminence, capable of setting a style, despite the predilections of the Virgin Queen.

In the next Sonnet we hear the poet murmuring his pleasure over the skill with which his mistress performed on the virginals. Her music excited him erotically. He pretends to think the keys ("jacks") dance for joy under her touch. The line about "saucy jacks" reminds us of a sarcasm Oxford once flung at Sir Walter Ralegh while they were watching the Queen play, in the hour of the execution of Essex. Her Majesty and everyone standing by the instrument knew how active and eager Ralegh had been for Essex's death. When the report of it was brought to the Queen she went on with the music, and Oxford remarked, "When jacks start up heads go down." (Ward, 336). He used the word in the derisive sense that the Nurse uses it in *Romeo and Juliet* (2.4), but with his typical word-trickery.

Sonnet CXXIX voices the dramatist's anger and remorse for his lust, as if he had just come from a sexual achievement (undoubtedly adultery) which left him dissatisfied, revulsive, in a temper to flagellate himself. He wishes he knew how "To shun the heaven that leads men to this hell." The forepleasure he calls heaven is cunningly indicated in the ensuing poem, which expresses his happiness on contemplating the head and breasts of his woman. He loves to look at her, to listen to her talk, though her breath is not redolent of Arabia. Yet her power over him, he implicitly affirms, cannot be traced to her external graces. He has heard people of fine taste and judgment say that her face "hath not the power to make love groan" (CXXXI). But she can break Shakespeare's heart. Unbeautiful by conventional standards, she also repels people by her unconventional deeds. Like her lover she disdained the morality of her critics and calumniators. The freedom of this woman frightened him, and in her presence he felt the criterions of truth which he had been taught turn into absurdities. She seemed to make fair foul and foul fair. Shakespeare does not analyze her attraction in the Sonnets: he kisses and curses, that is all. He set her, however, in the forefront of nearly all his dramas, and produced in them as complete an analysis of the Dark Lady as was humanly possible. (Frank Harris assembled the details in *The Man Shakespeare* and *The Women of Shakespeare*, and spoiled the resulting portrait by insisting it was a picture of Mary Fitton, a court lady whose extant pictures prove her brown of hair and gray of eye.)

In the hundred-and-thirty-third Sonnet we learn that the Dark Lady seduced his friend, that is Southampton. She has bereaved me, Shakespeare cries, of "my next self." Their union must be the sin of which he complains in the early poems to Southampton, where he playfully denounced the Earl as a "sweet thief". In the poems to his mistress, on the contrary, he denounces her as the thief, making out his friend a mere victim of superior force. In CXXXIV the poet hints that Southampton became acquainted with her on a visit he made to please the elder lover: the friend "came debtor for my sake," and she greedily took him, like a member of the detested profession of finance to which William Shakespeare of Stratford belonged. How the poet hated usury! "Thou usurer" was the worst insult he could throw at the woman who held him captive.

The next two sonnets display a veritable riot of puns on the name "Will," which the poet converts into a synonym for sex. If she wishes to have her way, to gratify her will, very well, he writes: "then thou lovest me, for my name is 'Will'." If orthodox erudition wants to embrace the assertion literally, it will have to be taken together with the poems' puns on the penis, and then the gullible scholar will kindly explain why the poet should have showered his name so with smut. I have already made the suggestion that the name "Shakespeare" itself may be viewed as a comedian's banner of virility, just as "Falstaff" could be interpreted as a symbol of impotence. Sexual equivocation on the word "will" was child's play to the mind that invented Shakespeare, and we must admit that his childishness sometimes appalls.

The Sonnet we have just quoted charges the Dark Lady with enterprises tantamount to nymphomania. In the following Sonnet she is branded "the bay where all men ride." Shocking as this insult may be, we have to thank Shakespeare for casting it in his immortal verse, for it enables us to identify the Dark Lady. Which of us would not care to know the kind of woman who moved the supreme dramatist so terribly? Curiosity about her character and culture has already evoked an abundance of opinions and conjectures toward her biography. My own inquiry has persuaded me that Shakespeare's black mistress was the Anne Vavasor we have encountered as the mother of Oxford's first son and the disputed prize of his fight with Sir Thomas Knyvet. A painting of Anne, said to be by Marcus Gheeraerts, shows that she was extraordinarily pallid and dark, with more strength than sweetness in her countenance. She was not one of the Virgin Queen's Maids of Honor, as many chroniclers have said, but just a Gentlewoman of the royal Bedchamber. Being niece of Knyvet, and allied by blood and wedlock to the Howards and Southwells, she became a factor in their Roman Catholic intrigues at Court. She must have met Oxford shortly after he separated from his first wife (Anne Cecil) and secretly turned Catholic, in 1576. On discovering that her kinsmen, at least Lord Henry Howard and Francis Southwell, were acting in the interests of Spain, he turned against them violently, and started a feud which did not end until the streets of London were reddened with his blood, Knyvet's, and their servants'. The non-Oxfordian scholar Albert Feuillerat, writing his life of Oxford's fellow playwright John Lyly, was struck by the similarity of this feud and the one in *Romeo and Juliet*. In the course of it De Vere and his Vavasor spent some days in the Tower of London (1581), after the birth of the boy whom she named Edward Vere. This illegitimate son grew up to become a gentleman of considerable renown, for classical learning and soldiership in the Dutch war against Spain. So far as we know, his mother took care of his upbringing, and his father's cousins, the "fighting Veres," gave him the opportunity to win military honor. Meanwhile Anne Vavasor's honor served as a target for all sorts of lewd and hostile wit. In 1584 the Roman Catholic tract known as *Leicester's Commonwealth* spread vicious rumors about her. Her brother Thomas blamed her bad reputation on Oxford, and in January 1585 challenged the Earl to a duel, saying, "If thy body had been as deformed as thy mind is dishonourable, my house had yet been unspotted, and thyself remained with thy cowardice unknown." (Ward, 229.) Oxford refused to fight him. Brother Thomas too gained high praise for his valor in the Low Countries, and his sister may have named her illegitimate child Thomas Vavasor after him. Prior to 1590 she married a merchant, John Finch, who helped to open England's commerce with Russia. It is doubtful whether her assumption of the bonds of matrimony altered Lord Burghley's decision that she was nothing but a "drab". (E. T. Clark, *The Man Who Was Shakespeare*, 1937, 82.) The duties of wifehood did not interfere with her amorous experiments. In 1590 her initials began to appear in the records of the gallant Sir Henry Lee, records of payments for nameless services she had rendered him. Later she became Lee's mistress candidly, without ostentation. About 1601 another Anne Vavasor was appointed to the Queen's Bedchamber, and the older Anne retired from the Court. She resided with Lee, who in 1605 granted her husband an annuity which Finch sold. The next year Lee wrote his thankfulness for her "loving care and diligence" during a severe illness of his. His gratitude materialized by his last will and testament in a gift of a house and land, with a request that she be buried in his tomb. His family contested the will, accused her of stealing costly cloth, jewels, linen, and corn from the estate, and she revealed that much of these wares had gone to Sir Edward Vere in the Netherlands. In 1618 she was officially charged with having two live husbands, John Finch and John Richardson, the latter a Durham gentleman who shared a farm lease with her. Early in 1621 a High Commission found her guilty of bigamy and sentenced her to pay a fine of 2000 pounds, but the King was merciful and granted the old lady "dispensation from public penitence or other bodily penalty." She lived until 1658. (We are indebted for this account of the amazing Anne to E. K. Chambers' life of Sir Henry Lee.) Historians have as yet unearthed no record of a connexion between her and Southampton. When the gaps in her life-story between 1590 and 1601 are filled in, we may be sure the connexion will come to light. Meanwhile we shall have to rest content with whatever we can glean from Shakespeare's plays and contemporary chronicles of scandal which seem to allude to the adventurous Anne Vavasor.

We know enough of Oxford's untamed love to understand that he lied when he called her "the wide world's commonplace" (CXXXVII). She was not a nymphomaniac, but a woman who combined strong passions with a cool and keen intellect, fond of remarkable men, and disdainful of her age's judgment on feminine integrity. We have the testimony of Sir Henry Lee that she could be gentle, patient, and kind. Shakespeare himself bears witness (in CXXXII) that her eyes showed pity in a heavenly way. He scorns her as a liar (in CXXXVIII, which first appeared in print in *The Passionate Pilgrim*, 1599). Yet she was unquestionably faithful to each of her lovers—in her own fashion. "On both sides thus is simple truth supprest," says he. The truth of the Dark Lady's character was as complex as Shakespeare's. He fancied that he was speaking the plain truth when he asserted, "She knows my days are past the best." Past youth, yes; but not past the days when he conceived and carried out his designs for *Antony and Cleopatra*, the tragic history of their romance. The truth about his insults to her is told in Sonnet CXL, where he begs her for more tenderness:

> For if I should despair, I should grow mad,
> And in my madness might speak ill of thee.

CXLII offers us ground for surmising that the Lady endeavored to dissuade the dramatist from his mad pursuit of her. She voiced her hate of his adulterous yearning, apparently sorry for his wife as well as piteous to him. He seized her rebuke in order to exercise his dialectic, and challenged her to justify the antagonism to his adultery in the face of her own breaking of wedlock laws. She cannot deny that she has "Robb'd others' beds' revenues of their rents." One can discern something like a note of pride in this revelation of his love's accomplishments with men.

In the following poem we learn that her man-nets were not inescapable. The poet attempts to rouse her sense of shame by drawing a comic comparison of her chase of lovers with a housewife's chase of some fowl that has eluded her clutch. Shakespeare compares himself to a baby whom the housewife puts down and neglects while pursuing the bird. Vividly, compassionately, he pictures the infant's predicament, struggling to follow the distracted mother. He pleads with his dark mistress:

> But if thou catch thy hope, turn back to me.
> And play the mother's part, kiss me, be kind:
> So will I pray that thou mayst have thy 'Will,'
> If thou turn back and my loud crying still.

My contention that the choice of simile is not accidental, but an utterance of Shakespeare's deepest pain, the sorrow of his bereavement of mother-love, will convince only those who are prepared to think so. Readers acquainted with Ella Freeman Sharpe's analysis of the infantile qualities in *King Lear* (*Collected Papers on Psychoanalysis*, 1950, ch. xi) will have little difficulty in grasping this notion. As I remarked before, the proof of it is copiously supplied by the plays, whose conflict-structure permits ample scope for the poet's ambivalences, whereas the sonnet, with its bare antithesis of octet and sestet, holds them by short tight reins. As a matter of fact Shakespeare's lyric is less personal than his drama, where absorption in the masquerade-struggle, the plot, induced unconscious betrayal of himself ever and anon.

Sonnet CXLIV, which presents the two loves of Shakespeare, the "man right fair," and the "woman colour'd ill," as angels always hovering by him, comes closest of all the poems to expressing the idea of the author's ambivalences which I have tried to convey. By translating the images of Southampton and the Dark Lady into spiritual forces over his destiny Shakespeare in effect told us that they both represented aspects of his ego. It will be observed that the formal male aspect ("right fair") is actually the more feminine, and the female aspect ("colour'd ill") is not only manly but dominant. The poet's sole hope of seeing the salvation of his friend from "hell" is based on the expectation that his "bad angel" will fire the "good one" out. His own subservience to the she-devil of his unconscious is made plain in the breathless quatrains and last gasp of a couplet in the lyric that follows (CXLV). The whole thing is an effusion of relief on hearing his mistress hesitate after pronouncing "I hate—" and then rescue him from despair with "Not you." He compares his relief to the clearing of the air when a fiend flies away from heaven to hell. The fiendish attributes of the lady were obviously concepts of Shakespeare's tortured ego religiously defending itself against "supernatural" cruelty, the antipathy of the divine mother he kept in his mind's cathedral, the love-thirst-thwarting superego. From this maternal image flowed the stuff that envenomed Shakespeare's narcissism.

Sonnet CXLVI is a pathetic expression of his narcissism, laughing at himself—"the centre of my sinful earth"— for squandering on clothes, garbing his aged body "costly gay." Ordinarily men dress themselves fancifully to attract the opposite sex. Shakespeare dressed to please himself. Yes, but which part of himself? The presence of this sonnet in the Dark Lady series indicates that it was the maternal goddess in his soul whose approval he coveted, without knowing it. If he denied himself gorgeous garments he suffered pangs of deprivation, like "an impatient child that hath new robes And may not wear them" (*Romeo and Juliet*, 3.2).

There is no use in dwelling on the pathological melody of the ensuing Sonnets, CXLVII-CL. They show how utterly powerless the poet was to liberate himself from his lady's spell. He keeps on asking himself, where is the secret of her potency over him? But his wits are too obsessed with fury and frustrated lust to be useful in exploration of her power. He can only repeat his wonderment that a woman so wicked, so stern, and unpretty, should captivate him. In words that remind us of the unforgettable description of the gypsy queen in *Antony and Cleopatra* (2.2) Shakespeare confesses that evil becomes his love: he finds a magic of energy and skill in "the very refuse" of her deeds,

That in my mind thy worst all best exceeds.

How profoundly his sex fever affected his metaphysics may be seen in CLI, which interrupts a song about conscience to crack meretricious jokes. Apart from the sick fun over the antics of his penis, the Sonnet has no interest except in the two lines which declare that when the beloved betrays him, he inwardly abandons his "nobler part" to the body's treason. Here is an unfunny identification of Shakespeare's superior self with the true "master-mistress" of his life. I interpret the poem as an effort to explain humorously how the writer reconciles his conscience with desire for the black wanton. "Conscience is born of love," he says, and his body is too blind to discriminate between the sorts of love that lure his soul.

Shakespeare reveals that the wanton is a married woman (in CLII) who has broken her bed-vow. But her lies are surpassed by his, he vows, since he has sworn that she was deeply kind, loving, truthful, constant. But now—"all my honest faith in thee is lost." He ends by damning her in a most unchristian manner, without a hint of the pardon which Shakespeare in his plays found divinely available to sinners. We may take this final sonnet as the parting shot of a lover who had been irrevocably banished, ordered to go home— for good.

The last two Sonnets of the volume were probably composed long before the break. They are alternative versions of a minor epigram in the *Greek Anthology*, which Shakespeare may have read in a Latin translation (of 1529). He changed the original for the sake of turning a compliment to the hygienic virtues of the town of Bath, to which he came—"a sad distemper'd guest"—hoping to get a cure for his love-sickness, only to discover that his mistress's influence sparkled in the healing water and mocked him. He was beyond the aid of physic. The two epigrams may have been attempted for the amusement of the "nymphs that vow'd chaste life to keep" as Maids of Honour to Queen Elizabeth, who is glorified as Diana, as usual. To imagine William Shakespeare of Stratford-on-Avon writing these vacation verses is a feat equivalent to believing that Nicholas Bottom— the brazen ass of the *Midsummer Night's Dream*—crooned Shakespearian sonnets into the ears of Queen Titania.

4

When Freud came to England for refuge he received a letter of welcome from J. Thomas Looney. The founder of psychoanalysis answered in June 1938, with a letter beginning: "Dear Mr. Looney, I have known you as the author of a remarkable book, to which I owe my conviction about Shakespeare's identity, as far as my judgment in this matter goes." Freud concluded by "confessing myself to be a follower of yours." This letter (kindly communicated to me by Mr. Charles Wisner Barrell, Secretary of the Shakespeare Fellowship of America) should be more widely known, among psychoanalysts of literature as well as professors and practitioners of poetry and the theatric arts.

Chapter 10–The Marlowe Mystery

I

Of all the theories offered us to identify the real writer of the plays and sonnets credited to "William Shake-speare", perhaps none is so funny as the guesswork proposing that we grant his laurels to Christopher Marlowe. One Wilbur Ziegler first suggested it was Marlowe in the title of a novel he published in 1895. His little monument to ignorance got gratifying attention from Dr Thomas Corwin Mendenhall, who in 1901 tried to support Ziegler's nonsense with statistics. Dr Mendenhall counted all the letters in 400,000 words used by the archdramatist, and announced that the latter's "word of greatest frequency was the four-letter word" (a discovery made in entire innocence of the euphemism "the four-letter word" has become). At the same time, he announced that Marlowe had a predilection for words of the same number of letters. The industrious doctor's discoveries were made in the unwavering belief that both Shake-speare and Marlowe used the spelling of Mendenhall's schooldays. Calvin Hoffman's book *The Murder of the Man who was Shakespeare* (1955), published in England as *The Man who was Shakespeare*, attracted more attention and multitudes gladly gave allegiance to his claim, because he offered to Anglo-American admirers of mystery fiction the lagniappe or frisson of his portrayal of the world's grandest poet as a pederast. None of the enthusiasts for the Calvinite claim have shown any but a superficial knowledge of Marlowe's work; all appear to be destitute of literary and psychological insight.

If there is one fact that reason is forced to contemplate in reviewing the writings of Kit Marlowe, it is this: he displayed an interest in politics intenser than his interest in poetry. All of his plays that we are aware of concentrate vision on state power. Religion seems to mean a primitive passion for Marlowe, lusting for sovereignty over human souls, its main usage being to disguise the desire to exploit and police. And art he cheerfully accepted as a prime political tool. Never would Marlowe have described statesmen in the language of disdain that Shake-speare flung at them.

Kit Marlowe was nearly twenty-two years old when he became a Bachelor of Arts at the college of Corpus Christi in Cambridge University. A month later, on 1 October, 1585, Queen Elizabeth proclaimed her intention of joining the Dutch republic in its war with Spain. The royal resolve may have contributed to Marlowe's own resolve to give up the prospect of becoming a minister in her Majesty's Church, for which, as a schoolboy in Canterbury, this son of a shoemaker and the daughter of a Papist priest had earned one of Archbishop Parker's scholarships. On 5 November, when Marlowe obtained the Bachelor's degree, he enrolled for courses toward the degree of Master of Arts, which the Parker scholarship meant to prepare men for divine service permitted him. This hiding of his university intention from the authorities was surely not the first falsehood of his career. Men of strong influence in the government encouraged his dissembling, and he worked for them faithfully in obscure missions during long absences from college in 1584, 1585 and 1586. Meanwhile his weekly expenses were recorded at Corpus Christi as larger than ever.

We do not know how deeply the Queen's account of the "just and reasonable grounds" of her declaration of war on King Philip stirred him. I doubt whether he cared much for the pathos of her report of the long bloodshed and persecutions the Low Countries had suffered under Spanish rule. His heart, it is safe to assume, throbbed no response to her survey of English commerce with the Netherlands and the losses incurred by their country from the war. If Marlowe felt an impulse of compassion on reading of the royal indignation over the Spaniard's design to bring the Dutch into perpetual servitude, the impulse did not stay in his mind as long and as vividly as the emotion he must have felt on reading of the peculiar appetite of the Spanish warlords for spectacles of carnage: "some of them," Elizabeth said, "notably delighted in blood" (1). Christopher could comprehend this delight. There was a thick streak of cruelty in his nature which would have glowed in covert sympathy with the sadism of Spain.

In my judgment, young Marlowe already had the wisdom requisite to understand that the Queen and her counsellors had to leave out of their war declaration their major motive. "There is perhaps no more constant factor," wrote Professor Conyers Read, "in the whole history of English foreign policy than the determination on the part of the English to prevent the union of the Low Countries with France." Lord Burghley saw the incursions of the French with military help for Holland as a menace to England's wealth: "our sovereignty upon the Narrow Seas," declared the Lord Treasurer, "will be abridged with danger and dishonour," if the French troops marching to aid the Dutch were not turned back (2).

But her Majesty's proclamation and shipment of men, arms and money arrived too late to prevent the fall of Antwerp into Spanish hands. While Philip's deputy in the battlefield, the Prince of Parma, built his fabulous bridge of boats to that metropolis, she was hotly or gloomily debating with herself and her ministers, particularly the labyrinthine-routined Cecil, the costs in blood and treasure, and spread of republican beliefs, of an English alliance with the Low Countries. The debate went on after Brussels, in March 1585, surrendered to the Prince of Parma. For a moment the English friends of the Netherlands thrilled with hope of Antwerp's rescue when the Italian engineer, Federigo Gianibelli, contrived a method of blowing up Parma's pontoons with drifting boats of gunpowder, and actually produced a marvellous havoc at the mouth of the Scheldt river, knocking Prince Alessandro unconscious. But the intrepid Spaniards repaired the breach. In June, while Philip parleyed with Pope Sixtus V about a project for invading England, twelve deputies from seven Dutch provinces came to London, went to Greenwich Palace and fell on their knees before Elizabeth. They remained in the beggars' posture for the duration of Josse van Menin's speech, pleading the necessity of her sovereignty in their homeland. Her Council was convinced that Antwerp should be helped, for the health of English economy, but she persisted in arguing the propriety of her heading a vulgar revolution. At last, in August, she agreed to send five thousand auxiliaries to the embattled States, who promised to repay their wages five years after making peace. As security for the debt she took the castle of Ramekins and the cities of Flushing and Brill, thus gaining control of the strategic isle of Walcheren. Later the Dutch delivered Ostend to her. The States Council also admitted to membership whatever general she appointed for the soldiers sent, and two other Englishmen she would name. The dice were cast. Her Rubicon however was crossed too late to save the most important town of the Low Countries, the banking capital of the world, from falling into Philip's net.

No English poet burst into public song in praise of her Majesty's action. At the end of October 1585 London held a pageant in honour of the new mayor Wolstan Dixie, a show for which George Peele wrote lyrics and was well paid. With his usual mellifluous facility and shallowness he alluded to the declaration of war:

Armour of safe defence the soldier hath:
So lovely London carefully attends
To keep her sacred sovereign from scath,
That all this English land so well defends;
And so far London bids her soldiers go,
As well may serve to shield this land from woe …

In the atmosphere of martial warmth that gradually enveloped the land, Marlowe's own poetry shifted from translation of Ovid's amorous elegies to the writing of *Lucan's first book of the famous Civil War betwixt Pompey and Caesar*, which John Wolf noted in the Stationers Register in September 1593 was "Englished by Christopher Marlow". Characteristic of the poet was the interpretation of contemporary experience in terms of his favourite classic poets, in images of Latin myth. He found in Virgil a way of happily combining the two passions that divided his intellectual energy, the erotic and the warlike, into a single shining work. He wrote *The Tragedy of Dido, Queen of Carthage*, evidently with the expectation of having it staged by one of the companies of chorus lads in London. It was accepted—I surmise in 1584—for production by the Children of Her Majesty's Chapel, who were then acting at the Blackfriars theatre under the direction of Henry Evans and John Lyly, under the master-eyes apparently of Edward de Vere, Earl of Oxford (3). On 27 December 1584, the Earl of Oxford's boys appeared with Evans at Greenwich Palace to play *The History of Agamemnon and Ulysses* for the Queen. This lost drama of the Trojan war, whose conclusion Marlowe pathetically and lengthily described in his *Dido*, may well have inspired that play [J. Thomas Looney argued that this lost play was by Oxford and his revision of it became Shakespeare's *Troilus and Cressida*—W.H.].

The hero Eneas is called both lovely and warlike. John Lyly had declared in the Prologue to his *Midas*, a satire on Spanish policy: "At our exercises soldiers call for tragedies; their object is blood: courtiers for comedies; their subject is love." Marlowe, composing for the same public and the same players, also tried to satisfy both groups of customers. He was, however, uncomfortable in the work of picturing the way of a man with a maid or a widow, like the Queen of Carthage. When he made her speak like a virile warrior he felt more at ease. "Humility belongs to common grooms," she cries when Eneas bends before her with gesture Christianlike, thanking her for queenly loving-kindness. The poet's own antipathy to the religious virtue rings from the line.

In Dido's mouth he also put a speech expressing the Queen of England's private creed about her government, and the state conviction of the King of Spain:

> Those that dislike what Dido gives in charge,
> Command my guard to slay for their offence.
> Shall vulgar peasants storm at what I do?
> The ground is mine that gives them sustenance,
> The air wherein they breathe, the water, fire,
> All that they have, their lands, their goods, their lives.

Here is the doctrine of absolute monarchy, popularly known as tyranny, which John Cowell, Doctor of Civil Law at Cambridge, cherished within range of Marlowe's hearing in 1584. Decades would pass before a Parliament would dare to silence the preaching of a Cowell on the royal prerogative in making laws. A republican of Athens in the days of Aeschylus might have said that Dido's downfall was the natural result of her despotic vanity. Yet Marlowe uttered not one word to show that he disagreed with her Majesty. He was, if possible, more royalist than Elizabeth herself. She always endeavoured to appear her loveliest, in exhibition of maiden modesty and spiritual kinship with the lowliest, when she went among the vulgar peasants and artisans who upheld her throne.

What Dr Cowell and Mr Marlowe taught the people in schoolroom and playhouse, Bishop Thomas Bilson taught them from pulpit and press. He issued in 1585, from Winchester, the main contention in favour of the state's ferocity toward Catholics who denied the official doctrine that she was the vicar of Christ, an argument that served to justify her savage treatment of Puritans too, and all adversaries of her claim to demidivinity. Bilson's book, *The True Difference between Christian Subjection and Unchristian Rebellion*, printed in 1586, affirmed that tolerance of dissent in religion was absolutely sinful. "A Christian prince," he scolded the Catholics, "may not pardon or wink at your falsehood." No statesman protested against Bilson's confession that the people had the right to resist other shapes of imperial oppression (4). Nor did the Bishop's cringing before the Crown arrive at the level of servility that John Aylmer, Bishop of London, reached when he wrote to his patron Christopher Hatton on 8 June 1578: "I trust not of God, but of my Sovereign, which is God's lieutenant, and so another God unto me" (5).

Bishop Bilson did not see the need to prove that the Elizabethan throne held a monopoly of truth. The holy oil on her head sufficed to prove it to him. But while Kit Marlowe believed in the divine privilege of monarchs, he did not believe in the coronation oil. The divinity that hedged a king, in his opinion, had no existence apart from arms, stark force. "For kings are clouts that every man shoots at," says the imbecile monarch Mycetes in the first part of *Tamburlaine the Great* (1.4). It was a widespread saying when Marlow wrote the verse, since the dominant factions of Christendom all rejected the sanctity of royal anointment if the head anointed belonged to a rival sect. Regicide had even become an act of theological merit, despite St Paul's commandment for obedience to masters of public powers. The commandment did not cover heretics, Jesuit savants insisted. And the Calvinist church version of the New Testament explained that the Apostle Paul referred to "civil magistrates; so that Antichrist and his cannot wrest this place to establish their tyranny over the conscience". That sturdy son of the Genevan church John Knox wrested it against the civil magistrates of Scotland who revered the "synagogue of Satan" in Rome.

Kit Marlowe despised the commandment. He considered the Apostle "a timorous fellow in bidding men to be subject to magistrates against his conscience" (6) Yet the poet's heart was by no means hostile to the principle of civil rank and dominion. He could easily imagine himself gripping the reins of authority and did not care whether the subjection of those below him would be based on Christian or anti-Christian dogmas. The fear voiced by Sir Edward Stafford in July 1584, after the assassination of Prince William of Orange, that Elizabeth might be the next victim of Romanist rage, made English politics a game full of exhilaration for Marlowe. "There is no doubt," Stafford asserted, "that she is a chief mark to shoot at" (7). Some of the young dramatist's intimate companions after he left Cambridge were men oddly familiar with the idea of shooting at the Tudor target.

Most of these meditators on assassination belonged to the faction of Robert Dudley, Earl of Leycester. Lord John, his father, they all knew, had played monarch-maker after the death of the boy Edward VI; he had proclaimed Elizabeth a bastard and usurper, and set the crown on the head of his daughter-in-law, Lady Jane Grey. For nine days Leycester's father had drunk the wine of majesty. The Earl himself got more than a taste of it after the coronation of Elizabeth, for he was always her dearest courtier. She never forgot his devotion and generosity during her girlhood. She sent him to the Netherlands as commander of the new army which was supposed to halt the triumphal advance of Parma. His nephew, Sir Philip Sidney, she appointed governor of Flushing. And his youngest noble partisan, Robert Devereux, Earl of Essex, then only nineteen years old, became the general of the Queen's cavalry in the Low Countries. We shall find nearly all of Kit Marlowe's murderous companions close to the family circle of Sidney and Devereux. Sidney's father-in-law, Sir Francis Walsingham, held the post of chief officer of espionage and legitimate murder, captain of the agents provocateurs of the empire, under the direction of William Cecil, Lord Burghley, who makes old Nic Machiavelli look today like a saint among statesmen by comparison.

In 1584 a group of Catholic exiles from England printed in Paris a sensational attack on Leycester's politics and character. *La Vie Abominable du Comte de Leycester* appeared in English next year as *A Copy of a Letter alleged to be from "a Master of Arts of Cambridge"*. Although the Privy Council banned the booklet on 28 June 1585, copies of it may have reached Kit Marlowe at the University. He would have been profoundly entertained by its accusations of state intrigue and lechery, social climbing over bodies broken and poisoned, it was said, by hirelings of the Earl. Simultaneously the Romanists accused him of being an offshoot of Calvinism and a patron of the Puritans. In Naples (also in 1585) the tract appeared as part of a polemic by one Julius Brieger entitled *Flores Calvinistici*. The Earl's own theology they defined as atheist. Leycester believed the little work was composed by John Leslie the Bishop of Ross, Mary of Scotland's main counsellor, with Charles Paget and Thomas Morgan, adherents of the imprisoned Queen of Scots, one English, the other Welsh. In the judgment of the Catholic Record Society, *Leycester's Commonwealth*, as the booklet is commonly called, was made by Charles Arundel, "with assistance of other exiled followers of Mary Stuart" (8). *An Addition du Translateur de ... la Vie Abominable* in 1585 singled out for laudation Lord Henry Howard, brother of Philip, Earl of Arundel, and his comrade in treason and scandal-spreading

Charles Arundel. The Earl of Oxford, in the Christmas of 1580, had attempted to expose these two as agents of the Vatican and Madrid. In private libels, written to enrage the Queen and Oxford's critics at Court, they executed a literary revenge which ought to be better known, because they illuminate one of the most creative minds of the time. But the chief clout of Arundel's polemics was Robert Dudley, the most active antagonist of the appeasement of Spain in the Privy Council.

Leycester's compatriot, the Secretary of State Francis Walsingham, learnt that a certain Robert Poley, a former servant of the Earl, possessed copies of the calumny tract. The Secretary had Poley brought where he could question him for two hours about its circulation in London. Poley was well acquainted with Walsingham's methods of cross-examination. Also he himself was an accomplished liar and student of deceit of state. "I will swear and forswear myself," he once declared, "rather than I will accuse myself to do me any harm" (9). He retained enough of the Secretary's confidence to get a job as a spy and instigator of political violence. He was energetic in these paths when he became intimate with Kit Marlowe. In 1580 Poley's name appears in Walsingham's correspondence with Burghley as a messenger, apparently to Thomas Morgan in Paris, concerned with "the secret cause that your Lordship and I are only made acquainted al" (10). The affair seems to have involved the bribing of cardinals in Rome. At that time the Secretary of State's cousin, Thomas Walsingham, also carried messages from France to London. On 12 November 1581, wandering soldiers on the mainland took hold of Thomas Walsingham in the company of one "Skeggs", considering their behaviour suspicious, but released them when the former showed that he carried "Monsieur's packet" (11). Monsieur was then the popular nickname for François Hercules de Valois, the Duke of Alençon, later Anjou. In those days the poet Thomas Watson, who also turned playwright, enjoyed consorting in Paris with Thomas Walsingham.

In the summer of 1585 Robin Poley or Pooley was nominally a servant of Christopher Blunt, younger brother of William, Lord

Mountjoy, and therefore in a position to find out the British connexions of the Arundel-Paget-Morgan cabal. For Kit Blunt was a fervent Catholic, devoted to the cause of Mary Stuart. Yet Leycester liked him and gave him a post of trust in the English army in the Netherlands. He knighted Blunt for his gallant services in the Flemish war, and later elected him Master of the Horse. Not long after the Earl's death Blunt married his widow. So it was simple to trick him into thinking that by his influence Poley gained employment in the household of Sir Philip Sidney, Leycester's nephew, early in 1586. The spy went to work for Lady Sidney in reality, it seems, to be in daily contact with her father, Francis Walsingham. The Secretary was not disturbed by reports of Poley's zeal among London Catholics. He knew his man. A year later the Romanists were denouncing Poley as a zealot for Walsingham's worship and statecraft. They charged him with poisoning Richard Creagh, the Archbishop of Armagh, when that prelate lay a prisoner in the Tower of London in 1585 (12). And they charged him with instigating a plot for the murder of the Queen.

Another member of Marlowe's last circle, Nicholas Skeres, appears to have been engaged in less patriotic activity in the summer of 1585. On 7 July the magistrate William Fleetwood named him as one of the "masterless men and cutpurses whose practice is to rob gentlemen's chambers and artificers' shops in and about London" (13). This Skeres was not an ordinary thief. He had studied law at Furnival's Inn in 1582, and signed a bond for forty pounds while there with another member of Marlowe's postcollegiate ring, Matthew Roydon, also of Holborn, studying at Davys Inn. Roydon became a rimer and dramaturge too. Possibly Nicholas was the government agent called Skeggs who ran errands with Thomas Walsingham in 1582 and 1583, when the latter served as a courier between London and Paris. To Sir Thomas Walsingham was dedicated, five years after Marlowe's brutal death, his poem "Hero and Leander," with a note by the printer Edward Blunt describing the poet as a man "that hath been dear to us". Companionship with cutpurses held few qualms for Sir Thomas, who in his prime befriended the swindler Ingram Frizer, the very man accused of killing Marlowe.

Collegiate life must have had strong allurements for the future dramatist. He stayed at Corpus Christi for the full six years allowed by his scholarship, ostensibly working toward holy orders with the degree of Master of Arts. Yet his absence from school increased in length in the years 1585 and 1586, together with the costs of his maintenance. Doubtless he spent many hours away from Corpus Christi among the pleasures of the capital, particularly the theatres and the "stews". The royal Council vouched for certain services he did for the government in this time. My guess is that he came to employment by Cecil and Walsingham on recommendation of a Cambridge doctor like John Cowell, and first learnt about the business of espionage working as a courier. They may have tested his agility, alertness and discretion, in journeys to Scotland. In July 1584 Walsingham remarked that political orbs in Britain did not expect Elizabeth to last much longer, and speculated on the bright prospects of King James Stuart. "I find that men begin to look to the sun rising," the Secretary of State observed (14). He was aware of Lord Hunsdon's hopes that the Scottish King would marry his daughter or his niece. Of course, he knew that Leycester schemed to marry his own infant son to Arbella Stuart, also a baby — evidently a resurrection of his father's grandiose dream about Jane Grey. Unluckily Leycester's boy died in July. In January 1586 Thomas Morgan reported that Robert Poley had been in Scotland and "knoweth the best ways to pass into Scotland" (15). For some tenebrous reason Walsingham also sent "Pooley" with messages to "Heilsignore" in Denmark. And on 18 January 1586, Thomas Morgan wrote to the captive Queen of Scots: "Charles Paget and I recommended some English in London to the French ambassador, to do him pleasure and service there; and amongst others one Robert Poley, who hath given me assurance to serve and honour your Majesty to his power, being but a poor gentleman." Morgan reported that Poley resided at Tutbury with Christopher Blunt, who "hath given credit to the said Poley" (16). The French ambassador described Poley as a small blond fellow employed in Sir Edward Stafford's embassy in Paris (17). It would be pleasant to have at least three words to sketch Christopher Marlowe for us.

II

The stages in and outside of London in the summer of 1586 were busy regaling the groundlings and their overseers in the galleries with propaganda against the empire of Spain. King Philip was furious at Elizabeth for her massive intrusion in the Low Countries. "But what has enraged him more than all else," wrote the Venetian ambassador in Madrid, "and has caused him to show a resentment such as he has never before displayed in all his life, is the account of the maskerades and comedies which the Queen of England orders to be acted at his expense" (18). His Majesty received a summary of one of these plays, recently performed, "in which all sorts of evil is spoken of the Pope, the Catholic religion, and the King, who is accused of spending all his time in the Escurial with the monks of St Jerome ..." The Venetian scorned to write any more of the English theatrical insolences. Since the "Philippic" comedies were produced by royal command, we may be sure the Queen's Company was most instrumental in their performance. The troupe had been organised under Francis Walsingham's direction with stars formerly in the service of the Earls of Leycester and Oxford. The leading clown of the company, Richard Tarlton, carried the agitation against Philip's imperialism offstage. A cobbler in Carter Lane asked him about the nationality of the Devil; he replied, "A Spaniard, for Spaniards, like the Devil, trouble the whole world" (19).

In this period the Earl of Oxford resided in the luxurious mansion called (after its goldsmith builder) Fisher's Folly. Here he pursued the mysterious work, never divulged, for which the Queen granted him, under privy seal warrant on 26 June 1586, one thousand pounds a year from the secret service fund (20). And here he acted as prime patron of the finest poets and playwrights of the age. Thomas Watson, who later came to live at the Folly as tutor in the household of William Cornwallis, who purchased it from the Earl, John Lyly, and Robert Greene submitted books to the judgment of De Vere. The mansion stood on the fringe of Bishopsgate, a short walk from the Theatre and the Curtain, not far from the Bell Inn and the Bull in Gracechurch Street where famous plays were staged. (On 22 April 1583, St Helen's church in Bishopsgate witnessed the baptism of Anne, daughter of "Robert Pollye," who, I presume, was the Robert Poley who witnessed Marlowe's murder.) Adjoining Oxford's house were four messuages owned by the actors Edward and John Alleyn. The brothers Alleyn belonged to the company wearing the livery of Charles Howard of Effingham, who became Lord Admiral in May 1585. The troupe seems to have been organised by former servants of William Somerset, Earl of Worcester, a man whose Catholic intellect interfered in no way with his loyalty to the Crown or his country. We have no information about his acquaintance with Edward de Vere, but we do know that his son and heir Edward was sufficiently friendly to the Earl of Oxford to promote the union of their players in 1602, and he used his influence in the Privy Council to obtain them special liberties (21).

Before the amalgamation of Oxford's and Worcester's men, the former parted with an old play of theirs, *The History of George Scanderbeg*, which was registered for printing in 1601 at the Stationers Hall but unfortunately has disappeared. The drama dealt with the struggles of the Christians in Albania, under their chief George Skanderbeg, to free themselves from the Turkish yoke. A consensus of critics dates the lost play about the time of Marlowe's *Tamburlaine*, which also extols war against Turkey. *Scanderbeg* seems to have been composed in a lofty and sonorous verse comparable to the style of *Tamburlaine*. When the Cambridge pedant Gabriel Harvey wrote his cryptic obituary on Marlowe, "Gorgon", he associated the poet with "Scanderbegging", as though the word would summon to his readers' thought the strut and thunder of the Marlovian line. Harvey says that when the news of Marlowe's sudden death reached him at Cambridge he could hardly believe it.

Jesu (quoth I) is that Gargantua mind
Conquer'd, and left no Scanderbeg behind?

Then he recalled a close friend of the dramatist, in whom he pretended to see the successor to the dead arts-master: "Have you forgot the Scanderbegging wight?" It is plain from the context of "Gorgon" that the wight Harvey had in view was Thomas Nashe (22). Perhaps Nashe was the author of *The History of George Scanderbeg*, evidently in imitation of Marlowe's epic tragedy. Nashe's name appears on the title-page of *Dido, Queen of Carthage* (printed in 1593) as co-author; however, it is questionable whether the tragedy owes anything substantial to the talents of one who aspired to become the English Aretino or Aristophanes. He could have collaborated with Marlowe on the epic story of Skanderbeg, after he came down to the capital from Cambridge in 1586, and found his fellow scholar revelling in the triumph of his Tamburlaine.

(In June 1586, according to detective wits of the Catholic Record Society and my own researches, the Privy Council, under the adroit and sinister guidance of Lord Burghley, set the trap for decapitating the Queen of Scots, employing the bat-witted priest John Ballard, and gentry of inferior brains led by the incredibly gullible Anthony Babington, lover of Robin Poley. On 6 July 1586, English diplomats concluded the treaty with Scotland in which the polymorphously perverse King James consented to stop his attempts to save his mother from her fate. Burghley strove to make the conspiracy of Babington and his strange bed-fellows a plot to kill Queen Elizabeth. We can see clearly all they aimed to do from the letter the miserable Mary wrote on 17 July to Babington: "The affairs being thus prepared and forces in readiness both within and without the realm, then shall it be time to set the six gentlemen to work, taking order, upon the accomplishment of their design, I may be suddenly transported out of this place" (23).)

In the year 1586 educated Englishmen felt an interest in the affairs and forces of Turkey that lost none of its heat in their concern with the wars of the West. When the armies of the Amuraths knocked at the gates of Christendom in the Balkans or the Carpathians, English believers in the old mother-faith considered their own doorways in danger. The ambition of many a brave and bright young man of the realm in this period was to serve his country by fighting the Turk. In 1543 the churchwardens had managed to collect a goodly sum of money for Henry VIII in the name of national defence "against the Turk" (24). There were always eager readers for books like John Shute's translation of Andrew Cambine's *Turkish Affairs*, which appeared in 1562 together with an account of George Skanderbeg's battles, under the title *Two Notable Commentaries*.

Marlowe's imagination luxuriated in such books, charmed by the colour, the eloquence and ferocious impulsiveness of their personages, the pomp and circumstance of their heroic deeds. They thrilled the barbarian in his brain, letting his fantasy run riot with visions of carnage. He must have devoured the news brought from the Orient in 1585 of the bloody defeats suffered by Sultan Amurath in his efforts to conquer Persia. Desire for horrible details of the campaign in Iran could be safely indulged among Englishmen and Christians who were anxious about the effect of the war on the religious struggles in Europe. Many of them were grateful to the Persians for relieving the Mediterranean and the Danube of the Turkish terror's ancient weight. Roman Catholics, admirers of Spain and the Hapsburgs, were especially pleased, because the defeats of the Sultan left the Pope and Philip more free to pursue their designs for the unity of the continent under the Cross. The Holy Roman Emperor Rudolph heard the news of the Persian victories with mixed emotions. "The Turk is the good fortune of the Lutheran" was a common saying in his empire, for every triumph of the Turk weakened the imperial government in the east and forced larger concessions to the heretics who paid taxes to Rudolph. Yet the Turkish defeats did not automatically signify the strengthening of his rule. His ambassador Busbecq pointed out that Amurath's misfortune meant opportunity for King Philip's encroachment on the Holy Roman Empire. "The Spanish nation," Busbecq affirmed, "greedy for empire, will never be quiet, even with their great power, but will seek for the dominion of the rest of Christendom." So even devout Catholics could experience a feeling of sadness on contemplating the Sultan's failures in Iran. Astute Anglicans like Sir Francis Walsingham were also worried by his distress. Walsingham's friend William Harborne, the first English ambassador to Constantinople, toiled indefatigably to divert the Turkish weaponry from Persia to Spain. Queen Elizabeth's agent at Strasburg in 1568 voiced their policy in assuring fellow Protestants of Germany that "the cruelty and impious domination of the Spaniards will be retaliated by the avenging arms of the Turks" (24a).

Marlowe's hero Tamburlaine (Timur Lenk) was a Tartar shepherd who became warlord over Persia and crushed the troops of Turkey sent against him in 1402. Christian historians glorified "Tamerlane" because he reduced for decades the Ottoman pressure on the perishing Byzantine despotism; they saw in Timur a saviour of "Romania". Pedro Mexia's *Silva de varia lecciones*, published at Seville in 1543, presented the barbaric conqueror almost as a demigod, full of nobility, bursting with heathen virtues. The book was translated into German and Flemish and French. From the French version Thomas Fortescue made his English edition, *The Forest* (1576), which Marlowe unquestionably perused with passion in the making of his play. Mexia's portrait of the Scythian shepherd made a magical impression on more than one English poet and playwright. George Whetstone, whose play *Promos and Cassandra* and collection of novels, *Heptameron of Civil Discourses*, furnished Shakespeare with the plot of *Measure for Measure*, voiced his enthusiasm for the Spanish history several times. In the *Heptameron* (1582) he spoke warmly of "Peter Mesiere his Chronicle of Memorable Things", in particular the "rare history of Tamburlaine the Great" (25). In *The English Mirror*, licensed for publication on 29 April 1586, Whetstone introduced many of Mexia's details in picturing the military accomplishments of the great Tartar. This book included a chapter entitled "A Brief Report of the Calamities of France, Flanders, and Scotland", but its fascination for Marlowe lay mainly in the section dealing with the calamities of Turkey under the hands of the "Rogue of Volga", Tamburlaine. *The English Mirror* stated that none of the illustrious captains of Greece and Rome, "none of all their martial acts, deserve to be proclaimed with more renown than the conquest and military disciplines of Tamburlaine". In his army, according to Whetstone, mutiny never lifted its fist, for "he was wise, liberal, and rewarded every soldier with his desert". This remark rang pregnant to English hearts with sharp sentiment, laughter and tears. Their Queen's miserly treatment of soldiers distracted her best captains and frequently goaded her troops to revolt. The royal shilling-pinching wasted untold quantities of the people's blood and treasure in the wars in Ireland and the Low Countries, and their generals never wearied of complaining about its ruinous effects on national defence. Incalculable are the funds the officers supplied out of their own family incomes, to keep up the soldiers' spirits with bread and beer. Leycester and Sidney spoke out boldly against Elizabeth's avarice and the way she starved the men who guarded England against Spain. Whetstone's words concerning his Tartar hero's love of the brave, how he constantly "praised and paid the virtuous and valiant soldier", carried in their wake a critique of the stingy Queen (26).

For the sake of Timur Khan's fabulous generosity and his destruction of Turkish fortresses and troops, Europeans could overlook his reverence, the favour he showed the religion of Islam. Marlowe left that out of his play. Instead he gifted Tamburlaine with a surprising adoration of a God practically pantheist:

> he that sits on high and never sleeps,
> Nor in one place is circumscriptible,
> But everywhere fills every continent
> With strange infusion of his sacred vigour.

Moreover, there are moments in the drama when the writer experienced a thrilling regression to the frame of childhood mentality when he adored the God of the Old Testament in the cathedral of Canterbury and heard

The Cherubins and holy Seraphins
That sing and play before the king of kings,
Use all the voices and their instruments

for his delight alone.

The personal motive for writing *Tamburlaine the Great* sprang, we
may suppose, from the dramatist's own wish for a worldly promotion that would drown the memory of his origin as a cobbler's son.
Fortescue's *Forest* urged young men of humble parentage to follow
Tamburlaine's example, and "aspire to the seat of virtue and honour". Whetstone seconded his motion, with a sentence that doubtless sounded in Marlowe's mind's ear like a disclosure of his naked
soul. "Notwithstanding the poverty of his parents," wrote Whetstone in eulogy of the shepherd from Samarcand, "even from his
infancy he had a reaching and an imaginative mind" (27). The mind
of our dramatist aspired to a pinnacle of happiness beyond the
dreams of his mother and father. The cobbler's boy fancied himself
as worthy to steer a state. In the person of his hero, in the theatre,
he attained the fruition of his fantasy. "I am a lord," says his protagonist, "for so my deeds shall prove;/ And yet a shepherd by my
parentage."

Nature, that fram'd us of four elements
Warring within our breast for regiment,
Doth teach us all to have aspiring minds:
Our souls ...
Will us to wear ourselves, and never rest,
Until we reach the ripest fruit of all,
That perfect bliss and sole felicity,
The sweet fruition of an earthly crown.

The poet compared this frenzy for a crown and throne, which he
thought obsessed every human soul, to the "thirst of reign" which
provoked the mythic oldest son of Ops "To thrust his doting father
from his chair" (1.6). No profound psychology is required to dis-

cern here an almost conscious hatred of the poet's father, a hatred whose fire extended to all the members of his class. It made an absolute royalist of Marlowe. He was indeed more monarchist than Leycester, whose contempt for the "churls and tinkers", the "bakers, brewers, and hired advocates", that dominated the States-General of the Netherlands, did not prevent him from working cordially together with them (28). The Tudor dynasty, in fact, depended for its basic nourishment on gentry of the same rank; upstart burgesses provided the salt of the Tudor earth. To despise them as Marlowe did was sheer madness. His kind of monarchism cast him out not only from his father's class; it barred him from the whole social order: it made him an isolate outlaw. Like his protagonist he wanted to threaten and overthrow the gods. He yearned to rid his realm of the Bible and other tomes of theology that had fretted his wits, burning them as Tamburlaine burns "the Turkish Alcoran,/ And all the heaps of superstitious books,/ Found in the Temples of that Mahomet …" A practical monarchist would have explored the political uses of the worshipped and their works.

At the same time that the cobbler's boy preached his evangel, "A god is not so glorious as a king" (2.5), he made his drama palatable to his Christian public by advocating the conventional view of kings as agents of divinity. He portrayed "The rogue of Volga" as a scourge of God, like any pastor of Catholic or Protestant flock explaining war as the rod of deity in the hands of princes. The same Tamburlaine who defies the gods in general talks mystically of "The chiefest god, first mover", in the phrase of Aristotle, and says this celestial power protects him against his enemies (4.2). The contradiction is too glaring to be a product of hypocrisy. I believe that it sprang from the deeps of Marlowe's character, the essential conflict that made him a dramatist.

He fought so hard against the thought of deity because he could not free himself from its mysterious terrors. All his trumpet-tongued harangues on theology and nose-thumbing at churches and their statues expressed the bravado of a boy who had acquired early a real fear of the Lord, and His Hell, as well as imagery of His Paradise throne surrounded by stars. It was not Marlowe, the bombastic sadist of the London taverns, but poor Christopher of Canterbury, whose soul secretly cried for pity and tenderness, who made Tamburlaine denounce the cruelty of the Algerians in these anguished words:

> I that am term'd the scourge and wrath of God,
> The only fear and terror of the world,
> Will first subdue the Turk, and then enlarge
> Those Christian captives which you keep as slaves,
> Burdening their bodies with your heavy chains,
> And feeding them with thin and slender fare;
> That naked row about the Terrene sea,
> And, when they chance to rest or breathe a space,
> Are punish'd with bastones so grievously
> That they lie panting on the galleys' side,
> And strive for life at every stroke they give. (3.3)

Not Timur Khan but Christopher Marlowe utters this indignation against "the cruel pirates of Argier ... That make quick havoc of the Christian blood". Verses like these enable us to understand how the poet, in spite of his beastly fantasies and outbursts enchanted some of his countrymen into becoming his lifelong friends. They could appreciate the charming child in him that made his savage hero compare his army to "Julius Caesar's host" in Lucan's epic: "Nor in Pharsalia was there such hot war" (3.3). Even more they valued his lyric genius, which would suddenly intrude on speeches of astounding conceit with allusions to the "silence of thy solemn evening walk", and the magnificent meditation beginning "What is beauty? saith my sufferings then" (5.2). Kit Marlowe interrupts that reflection on the "Quintessence" of literature, to be precise "Poesy", with the warning that continuance in that vein will vanquish his virility, which he had early learnt to consider as proved by savagery

> But how unseemly is it for my sex,
> My discipline of arms and chivalry,

My nature and the terror of my name,
To harbour thoughts effeminate and faint?

Fear of the feminine in his nature drove Marlowe to the hairy sort of assertion of his sex that homosexuals confuse with manliness.

The chief intellectual appeal of *Tamburlaine* rang, as we have already indicated, in its verses of exultation over the defeats of the Turks at the arms of their Persian foes. The First Part of the tragedy concludes in a scene of Persian peace, with Baiazet, the emperor of Turkey, self-slain in a cage, with his wife a suicide nearby. Over their bodies the young queen Zenocrate, who is drawn too lovable to be believable, pronounces a funeral moral that flatly contradicts the pervasive passion of the play:

Those that are proud of fickle empery
And place their chiefest good in earthly pomp,
Behold the Turk and his great emperess!

With this moral and the vision of the Mahometan humiliation Marlowe probably satisfied the players to whom he brought this tragedy that it was a pious and patriotic work. The groundlings and gentry who watched the play were equally satisfied and more, entranced and intoxicated by the gorgeous rhetoric and giant-striding rhythm with which its ambivalent themes were proclaimed. They could grin with devout felicity when the fellow who acted Baiazet raged in the dust before the victorious Persians:

Now will the Christian miscreants be glad,
Ringing with joy their superstitious bells. (3.3)

The players who welcomed Marlowe's masterpiece were the servants of Admiral Howard, headed by the tall stentorian Ned Alleyn. It might have been written with Alleyn and his men in mind.

The First Part demands no more complex stage than a London inn such as they commonly used could afford, and a small troupe would have comfortably managed all the roles, with properly coloured costumes and drums. It is noteworthy that Marlowe did not submit his play to the supreme actors of the age, the Queen's company. Indeed, I suspect that he regarded her Majesty's men with some contempt, and threw a barb at them in the opening lines of *Tamburlaine*, ridiculing the plays of triviality their star Dick Tarlton excelled in:

> From jigging veins of riming mother-wits,
> And such conceits as clownage keeps in pay
> We'll lead you to the stately tent of war ...

The Admiral's actors almost certainly performed The First Part of *Tamburlaine the Great* in 1586 (29). It stirred up a clapping and cheering such as London theatres had seldom heard; it came close to eclipsing the popularity of *The Spanish Tragedy*, which I have elsewhere tried to demonstrate was Thomas Watson's work (30). [See Chapter 13–W.H.]

Before we look further into our playwright's progress, I would like to review certain historic events of 1586, which no documents depict him as partaking in, but surely had a hellish influence in his life.

On 2 August 1586, Anthony Babington and his comrades in conspiracy to rescue Queen Mary from her castle prison, met for supper in a garden belonging to Robert Poley. Among them moved his friend "Skyrres", for what function, we are not informed. On the next day Poley went to Sir Francis Walsingham to get instructions for the following day. 4 August saw Thomas Walsingham visiting Poley and then the arrest of Father John Ballard in Poley's house. Learning of the priest's capture by police, Babington endeavoured to conceal himself, and sent Poley the brief epistle that reveals to us the fragile ego of the author, desperately adolescent if not verging on idiocy.

> Farewell, sweet Robin, if as I take thee, true to me.
> If not, adieu, *omnium bipedium nequissimus*. Return me

thine answer for my satisfaction, and my diamond, and
what else thou wilt. The furnace is prepared wherein
our faith must be tried.

Poley did not deserve the superlative, "of all bipeds the wickedest".
But Babington could outstrip most competitors for the prize which
might be awarded to the stupidest. Yet Cecil succeeded in persuading Queen Elizabeth that the Babington ring of mooncalves actually
imperilled her life under direction from the prisoner Mary Stuart.
To give an air of verisimilitude to his claim that the Spanish forces
in the Low Countries were nearly on tiptoe for invasion of England
to support the Catholic conspirators, Burghley called a halt to nego-
tiation he had begun for peace-talk with statesmen of Spain. To
show the Spaniards how earnestly they should deem his game, he
ordered a stoppage of supplies for the English and Dutch troops
(31). Philip responded by noting on a letter about the plot that Cecil
should not be a major target for attack: "It does not matter so much
about Cecil, although he is a great heretic, but he is very old; and it
was he who advised the understandings with the Prince of Parma,
and he has done no harm" (32).

On 16 August Walsingham's hunters captured Babington and
took him for questioning to Sir Christopher Hatton's house. Burghley put Poley on the trail for seizure of the other six conspirators.
On 18 August, Burghley, Hatton and Lord Bromley examined the
forlorn Anthony, presumably advising him about the modes extort-
ing confession recommended by the Lord Treasurer in his treatise
The Execution of Justice (printed in Latin in March 1584). Babington's
confession indicates no sign of torture.

On 21 August, the merry Roger Manners, from the Court at
Windsor, wrote his brother John as usual, but without his customary gossip: "For news, I know none and if I did it is not good to
write of these perilous causes" (33) Mary Stuart was moved from
the Chartley chains to her final resting place at Fotheringhay, on 25
August. The "Sicilians", as witty Catholics termed the Romanesque
rackmasters employed by Burghley (34), found scarcely any difficul-

ties in collecting Babington's cronies and wringing crooked confessions from them. Anthony Tyrrel told them what they wanted to hear, the so-called plans of the group for killing the Queen. On the same day, 9 September, the Privy Council summoned the Lords selected by Cecil to be the judges of the Queen of Scots to Windsor. On the 12th Burghley composed a flattering frisson for Leycester: "Your Lordship and I," he scribbled, "were very great motes in the traitors' eyes, for your Lordship there and I here should first, about one time, have been killed. Of your Lordship they thought rather of poisoning than of slaying" (35).

Historians have regularly copied the contentions of William Camden and other scribes in the service of Cecil when they come to deal with the Babington plot. Mechanically they copy, and doggedly they ignore the argument of the priest Rob Southwell in *An Humble Supplication to Her Majesty* (dated at the end 14 December 1595). Southwell forgot about his calling to be a poet when he wrote this little volume charging that Robert Poley penned at the command of Sir Francis Walsingham the letter sent to Queen Mary by Babington which became the principal ground of her condemnation to death. This letter, mailed on 12 July, offered to murder Elizabeth. Mary Stuart's two secretaries, Nau and Curie, answered it with encouragement, bribed for the job, according to Southwell. "Poolie," he declared, "being Sir F. Walsingham's man, and thoroughly seasoned to his master's tooth, was the chief instrument to contrive and prosecute the matter, to draw into the net such green wits ..." And Poley, he points out, was never indicted for any crime even though he furnished the main brains of the conspiracy.

On 30 September, Babington and his six friends, in accord with their court sentence, were hanged for an instant, then taken down and cut in pieces with long agonies. On 1 October, more alleged plotters were hanged until dead. Seven days later the Lords assembled at Windsor to serve as commissioners for the trial of Queen Mary heard the incriminating letters read and were shown ciphers, but naturally not told about the forgeries of Walsingham's servant Thomas Phelippes, and the pains taken by William Cecil in his webwork for the neck of the Scottish queen. When the peers delivered the "verdict" expected by Burghley and his Privy conspirators, William Davison expressed his fear to Walsingham that Elizabeth would be reluctant to behead her cousin: "She will keep the course she held with the Duke of Norfolk," he predicted, "which is not to take her life without extreme fear compel her" (36). Burghley and Sir Francis gave her Majesty the necessary fillips. Early in January 1587 they hatched a plot involving Des Trappes, a servant of the Ambassador Chasteauneuf, and William Stafford, brother of the English ambassador to France. Both men were branded schemers for the murder of Queen Bess. Burghley insisted that such plots would continue springing up so long as Mary Stuart lived. He obtained the Queen's signature to the death warrant by a trick, says one biographer of Walsingham, that bears definite marks of the Secretary's weird talent (37). On 8 February the Queen of Scots knelt to the royal axe. The government made strenuous gestures to convince the people that Mary's execution was an event of national need. Henry Herbert, Earl of Pembroke, whose wife Catherine (born Grey) had been sister to an English queen for nine days, and London officials rode through the streets denouncing Mary as a traitress worthy of death. In the same moment all the bells in the capital began to ring; and they rang for twenty-four hours, over bonfires of rejoicing for her death. Quietly Des Trappes was released. In March Sir Francis informed the French ambassador that the whole business involving his servant had been nothing more than an effort by William Stafford to extort money from Chasteauneuf (38).

On 16 February 1587, to divert English minds from the tragedy of Mary Stuart, the government furnished London with a funeral designed to excite patriots with hate for all local souls desiring peace with Spain and pitying the victim at Fotheringhay. Sir Philip Sidney had died on 16 October of a thigh wound from the battle of Zutphen, and his father-in-law transported his body to London for burial. Walsingham kept the corpse for three months in the Aldgate Church of the Minories, until the patriotic purpose could be served.

He arranged for the burial of Sidney, like a national idol, at Paul's Cathedral yard, in an affair which cost six thousand pounds. Meanwhile Cecil and he seem to have instigated the performance of farces about Mary Stuart in the weeks before her death. All through January, the envoys of her son King James told him, "in divers plays and comedies in public they have brought your mother in a rope to the Queen of England in derision" (39). The wonder of the Scottish King over Walsingham's wizardry prompted the former to affirm that the Secretary of State, notwithstanding his outward profession of Christian austerity, was indeed "a very Machiavel" (40).

III

London sentiment against the Catholics ran especially high in January because two of Leycester's officers, Sir William Stanley, the governor of Deventer, and Rowland Yorke, commander of the English fort at Zutphen, on 19 January, suddenly avowed themselves contrite Catholics and surrendered their stations to the enemy. Cardinal William Allen wrote a treatise trying to prove "how lawful, honorable and necessary that action was; and also that all others, especially those of the English nation, that detain any towns, or other places in the Low Countries, from the King Catholic, are bound, upon pain of damnation, to do the like" (41). The Cardinal's argument did not seriously impress the English nation, whose main opinion appears to have been that "King Coin", not the Prince of Peace, had converted Stanley and Yorke from their duty. The national anger had numerous sparks for them when John Lyly had one of the characters in his *Midas* recall "how many gates of cities this golden key hath opened". Richard Jones, the printer of *Tamburlaine*, issued *A Short Admonition upon the Shameful Treason....*

Of course, Puritans viewed these betrayals as scourges from Heaven for England's sins. Not the least of the sins, in their eyes, were play-acting and play-going. On 25 January 1587, Maliverny Catlyn, a spy for Walsingham, lamented to his master: "The daily abuse of stage plays is such an offence to the godly and so great a hindrance to the gospel as the Papists do exceedingly rejoice at the blemish thereof." "And not without a cause," he mourned, "for every day in the week the players' bills are set up in sundry places of the city, some in the name of her Majesty's men, some the Earl of Leycester's, some the Earl of Oxford's, the Lord Admiral's, and divers others, so that when the bells toll to the lectors, the trumpets sound to the stages, wherat the wicked faction of Rome laugheth for joy." Catlyn admitted that the theatre no longer profaned the Sabbath as they used to do, but still acted like magnets to pull the folk from the churches. He proposed that the affluent actors should contribute weekly from their profits for the support of the poor. "It is a woeful sight," he remarked, "to see two hundred proud players go in their silks where five hundred poor people starve in the streets" (42).

In January the moneylender Philip Henslowe, having observed the profits of the Theatre and the Curtain and the various inn stages, erected his playhouse, the Rose, by the Thames among the brothels of Southwark. It became the headquarters of the Lord Admiral's men. Edward Alleyn married Henslowe's daughter. The company clamoured for more dramas by Kit Marlowe, but his genius had no affection for facility and could not drum forth its decasyllables for pence.

He seems to have turned from the rapture of *Tamburlaine* early in 1587 to lilting erotic poetry. He translated into English metre and rime the *Raptus Helenae*, a Latin paraphrase that Thomas Watson made in 1586 from the Greek "Rape of Helen" by Coluthus. Richard Jones registered the Watson work at the Stationers Guild on 16 April 1595, long after both poets were dead, but none of the verses have come to our light. Kit Marlowe's friendship with Tom Watson is one of the most attractive features of the former's short life. It deepened with the years, and even came to be sealed in blood. Their mastery of the classics did a great deal to elevate the popular drama far above the level of jigs and tales of bawdry on which it chiefly flourished before.

Marlowe penned the second Part of *Tamburlaine the Great*, as the Prologue declares, in response to the general enjoyment of the First.

To work up a plot for the Second was not an easy task, since the poet had exhausted the historic materials about Timur Khan within his reach in the first five acts. For the last five he had to combine sources as remote and exotic as Nicholas Nicholay's *Navigations* (in Turkey) translated by T. Washington (1585), and Ariosto's epic romance *Orlando Furioso*. He took the battle of Varna out of its chronological order to shape the first striking episode of the new play, the scene where King Sigismund of Hungary violates the oath he made to Christ for a peace treaty with Orcanes of Anatolia. Sigismund is convinced that

> with such infidels,
> In whom no faith nor true religion rests,
> We are not bound to those accomplishments
> The holy laws of Christendom enjoin. (2.1)

Here we have the doctrine of perjury which the Huguenots accused the Pope and his cohorts of practicing, and ordaining as duty toward infidels at the Council of Constance in 1415. The Huguenots are said to have got their name from being Eidgenossen (oath-united) at the Calvinist nucleus of Geneva. According to the Protestants, the Council of Constance used the doctrine to justify the burning of John Huss after Sigismund had pledged the word of the Holy Roman Empire for his safe-conduct. In Marlowe's tragedy the Christian king suffers a terrible defeat under the fury of the Mahometans he betrayed. "God had thunder'd vengeance from on high," the poet makes him cry out, "For my accurs'd and hateful perjury." The heathen Gazellus however is not impressed by the evidence of heavenly justice. " 'Tis but the fortune of the wars, my lord," he remarks to Orcanes, "Whose power is often prov'd a miracle" (2.3). Orcanes insists on avowing his gratitude to Christ for punishing Sigismund's crime of taking his name in vain.

In the next scene Tamburlaine himself is shown mourning for his queen Zenocrate with a speech that mounts in its sad ecstasy to a vision of Biblical bliss. He fancies his bride in Heaven, listening to the tongues of angels chanting and strings of seraphic melody. One might think that the Tartar conqueror had been converted, just as the English king Henry IV had wished, and turned into a champion of the prophets of Israel! Marlowe nowhere manifests any knowledge of King Henry's hope. But the Second Part of *Tamburlaine*, more shrill and artificial than the First, presents the hero not merely termed the scourge of the Lord but plangently announcing himself as a man destined "from above,/ To scourge the pride of such as Heaven abhors" (4.1). That he should be the first among the abhorred never occurs to him or his creator. So deep is the dramatist's identification with his protagonist.

Tamburlaine builds a bonfire on the stage for the Koran and other books of the Turkish creed from shrines of Mahomet: "Whom I have thought a god." In calmer mood afterward he commands his warriors to worship a different deity:

> The God that sits in heaven, if any god,
> For he is God alone, and none but he.

"If any god …" There is much vicious in that "If". It preludes the conclusion of the tragedy, where the sick and half-crazed hero challenges God to a duel and wants to march to the storming of Heaven, the Heaven he once said he served. He cries again for the slaughter of the gods, all the gods. And at the end he sinks once more into the fatal ambiguity of his creator: "For Tamburlaine, the scourge of God, must die."

When Marlowe burnt the bible of Islam in his play, and sneered at its "foolish laws", he had probably made up his mind that he would not live by the statutes of Christianity. For five and a half weeks after Christmas of 1586 he resided for the last time at Corpus Christi College, and then went hunting his fortune in the dark roads his heart coveted.

In the anonymous comedy *The Return from Parnassus*, composed by a student of St John's College (perhaps the gay graduate Thomas Nashe?), Studiosus and Philomusus parley about their chances of careers after graduation from Cambridge. They despair of making a good and godly living as scholars in England, whose schools were scarce and whose churches were more than adequately staffed by frequently illiterate ministers. Their decision is to accept the temptations held out by Papists, who promised glory both eternal and temporal to talented English youth who would go to study how to serve the cathedrals at Rome or Rheims. From the English seminaries in these cities came the young Jesuit fathers who entered England clandestinely and laboured to restore the lost sheep in the Anglican fold to the shepherd in the Vatican. They knew the penalty of their labour under Elizabeth's law could be frightful death. But their blood flamed for martyrdom. Marlowe never evinced a single sign of wish for their outlaw lustre. Yet, before he took the degree of Master of Arts in June 1587, a rumour circulated in Cambridge that he intended to cross the sea and study the sedition taught at Rheims (43). I conjecture that he started the rumour himself, to shock the dons and to cloak his true purpose in leaving the University.

Writing about 1870, Lieutenant-Colonel Francis Cunningham decided after a survey of Marlowe's works that the poet had gone to seek fame if not fortune in the Dutch war. Cunningham asserted confidently that Marlowe showed familiarity with the soldier's skill in trailing a pike or managing a charger with the English force in the Netherlands. As proof he set forth the poet's employment of military terms, and his fondness for employing them. "In the rough school of the march and the leaguer", Cunningham said, "he was more likely to have acquired the habit of using profane oaths and appealing to the dagger than in the quiet halls on the banks of the Cam." A. H. Bullen considered this a most plausible view (44). The testimony of Marlowe's plays will not uphold the surmise that he had ever trailed a pike or galloped with the Earl of Essex in Holland. Military terms abound in them, but they all come from bookish theory. "Mere prattle, without practice," as Ensign Iago would say, "is all his soldiership." For example, the lecture on war-craft in the Second Part of *Tamburlaine* (3.2) is probably derived from the second chapter of Paul Ive's *The Practice of Fortification*, not printed until 1589. Marlowe surely read this before the printing of his tragedy in August 1590. Ive's book was dedicated to Sir Francis Walsingham. He too was a Cambridge graduate, from Marlowe's college, and, although an engineer by profession, did secret service work, in August 1587, when Marlowe was similarly employed (45).

How the dramatist gained admission to the retinue of secret state agents, we have not the least idea. He may have been allured to join them after Walsingham had demonstrated by his handling of the Babington bunch how widespread and secure his spies were.

On 31 March 1587, the authorities of Corpus Christi College noted that he had completed the requirements for the Master of Arts degree, and they granted him their "grace". The rumour emerged that he had turned disloyal to the Queen's church and taken steps to enter the Romanist seminary of Rheims. The college heads felt impelled to delay the degree. On 29 June the Privy Council intervened, sending a message to Cambridge that requested his advancement to the degree and the quieting of hostile talk about him. "Whereas it was reported," ran the Council letter, "that Christopher Morley was determined to have gone beyond the seas to Rheims and there to remain, their Lordships thought good to certify that he had no such intent, but that in all his actions he had behaved himself orderly and discreetly, whereby he had done her Majesty good service, and deserved to be rewarded for his faithful dealing … it was not her Majesty's pleasure that anyone employed as he had been in matters touching the benefit of his country should be defamed by those who are ignorant in the affairs he went about" (46). Lord Burghley himself, as Chancellor of Cambridge University, may have prompted this intervention. Marlowe got the degree.

It has been surmised that Marlowe's service for the "country" consisted in a mission to the Netherlands or France. On 26 June the Earl of Leycester, who had been visiting England, returned to his troops in the Low Countries. Walsingham sent his agent Francis Needham to act as the Earl's secretary and incidentally to spy on him (47). Kit may have been sent as a courier to Lord Buckhurst, the poet of *Gorboduc*, the first academic tragedy in English; Thomas

Sackville then served as ambassador to the Netherlands. Elizabeth dispatched Buckhurst to learn the terms on which the Prince of Parma would agree to a truce. She corresponded with Parma from her palace at Greenwich, while he occupied his veterans with the siege of Sluys. Englishmen brilliantly defended that city, led by the Earl of Oxford's cousin Francis Vere, his dear friend Sir Roger Williams, and others famous in the history of the war. Elizabeth gave little thought to their welfare. She displayed more interest in the soul-syrup Parma sent her this month from the mouth of one Morris, a servant of Sir James Croft, one of the Privy Councillors who secretly favoured the Spanish cause. Morris came posthaste from Holland with news for her Majesty that the Prince was prepared to arrange an armistice. The news had no other warrant than Morris's mouth. But she was avid to believe it, the Buckhurst "most plainly dehorted her from such posthaste," and urged that "she should never make good peace without a puissant army in the field" (48). Leycester's fresh troops and funds came too slow and thriftily to save Sluys. He ordered fireships to destroy Parma's bridge to the town; when they finally arrived, they failed to explode the bridge. Sluys yielded to the Spaniards in July, giving them a port of power opposite the English coast.

The Queen's relations with the tyrant of France were quite genial in June 1587, despite her gestures of help to King Henry of Navarre and her other Huguenot friends in the civil war. With the promise of English finance, the German mercenaries under Casimir the Palatine had joined Navarre's army, but the Lord Treasurer Cecil left them unpaid.

A letter from Utrecht to Lord Burghley, dated 2 October 1587, mentions "Mr Morley" as one of his messengers in a journey to Northumberland (49). The elder statesman must have been well satisfied with the poet's speed and silence in running errands, for we find "Mr Marlin" acting as messenger for the English ambassador in Paris when Sir Edward Stafford accompanied the King of Navarre during his battles in 1591-92.

Robert Greene observed Kit Marlowe riding the literary tide of the time and amused his own admirers by turning green with envy. For a while he quit writing love stories and scribbled instead *Euphues his Censure to Philautus* (licensed for printing on 18 September 1587) aiming to win a reward for it from Essex with a dulcet dedication, and amaze his readers with "the exquisite portraiture of a perfect martialist", which he "interlaced with diverse delightful tragedies".

In November the Admiral's players had an accident that shed real blood by the stage they had dripped with scarlet for the Second Part of *Tamburlaine*. They were performing the first scene of Act 5, where the Governor of Babylon is hung in chains on a wall to be shot at by the warlord's men. With one of their borrowed calivers an actor's hands swerved, discharging the bullet not at his fellow-tragedian but a child in the audience. The shot killed the infant, and a woman big with pregnancy nearby died from the blast, and one man was hurt in the head (50). These disasters provided fuel for Puritan sermons against the stage, yet hardly lessened the London demand for plays like *Tamburlaine*.

The unknown author of *The Troublesome Reign of King John* invited his audience to behold the exploits of his hero Falconbridge with the same gusty attention they gave Marlowe's idol and idolater:

> You that with friendly grace of smoothed brow
> Have entertain'd the Scythian Tamburlaine,
> And given applause unto an infidel:
> Vouchsafe to welcome (with like courtesy)
> A warlike Christian and your countryman.

George Peele anticipated the decline of Marlowe's play from popularity, reminding his listeners that the world's mightiest conquerors have ended content with a few feet of earth:

> Tamburlaine, triumph not, for thou must die,
> As Philip did, Caesar, and Caesar's peers.

The memory of the Scythian shepherd died hard. It is questionable whether anyone who had ever seen Ned Alleyn mounted on his chariot, drawn by harnesses & kings, could forget his music and imagery. Sir Walter Ralegh apparerently had Marlowe's magic in mind when he wrote his *History of the World* decades later, portraying God as "the author of all our tragedies", Who "hath written out for us and appointed us all the parts we are to play". Spellbound by this Genevan conviction, Ralegh declared that God assigned the sultan Bajazet "to play the Grand Signior of the Turks in the morning and in the same day the footstool of Tamerlane". The Tartar's name almost became proverbial in England, and when the humble historian John Stow searched for a simile to glorify Sir Francis Drake, he exulted the great pirate was "as famous in Europe and America as Tamburlaine in Asia and Africa" (50). Sheer guesswork leads me to imagine that the play which the Admiral's company performed on 29 December 1587, for the Court at Richmond, was the tragedy of *Tamburlaine*.

The contrast that Maliverny Catlyn had observed in London at the beginning of 1587, between the frivolity and fat of the players and the hunger of the city paupers increased in bitterness at the end of the year. English soldiers followed Leycester home, and came begging for bread at the gates of Greenwich Palace. The royal guards drove them away as vagabonds, threatening them with the stocks. Even the multifariously useful Robert Poley suffered from unemployment. He wrote to Leycester pleading for work at home or abroad, evidently in vain. He visited Thomas Walsingham's house in Seething Lane, a short distance from the Tower, hoping for a renewal of "secret recourse to Mr Secretary", but Sir Francis had no occasion to use him: "all to lost labour." (52). Yet the industries of the nation were busy as could be getting ready for the "Invincible Armada" that the Spanish autocrat was manning his long-schemed invasion of England. On 9 October Burghley laid before the Privy Council his plan for defence by sea against Philip, and measures for internal defence against the Catholic recusants who might rise to welcome the Spanish fleet. On 27 November Ralegh, Drake and other military leaders held a council to determine their means of resisting the Spanish invasion. Elizabeth however felt her kingdom too poor to encounter the might of Madrid, soaring as it seemed on wings of American silver. She continued to talk of a pacific mission to Madrid.

Early in January 1588 the Council discussed her Majesty's hopes of placating King Philip. Leycester boldly opposed her plan, and so spoiled her enjoyment of a play, as Antonio de Vega informed his master in Madrid. "At 11 o'clock at night," he wrote (on 9 January), "after the Queen had heard a comedy, she flew into a passion with the Earl of Leycester, who was present, and told him that it behooved her at any cost to be friendly with the King of Spain. 'Because,' she said, 'I see that he has great preparations made on all sides. My ships have left to put to sea, and any if evil fortune should befall them, all would be lost, for I shall have lost the walls of my realm.' " Earl Robert strove to calm her by cheering talk about Drake; she replied that all Drake did was annoy the enemy (53).

We cannot help wondering what comedy it was that left her imperial brain a prey to such gnawing thoughts. There is no record of a Court play between 6 January, when the Queen's men acted for her, and 2 February, when the Children of St Paul's performed. I imagine that it was the former who left her in bad humour, and that the play was Robert Greene's *Comical History of Alphonsus, King of Aragon*. This piece appears to be an unhappy effort to equal the success of *Tamburlaine* with straining imitation of its oratory. "Mighty Tamburlaine" is mentioned in it with poorly concealed envy, and Greene let the world see that his heart was not in the work:

> And this my hand, which used for to pen
> The praise of love, and Cupid's peerless power,
> Will now begin to treat of bloody Mars …

Tom Nashe may have had this failure in his mind's eye when he wrote that Greene was the "chief agent" for the Queen's company, composing more plays for them than four other authors: "how well I will not say" (54).

Greene plainly voiced his jealousy of Marlowe's splendour in the preface to his novel *Perimedes the Blacksmith* (licensed in March 1588). He complained about a satirical treatment of his motto, taken from Horace, *Omne tulit punctum qui miscuit utile dulci* — All points (of praise) he wins who mingles the useful and the sweet. His grievance runs thus: "lately two Gentlemen Poets made two mad men of Rome (meaning two clowns of London) beat it out of their paper bucklers (punning on points): and had it in derision, for that I could not make my verses jet upon the stage in tragical buskins, every word filling the mouth like the fa-burden of Bow-bell, daring God out of heaven with that Atheist Tamburlan, or blaspheming with the mad priest of the sun" (55). This reference to the Second Part of Marlowe's tragedy is the first time the charge of atheism was flung at him in print. Greene left no doubt as to the man he accused, pretending a rage of religion against writers who "wantonly set out such impious instances of intolerable poetry, such mad and scoffing poets that have prophetical spirits as bred of Merlin's race." The pun on Marlowe's name — contemporaries often pronounced it Marlin — is unmistakable. The word atheist in those days covered a multitude of theological opinions. A court hurled it at Francis Wright, alias Kit of Wymondham, who was burnt alive at Norwich on 14 January 1588, for "judaising" ideas, harping tirelessly on the pure unity of God and the humanity of Jesus called Christ. Judging from the testimony of Marlowe's plays, critics maintain his own religious beliefs were like Wright's, unorthodox — in peril of Elizabeth's blazing stakes if not the Almighty's — but certainly not atheist.

The phrase "the mad priest of the sun" is generally taken to be an allusion to the lost tragedy *The Life and Death of Heliogabalus* (registered for the press in 1594). One of Marlowe's learned friends composed it of course; my guess is Thomas Watson, because he had the Latin and Greek lore to write better about the epicene emperor than any of the other University-trained artists of the period working along Senecan lines. Greene scorned both scholars: "If there be any in England that set the end of scholarism in an English blank-verse I think either it is a humour of a novice that tickles them with self-love, or too much frequenting the hot-house (to use the German proverb) hath sweat out all the greatest part of their wits" (56). Greene's suggestion will have to be viewed literally: his points about the novice Marlowe's narcissism and Watson's wanderings out of wedlock among the non-nuns of Shoreditch and the Bankside smite their marks.

IV

When Green inscribed his attack on Marlowe's prophetic soul, the greater dramatist was presumably absorbed in the problems of his tragical history of *Doctor Faustus*, which German erudition has conjectured he wrote in the winter of 1587-88 (57).

The scene of the dukedom of Vanholt is dated in January, and this seems to me a likely time for the writing of this spirit-frosting play. I find a reference to the triumph of the drama in Richard Bancroft's sermon delivered at Paul's Cross on 9 February 1588, whose text the clergyman took from the First Epistle of John: "Beloved, believe not every spirit, but try the spirits whether they are of God" (4.1). Bancroft's rhetoric, primarily darted against Puritan antagonists, ventured once to allude to ancient lewdness. The Devil, said he, might come to tempt the amoured in purity "in the shape of Helena of Greece". I would venture to suggest that the play the Admiral's troupe enacted for the Queen and her Court at Whitehall on 11 February 1588, was the mint version of *Doctor Faustus*.

A year later, on 28 February 1589, the "Ballad of the life and death of Doctor Faustus the great Conjuror" entered the Stationers Register, done, I guess, by some enchanted minstrel-hack who had witnessed the play.

Its primary source is known to be the *Historia von D. Johann Fausten* published at Frankfort in 1587. The publisher said that the legend had lately been sent to him from Speyer, in the Rhineland Palatinate, the home country of Elizabeth's ducal mercenary Casimir. Marlowe might have learnt the story there while travelling on an errand for the Privy Council. They were certainly desirous, at the close of 1587, to get information on the little war the valiant Martin Schenck was conducting against Catholic strongholds on the Rhine. He captured the city of Bonn near the end of the year, and forced the lord of Parma to dispatch an army under the Prince of Chimay to recover it. It is possible that Marlowe had seen "the stately city of Trier" which he mentions in the drama. But his knowledge of German geography was curiously weak for a poet who had exhibited a loving accuracy in maps while composing his *Tamburlaine*. His protagonist Faustus dreams of making the Rhine flow around Wittenberg, the University town on the Elbe. This confusion of the Elbe and the Rhine may have been induced by a surfeit of Rhenish wine in the cellar tavern of the Steelyard, the German emporium in London.

If the poet did not obtain his material in the fatherland of his hero, then he must have read it with the help of his friends among the book-sellers close to Paul's Cathedral. The only extant translation of the German source in English is P. F.'s *History of the Damnable Life and Deserved Death of Doctor John Faustus*, published by Edward White in his shop at the "little north door" of the Cathedral, in December 1592. The publication of this pamphlet was delayed, I believe, to let White's friends, the players make their full purses from the tale on the stage.

At all events, the climate of Marlowe's *Faustus*, even in its present mutilated form, is richly suggestive of the Low Countries and their war as well as of German folklore. At one moment indeed the protagonist talks like a Dutch patriot. In the opening scene he speaks of compelling devils by his magic to "tell the secrets of all foreign kings" -- a natural idea for a dramatist in secret service. Then he thinks of national defence: he will have the hellions wall his country with brass. Suddenly the Doctor's devils are changed from defenders of Germany to financiers for the Netherlands:

I'll levy soldiers with the coin they bring
And chase the Prince of Parma from our land.

In the next instant Faustus reveals the Tamburlaine in his soul, or the Machiavellian in Marlowe's. He dreams of prevailing as "sole king of all our provinces." As monarch of the Dutch he would be a king of mechanics. Marlowe remembers the gunpowder ships that the engineer Gianibelli of Mantua had floated against Parma's pontoons to Antwerp in April 1585. He may have heard how the Flemings swore "that invisible demons had been summoned to plan and perfect this fatal and preterhuman work", the Prince's boat-bridge (58). The demons of Faustus were bound to surpass those of Parma or Gianibelli:

> Yea, stranger engines for the brunt of war
> Than was the fiery keel of Antwerp's bridge,
> I'll make my servile spirits to invent.

Marlowe may actually have met the inventor of the fiery keel, since Gianibelli belonged to the engineers serving the Queen at the time when I imagine *Faustus* was composed. The ingenious Mantuan worked under the direction of her Council constructing defences on the Thames to bear the brunt of Spanish invaders.

The main action of Marlowe's tragedy swings between poles of divine and devilish conflict for the soul of "the studious artisan", into whose creation Marlowe poured so much of himself. The lusts and fantasies of Faustus are obviously Marlowe's lusts and fantasies, as we can see from the instant the protagonist is introduced: "his parents base of stock", his youth "excelling all whose sweet delight disputes/ In heavenly matters of theology". In the figure of the hero, who brags how he "with concise syllogisms/ Gravel'd the pastors", who was "wont to make our schools ring with Sic probo" (So I prove), we plainly recognise the young logician whom Thomas Kyd later described as always glad to "strive in argument to frustrate and confute what hath been spoke or writ by prophets and such holy men" (59). And it is the shoemaker's lad from Canterbury whose fancy dwells fondly on the wish that he could "fill the public schools with silk,/ Wherewith the students shall be bravely clad".

To realise such dreams he would have ventured a bargain for his soul with Lucifer, if the Devil had come to his poetic conjuring, as he was said to have done once when Doctor Faustus invoked him on the stage. This freethinker Christopher took conceptions of the Fiend more seriously than the learned and merry old gentleman whom Burghley's son Robert met in Flanders in March 1588. The old man lived in the shadow of the English guns at Ostend but told young Cecil he was "as little in fear of the garrison of Ostend as he was of the Turk or the Devil" (60).

Young Cecil had been sent by his father with the commissioners of the Privy Council dispatched to Ostend in February 1588 to discuss terms of peace with Philip's commander-in-chief. "So it came about that at the very moment that Howard and Drake were pouring their broadsides into the Spanish Armada in the Channel ... [Sir James] Crofts was writing home to Burghley that he felt convinced of Philip's sincere desire for peace" (61). Young Cecil did not find the meeting with Parma's diplomats entirely valueless. His father's son laid the foundation at Ostend of the peace treaty he ultimately made with Spain when Elizabeth and her bravest courtiers were quiet in their graves. They died ignorant of the esteem in which Robert Cecil was held at the summit of the Spanish empire. What shall it profit a man if he gain the whole world and lose his own soul?

The author of *Faustus* had experimented with such an exchange in imagination in his *Tamburlaine* to more vivid purpose than can be seen in this tragedy of magic wantonly wasted. The best his new hero acquired was the love of Helen of Troy, a ghost. All his raptures over the riches and power to be gotten on our globe end in bare words. At the outset of his magic he wished to be served as "Indian Moors obey their Spanish lords", meaning the "white Moors" whom Sir Walter Ralegh had seen in America. Ralegh captured two specimens for the curiosity of the Court. The idea of employing devils for armaments did not fascinate the dramatist as intensely as the thought of wealth. When his protagonist thinks of turning physician, his goal is to "heap up gold". The first enterprise he conceives for his magic spirits is to "fly to India for gold". The obsession of money gripped Marlowe at this time almost to the verge of monomania; his genius was already on its road to *The Jew of Malta*. Faustus keeps returning to the topic when he dreams of supernatural forces at his command:

> From Venice shall they drag huge argosies,
> And from America the golden fleece
> That yearly stuffs old Philip's treasury.

In more modest temper he visions a monopoly of the grand market city of Emden in East Friesland: "The signiory of Emden shall be mine." But he squanders his energy instead on some childish legerdemain, practical jokes (particularly at the expense of the Pope), and the love affair with the phantom Helen. His book-braced knowledge left him boyishly unable to deal with the root-riddles of his tragedy. So he ended it with the effort of his hero to clutch the sky, where he sees the blood of Christ streaming (to the immense admiration of Edith Sitwell) — without one drop of pity for the blind brute except what a charitable public might supply, before Faustus plunges to the hell to which he purchased admission.

Gabriel Harvey may have witnessed a performance of *Faustus* that was more spectacular than the play we now possess. In a marginal note to Richard Morysine's translation of the *Strategematicon* by Frontinus, which the pedant bought in 1578 and scribbled notes in until 1590, he pondered: "If Doctor Faustus could rear castles and arm devils at pleasure, what wonderful and monstrous exploits might be achieved by such terrible means" (62). This reflection offers testimony of some reliability in John Wright's edition of the tragedy (1616), which contains an episode of soldiers ambushing the magician and being routed by an apparition of devils with drum, ensign and arms. Perhaps Harvey saw a wizardry of stagecraft where we today can hear only the words, "erecting that enchanted castle in the air".

The popular favour which the Admiral's men won with *Doctor Faustus*, the Queen's men strove to rival with *Friar Bacon* by Robert

Greene. This comedy neatly dovetailed a pastoral romance in Greene's happiest manner with a patriotic fantasy of the defeat of German magic by English art. The heroine Margaret, a rustic beauty, compares herself to Helen of Troy, and mocks Marlowe's famous verse by suggesting that she might set the county of Suffolk afire with her face (scene 10). The date of *Friar Bacon*'s first appearance seems to be indicated by at least three facts. Greene named his German wizard after Jacques Vandermast, a foreigner imprisoned in the Tower of London in 1585 and still there in the summer of 1588 (63). Greene set the time for Harleston Fair in the play on Friday 25 July (scene 1), St James's day, which fell on a Friday in 1589. And the Marlovian strains the rival poet produced for his Friar's resolution to ring the kingdom with a wall of brass sounds like a bid for plaudits after the havoc suffered by the Spanish Armada:

> I will strengthen England by my skill,
> That if ten Caesars lived and reigned in Rome,
> With all the legions Europe doth contain,
> They should not touch a grass of English ground.

In July 1588 the dread navy arrived at last, with the Pope's benediction. Cardinal William Allen from Rheims laboured to convince the English people that Armada was the bearer of an evangel of freedom from Tudor tyranny. His Admonition to the Nobility and People of England and Ireland, concerning the present wars for the execution of his Holiness' sentence, by the high and mighty King Catholic of Spain, did not help Philip much. The latter's big "Invincible" vessels were no match for the swift little English ships. Driven past Calais by blazing boats, the Spanish fleet (shouting "Antwerp fireships!") went on 29 July to encounter Admiral Howard's sea-dogs and met unforgettable disaster. The survivors fled round Scotland and Ireland, through storms of a fury they had never felt, and by September a remnant of the Armada reached home ports. The disconsolate Parma broke up the camp at Dunkirk where he had kept regiments waiting for Philip's fleet to clear a way to the English coast. Through the entire fight the Prince pursued with customary solemnity the comedy of his Ostend conversations about peace with Elizabeth's commissioners.

On 4 September the Earl of Leycester died, worn out by his exertions as commander-in-chief of the land forces mobilised to meet the Spaniards. The day before, the jester Richard Tarlton was buried. Doubtless her Majesty missed both of them deplorably when she walked on 24 November in her thanksgiving procession to St Paul's. However, she consoled herself by sending auditors to scrutinise the property Leycester left and determine exactly what funds he was fancied to owe the Crown.

It would be both dramatically and psychologically illuminating to have Marlowe's impressions of the English victory. If the fleeting images and references to the naval battling of Spaniards in *The Jew of Malta* were designed to refresh memories of Admiral Howard's triumph, they yield extremely little insight into the poet's ideas of the Armada and its wreck. The Spanish vice-admiral in the tragedy, Martin del Bosco, vividly describes a battle with Turks, and canvas-climbers in the playhouse who had taken part in the Channel duels would have warmly appreciated Marlowe's portrayal. But we find no personal or political remarks in the description of the other allusions to Spanish war at sea. Naming Del Bosco's ship "The Flying Dragon" may have denoted an irony for admirers of Drake.

V

The central problem in *The Jew of Malta* is one of money. The Turks demand tribute from the Maltese, but the rulers of the island protest that they are too poor to pay, "by reason of the wars, that robb'd our store". On the Jewish population of Malta is inflicted the task of raising the complete sum required, and by means of this injustice the poet is able to hurl another dart at Christianity at the same time that he subjects Judaism to the same vitriol that he applied to Islam in *Tamburlaine*. After the money is collected, the Spanish vice-admiral persuades the Maltese to keep it, promising protection against the Turks from his master, the "Catholic King", who claims title to the island. The protection fails to arrive, and Calymath, the Turkish commander, taunts the Christians for trusting in "haughty Spain". Meanwhile Barabas, "The Jew of Malta", plots the trapping of the Turks so that he can recover his original status among the Maltese, but they drop him into his own trap, imprison Calymath, and close the play with the warning to all the island's enemies:

> So will we guard us now,
> As sooner shall they drink the ocean dry,
> Than conquer Malta, or endanger us.

Triumphantly the Christians march away, with choral thanksgiving: "Neither to Fate nor Fortune, but to Heaven." There is of course no hint in the tragedy that Maltese merchants might have taken advantage of the war to trade clandestinely with the Turks, as Lord Willoughby, the English general who took Leycester's place in the Low Countries, complained the Dutch did. "If I should say truly," he wrote to the Privy Council in October 1588, "they send as much [victuals] to the enemy as to us" (64).

In a 1633 eulogy of this sadly spoiled play, which opens as if it was going to become Marlowe's mightiest, Thomas Heywood declared that *The Jew of Malta* was made by "the best of poets in that age" (65). It did not represent Marlowe at his best.

Midway in the tragedy Marlowe changed his hero to a caricature, and embroidered his plot with patches of wit and purple in mimicry of *The Merchant* (formerly named *The Jew*) *of Venice*, and *Romeo and Juliet*. When Barabas howls "My girl! My gold!" it seems perfectly plain to me that Marlowe merely translated into terser idiom Shakespeare's "My daughter! My ducats!" And Marlowe's verses, "The sweetest flower in Cytherea's field," "But stay, what star shines yonder in the east?" sigh to my ears a poet's tribute to his superior. After the opening soliloquy, Marlowe's blank verse sounds even more impoverished. The weakening of imaginative power the drama displays can be blamed on the progress that the dramatist was manifestly making in his observation of reality. In the person of Barabas he unmasked the infantile character of his early aspiration to power and glory, and pointed out the substantial things behind the emblems of majesty he once revered. "I must confess," the hero remarks, almost with a sigh, "we" (rich Jews) "come not to be kings." Yet for the lack of this uncertain splendour there is a recompense of perhaps greater and more worshipped weight.

> What more may Heaven do for earthly man
> Than thus to pour out plenty in their laps,
> Ripping the bowels of the earth for them,
> Making the seas their servants, and the winds?
> Or who is honour'd now but for his wealth?

The dramatist simply found it beyond his powers to sustain a point of outlook so unwarlike, so alien to Tamburlaine's, or so foreign to the enthusiasm for wisdom, the lust of Faustus, as the pivot vision of the financier. He fabricated his Barabas from records and rumours concerning the famous money master of the Levant, Joseph Nasi whom the Sultan of Turkey appointed Duke of the Greek island Naxos. Joseph Nasi possessed the riches, and consanguine and synagogue relations, which made unadorned fact of Barabas's boast:

> In Florence, Venice, Antwerp, London, Sevill,
> Frankford, Lubeck, Mosco and where not
> Have I debts lying; and in most of these
> Great sums of money lying in the bancho.

The Jewish Duke of Naxos dealt luxuriantly, exactly like Marlowe's protagonist, in "the wines of Greece", and sailed an "argosy from Alexandria,/ Laden with spice and silks". Fragments of Spanish decorated his speech too; but he was born in Portugal and baptised João Miguez, by parents who cunningly concealed from their Catholic world the obstinacy of their fidelity to the Judaic creed. In emulation of his rise to the dukedom of Naxos, Marlowe made his Jew governor of Malta in the service of the Sultan and "Selim Calymath, son to the Grand Seignior". What the poet lacked that Joseph Nasi had abundant in his sixty years was a voluptuous delight in material things, caring more for works of exotic value, talent and loveliness than for the excrementlike minerals that represented their prices, yet enjoying the mathematics that made finance a finer game than Persian chess. The latter, with its supreme purpose of killing a king (checkmate is English for Shahmat) would have appealed to Kit Marlowe more keenly than to Joseph Nasi, a man of strong family affection, and of loyalty to the Sultan. Kit Marlowe could not bring himself to stoop from his perch of Platonic delusions of spirituality to the passionate interest of many Jews in the world's best wines, nonpareil textiles and precious stones, paintings, manuscripts. The poet could apprehend Jewish ambition, the well veiled delight in moving potentates like pawns, especially in moving Mahometans to the destruction of Christian arrogance. But his idealism spurned the subtlety of Hebrew brains dreaming of a divine kingdom amid base earth. He preferred to embrace in fantasy the brutality of Asiatic genocides.

Nevertheless, *The Jew of Malta* easily became the most popular of his plays. It appears to have equalled *The Spanish Tragedy* in the hearts of his countrymen. Scholars conjecture that the poor play attained this lustre on account of the brilliance of Edward Alleyn in the title role. Alleyn shone more spectacularly and eloquently in *Tamburlaine the Great*. The fascination he exerted in the part of Barabas, I believe, came from the peculiar spell unconsciously radiated by Jews to the imagination of English, maybe all European, Christians, who found themselves utterly mystified by the survival of Jewish vivacity, the skill of Jews in the mysteries of commerce, medicine and other black and white arts. The monster that Barabas turns into at the ruinous end of Marlowe's play is a pale reflection of the Prince of Hell that Christians almost universally conceived as the paramount Jew under the sun.

I think it is a note of personal sarcasm, rueful laughter from the poet's heart, that we hear in Ithamore's declaration of independence: "I scorn to write a line under a hundred crowns." The villain

Pilia-Borza tells him, "You'd make a rich poet, sir". Indeed, Ithamore is temporarily enriched by Marlowe making him a mouthpiece for his own lyric gift.

The tragedy seems to have been written by the summer of 1589. The mockery of Machiavelli which opens the play announces, "now the Guise is dead". This refers to the murder of Henri Balafré (Scarface), Duke of Guise, towards the end of December 1588. The event gave English Protestants hopes of the downfall of the Catholic League he led. The crime was committed to oblige King Henri III, who yearned to prove himself the sole master of France, not a puppet of the League. A week later the real brains of French royalty were stilled: Henri's mother, Catherine de'Medici, died. Guise's brother, the Duke of Mayenne, rallied the League for renewal of the war with Navarre, but the last of the Valois kings was anxious for conclusion of civil war. He negotiated with Navarre for a treaty, and drew down on his lonesome head the wrath of Philip and the Pope. "The state of the world is marvellously changed," Burghley confided to the Earl of Shrewsbury in May 1589, "when we true Englishmen have cause for our own quietness to wish good success to a French king" (66).

No Jesuit logic nor hortatory fire could stop Henri III from compromising with the Huguenots. In July the young monk Jacques Clement thrust his dagger into the King's bowels, and the Valois dynasty perished under the curses of the Church it had sacrificed incalculable wealth and blood for. Pope Sixtus V had only twelve months more to sway his monarchy, and rivalry for his tiara burnt fiercely among the Cardinals. William Allen hoped that Philip would lean the strength of Spain to his election, in view of the great services he had rendered the Catholic King. The discussion of the next occupant of the Vatican throne appears to have an echo in the Prologue to Marlowe's *The Jew of Malta*, where Machiavel sneers,

> Though some speak openly against my books,
> Yet will they read me, and thereby attain
> To Peter's chair; and, when they cast me off,

Are poison'd by my climbing followers.

Marlowe could have written this with the Huguenot tract, *The Restorer of the French Estate* (1589) before his eyes. It fumed against the Popes in a similar fashion: "most of them climbed up to the Holy See by lies, hypocrisy, guiles and deceit, by money, arms, massacres, poisonings, and magical arts."

Another booklet of 1589, Paul Ive's translation of the *Instructions for the Wars* by Jean du Bellay, probably supplied our playwright with his device for secretly admitting the Turks to Malta by means of a sewer or cave. When he wrote the scene, he might have remembered the siege of Sluys in July 1587, when the Spaniards mined their way to extensive wine vaults under the town, and fought with the English defenders there for eight days, hand to hand underground, with pike, pistol and knife.

Robert Greene did not attempt to compete with Marlowe's Maltese tragedy. A manuscript play at Alnwick Castle, the Northumberland library, seems to be a sequel to his *Friar Bacon*. It is entitled *The Wasp* but has been printed (by W. L. Renwick in 1936) under the name John of Bordeaux. It presents the magician Bacon at the German emperor's court stirring up militancy against the Sultan Amurath and his Ottoman armies. In January 1589 Greene delivered to the press *The Spanish Masquerado*, "Wherein under a pleasant device is discovered effectually, in certain brief sentences and mottos, the pride and insolency of the Spanish estate: with the disgrace conceived by their loss, and the dismayed confusion of their troubled thoughts." Here he attacked professional warfare as deadly to every commonwealth: "The Soldiers eat all." In this pamphlet Greene commenced a new approach to his readers: "lest I might be thought to tie myself wholly to amorous conceits, I have ventured to discover my conscience in Religion." To the end of his literary days he remained a preacher out of uniform, but more fervent than most of the Homilies.

In the season when, by our reckoning, *The Jew of Malta* was composed, English nerves were cheerily vibrated by the expedition of

Sir Francis Drake and Sir John Norris to carry war to the shores of Spain. George Peele manufactured "A Farewell" to their troops. He summoned them to say goodbye to the theatres and proud tragedians, and thus got an opportunity to advertise a few of his current scriptures for the stage, as well as "mighty Tamburlaine". According to Peele, the purpose of the expedition was "To propagate religious piety ... deface the pride of Antichrist,/ And pull his paper walls and Popery down". He identified the Papacy with avarice:

A famous enterprise for England's strength,
To steel your swords on Avarice' triple crown.

Norris and Drake failed to satisfy the expectations of their promotors and well-wishers. Disappointment vented its spleen in the autumn campaign launched by the Queen in France, when Lord Willoughby and Sir Roger Williams came with money, troops and supplies to join the King of Navarre in his battles for the crown against the house of Guise and their candidate Charles de Bourbon. To this war effort Marlowe's own contribution appears to have been *The Massacre at Paris*.

For the first six scenes of this hasty tragedy he apparently went for material to François Hotman's *De Furoribus Gallicis* (1573). For the rest he scoured contemporary Protestant pamphlets, such as *La Vie et Faits Notables de Henry de Valois* (1589), Hurault's *Anti-Sixtus* (published in London 1590), and cursory pamphlets in like vein. As propaganda Marlowe's work suffered from all the faults of an artist trying to paint human nature in shades of black or blank-white. His protagonist, the Duke of Guise, is drawn without a single redeeming trait. Not only is one of the most courageous warriors of the age defaced; history is distorted in order to draw his villainy darker. Marlowe converted him to a mere agent of Madrid: "Philip and Parma, I am slain for you!" Guise is blamed for bringing the English priests to the seminary at Rheims "To hatch forth treason 'gainst their natural queen." He is accused of inspiring "the King of Spain's huge fleet/ To threaten England"! In the author's zeal for polemic against the Guises and their Holy League he finds phrases of sympathy for the Puritans who despised his art. True, the sympathy is squeezed up only by the horrors which the Huguenots — whom he terms Puritans — endured in the slaughter of St Bartholomew's eve, a massacre depicted by Marlowe with obvious sadistic delight. Yet his individual feeling for their cause emerges clearly in the line spoken by Anjou when he stabs the Protestant philosopher Peter Ramus, whose dialectic revolt against scholastic authority had entertained Marlowe at Cambridge.

"Ne'er was there collier's son so full of pride," says Anjou.

Substitute cobbler for collier and you have one of the most familiar sneers of London intellectuals, gentry envious of the genius from Canterbury. It was a commonplace of orthodoxy, Anglican as well as Catholic, to spill contempt on heretics because of their trades. "None are schismatics," the exile Nicholas Sanders declaimed in writing about the English commons, "except those who have sedentary occupations, as weavers and shoemakers, and some idle people about the Court" (67). Marlowe thirsted for revenge on the aristocrats and their lackey-writers who laughed at his father's industry and the liberties of religious thought associated with its sit-and-tarry life and toil. In *The Massacre at Paris* he voiced his craving to "keenly slice the Catholics"! It would not surprise us to learn that he enjoyed the martyrdom of the two Romanist priests who were hanged in August 1588, at Holywell Priory, across the Shoreditch road from the Theatre. Marlowe's residence was a short walk southward in Norton Folgate.

Poor art or not, *The Massacre* held the stage for several years, thrilling thousands with its clarion for war against the triple terror of the French League, the Spanish autocracy, and the Vatican. When the poet made the bloodthirsty Guise exclaim,

The Pope will sell his triple crown,
Ay, and the Catholic Philip, King of Spain,

Ere I shall want, will cause his Indians
To rip the golden bowels of America.

he actually appealed for Elizabeth to hazard her treasury, replete
with plunder from the Spanish galleons of Peru and Mexico, for the
sake of Protestant Europe. The play was propaganda for a military
alliance between England and Huguenot France. In the interest of
this alliance Marlowe put into the lips of Henry of Navarre a bless-
ing for the Queen of England "for hating Papistry". The real hero
of the tragedy is this founder of the Bourbon dynasty, represented
as a champion in the struggle with the Roman Church at the very
time when he contemplated rejecting the Huguenots to purchase
the Pope's endorsement of his claim to the French crown. Marlowe
embarrassed the Bourbon king by the laudation poured for him in
the play. In July 1602, when Sir Ralph Winwood objected to his
Majesty about a Parisian play that had featured Queen Elizabeth
among its characters, Henry IV let the Englishman feel his displeasure because "the death of the Duke of Guise hath been played at
London ... the Massacre of St Bartholomew hath been publicly
acted, and this King represented upon the stage" (68). Henry was
not unwilling to be imitated in buskins as a hero at war with Spain.
But the dramatist vexed him by making his stage-image say,

Spain is the council-chamber of the Pope,
Spain is the place where he makes peace or war.

Navarre was eager for concerted action with England; the poet
however wished that he would unite forces with the Queen "to beat
the papal monarch from our lands". On the contrary, the King believed, Paris was worth a mass, and the unity of France wisely purchased with genuflexion to the Pope. For him the war with Philip
was a dynastic and commercial affair, best fought without question
of the soldiers' creeds. He wanted to substitute nationalism for the
theological cement that had warmly held his armies together in his
Calvinist years. Elizabeth nourished a like desire. One doubts

whether she relished the praise of her that Marlowe put on his Na-varre's tongue, vowing eternal love

to the Queen of England specially
Whom God bless'd for hating Papistry.

Plays like *The Massacre at Paris* were calculated to please firebrands against Spain and the Papacy like the Earl of Essex. Earlier in the year 1589 Essex had outraged her Majesty by quitting the Court without her consent to go with Norris and Drake to ravage the coast of Portugal. Hardly had she forgiven him for this when he began begging her for permission to risk his handsome neck in the French war.

In this year, by the way, we find the shadowy Nicholas Skeres getting pay from the government for carrying mail between Essex and the Court (69). I wonder if Skeres haunted the corner of the poet's eye when he created the figure of Pilia-Borza in *The Jew of Malta*? At the start of Act 3 he shows up, bragging of his burglaries, skulking "the back lanes". In the fourth act we hear his individual voice, outraged "that such a base slave as he should be saluted by such a tall man as I am, from such a beautiful dame as you". "And so I left him, being driven to a non-plus at the critical aspect of my terrible countenance." But Marlowe saw no need to define the fate of Pilia-Borza in his final act.

A more charming but hardly less discreet member of the Earl's circle was the Huguenot refugee, François Hotman's son Jean, who had served Leycester and after his death became one of the most devoted members of the Essex faction at Court. The Earl trusted Jean Hotman with messages to Scotland bidding for the benevo-lence of King James. In the fall of 1589 Essex's sister, Lady Pene-lope Rich, wrote to Hotman about their progress in the courtship of the Stuart dynasty, and incidentally alluded to the energy of the poet Henry Constable for their cause (70).

VI

In September 1589 our impulsive dramatist finally got into trouble with the law. On Thursday the 18th, in Hog Lane, near Norton Folgate, where he lived, he encountered a ruffian named William Bradley, who had a grudge against him. The earliest record of the quarrel extant is from the summer of 1589, when William Bradley asked the lawcourts for security of peace against Hugo Swift, John Allen, and Thomas Watson, whose wife's maiden name was Anne Swift. The Sheriff of Middlesex received instruction to summon the three men to Westminster Hall on 25 November. As Watson's close friend, Kit Marlowe would have looked just as repulsive in the eyes of Bradley, and may have already indicated menace to the seeker of security. Their swords were endeavouring to end it when Marlowe's neighbour Thomas Watson came on the scene. Bradley shouted to the newcomer, whose sword, Watson afterward contended, was drawn to part the duellists, "Art thou now come? Then I will have a bout with thee". The bout concluded with Watson's blade in his breast. Bradley was killed as a crowd gathered to break up the fray. It occurred near the Curtain, but the coroner's inquest did not report any witnesses from the playhouse. We do not know if Robert Poley, a resident in Shoreditch close to both poets' homes, saw the constable take them to Newgate prison, where they claimed self-defence.

On 1 October Marlowe was released, after his bail had been paid by a lawyer, Richard Kitchen, and Humphrey Rowland, a maker of lantern horn. Rowland dwelt in East Smithfield and had two foreigners working for him, John Carpenter and John Cornelis of Antwerp, men recorded as belonging to no church. The horner was a kinsman, perhaps the son, of John Rowland, another "stranger", listed in 1544 as an inhabitant of East Smithfield. How Marlowe made the acquaintance of Rowland and Kitchen is unknown. He may have met Kitchen at the Rose theatre, for the lawyer sometimes took part in the enterprises of Philip Henslowe, Ned Alleyn's father -in-law. Rowland enjoyed the good-will of Lord Burghley himself, and his Lordship possibly encouraged the horner to help the playwright, remembering Marlowe's diligence for the Privy Council. At any rate, Marlowe was cleared of responsibility for Bradley's death on 3 December, when he and Watson came before the Old Bailey justices, one of whom was Sir Roger Manwood, a Kentishman whose epitaph Marlowe composed in elegant Latin. Watson went back to Newgate jail to wait for her Majesty's long delayed pardon (71).

While making the acquaintance of Newgate's more or less dramatic personalities Marlowe's anarchist convictions lost some of the impartial veneer. He discovered that he had "as good right to coin as the Queen of England". John Poole, a fellow prisoner, gave him exciting glimpses into his own craft of mixing metals so that they resembled the royal currency. The poet evidently departed from the prison with Midas epiphanies parading in his head. He wanted to enlist as a disciple of Poole and, "with the help of a cunning stamp maker, to coin French crowns, pistolets and English shillings". The scheme did not advance beyond the visionary stage. The sole use that Marlowe seems to have made of his first lessons in Poole's alchemy is the production of one metaphor in his love-poem "Hero and Leander": "Base bullion for the stamp's sake we allow" (72).

Want of money must have hurt the poet's feelings severely in the fall of 1589, particularly after 6 November, when the Lord Mayor of London acted on complaints from the Master of the Queen's Revels and stopped all performances of the Admiral's company. Robert Greene's romance *Menaphon*, registered on 23 August, with its prefatory epistle by Thomas Nashe, would only have made him laugh if its polemic had been confined to Nashe's joke about "kill-cow conceits and the spacious volubilities of a drumming decasyllabon" (73). But Greene's venom against Marlowe exacted a drastic answer that Marlowe never delivered, which I take to be evidence that the latter's sadism was mainly imaginary, and indeed internally oriented, so that it changed into masochism. Kit's nerves would not have vibrated painfully at Greene's allusion to his first theatrical triumph: "I read that mighty Tamburlaine, after his wife Zenocrate (the world's fair eye) past out of the Theatre of this mortal life, he chose stigmatical trulls to please his humorous fancy." Marlowe would have laughed over the parody of his verse: "her front curled like to the Erimanthean Boar, and spangled like to the worsted stockings of Saturn, her face like Mars treading upon the milk-white clouds: believe me, shepherd, her eyes were like the fiery torches tilting against the moon ..." (74). Greene could not refrain from making his satire more personal and poisonous.

> Whosoever, Samela, descanted of that love told you a Canterbury tale; some prophetical full mouth that, as he were a Cobler's eldest son, would by the last tell where another's shoe wrings, but his souterly aim was just level, in thinking every look was love, or every fair word a pawn of loyalty.

The mockery of Marlowe's home and upbringing is plain. What is new here is the revelation of Christopher as an innocent, lamblike, believer in his lovability, trusting in the pledges of prostitutes.

This jest is one of those promised by Greene "To the Gentlemen Readers" of his pastoral tale: "if you find dark enigmas or strange concepts," he advises them, "as if Sphinx on the one side and Roscius on the other, were playing the wags [T would] desire you to take a little pains to pry into my imagination" (75). The reference to Roscius deliberately leads us to woolgathering for our eyes; his chief target of ridicule was no actor like the renowned Roman, but the writer whose father had been a Canterbury cobbler. So far as we know, that writer did not retaliate.

Looking about for new sources of income, Marlowe developed certain theatrical powers of his which had lain rather dormant when he worked for the domain of Edward Alleyn and for naive narcissism. He commenced to write plays with more than one outstanding character, with some probing into dark nooks of human nature, even with pity for mortal shortcomings, and blank verses glowing with colourful conflict in dialogue rather than exalted for sheer lyric and soliloquy over the heads of everyday speech.

The first of his efforts in the new vein appears to have been *The Troublesome Reign and Lamentable Death of Edward the Second, King of England,* "with the tragical fall of great Mortimer: As it was sundry times acted in the honorable city of London, by the right honorable the Earl of Pembroke his Servants". This tragedy, according to one scholar at least, cannot have been produced later than 1589 (76). The Earl of Pembroke in the play is treated with particular care and admiration, in a style worthy of his servants. King Edward singles him out to bear the sword of state before his Majesty "in solemn triumphs and in public shows". Marlowe would have us recall how Henry Herbert, the Earl of Pembroke, who patronised his company of actors, rode solemnly through London proclaiming the Scottish Queen a traitor, while the city church bells rang to enforce his words.

Edward the Second contains a few passages that may be taken as expressions of sympathy for the English campaigners in northern France. One of the prime motives of Mortimer's revolt in the play is his anger at the King for letting the Lord Valois overrun Normandy. From the tongue of Lancaster comes a couplet of sorrow over the condition of wounded veterans which gives us a glimpse of the undercurrent of compassion for the downtrodden that flowed (from self-pity?) in Marlowe's soul. The couplet evokes acrid memory of the soldiers whom the Queen's guards had thrust away from Greenwich Palace when they had gathered at the gates to beg food.

Thy garrisons are beaten out of France,
And, lame and poor, lie groaning at thy gates.

Immediately after this couplet, Lancaster laments a rebellion of Ireland which also echoes English imperial perplexities of Marlowe's own day:

The wild Oneil, with swarms of Irish kerns,
Lives uncontroll'd within the English pale ... (Scene 6)

This would have reminded the crowds who saw and heard *Edward the Second* of Sir Walter Ralegh's voyage in mid-August 1589 to crush the Irish kerns and gallosasses. Few however would have believed that Ralegh sailed against his will, as Sir Francis Allen asserted to Anthony Bacon on 17 August: "My Ld of Essex hath chased Ralegh from the Court, and confined him into Ireland." The dashing Essex and his extremely clever counsellor, Anthony Bacon's brother, did not foresee that his Lordship would, in the near future, blunder as though banished to Ireland.

The sad lines about the war veterans I have quoted remind us that Marlowe is said to have had a hand in the anonymous drama *A Larum for London or The Siege of Antwerp*, which makes a touching plea for the maintenance in comfort and affection of the soldier whose occupation is gone. That play contains reminiscences of *Edward the Second*; "silver Rhodope" and "swilling epicures" come directly from Marlowe's history. *The Siege of Antwerp* seems to be written with the Marlovian method as the standard of histrionic art; the hero, Lieutenant Vaughan, called "Stump" because of his lameness, is virtually faultless in his virility. And the play burns with hatred for the avarice and savagery of Spain in the Low Countries. Nevertheless I think Thomas Watson wrote most of the play, because it is pungently thick with reminders of *Jeronimo*, the companion piece of *The Spanish Tragedy*, which I have argued were both the work of Watson (77).

Incidentally, in Robert Greene's little book *Ciceronis Amor: Tullie's Love*, printed in 1589, there are six lines in Latin "Ad Lectorem" complimentary to Greene's pen-play, by Thomas Watson. I consider the verses an attempt of the witty and wily Watson to mollify the pastoral writer's antagonism to Marlowe.

The rage against Romanism that flames through *The Massacre at Paris* flings a few sparks in Marlowe's tragedy of medieval England. He makes his English monarch echo his French king in *The Massacre*, swearing incessant war on the church of Rome. The latter vows that his bloody hands will combat the "antichristian kingdom" until he can tear the Pope's triple crown off and burn the Eternal City:

> I'll fire his crazed buildings, and enforce
> The papal towers to kiss the lowly earth.

Edward II, in nearly identical language, dreams of sweeping Rome's "superstitious taper lights" from her multitude of "antichristian churches", and shouts to the city:

> I'll fire thy crazed buildings, and enforce
> The papal towers to kiss the lowly ground.

Is it possible to believe that the mind of Shake-speare reverberates in this barbarism? He, who shuddered to think of "sweet religion" being abused in "rhapsody of words"? From what we know of Marlowe's intransigent enmity to religious authority, it is reasonable to assume that these verses express what modern psychology calls a repetition compulsion, the twanging of heartstrings which were never able to overcome an infantile fury toward churches that the child of Canterbury transferred to "Papistry", in accordance with the legitimate direction for anticlerical sentiments provided by Elizabethan policy. The monotony of the pattern shows us how profoundly fixed, how inextricably it was webbed in Marlowe's brain. But only Freudian guesswork would dare to trace the obsession from ideological indignation against the "Mother-Church", which to the Canterbury boy denoted the ecclesiastic body persecuted Puritans called "the church that is planted in the blood of her mother" (78) down to the primitive rancour of the infant against his own maternal ruler, whom he wished to believe a dissembler of evil against him; constantly he announced his independence of her, psychoanalysis would say, but refused to search anywhere else for a sunny-natured woman desirous of a home with him. He pretended to have the conviction that no such creature existed, and therefore he would have to make milk for himself miraculously, satisfying the baby-greed his mother had rejected by the sorcery of verbal bliss. You can see the whole structure of the Freudian doctrine of the origin of literature in Dr Edmund Bergler's bitter book *The Writer and*

Psychoanalysis (New York 1950). Since we know absolutely nothing about Marlowe's mothering, analytic psychology must keep reasonably mum about it.

Memories of Canterbury and Kent must have been refreshed and sharpened for the poet by events in the shire during the spring of 1590 in which his friend, the curiously crooked judge Sir Roger Manwood took an active part. Kent, in particular the town of Faversham, was excited this season by feats of two bandits named Curtail and Manwaring, whom Manwood tried to hunt down. It has been plausibly suggested that the case of these two criminals prompted the writing of the anonymous tragedy *Arden of Feversham*. On grounds of style and knowledge of locality *Arden* is ascribed to Marlowe, a judgment for which I submit some testimony of my own. [See Chapter 11–W.H.]

Raphael Holinshed's history of England furnished Marlowe with his material for the tragedy. But the chronicler pictured Black Will, the partner of the murderess Alice Arden, as a stern brave homicide. In the play he shows up a derided braggart. His accomplice George Shakebag is shown as stronger and fiercer. "Two rougher ruffians never lived in Kent" — yet the poet presents them no less at home in London. Will and George, I consider, were made in the image of William Bradley the unlucky duelist, and his companion, George Orrell of the twisted neck, a war veteran mentioned in a state account of the downfall of the Earl of Essex as "a most desperate rakehell as lives". He seems to have been brave rather than thrasonic. I suspect that he is the "notorious coiner" Orrel reported in 1584 as living with his Puritan father-in-law, a Cartwright. In the summer of 1589 Thomas Watson's brother-in-law Hugo Swift petitioned for the law to guard him against George Orrell, *ob metum mortis*. The likeness between Black Will and Will Bradley appears in the law record of the latter's assault on Robert Wood in the autumn of 1589, cudgeling him nearly to death. Wood had condemned Bradley on that day as a bully and worthless fellow (79). Perhaps Marlowe loaded the nickname Black Will with a private joke about the law student Blackwell, who married the daughter of Richard Kitchen, the poet's benefactor, and resided in the lawyer's chamber at Gray's Inn in 1587. The dramatist kept the name of Bradshaw for a minor figure in the *Arden* ferocity, but changed another shady person's name from William Blackburn to Clark, we know not why. Maybe he deemed he had done enough to bury the reputation of William Bradley. Orrell the rakehell, by the way, lived to win honour for his courage in ordeal of duty in Ireland.

There was a poor gentleman named Greene among the conspirators who killed Arden of Feversham. The dramatist went to odd lengths to make the miserable Greene detestable. He changed his name from John to Richard, reminding us at once of Marlowe's antagonist, the pastoral romancer. Robert Greene was well known in London for consorting with malignant persons, notably "Cutting Ball", whose sister Em lived in sin with Robin not long before his agonized death. Richard Greene appears in the tragedy after Alice Arden has pronounced the lines,

> In London many alehouse ruffians keep,
> Which, as I hear, will murder men for gold.

He offers to free her from domestic bondage and Master Arden; he will "hire some cutter for to cut him short". Supposed to be a citizen of Feversham, this Greene is alleged to have known Black Will in the metropolis for twelve years. Yet, like the literary Robin, be is blatantly pious. And he is fond of the fables of Aesop, precisely like Robert Greene, who, in *Never Too Late* and in the *Groatsworth of Wit* (which has been demonstrated the work of Henry Chettle) appears taunting gentlemen of the stage with comparisons of their showmanship with the vanity of Aesop's crow. In *Never Too Late* (published in 1590) Greene threw sarcasms at the great Roman actor Roscius, to whom Ned Alleyn was often compared: "Why, Roscius, art thou proud with Aesop's crow, being pranked with the glory of others' feathers? Of thyself thou canst say nothing; and if the cobbler hath taught thee to say Ave Caesar! disdain not thy tutor because thou pratest in a king's chamber" (80). Roscius of Rome never declaimed for a king, and no cobbler educated him. The jibe simply alludes to Alleyn who rejoiced in performances for the Queen's Revels. His hailing of Caesar echoes to my ear a mysterious passage in the preface by Nashe to Greene's *Menaphon*; warning actors to conduct themselves more modestly: "Yet let subjects, for all their insolence, dedicate a *De profundis* every morning to the preservation of their *Caesar*, lest their increasing indignities return them ere long their juggling to mediocrity, and they bewail in weeping blanks the wane of their monarchy." Nashe appears to have in mind a patron or supervisor on whom the Alleyns, perhaps all the actors of England, were dependent for leadership and light as well as the favour of her Majesty. The play-lord evidently worked as an invisible emperor of drama, choosing to be unnamed and shadow-sheltered. There is no aristocrat of the age whom this description fits better than Edward de Vere, Earl of Oxford, with his annual thousand pounds for secret enterprise.

The play *Arden* is manifestly a labour of haste. It slides from grimness to the brink of gaiety when Black Will goes off with brevity like this: "We have our gold; mistress Alice, adieu; Mosby, farewell, and Michael, farewell too." The poet probably laboured in hot weather; in the second act Black Will declares:

> I tell thee, Greene, the forlorn traveller,
> Whose lips are glued with summer's parching heat,
> Ne'er long'd so much to see a running brook
> As I to finish Arden's tragedy.

None of the extant editions of *Arden* tells us which of the noblemen's companies played it. On the basis of parallels between *Arden* and the plays credited to Thomas Kyd the conjecture has been favoured that this play was composed at the time when Kyd and Marlowe were "writing in one chamber", in the service of an unnamed Lord.

According to Kyd, Marlowe was "bearing name to serve my Lord" in 1591, "although his Lordship never knew his service but in writing for his players" (81). In the course of their collaboration, the nature of which is never made clear (I have contended that Marlowe was dramatist and Kyd scrivener or copy-clerk for the company), Marlowe left among Kyd's papers some notes he had taken from a critique of the Athanasian creed in John Proctor's *The Fall of the Late Arian* (1549). The Arian in question seems to have been John Ashton, whom a clerical inquisition persuaded to recant his arguments against the existence of the Trinity in 1549. Proctor's pamphlet included the arguments and Marlowe seized on them for a book he had dreamed of writing against the teachings of Christianity. His agitation on the metaphysical mysteries became so intense that he could no longer restrain it to verbal combat. He lost his temper frequently and craved blood, "attempting sudden privy injuries to men," says Kyd. The paranoiac frenzy apparently occurred with special violence toward the end of 1591. Perhaps the unhappy Christopher experienced onsets of unconscious terror and yearning for prostration before the men *ex cathedra* who symbolised for him masculine might and paternity. Such attacks could have been provoked by repressed vile thoughts on the death of the Holy Father Gregory XIV on 15 October. Two months later, on 29 December, Pope Innocent IX died, of Spanish poison, it was whispered. Marlowe's upflares against divine authority finally compelled his noble master to discharge him. "For never could my Lord," Kyd affirms, "endure his name, or sight, when he heard of his conditions." His Lordship had the habit of daily prayer together with his servants. So, "by my Lord's commandment, as in hatred of his life and thoughts, I left and did refrain his company" (82).

VII

On 6 April 1590, the astrologer Dr John Dee recorded in his diary: "Good Sir Francis Walsingham died at night," eleven o'clock. William Camden reports that the Principal Secretary of State perished with a fleshy growth in his testicles, or the violence of his medicines. He suffered almost all his life from hardship in passing urine. The next night this quietly aggressive, tight-mouthed man was deposited in earth at Paul's Cathedral. Before the funeral finished, his master William Cecil, Lord Burghley, did a ghoulish but characteristic thing, described by Robert Beale, brother-in-law of the dead Secretary: "all his papers and books, both public and private, were seized and carried away, perhaps by those who would be loth to be used so themselves" (83). Cecil always made sure that no documents would remain out of his grasp which might incriminate him as contriver of the judicial murders of Thomas Howard, Duke of Norfolk, Mary Stuart, Queen of Scotland, and others of their sort. Burghley managed to control records of nobles who presented him in lights he did not desire to appear in, as the Historical Commission Calendar of the Salisbury (family) manuscripts at Hatfield sufficiently testify.

Sir Edward Stafford died toward the end of 1590, and Sir Henry Unton took his place in the English embassy in France. During the years 1591 and 1592 "Mr Marlin" was employed as a messenger for Unton, who could usually be found at the camp of King Henri of Navarre.

Sir Edward's correspondence tells how for some time he had been afflicted by an agent of Walsingham who had much in common with Kit Marlowe and complained about him in vivid detail. The spy said his name was Roger Walton, and he claimed to have been a page or ward of the Countess of Northumberland, whose staunchly Catholic husband had been killed in the Tower of London in June 1585. To some people in Paris, Walton exhibited himself as "a great Papist, to others a Protestant, but as they take him that haunteth him most, he hath neither God nor religion, a very evil condition, a swearer without measure and tearer of God, a notable whoremaster" (84). What Stafford or Unton thought of Kit Marlowe, no state document has yet disclosed.

The poet had long ceased to be the politically aspiring youth whose orderly and discreet behaviour the Privy Council had commended in his last term at Cambridge. His quick-kindling temper made him notorious in the fashionable walkways at Paul's Cathedral and in London inns. His name is not connected with the quarrel of May 1591 that closed with the Admiral's men quitting James Burbage's Theatre. Nor do we find it linked with the fury of the Essex faction against Robert Cecil, who, in December 1591, chagrined the Earl by depriving him of the Chancellorship of Oxford University. "Whether you have mistaken the Queen," Essex wrote to young Cecil, "or used cunning with me, I know not" (85). His followers felt sure that Burghley's successor had dealt treacherously, Lord Henry Howard craftily lifted the temperature of their hate, hoping to behold the destruction of the Cecils, while indefatigably fawning on Robert, and assisting him in secret intrigues with Scotland and Spain, which eventually gained him the Earldom of Northampton.

On 9 May 1592, the constable Allen Nichols and the sub-constable Nicholas Helliott begged Sir Owen Hopton for legal protection against threats of Christopher Marlowe, apparently made in Holywell Street, near Burbage's playhouse. They declared at the Middlesex Sessions that he behaved contemptuously and pugnaciously toward the Queen's officers of the peace in the Shoreditch district (86). On 23 June London magistrates ordered the city theatres to shut in order to prevent the rioting of prentices expected on Midsummer Night (24 June). Kit's character was not rendered any kinder or milkier by the companionship of Robert Poley, his perfidious neighbour, who also carried messages for the government this year. In October Poley travelled with letters from Hampton Court to Edinburgh, and stayed at the Scottish court for two months, probably busy with espionage. Early in the following year he received pay for "special and secret afairs" in Scotland. The playwright's interest in the Stuart dynasty meanwhile grew more torrid, despite the Tudor virulence against English questing for complacency from King James. Presumably Marlowe heard hints of the Earl of Essex's own concern with Jacobean politics, since he moved in the orbit of the Earl's servants and admirers, and could not refrain from depicting his interest in the Stuart claim to Elizabeth's throne prematurely. Marlowe, in fact, courted disaster.

In 1592 the parsimonious Philip Henslowe recorded in his accounts of the Rose theatre, he had paid 13 shillings for repair of the ceiling in "my Lords Roome". This item may help us to identify the

Lord whom Marlowe had served for the sake of his players. Anyone fairly acquainted with the history of the Elizabethan stage knows that a single solitary Lord was so friendly with players and writers for them as to have a room for himself at the Rose. This was Edward de Vere, Earl of Oxford, who enjoyed a modest fame as author of comedies, and more fame as the patron of John Lyly, Thomas Watson, Anthony Mundy, Robert Greene: the list has no end. That both Kyd and Henslowe should not refer to him by name indicates the force of his resolution that the world should connect him no more with their butterfly literature.

On 26 September 1592, one of the few sobering forces of Marlowe's life, the pacific scholar, poet and playwright Thomas Watson was buried in the graveyard of St Bartholomew the Less, in West Smithfield, not far from the Curtain and the Theatre, and the Boar's Head playhouse. On 10 November Watson's Latin lyric "Amintae Gaudia" was licensed for printing. It came from the press with a dedication in the same tongue to Mary Herbert, Countess of Pembroke, Sidney's famous sister, signed "C.M." In December Marlowe produced his Latin eulogy of Sir Roger Manwood, who had died on the 14th under the shadow of Privy Council charges of malpractice in his judge's office, as Lord Chief Baron of the Exchequer. A relative of the Walsinghams by marriage, and one of the most successful Elizabethan lawyers, Manwood had little to learn from the statecraft of Machiavelli, and certainly did not agree with Marlowe that Justinian's Institutes held nothing to attract a self-adoring and daring young man. The study of law, says Doctor Faustus, "fits a mercenary drudge,/ Who aims at nothing but external trash,/ Too servile and illiberal for me". But the poet had acquired a large deal of information about the romance and mystery of the "external trash" by the time he composed *The Jew of Malta*. Then he understood that the posture of servility might be an immensely amusing disguise for human nature cunningly in quest of lordship and wealth. By the time Marlowe composed his obituary for Manwood he had lost much of the idealism that entranced him into dreams of using wealth for such purposes as clothing boys in public schools with silk and bravery. Manwood spent considerable funds in building a house of puerile "correction" in Canterbury. Marlowe must have realised that, if he wished to mingle intimately with men like Manwood, he would have to abandon childish ideals for the schools and advocate the righteous regimen that had made Sir Roger an eminent Cambridge Master of Arts and well-paid servant of the state. It would have been wonderful to hear the creator of *Faustus* contending for the virtues of the school dominie's magic wand. Yet the poet had the nerve and sophistry necessary to argue thus. If he ever heard the jolly Sir Roger preaching his gospel of corporations, gloating on the notion that they had no bodies to kick nor souls to damn, the dramatist surely thrilled and laughed at his devilish cleverness, and envied the energy that could utter its secret sadism with such liberty of wit (87).

There is no evidence that Marlowe was going ahead with his theatrical writing at the beginning of 1593. A new version of the tragedy of "Tamber Cam" drew big crowds to the Rose, and *The Jew of Malta* and *The Tragedy of the Guise* continued to put plenty of shillings into the pockets of Henslowe, Alleyn, and their partners. None of their profits went to relieve Marlowe's consumption of the purse, and none of the new plays of the season bear any plain marks of our poet's hand. The Earl of Pembroke's company, whose first record of performers comes from the town of Leicester at the end of 1592, made deep impressions with his *Edward the Second*, but apparently stronger impressions with *Titus Andronicus* and Parts 1 and 2 of *Henry the Sixth*. They acted for the Queen and the Court on 26 December 1592, but we know not what.

In my opinion, he spent the wintry nights between the Yuletide of 1592 and March or April of 1593 in composition of his long poem on "Hero and Leander" – "Whose tragedy divine Musaeus sung". This unfinished romance gave him abundant opportunity to unfold fresh philosophy concerning the mainsprings of the universe. He revealed here his knowledge of Empedocles's doctrine of the origin of the world in struggle. But the Greek sage had conceived of strife as evil and called the energy that combined elements and produced harmony Love. In *The Conquests of Tamburlaine* already Marlowe rejected this view. He imagined (2.7, 12-29)

> Some powers divine, or else infernal, mixt
> Their angry seeds

when warlike life was born. In "Hero and Leander" he portrays the "silly maiden" being carnally conquered, and warns us:

> Love is not full of pity (as men say)
> But deaf and cruel, where he means to prey ...
> She trembling strove, this strife of hers (like that
> Which made the world) another world begat
> Of unknown joy.   (Sestiad 2, 291ff.)

Marlowe heartily concurred with the principle of Heraclitus: 'War is the father of all and the king of all." The master of blank verse indicates his delight in riming and weaving couplets for storytelling and side-remarks to the reader, but always from his strictly narcissistic point of view, indulging pederastic fantasy, revelling in erotic wit, and tossing as many barbs of sarcasm as he pleased. Some poets, he declares, "their violent passions to assuage,/ Compile sharp satires". He himself prefers to rime a tragedy of ancient Grecian love. As he warmed to the work, however, the old lusts in him woke. Once more he voiced the wish

> That Jove, usurper of his father's seat,
> Might presently be banish'd into hell.

This time the rebellious idea obtrudes with patina of melancholy and humour, as if he mocked his Lucifer impulse, with its cradle delusion of the ego's grandeur. His mind had reached the ripeness where it could aver without bitterness:

> It lies not in our power to love or hate,
> For will in us is over-rul'd by fate.

Hate remained the strongest of his moods. Even when he sighed for a golden age in which "Murder, rape, war, and lust, and treachery", could be buried with Jupiter in "Stygian empery", he lingered melodiously on thoughts of hate. He spoke acridly of lords who choose a "garish toy" before "virtuous deeds",

> And still enrich the lofty servile clown,
> Who with encroaching guile keeps learning down.

The idea of learning living in poverty moved him to several of his most musical and memorable verses, and the blissful contradiction of his own couplet on will and destiny:

> Learning, in despite of Fate,
> Will mount aloft, and enter heaven-gate,
> And to the seat of Jove itself advance ...

Unfortunately, the climbing to paradise took place under conditions where the body was abased, and for this the poet blamed the feminine divinities of fate:

> And to this day is every scholar poor:
> Gross gold from them runs headlong to the boor.
> Likewise the angry Sisters, thus deluded,
> To venge themselves on Hermes, have concluded
> That Midas' brood shall sit in Honour's chair,
> To which the Muses' sons are only heir ...

Hermes, the god of commerce and larceny, Marlowe fancied, had angered the Sisters of Destiny by despising their love. They determined that "he and Poverty should always kiss".

Fabricators and magicians fascinated the poet. He could not resist the lures of companionship with people whose purses seemed to swell without work, who disdained to live by servile and "illiberal" means, making their ways by their wits. The infantile parasite in him stood in awe of the tricksters. When, in "Hero and

Leander," he poured his indignation on the "vicious, hare-brain'd, and illiterate hinds", who alone among men, in his judgment, "have hard hearts and obdurate minds", he was not thinking of playmates like Nicholas Skeres. Toward these scoundrels Marlowe's heart went out with an ill love, tempting calamity.

Especially in their company he disburdened his intellect of its old theological antipathies. "But almost into every company he cometh," wrote Richard Baines, "he persuades men to atheism, willing them not to be afeared of bugbears and hobgoblins." He proudly informed Richard Cholmley that he had read his "atheist lecture" to Sir Walter Ralegh, and skeptic gentlemen close to that great adventurer. Marlowe affirmed that "Moses was but a juggler", and that Thomas Harriot, Sir Walter's gifted servant in sciences, could do more than the law-bringer of Israel. Marlowe seems to have been familiar with Harriot's account of the colonial enterprise of Ralegh in "Virginia". *A Brief and True Report of the New-found Land of America* (1588) inspired the poet with capricious ammunition for his critique of Christianity. In it, Harriot described the use of tobacco in the cult sacrifices of Indians; Marlowe remarked, if the Eucharist were administered in a pipe of tobacco it would be more acceptable. He shared with Harriot the heretic belief that the traditions of the primitive Americans surpassed the book of Genesis in age. "Impudently they persist in it," Thomas Nashe declared, referring to freethinkers he had heard in London, "that the late discovered Indians are able to show antiquities thousands before Adam" (88).

The evidence from the new western world as well as the classical witnesses Marlowe adduced in his tavern controversies had a spellbinding effect on various underworld brains. One of the most notorious of these was Richard Cholmley, for whom the Privy Council issued a warrant of arrest on 19 March 1593. A government agent warned the Council, "This cursed Cholmley hath sixty of his company and he is seldom from his fellows", young villains with "resolute murdering minds". They tickled themselves with speculations of a utopia they wished to establish after the Queen's death, hoping to elect a monarch of their own, and to live according to their own laws, thumbing their noses at Old Father Antic, the legislator of yore. A member of the gang, Henry Young of Kent, vowed that he was willing to kill the Queen. He appears in the state records as a professional informer, perhaps a provocator. Cholmley too is found among the employees of her Majesty's Council, "for the apprehension of Papists, and other dangerous men". He was accused of taking money from such outlaws in exchange for relaxing his vigilance and letting them escape. In fact, he saw no reason why he should keep faith with the royal ministers, since they had no respect for truth or fidelity themselves, being "all atheists and Machiavellians" (89).

It may have been one of these informers — "some outcast Ishmael," Kyd called him — who guided constables to Kyd's door on 12 May 1593 and saw him carried off to Bridewell prison under arrest for alleged authorship of a libel inciting citizens of London to riot against foreigners. In this month a survey was made in the city to count the aliens in residence. The survey prompted some patriotic wretch to compose a set of incendiary rimes which were stuck on the wall of the Dutch churchyard in Austin Friars on the night of May 5. The first quatrain has been preserved:

You strangers, that inhabit in this land,
Note this same writing, do it understand;
Conceive it well, for safeguard of your lives,
Your goods, your children and your dearest wives (90).

The bloodcurdling threats led, on 11 May, to a Star-Chamber decision to search out and punish the individuals responsible for the "lewd and mutinous libels set up within the city of London", of which the outrage at the Dutch church was deemed the most lewd. The government delivered a command to magistrates, desiring "extraordinary pains" to be taken in the examination of any persons they suspected of producing the diatribes. They were instructed to enter all houses and places where suspected persons dwelt, and, "upon their apprehension, to make like search in any the chambers, studies, chests, or other like places for all manner of writings or papers that may give you light for the discovery of the libellers".

"And after you have examined the persons," the Star-Chamber decree added, "if you shall find them duly to be suspected, and they shall refuse to confess the truth, you shall by authority hereof put them to the torture in Bridewell, and by the extremity thereof, to be used at such times and as often as you shall think fit, draw them to discover their knowledge concerning the said libels."

So they arrested Thomas Kyd the next day, and confiscated his papers, among which they found certain "vile heretical conceits denying the deity of Jesus Christ", which had been shuffled into his belongings when he and Marlowe were writing together two years ago. The luckless Kyd toiled piteously to clear himself of the stigma of atheism, which accusation overclouded in the Privy Council's vision the original charge of 12 May. On the Bridewell rack he protested innocence in the affair of Austin Friars, and cast all guilt for the unitarian "conceits" discovered among his papers on Christopher Marlowe. Kyd charged Kit, not only with being "irreligious", but also "intemperate and of a cruel heart". He told his inquisitors, "it was his custom when I knew him first and as I hear say he continued it in table talk or otherwise to jest at the divine scriptures, gibe at prayers, and strive in arguments to frustrate and confute what hath been spoke or writ by prophets and such holy men". The Council knew that Marlowe was not in town to answer questions about his alleged blasphemies. They sent no police to his residence in Norton Folgate to collect his papers. Instead, on 18 May, they sent Henry Maunder to the house of Thomas Walsingham at Chislehurst in Kent, "or to any other place where he shall understand Christopher Marlowe to be remaining"; Maunder went with a warrant to fetch the poet before the Council, "and in case of need to require aid".

On 20 May, the Council secretary noted, "Ch. Marley of London, gent., being sent for by warrant from their Lordships, hath entered his appearance accordingly for his indemnity therein, and is commanded to give his daily attendance on their Lordships till he shall be licensed to the contrary" (91). The summons apparently did not disturb Kit. He must have heard tales of Kyd's imprisonment and torture and guessed that poor Tom would tell calamitous tales of him and his rhapsodies on religion, and the future of Britain. He knew that Kyd could unfold a fantastic tale of his endeavours to persuade men of quality to go up to Edinburgh to offer their services to the King of Scots. The last time that Kyd saw him he had asserted he would make the pilgrimage to the northern capital. Later Kyd heard that Matthew Roydon, the Kentish comedian, friend of Marlowe and Nicholas Skeres, also intended the journey to James.

Less than two weeks after Marlowe's coming before the Privy Council, presumably after ten days of dutiful daily appearance before their Lordships, he died, falling among thieves. He went down to Deptford on 30 May, the day after the Puritan John Penry was hanged for inciting his fellow-Welsh and other folks to rebellion by speeches and books for the overthrow of bishoprics. It seems that Marlowe never knew that Richard Baines tried to bring him to a similar fate by submitting to the Privy Council "A Note Containing the Opinion of one Christopher Marly, concerning his damnable judgments of religion and scorn of God's word". According to the Puritan William Vaughan, the dramatist was invited to Deptford to a feast by the man who accepted the blame for murdering him, Ingram Frizer, a servant of Thomas Walsingham. Frizer and Marlowe were accompanied by Robert Poley and Nicholas Skeres, men with reputations more malodorous than Frizer's. The four men spent the whole of Wednesday 30 May, at a tavern owned by a certain Eleanor Bull, but what they conversed about, the motive of their meeting, the witnesses of their talk and turbulence, are all unknown. The Privy Council evinced no curiosity about Marlowe's truancy this day.

The coroner's inquest on 1 June found that Ingram Frizer killed the poet in self-defence, because Marlowe had tried to knife him in a quarrel over the cost of the day's eating and drinking. As proof of Marlowe's murderous purpose, the jury had the spectacle of slight cuts on the killer's head and the words of Poley and Skeres, the agent provocateur and the cutpurse. The inquest took equally careful note of the size and price of the fatal weapon, for, as Marlowe's expert murderer Barabas says, after he has stricken a priest dead with his cane and summoned constables to the scene, the weapon must be shown at the inquest: "Law wills that each particular be known." (*The Jew of Malta*, 4.1) Each particular trifle, to be exact. The jury exhibited no desire to find out why the four men were together in Deptford instead of London, their hometown, how intimately they were acquainted, whether there might have been a different motive for piercing the poet's eye and brain from the one alleged. Nor was any interest manifested in the fact that Poley, on the deadly day, was carrying letters from The Hague intended for the Court (for whom?) which was then at Nonesuch Palace in Surrey. He had left the Court at Croydon on 8 May, and delivered his Holland mail on 8 June, "being in her Majesty's service," the Court accounts affirm, "all the aforesaid time." Does this not sound as though the Court secretary were inscribing an alibi? Poley's employers were not perturbed by his dallying in Deptford for an entire day, when Sir Robert Cecil, who acted as principal secretary of state without winning appointment to Walsingham's place until 1596, was waiting for the Dutch news.

Ingram Frizer, the future churchwarden, Thomas Walsingham's servant, got the Queen's pardon for homicide in self-defence on 28 June, more rapidly than Watson received it after he killed William Bradley, in a duel.

On the day after the Queen's pardon arrived, Richard Cholmley was at last arrested and brought to gaol. The event does not seem to have daunted him. On the road he boasted that he was ignorant of all law but in case of necessity "he could shift well enough". A few months later the Earl of Essex wrote his thanks to three gentlemen of legal talent for their trouble-taking in the matter of his servant Cholmley, and he urged them to persevere until his innocence was plain to his judges.

On the day of Cholmley's departure to jail, a rural fool named Drew Woodleff bound himself in debt for the sum of £200 to Thomas Walsingham, whose servant Frizer was then busy swindling Woodleff for a tempting patrimony. The astonishingly stupid Woodleff had come to the capital in quest of financial assistance, and by the advice of Nicholas Skeres he entrusted his affairs to Frizer. The mulcting was immense (92). Frizer seems to have been a remarkably humble man, with no desire for fame, contrary to the claim made by Shake-speare in the opening lines of *Love's Labour's Lost*. Marlowe had not lain very long in his Deptford grave before the name of his alleged killer was forgotten or oddly distorted by clerks and historians. A veteran actor informed the biographer John Aubrey that Ben Jonson killed Marlowe! William Vaughan, telling about Marlowe's invitation to the feast of his finish, in his book *The Golden Grove* (1600) simply calls the murderer Ingram. When Gabriel Harvey heard the news of the poet's death, in the cloisters of Cambridge University, the killer was said to be Plague. Gabriel's brother Richard served as rector in the church at Chislehurst, Kent, where Thomas Walsingham worshipped. The Cambridge pedant appears to have wasted no time in research; he penned an obituary for poor Kit, one of the university wits and artists he deeply detested. He entitled the poem "Gorgon", perhaps remembering how the Sultan of Egypt in *Tamburlaine* swore to face the Tartar shepherd even if he were "As monstrous as Gorgon, prince of hell". When Harvey thought of Marlowe, he invariably recalled *Tamburlaine*:

> Magnific minds, bred of Gargantua's race,
> In grisly weeds his obsequies lament,
> Whose corpse on Paul's, whose mind triumph'd on Kent,
> Scorning to bate Sir Rodomont an ace ...
> Is it a dream? or is the highest mind
> That ever haunted Paul's, or hunted wind,
> Bereft of that same sky-surmounting breath,
> That breath that taught the tympany to swell?

In like doggerel the pedant went on to gloat over the dead poet's defeat in his final struggle, fancying Marlowe's "Tamburlaine contempt" of death silenced under the stroke of "the grand disease".

The fall of Marlowe as a victim of plague seemed to Harvey one of the main events of the year, and as such he celebrated it:

> The Christian Neptune Turkish Vulcan tames ...
> Navarre woos Rome; Charlemagne gives Guise the Fy:
> Weep, Paul's, thy Tamburlaine vouchsafes to die (93).

Dread of the plague oppressed more minds than Harvey's at the University. On 17 July 1593, Cambridge authorities made a plea for restraint of public shows and "Common plays", for fear of infection.

Thomas Nashe wrote an elegy for his friend in Latin, as a sort of prelude to an edition of *Dido, Queen of Carthage*. The loss of this poem is indeed deplorable. We would be grateful to know what "the Scanderbegging wight" whom Harvey ridiculed as Marlowe's successor had to say about his tragic death.

A greater dramatist introduced two or more of his reflections on the event in the comedy *As You Like It*. The play has long been lauded for its tribute to the "dead shepherd", who, in "Hero and Leander", had given the world the immortal line, "Who ever lov'd that lov'd not at first sight?" Actually Shake-speare writes about Marlowe and his fate in a spirit of irony. He puts the immortal line on the lips of the foolish shepherdess Phebe, who falls in love at first sight with the heroine Rosalind disguised as a boy. Rosalind herself alludes to Marlowe's poem with critical laughter. Leander, she remarks, "would have lived many a fair year, though Hero had turned nun, if it had not been for a hot midsummer night, for, good youth, he went but forth to wash him in the Hellespont, and being taken with the cramp was drowned; and the foolish coroners of that age found it was 'Hero of Sestos.' But these are all lies; men have died from time to time, and worms have eaten them, but not for love." (4.1) Marlowe presented his pagan heroine as a nun of Venus, and Shake-speare found the term just as useful for his fun at the dead poet's expense. He also made fun of scholars like Francis Meres, who spread the rumour that Marlowe had been stabbed to death by a servingman who rivalled him in a lewd love (94).

In the mouth of the clown Touchstone the greater poet placed his last judgment on the dead dramatist, regarding Marlowe's fate as less cruel than the fate of a poet (such as Shake-speare) whose work meets few minds able to embrace and master it. "When a man's verses cannot be understood," Touchstone grieves, "nor a man's good wit seconded with the forward child Understanding, it strikes a man more dead than a great reckoning in a little room." How could anyone familiar with Marlowe's magnificence miss the reference to his "Infinite riches in a little room" — from *The Jew of Malta*, the "reckoning" for which the coroner's jury said he died, and the allusion to the last lines of his *Doctor Faustus*, where the Chorus exhorts the wise,

Only to wonder at unlawful things,
Whose deepness doth entice such forward wits,

lines that Shake-speare turned into an epitaph for their own author? These abstruse passages in *As You Like It* (3.3) tantalise us with the hint that the superior artist knew or suspected more reasons for the murder of Marlowe than history is aware of. Certainly, the official narrative of the murder is a linkage of lies. Ingram Frizer was easily dismissed by the jury as a burgess incapable of such a crime, commended by both clergy and statesmen. Robert Poley was a cold-blooded scoundrel who never seems to have soiled his fingers with anything not favoured by the politicians he served. Therefore, I nominate Nicholas Skeres as the one who drove the blade into Marlowe's brain through his eye.

Skeres would have been motivated to the deed if, as I imagine, he had on distressing occasions been made a target for Marlowe's wit; I have suggested that the dramatist drew Pilia-Borza in *The Jew of Malta* with Skeres as model; I believe Marlowe viewed him as a caricature of mankind. Yet I can see no cause for the criminal lifting a knife against the writer unless it appeared more than revenge for jokes. It would have to be profitable. Who could have paid him the adequate price?

Various theories have been proposed to account for the mysterious death of the dramatist. One suggests that Sir Walter Ralegh instigated the assassination to stop a tongue that might have injured him fatally during the Privy Council's investigations of heresy and atheism. Ralegh is believed to have been the mastermind of the "School of Night" which scholars have constructed out of a recondite phrase in the text of *Love's Labour's Lost*. But Ralegh's religious opinions were fairly well explored by the government, and nothing was discerned in them that could seriously damage him. He was certainly more Christian than Christopher. Another hypothesis presents the family of Walsingham as the one most vitally interested in shutting Marlowe's mouth. It is argued that Thomas Walsingham's wife, Audrey (a lady bearing very little resemblance to Touchstone's bride), became involved in schemes with the court of King James while Elizabeth still lived and had strength to punish conspirators for her dynastic competitor. When the Walsinghams heard (so the argument goes) that Marlowe was going to be questioned by the Council, they resolved to silence him, for he must have had more than a glimpse into their "Jacobite" plot. The lease that James gave Ingram Frizer, after his English coronation, for the use of Lady Audrey, alleged to be a reward for her faithful service to the late Queen, is said to be a payment for the Walsingham's loyalty to the house of Stuart prior to Elizabeth's death. Each of these theories consents to the official judgment that Frizer was Marlowe's murderer. But we have yet to be convinced that this shrewd servingman, the most respectable of the three who surrounded the poet at his last supper, was truly the killer. In the worst of Frizer's business transactions he emerged in the odour of sanctity. If the imbecile coroners of the age accepted his confession of guilt, it was very likely with compassion for a mercantile-minded young man's suffering at the hands of a lewd intellectual, a writer and a rogue.

Dispassionate scrutiny of the characters involved in the Marlowe murder case, despite the testimony of the inquest, would have picked one of Frizer's two friends, the spy or the thief, as the most probable wielder of the blade. I surmise that Nick Skeres did it under the direction of Robert Poley, whose respectability as a witness would have overawed the Deptford jury in the moment he disclosed that he carried messages from Holland to the Court. The small blond fellow and the servile Frizer gripped the struggling poet's arms, after Poley and alcohol had led him to talk in his wild way about Nick's diabolic looks and short cryptic speech, his burglaries and blunders with whores, and about tobacco and buggery being better than amorous women (Marlowe's belief as recorded by Richard Baines), and the chances of Queen Bess quitting this sphere of tears before the "rising sun" of Scotland grew too old to renovate it. I believe that Marlowe was slain to prevent him from telling the Privy Council, perhaps from the Bridewell rack, about Robert Poley's transactions with the court of the Scots (95). Marlowe knew much, and could not be trusted to stay mute, about Poley's journeys to the north, made in obedience to his employers who looked to Edinburgh for preferment — "fruitful wits" (to use Marlowe's phrase in "Hero and Leander") who "discontent run into regions far". Poley's main master was Sir Robert Cecil.

In 1593 the son of the Lord Treasurer had but one rival to remove in order to take old William's place as the prime minister of her Majesty. Her fondness for Robert Devereux, Earl of Essex, was his chief obstacle. That, I think, is enough to explain the dedication, on 31 December, of *A Conference About the Next Succession to the Crown of England ... Directed to the Right Honorable the earl of Essex, of her Majesty's Privy Council,* which came from a Jesuit in the service of Spain named Robert Persons, working in Antwerp. Cardinal d'Ossat told King Henri IV about Persons and his publicity for the disgrace and downfall of Essex, whom he hailed thus: "no man more like to have a greater part or sway in deciding of this great affair" of the English crown (96). When the Queen showed the book to Essex, he changed countenance. "At his coming from Court he was observed to look pale and wan, being exceedingly troubled at this piece of villainy done unto him" (97). Little can be learnt of the connexion between the duel of Cecil and Devereux and King James's threat, on 13 April 1594, of breaking amity with Elizabeth. I have no doubt that Sir Robert got chief credit for renewing the royal endearments from Scotland.

On 6 December 1594, the informer Richard Baines went to the gallows for some felony not yet clarified, and on the same day an enterprising printer obtained license for "The Woeful Lamentation of Richard Baynes executed at Tyburne".

On 13 March 1595, "Nicholas Kyrse, alias Skeers, servant to the Earl of Essex", was arrested in "dangerous company" at the home of one Edmund Williamson, who seems to have been acquainted with Robert Poley. Skeres went to the Counter prison, under charges not known. In February 1601, when the Earl of Essex, spurred on by Lord Henry Howard, the secret supporter of Sir Robert Cecil, launched his foolhardy demonstration against alleged traitors environing Elizabeth, his supposed servant Skeres was a resident of Newgate prison. He could not be accused of aiding the "insurrection", as Richard Cholmley and George Orrell were. They were locked into the Counter and Poultry jails, but suffered no further for their enthusiasm in the Essex affair. On 31 July 1601, the Privy Council sent a warrant for removal of Nicholas Skiers from Newgate to Bridewell. After this date he dropped into oblivion, unless he is the "Nicholas Shere, a poor man, committed to Pope's ward to his great charge and probably undoing", for whose sake Francis Cotton wrote to Sir Robert Cecil on 8 February 1603, offering to give bail if the miserable man could be released. We are ignorant of the outcome of the appeal.

Meanwhile Robert Poley had fallen on desperate days. On 17 December 1600, he reminded Sir Robert of his services and begged to be restored to state favour and work. Cecil gave him two jobs in August and September 1601. On 3 June 1601, according to the Cecil manuscripts at Hatfield, he wrote to a commissioner for Channel passage control at Dover, asking for some kindness to "George Poly, my kinsman". Robin said he would be ready to receive George at the Black Bull inn in Southwark. On 10 July, we learn from the same archives, George Cotton confessed that he left the Catholic school at St Omers by the advice of his cousin Pooly, under whose name he travelled and was known at the seminary. But Henry Brooke, Baron Cobham, Cecil's political ally and brother-in-law, charged Poley with treachery in the Cotton case. "Your private reprehension," Cobham declared, "will be a sufficient warning". In the summer of 1602 Poley sent a letter to Cecil full of news about "seditious" priests and plangent with the pangs of his "necessities". Then the spy vanished from government archives (99).

Sir Robert went his stately way unharmed by the declaration of the French king: "it is alleged publicly of Cecil that he belongs to the party of Spain." In the spring of 1602 Lord Harry Howard amused him with a scheme to get Brooke, his brother-in-law, at his mercy: "Embark this gallant Cobham by your wit and interest in some course the Spanish way, as either may reveal his weakness or snare his ambition." The summer of 1602 seems to be the time when the deathward bound Elizabeth nearly caught the cunning Cecil in one of his exchanges with King James. We have it on the reliable authority of Sir Henry Wotton that, on a day undated, the Queen "going to take the air toward the Heath (the Court being then at Greenwich), and Master Secretary Cecill then attending her, a Post came crossing by, and blew his Horn. The Queen out of curiosity asked him from where the Dispatch came, and being answered, From Scotland, she stops the Coach, and calleth for the Packet.

"The Secretary, though he knew there were in it some Letters from his Correspondents, which to discover were as so many Serpents, yet made more shew of diligence then of doubt to obey; and asks some that stood by (forsooth in great haste) for a knife to cut the Packet ... at a pretty distance from the Queen, he telleth her, it looked and smelt ill-favouredly, coming out of a filthy budget ..." Sir Robert said he would air it, "because he knew she was averse from ill scents, and so being dismissed home, he got leasure by this seasonable shift, to sever what he would not have seen" (100).

As for Ingram Frizer, he lived to become a churchwarden at Eltham, Kent, near the Chislehurst mansion of his benefactors and died in the hope of a glorious resurrection in August 1627. Neither he nor his master Sir Thomas Walsingham considered worthy of permanent ink their opinions on the dedication that Edward Blunt wrote to the latter when he published Marlowe's "Hero and Leander" in 1598. Frizer's comment on the dedication would surely deserve century-lasting brass. Blunt declared that the poet's friends did not feel themselves discharged of the duty they owed him when they had "brought the breathless body to the earth". They still had the task of publishing the last masterpiece of "that beloved object", left incomplete by "the stroke of death". Blunt accepted the obligation of printing it, confident that Walsingham, who had bestowed many kind favours on the poet, "entertaining the parts of reckoning" in him with liberal affection, would take kindly the dedication of "whatsoever issue of his brain should chance to come abroad". The printer was humorously reputed to be blunt by nature as well as by name. His dedication of "Hero and Leander" may strike some of us as a product of subtlety almost as ingenious as the wit that created *As You Like It.*

APPENDIX

Some while after completing my analysis of Marlowe's life and scriptures, I overcame my aversion to the works of A. L. Rowse and perused *Christopher Marlowe: His Life and Work* (1964), which a friend had told me contained fresh information about the poet. I read its 215 pages and record the news I found here. The remainder of the volume, as I suspected, reeks with "vanity and vexation of spirit", along with numerous remarks that are simply untruths or half-truths, like Rowse's other writings concerning the era and art of Shakespeare.

Researches of Dr William Urry, noted in *The Times Literary Supplement* (13 February 1964), portray John Marlowe, father of the dramatist, as "a noisy, self-assertive, improvident fellow", frequently prosecuted for debt. John's mate, born Catherine Arthur of Dover, the daughter of a priest, failed to keep her house in kind and quiet order. Her daughters acquired unsavoury reputations, one of them pictured in her ripeness as a shrew, "scold, common swearer and blasphemer of the name of God". But Catherine was able to bequeath her "greatest gold ring" to Margaret, another gold ring granted to Anne in exchange for the ring with a double posy that Dorothy was to get for it, and a silver ring too for Anne. The shoemaker's widow also left silver spoons, various feminine garments and household commodities, and coins for charity. She wished to be buried in St George's churchyard in Canterbury, "whereat my husband John Marlowe was buried". Her will contains not a word about the boy Christopher, murdered thirteen years before the distribution of her worldly wares. She had two other sons, who died in early youth.

(The trustworthiness of Rouse's afflatus of facts can be estimated at a glance in his sentence on page 85 affirming that Queen Mary Stuart "had ultimately been caught red-handed in the Babington Plot for the murder of Elizabeth". A schoolman so stupified would of course present Sir Francis Walsingham as alone responsible for the Elizabethan networks of espionage and judiciary murder, actually organised and directed by William Cecil, Lord Burghley, whose name hardly appeared in Rowse's book.

The merit of Rowse's mentality is seen nakedly on page 122, where he refers to Thomas Kyd's exposure of Marlowe's sneering at the New Testament, beginning with "he would report St John to be our Saviour Christ's Alexis," and declares: "All this is authentic Marlowe, and represents an advance in rationality.")

"In the autumn of 1592," says Rowse, forgetting to tell us where he got the datum, Marlowe was visiting Canterbury and "engaged in a struggle at the Chequers Inn with William Corkine, tailor and musician". What sort of struggle? Rowse neglects to inform us, and leaves us wondering how he knows the Marlowe of the case was our Kit (page 127). (It is not difficult to tell how Rowse knew "that Shakespeare loved horses" (140). He remembered reading that the young fugitive from Stratford had served as a guardian of horses at the gate of the Theatre when he first came to London.)

Perhaps the most amusing page in Rowse's tome is 171, dealing with Shakespeare's alleged good fortune in 1592 of obtaining a patron. Rowse instructs us that the poet wrote his Sonnets to the young Earl of Southampton for "offerings of duty" in a "family campaign to incline the youth to marriage", wedlock with Elizabeth de Vere, the daughter of the Earl of Oxford, whom Southampton seems to have heartily detested. How William the runaway meat-chopper of Stratford, with what Rowse terms his "innate breeding and tact", would dare to advise the noble he wanted for patron to marry this Goneril of the Cecil household, we are left to figure out ourselves.

Rowse copied from Frederick S. Boas's research (reported in *The Times Literary Supplement*, 16 September 1949) the evidence that Richard Baines, Walsingham's informer, had been a seminary priest of Rheims, a student there from 1579 to 1583, ordained subdeacon in March 1581, deacon in May, and robed for altar service in September: he celebrated his first Mass in Rheims the next month. Then he commenced correspondence with Walsingham's office about the plots of William Allen, his Rector, for the overthrow of Elizabeth. He meditated plots of his own to poison the town well or the Rheims bath-water (192).

About Nick Skeres, we learn from Rowse that he was "a man of some substance", son of a prosperous merchant-tailor. What blinded Rowse to the material in his sources about the burglaries of Skeres? He copies from Leslie Hotson the inquest account of Marlowe's death without one question of its veracity. He even believes that "Marlowe in a passion suddenly drew Frizer's dagger" from that gentleman's scabbard, "and gave him a couple of cuts over the head". (199) Frizer's back, we are informed, was turned to the passionate playwright. However, "Frizer, rather constricted between Poley and Skeres, nevertheless struggled to get back his dagger and in the course of doing so inflicted a mortal wound ..." "That is all there is to it," concluded Rowse. He alluded to the phrase in *As You Like It*, "a great reckoning in a little room", as if the greater artist believed the official figment about the origin of the knife affair in Nell Bull's tavern.

Notes

1   R. Holinshed, *Chronicles of England, Scotland and Ireland* (London 1808) 622.
2   Conyers Read, *Mr Secretary Walsingham* (Oxford 1925) I, 202.
3   See Irwin Smith, *Shakespeare's Blackfriars Playhouse* (New York 1964) 151.
4   On Thomas Bilson, consult *The Dictionary of National Biography* V, 44.
5   Harris, Nicolas, *Memoirs of the Life and Times of Sir Christopher Hatton, KG* (London 1847) 59.
6   Richard Baines, Harleian MS 6853, f.320, quoted in *The Works of Thomas Kyd*, ed. F. Boas (Oxford 1901) cxv.
7   *A Collection of State Papers Relating to Affairs in the Reign of Queen Elizabeth* ed. Murdin (London 1759) 415.
8   *Lettres, Instructions et Memoires de Marie Stuart*, ed. Labanoff (London 1894) VI, 300. *Publications of the Catholic Record Society* XXI (1926) 58.
9   Frederick S. Boas, *Christopher Marlowe: A Biographical and Critical Study* (Oxford 1940) 123.
10 State Papers, Domestic, Elizabeth, CXXXIX, no. 38, quoted by Leo Hicks, SJ in *An Elizabethan Problem ... Two Exile Adventurers* (New York 1964) 109.
11 Calendar of State Papers, Foreign, 1581-2, 370.
12 See Hicks, *op.cit.* 247-9; J. H. Pollen, *Mary Queen of Scots and the Babington Plot*, Scottish History Society, 3rd series, 1922, cxxv.
13 See John Bakeless, *The Tragicall History of Christopher Marlowe* (Cambridge, Mass. 1942) 1, 182.
14 Conyers Read, *Lord Burghley and Queen Elizabeth* (New York 1961) 289.
15 Boas, *op.cit.* 120.
16 Calendar of State Papers, Scotland, VIII, 189; Murdin, *op.cit.* 470.
17 Hicks, *op.cit.* 245.
18 Calendar of State Papers, Venetian, VIII, 182.
19 *Tarlton's Jests*, ed. J. O. Halliwell (London 1844)
20 B. M. Ward, *The Seventeenth Earl of Oxford* (London 1928) 257f. Captain Ward's father, Rowland Ward, in 'Shakespeare and Elizabethan war propaganda', *Royal Engineers' Journal* (December 1928) and Captain Ward himself in 'Shakespeare and the Anglo-Spanish War, 1585-1604', *Revue Anglo-Americaine* (December 1929) contended that the Earl of Oxford received his secret service money for the purpose of promoting patriotism in the theatres.
21 E. K. Chambers, *The Elizabethan Stage* (Oxford 1923) IV, 335.
22 *Works of Gabriel Harvey*, ed. A. Grosart (London 1884) I, 295.
23 Pollen, *op. cit.* 41. Compare Francis Edwards, SJ, *The Dangerous Queen* (London 1964).
24 I am unable to locate the source of this item.
24a Christopher Mont, in *The Zurich Letters ...* ed. Hastings Robinson (2nd ed.,

Cambridge 1846) 319.

25 George Whetstone, *The English Mirror* (London 1586) Bk I, 79.

26 *Ibid.* 80.

27 *Ibid.* 79.

28 *Correspondence of Robert Dudley, Earl of Leicester, during his Government of the Low Countries*, ed. John Bruce (London 1844) 312, 424.

29 J. P. Collier, *History of English Dramatic Poetry* (London 1831) III, 112, approved by Alexander Dyce, Tycho Mommsen, Nikolai Ilyich Storojenko: *Works of Robert Greene*, ed. A. Grosart (London 1886) I, 169.

30 Bronson Feldman, 'Thomas Watson, Dramatist', *The Bard* 1(1977)129 f.

31 See Bakeless, *op.cit.* I, 172-5 and Pollen, *op.cit.* Compare Read, *Lord Burghley* 337.

32 Calendar of State Papers, Spanish, III, 608.

33 Calendar of Rutland Manuscripts I, 204.

34 Read, *Lord Burghley* 319; also J. Froude, *History of England* ... (London 1870) XII, 132n.

35 Read, *op.cit.* 345.

36 Calendar of State Papers, Domestic, CXCIV, 30.

37 Read, *Walsingham* III, 57; Read, *Burghley* 366.

38 Read, *Burghley, loc.cit.*

39 *King James's Secret*, ed. Rait & Cameron (London 1927) 171.

40 See Bakeless, *op.cit.* I, 159-60; Read, *Walsingham* II, 266.

41 J. L. Motley, *History of the United Netherlands* (New York 1860) 11, 167, 175, 400.

42 Read, *Walsingham* II, 323.

43 Bakeless, *op.cit.* I, 27-8, 82.

44 Lt Col Francis Cunningham, ed. *Works of Marlowe* (London, n.d. 1870) ix-x; A.H. Bullen, ed. *Works of Christopher Marlowe* (Boston 1885) 1, xiii.

45 Bakeless, *op. cit.* I, 211.

46 *Acts of the Privy Council*, ed. Dasent (London 1907) XV, 141. Cf. Tucker Brooke, *The Life of Marlowe* (New York 1920) 34.

47 Read, *Walsingham* III, 246.

48 Motley, *op.cit.* II, 250.

49 Calendar of State Papers, Domestic, Addenda 1580-1625, 217.

50 *Letters of Philip Gawdy*, ed. Isaac H. Jeayes (London 1906) 23; E. K. Chambers, *Times Literary Supplement* 28 (August 1930) 684.

51 Sir Walter Ralegh, preface to *History of the World* (London 1820) 11, xiii. John Stow, *The Annales, or Generall Chronicle of England* (London 1615).

52 Ethel Seaton, 'Marlowe, Robert Poley, and the Tippings', *Review of English Studies* 5 (1929) 273 f.; 'Robert Poley's ciphers', *ibid.* 7 (1931) 137 f.

53 Calendar of State Papers, Spanish, 1587-1603, 191.

54 Thomas Nashe, *Strange News of the Intercepting Certain Letters* ... (1593) in his

Works, ed. R. McKerrow (London 1910), I, 260.

55 Greene, *Works,* ed. Grosart VII, 7.

56 *Ibid.* VII, 8.

57 Gunther Venzlaff, *Textüberlieferung und Entstehensgeschichte von Marlowes 'Doctor Faustus'* (Berlin 1909) 22.

58 Motley, *op.cit.* I, 200 f.

59 Thomas Kyd, letter to Sir John Puckering, in Harleian MS 6848, f. 154, quoted by Bakeless, *op.cit.* I, 114.

60 Motley, *op.cit.* II, 363.

61 Read, *Walsingham* III, 276.

62 Quoted by F. S. Boas, ed., *Tragical History of Doctor Faustus* (New York 1932) 9 -10.

63 Calendar of State Papers, Domestic, Elizabeth, CLXXXII, 44; CCX, 30.

64 Historical MSS Commission: Ancaster MS 228.

65 Bakeless, *op.cit.* I, 193.

66 Read, *Burghley* 456.

67 Thomas McNevin Veech, *Dr Nicholas Sanders and the English Reformation* (Louvain 1935) 28. Compare Edward Seymour, Earl of Hertford, on the 'Martin Marprelate' tracts: "as they shoot at Bishops now, so will they do at the Nobility also, if they be suffered": Edward Arber, *An Introductory Sketch to the Martin Marprelate Controversy* (London 1880) 114.

68 Edmund Sawyer, *Memorials of Affairs of State* (London 1725) I, 425.

69 Boas, *Christopher Marlowe* 269.

70 *Correspondence inédite de Robert Dudley, Comte de Leicester, et François et Jean Hotman,* ed. Blok (Haarlem 1911)178. See the Calendar of Salisbury MSS (Cecil Papers) III, 441.

71 Mark Eccles, *Christopher Marlowe in London* (Cambridge, Mass. 1934).

72 Mark Eccles, 'Marlowe in Newgate', *Times Literary Supplement* 6 (September 1934) 33. Calendar of State Papers, Domestic, 1598-1601, 372.

73 Greene, *Works,* ed. Grosart VI, 6.

74 *Ibid.* VI, 119.

75 *Ibid.* VI, 7-8, 86.

76 Rupert Taylor, 'Tentative chronology of Marlowe's ... plays', *Publication of the Modern Language Association* 51(1936) 653.

77 Bronson Feldman, 'The Rape of Antwerp in a Tudor play', *Notes and Queries* 5 (June 1958) 246-8.

78 W.E.H. Lecky, *History of the Rise and Influence of the Spirit of Rationalism in Europe* (New York 1870) II, 48n.

79 Eccles, *Marlowe in London* 57; Boas, *Marlowe* 38. On Orrel the coiner, see John Strype, *Annals of the Reformation* (London 1709) III, 209.

80 Greene, *Works,* ed. Grosart VIII, 132.

81 Kyd, *Works,* ed. Boas cix, quoting Harleian MS 6849, f.218.

82 *Idem.* See Brooke, *Life of Marlowe* 104.

83 Read, *Walsingham* 1,431, quoting Yelverton MS CLXII; William Camden, *The History of the Most Renowned and Victorious Princess Elizabeth* (London 1675) 394.

84 Calendar of State Papers, Domestic, 1588, CCIX, 57.

85 Murdin, *op.cit.* II, 655.

86 Eccles, *Marlowe in London* 105.

87 Bakeless, *op.cit.* I, 92.

88 Nashe, 'Christs Tears Over Ierusalem', in *Works*, ed. McKerrow, II, 116.

89 F.S. Boas, *Marlowe and his Circle* (Oxford 1931)79 f; Boas, *Marlowe* 253.

90 Boas, ed., *Works of Thomas Kyd* lxix. See Tucker Brooke, *Life of Marlowe* 107.

91 *Acts of the Privy Council*, ed. Dasent XXW, 244 f. My account of the killing of Kit is of course founded on J. Leslie Hotson's *The Death of Christopher Marlowe* (Cambridge, Mass. 1925).

92 Bakeless, *op.cit.* I, 167-8. See Boas, *Marlowe* 269.

93 Gabriel Harvey, *Works.* ed. Grosart (London 1884) I, 295.

94 Francis Meres, *Wits Treasury*, in *Elizabethan Critical Essays*, ed. G. Gregory Smith (Oxford 1904) II, 324.

95 See Boas, *Marlowe* 120; Leo Hicks, *An Elizabethan Problem* 245; Eugenie de Kalb, 'Robert Poley's movements as a messenger of the Court', *Review of English Studies* 9 (1933) 13-18.

96 Robert Persons, *A Conference about the Next Succession to the Crown of England...* (Antwerp: R. Doleman 1594) quoted by Elizabeth Tenison in *Elizabethan England* (Leamington 1939) 492-3.

97 Sir Henry, Sir Philip. Sir Robert Sidney, *Letters and Memorials of State*, ed. Arthur Collins (London 1746) I, 359.

98 Bakeless, *op.cit.* I, 182.

99 Calendar of Salisbury MSS XI, 216, 278, 302; XII, 230.

100 *L'Ambassade de France*, ed. Laffleur 203; Edward Edwards, *The Life of Sir Walter Ralegh* (London 1868) II, 436 f.; Sir Henry Wotton, *Reliquiae Wottonianae* (3rd ed., London 1672) 169-70.

Chapter 11–A Preface to *Arden of Feversham*

First of the extant tragedies of middle-class life in England, *Arden of Feversham* is generally regarded as the best (1). It deserves cordial study as the forerunner of the domestic drama, or bourgeois tragedy (what you will); in it we may behold the ancestor of the kind of drama dominant in our time. But scholars have been less concerned with this aspect of the play (2) than with the question of its authorship. Ever since Edward Jacob of Faversham published, in 1770, his claim that the poet behind the anonymous drama was William Shakespeare, controversy about the authorship has been sustained. Although the verdict of most investigators is a denial of Jacob's claim, few critics have doubted that *Arden* was the product of a talent that worked under the spell of Shakespeare, perhaps Christopher Marlowe, perhaps Thomas Kyd. The following pages are devoted to tracing the theatrical history of this unknown talent and his "dreadful story of domestic woes." (3)

The Register of the London Stationers Company tells us that, on 3 April 1592, "Edward white, Entred for his copie vnder th andes of the Lord Bishop of London and the wardens The Tragedie of Arden of Feuersham and Blackwall." (4) The latter name was a mistake, as the title-page of the first quarto of the tragedy witnesses:

"The Lamentable and True Tragedie of M. Arden of Feversham in Kent. Who was most wickedlye murdered, by the meanes of his disloyall and wanton wyfe, who for the loue she bare to one Mosbie, hyred two desperate ruffins Blackwill and Shakbag, to kill him. Wherein is shewed the great malice and discimulation of a wicked woman, the unsatiable desire of filthie lust and the shamefull end of all murder. Imprinted at London for Edward White, dwelling at the lyttle North dore of Paules Church at the sign of the Gun. 1592"(5)

White was not permitted to enjoy the pence-appeal of his quarto in peace. His commercial zeal brought him into collision with a rival publisher, Abel Jeffes, and the clash led them into the court of the Stationers Company. The Company passed judgment on the competitors on 18 December 1592: "Edward White and Abel Ieffes have eche of them offended. Viz Edw White in havinge printed the Spanish Tragedie belonging to Abel Ieffes/ and Abel Ieffes in having printed the Tragedie of Arden of Kent belonginge to Edw White." The two editions were ordered confiscated and forfeited to "thuse of the poore of the companye." Both printers were fined ten shillings each, and warned that they were in danger of prison sentences (6). Apparently, they managed to straighten out their difficulties, for White was able to issue a second black-letter quarto of *Arden* in 1599, very similar to the first quarto (7). He seems to have parted with the copyright; the third quarto appeared in 1633, "Printed by Eliz. Ailde dwelling neare Christs-Church." The widow Ailde did a poor job: her edition omitted many words from the play (8).

Since the publications of White and Ailde, *Arden of Feversham* suffered only one more vicissitude at the hands of publishers, and then became a text for academic travails in what has been wrongly designated the Shakespearean 'Apocrypha'. I have already mentioned the vicissitude: the enterprise of Edward Jacob in the identification of the man who wrote *Arden*. Jacob was a citizen of Faversham, Kent, the scene of the play, and extremely fond of his home town and its traditions. He wished to pluck a Shakespearean laurel for Faversham's crown; so he reprinted *The Lamentable and True Tragedie of M. Arden of Feversham*, "With a preface in which some reasons are offered in favour of its being the earliest dramatic work of Shakespear now remaining; and a genuine account given of the murder from authentic papers of the time." (9) Jacob's "reasons" were exhausted in half a page of unhappy parallels between phrases of Arden and phrases of Britain's supreme poet, such as "taunting letter", "painted cloth", "Basilisk", "Precisian", "Mermaid's song", "lean-faced knave", "white livered", "wild cat", "horned beast", "A Raven for a Dove", "buy his merriment as dear", "swear me on the inter-rogatories", and "death makes amends for sin". The ignorance dis-played by Jacob in identifying Shakespeare as the author of *Arden* on the basis of terms like these, which could be paralleled from dozens of Elizabethan plays, was truly phenomenal, even for the amateur researchers of his age. Nevertheless, his claim found eru-dite support, despite the protest of the *Edinburgh Review* that *Arden* was quite unlike the "earliest" manner of the master-dramatist, both in conception and execution (10). Yet so astute a scholar as A. H. Bullen remained almost persuaded that our tragedy had been "retouched here and there by the master's hand." And Eva Turner Clark tried to confirm the Jacob theory, with more pages of parallel passages in her *Hidden Allusions in Shakespeare's Plays* (1931) (11). Certainly, Arden came from the hand of a skilled and daring poet. Swinburne's rhapsodies over the drama are not necessary to prove that (12).

Scintillations like those of Shakespeare's genius were manifested by the writer of *Arden* in the way he handled the raw material of his tragedy. His source was one of Shakespeare's favourite books, Raphael Holinshed's famous *Chronicles of England, Scotland and Ireland* (1578). Seven columns of print, in five pages – 1703 to 1708 – were occupied by Holinshed in reporting the plot of Alice Arden to kill her husband and her success, exposure and punishment. Men of gravity in the government had told the historian, they wanted to see the moral lessons of the affair broadcast. But if Holinshed or the dramatist was aware of the sordid record of the case in the *Wardmote Book* of Faversham, he showed no anxiety for accuracy. The poet followed the historian in both errors and embellishments (13). Con-sequently, the date of the drama must be looked for between 1578 and April 1592, when it was registered for the press.

In the year after Holinshed's *Chronicle* was published, Elizabeth's court was entertained with a play entitled *The history of Murderous Mi-chael*, which may have been founded on the Faversham affair. Alice Arden's servant Michael is a prominent figure in the tragedy, an as-sassin comical in his clumsiness, yet attracted to poetic flights. The role would have fitted the comedian John Adams finely; he was the star of the players serving the Earl of Sussex, who performed *Murderous Michael* on 3 March 1579 (14). The idea that *Michael* was a primitive version of *Arden* has appealed to learned and subtle critics (15). The idea is upheld by the fact that traces of connexion between *Arden* and the actors of the Sussex troupe can be demonstrated.

Those traces led the vexatious but indefatigable Frederick Gard Fleay to credit Thomas Kyd with the writing of *Arden*, mainly on the ground of three parallels with *The Spanish Tragedy*, which there is no valid reason to believe was the work of Kyd (16) [see Chapter 13 –W.H.]. Similar evidence of Kyd's authorship was offered by Charles Crawford, who exhibited numerous striking resemblances between *Arden of Feversham* and *Solyman and Perseda*, which is also ascribed rashly to Kyd (17). Compare these two passages, for examples, from the disputed plays:

> (1) I think the ouerplus thats more than thine
>   Would mount to a greater sommoe of money
>   Then either thou or all thy kinne are worth. (18)
>
> It (a precious chain - - F.) was worth more then thou and all thy kin are worth. (19)
>
> (2) What ailes you, woman, to crie so suddenly?
>   Ah, neighbors, a sudden qualm... (20)
>
> What ailes you, madam, that your colour changes?
> A suddaine qualme... (21)

What plausible denial could be made to the claim that one mind was behind these verses, or else that the author of one happened to be aping the other? Even Frederick Boas, who refused to believe that the sportive but unlucky Kyd wrote *Arden*, admitted that "in the cadence and diction of many passages, and in the combination of lyrically elaborate verse-structure with colloquial directness of speech, *Arden of Feversham* recalls the manner of Kyd." (22) Boas thought Marlowe was the author of *Arden*, because Kyd, he said, "so far as we can judge, was not given to repetition. Marlowe, on the other hand, was a frequent borrower, and he might readily have adapted Kyd's lines to his own use, especially at a time when they were in close contact." (23) This opinion prompts the question: do we have enough authentic products of Kyd's pen to enable us to say definitely that he was not given to repetition? *Solyman and Perseda*, which Boas included among Kyd's works, is a repetition on a big scale of the inner play of *The Spanish Tragedy*, which a majority of scholars deem the composition of Kyd. And Boas failed to explain why the sky-storming creator of *Tamburlaine*, *Faustus*, *The Jew of Malta*, and *Edward II*, should have turned his Muse to the miseries of mediocre persons.

Parallels or no parallels, we have good proof that the creator of *Arden* rejoiced in the liberty of copying from the creator of *Hieronimo* and *Solyman*, proof derived from analysis of the way the anonymous dramatist treated the stuff of Holinshed's history. The chronicler pictured Black Will, the accomplice of Alice Arden, as a grim fearless killer. In the play he turns out a ludicrous braggart, made in the image of Basilisco, the rascal of *Solyman and Perseda*. The allusion to Basilisco as "the braginest knave in Christendom" instantly reminds us of Dick Reed in *Arden*, who is called "the raylingest knaue in christendome." (24) Boas noted moreover that the villains of these two plays "might owe something to the creator of Pedringano and Serberine in *The Spanish Tragedy*," (25) In my opinion, they owe their very existence to that poet's closest comrade.

Kyd the scrivener for players probably was inspired by his handiwork on *Arden of Feversham* to write a characteristic booklet, licensed for printing on 28 June 1592: *The trueth of the most wicked and secret murthering of John Brewen, Goldsmith of London, committed by his owne wife, through the prouocation of one John Parker whom she loued: for which fact she was burned, and he hanged in Smithfield, on wednesday, the 28 of June 1592, two yeares after the murther was committed.* "Imprinted at London for

Iohn Kid, and are to be sold by Edward White, dwelling at the little North doore of Paules, at the sign of the Gun." This was a piece of journalism with a glaring likeness in theme and treatment to *Arden of Feversham*. The pamphlet was registered on the very day John Brewen's murderers went to their death. In the narrative Kyd included several expressions taken from Holinshed. He described an attempt by Mistress Anne Brewen to poison her husband with pottage; that recalls the scene where Alice Arden tries to kill her husband in the same way. The account of a quarrel between Parker and his paramour sounds like an echo of the quarrel of Mosbie and Alice. Both women were made to cry out that they would never have been tempted to turn strumpet if the quarrelling never had allured them (26). The very cry, "woe worth!" appears in both scenes of the pamphlet and the play. The Brewen tract may be classified according to the words used by the author of *Arden* to describe his drama:

> this naked Tragedy,
> Wherein no filed points are foisted in
> To make it gratious to the eare or eye;
> For simple trueth is gratious enough,
> And needes no other points of glosing stuffe. (27)

Nevertheless, Arden does contain some "points of glosing stuff," chiefly borrowed from Kyd's chamber-companion Kit Marlowe and Marlowe's intimate friend Thomas Watson. Close echoes of Marlowe's *Edward II* have been heard in our burgess tragedy (28). And the portrait of the thief Jack Fitten in *Arden* is a spitting image of Pilia-Borza in *The Jew of Malta* (29). I suspect that the allusions to Ovid's *Amores* in our play were inspired by Marlowe's version of the erotic Roman poems, done probably during his Cambridge years (1581-87). The earliest editions of Marlowe's *Amores* were undated, leading a clandestine existence as pornography. Kyd's own knowledge of Ovid was, to put it mildly, meagre. The poet of *Arden* was well acquainted with Tom Watson's erotic rimes, *Hekatompathia* (registered simply as *Passions* in 1582) and *Tears of Fancy*, posthumously printed in 1593. *The Spanish Tragedy* and *Solyman and Perseda* show adaptations of at least two of Watson's *Passions*. And the phrase "let my passions penetrate", used by murderous Michael in *Arden*, recurs in the *Tears*, which doubtless circulated among Watson's private friends long before his death in September 1592 (30).

I find evidence of the authorship of *Arden* in these three lines of comparison for a Kentish fog (which plays no part in Holinshed's history):

> This mist, my friend, is misticall,
> Lyke to a good companions smoaky braine,
> That was halfe dround with new ale ouer night. (31)

Kit Marlowe was a Kentishman. And his notorious alcoholic lectures on metaphysics have left vestiges in the squealings of state delivered by the gallows-haunted Richard Baines (reported in John Bakeless's biography and Tucker Brooke's account of Marlowe's life). The reference to smoke may be a reminiscence of Sir Walter Ralegh's Virginia revelation; under the influence of his tobacco and his man of science, Thomas Hariot, the dramatist must have often felt his brain "half drowned" and half-uplifted to mystical visions of heaven.

In the spring of 1591, according to the town annals of Faversham, the Queen's company of actors and the players of the "Earl of Essex" performed on the native ground of Arden. E. K. Chambers deemed it "conceivable" that Essex may have been a pen-slip for Sussex (32). It is tempting to imagine *Arden of Feversham* being produced in that very town in the year before it was delivered to the press. The records of Faversham tell us that the Sussex company acted there in 1589. They might have played *Murderous Michael* there, and afterward given Marlowe the old tragedy for reincarnation as *Arden of Feversham*. About the middle of 1590, I believe, when he was writing in the same room with Thomas Kyd, employed by a certain Lord about whom Kyd wrote to Sir John Puckering, but never named, Marlowe wrote *Arden* for their Lord's players (33). And the drama was done during some extremely torrid days (34).

The belief that our play was written for enactment in the summer of 1590 is supported by the fact that Faversham was excited during this time by the deeds of two bandits named Curtail and Manwaring, whose repute was much like that of Black Will and Shakebag in *Arden*. There is a scene in Act 4 which takes place on the Kentish coast opposite the Isle of Sheppey, where the two robbers sheltered themselves (35). Sir Roger Manwood of Kent, who later did some favours for his countryman Marlowe, hunted these criminals.

Among the conspirators against the life of Master Arden was a poor gentleman named Greene, and the poet did all in his power to make the name infamous. This could have been Marlowe's retaliation against Robert Greene for making fun of him among his tavern friends. The original Greene of the murder case was named John; the author of Arden changed it to Richard (36). Robert Greene was well known in London as a companion of criminals, in particular one "Cutting Ball". (37) Richard Greene makes his first appearance in the play right after the adulteress Alice has remarked,

> In London many alehouse Ruffins keepe,
> Which, as I heare, will murther men for gould.

Richard Greene promises to liberate her from husbandage, to "hyre some Cutter for to cut (Arden) short." (38) This Greene is supposed to be a citizen of Faversham, but the writer of *Arden* affirms that he has known the villain Black Will in London for twelve years (39). Despite his pleasure in consorting with cutthroats, Richard Greene, like Robert, was "religious", a fellow of "great deuotion"! (40) Let us observe also the affection of the two Greenes for the fables of Aesop. In the preface to Robert Greene's *Menaphon* (1588), where blank-verse bards are satirised with ill-concealed envy, the humorist Thomas Nashe had taunted Kyd with an alleged tale of a "Kidde in Aesop" – actually in Spenser's *Shepherds Calendar*. In *Arden* the "cutters" Will and Shakebag are lessoned by Richard Greene with a story from Aesop (41). Incidentally, this Greene is not made an actor in the scene of the stabbing of *Arden*, and the last we see of him is when he trembles in fear of arrest and pleads with the stronger spirited Alice, "But cleaue to us as we wil stick to you."

If the author of *Arden* had Robert Greene in mind when he drew the character of Richard Greene, he must have been thinking of two more sinister men of London's underworld when he created Black Will and George Shakebag. Although he described them as denizens of Kent ("Two Ruffer Ruffins neuer liued in Kent") (42) he pictured them as heartily at home in London's most evil streets. And London, at the time *Arden* was staged, had not yet cleansed her nostrils of the memory of two scoundrels whom these outlaws of *Arden* resemble. The two scoundrels were also named Will and George. Anyone who knew Kit Marlowe and Tom Watson well would have known about their murderous enemies, Will Bradley and George Orrell. The wry-necked soldier Orrell – portrayed in a state document of the Essex revolt in 1601 thus: "a most desperate rakehell as lives" (43) – appears to have been more brute than braggart. He could have snarled with Shakebag, "I cannot paint my valour out with words", and sneered at warnings of hell and ghosts:

Nay, then lets go sleepe, when buges and feares
Shall kill our courages with their fancies worke. (44)

Shortly after Tom Watson's brother-in-law, Hugh Swift, requested the protection of the law against George Orrell, in the summer of 1589, Will Bradley petitioned the Court of the Queen's Bench for security of peace against Swift and Watson: *ob metum mortis* (45). This Bradley, a tavern keeper's son, was probably the same Will Bradley who assaulted one Robert Wood in the autumn of 1588 with a cudgel, so that Wood seemed in peril of death. He had denounced Bradley on the day of the assault as a worthless fellow, a bully (46). Who could miss the likeness of this deadly Will to Black Will in *Arden of Feversham*, with his boasts of assault and battery?

"in Temes streete a brewers carte was lyke to haue runne ouer me: I made no more ado, but went to the clark and cut all the

natches of his tales and beat them about his head... . I haue broken a Sariants head with his owne mace." (47)

On 28 September 1589, bully Will Bradley fought a duel with Tom
Watson's brave friend Marlowe in the neighbourhood of Cripplegate. Watson arrived, and Bradley shouted hexameter iambics at
him: "Art thou now come? Then I will have a bout with thee!" (48)
With his sword and dagger he cut Watson severely. But the poet
retreating drove his sword into Bradley's chest, and thus abridged
the braggart's doleful days. Nearly five months after Watson entered
Newgate prison for killing Bradley, he received the Queen's pardon,
and in less than two years stopped all his sins. But the rakehell Orrell lived to win honour for gallantry in her Majesty's service in the
Ireland wars.

Arden of Feversham slowly commenced a series of plays concerned
with household tragedies of murder and adultery in middle-class
Britain. The tradition of what might be termed theatrical journalism
was continued by the anonymous success *A Warning for Fair Women*,
produced by the Lord Chamberlain's men (Shakespeare's company)
and published in 1599. This grim yet sometimes charming drama
has also been attributed to Kyd, but on very brittle evidence. Virtually anonymous was *The Yorkshire Tragedy*, printed in 1608, as performed by the King's troop, formerly the Chamberlain's men, and
advertised as the product of the pen of "W. Shakespeare"! Could it
have been manufactured by the maltdealer and moneylender from
Stratford? The paltry play is enlisted among the Shakespeare
'Apocrypha' merely because of the titlepage signature. Seven years
before, one Robert Yarington, about whom nothing else is known,
emerged in London as the writer of *Two Lamentable Tragedies. The one
of the Murther of Maister Beech. .. The other of a Young Childe murthered in a
Wood by two Ruffins*. The chief rivals of Shakespeare's troop, the Lord
Admiral's men, acted these plays, but nobody knows when. A lost
play alleged to be by John Webster and John Ford is believed to
have continued the mode of *Arden*; the tragedy was named *A Late
Murder of the Son upon the Mother*. Lovers of the poetry of pity and

terror, as well as detectives of the filial complexes, must regret the loss of this play. Who would not cheerfully pitch to oblivion a hundred Yarington tragedies for one drama by Webster and Ford?

The stage chronicle of *Arden* is soon told. There is no record of its enactment on the boards or after Edward White issued it in blackletter. It may have been revived shortly before the Puritan Revolution; there is a ballad of 48 stanzas in the Roxburghe Collection, dated about 1633 by Bullen, entitled "Complaint and lamentation of Mistresse Arden, of Feversham in Kent, who for the love of one Mosbie, hired certaine Ruffians and Villaines most cruelly to murder her Husband; with the fatall end of her and her Associates". A mysterious B. L signed the ballad before it was printed for C. Wright. It went to the ancient popular tune of *Fortune My Foe.*

Mrs Eliza Haywood resurrected *Arden of Feversham* and altered it considerably for a performance at the Haymarket theatre on 21 January 1736. She reduced it to three acts. Unfortunately, we have no report of the play's appeal (49). The successful burgess tragedian George Lillo attempted a third revival, in five acts for the Theatre Royal in Drury Lane. He died leaving the drama "imperfect", his pious editor Thomas Davies informs us, and Dr John Hoadly finished it. Its performance in the summer of 1762, Davies says, "though much applauded", did not earn more than one night's esteem. He fancied its failure might have been due to "adhering too strictly to our old chronicles." (50) There is an account of another production at the Drury Lane house on 19 July 1759, and a play of the same name was given at Covent Garden on 14 April 1790 (51). Then apparently the phantoms of Arden and his Alice and her Mosbie were allowed to stay dormant for more than a century. At last in 1906 A. H. Bullen printed a tragedy called *Lilies That Fester*, a one-act drama "Adapted from the old play *Arden of Feversham*", by the stage wizard William Poel. Since then the play has been left to the libraries. We have no evidence of any theatrical adventures of the three German translations of *Arden*, including the fine one by Ludwig Tieck, nor of the French version by Francois Victor Hugo, nor the Dutch edition by Kuitert.

Opinions on the merits of our tragedy vary extremely. The rhapsodic Swinburne thought it was worthy of Shakespeare, but offered no material proof. John Addington Symonds also judged it a masterpiece, but he was not so eager to discover the fingers of Shakespeare in the play (52). E. H. Oliphant argued, and F. S. Boas agreed with him, that, if Christopher Marlowe did not compose *Arden*, "there is no other known playwright of the time whose hand can be traced in its finest flights."(53) On the contrary side stands Adolphus W. Ward, and those who agree with him that "the play as a whole, is but a slovenly piece of work, and the characters carrying on its action are throughout either repulsive or uninteresting." (54) My inclination is to take a stance halfway between the two critical poles. Surely *Arden* is not grandly constructed; it exhibits frequent signs of writer's haste, reckless haste. It descends from the terrible to the ridiculous when, after the knifing of Arden, Black Will departs with this speech:

> We haue our gould; mistris Alice, adew;
> Mosbie, farewell, and Michaell, farewell too. (55)

Surely the author sympathised with Black Will when he made him blurt,

> I tell thee, Greene, the forlorne trauailer,
> Whose lips are glewed with sommers parching heat,
> Nere longd so much to see a running brooke
> As I to finish Ardens Tragedy. (56)

Moreover, the characters are not all repulsive or bereft of psychological concern, Franklin, Arden's friend, whom the dramatist seems to have invented, is compassionately portrayed. And the variety of villains in the quickly shifting scenes are sometimes fascinating or simply funny. There are times when the language of the play reaches incisive phrase and memorable cadence. And the portrayal of Mistress Alice is accomplished with genuine insight. Verily, in its finest flights *Arden of Feversham* deserves the praise of the *tragedia cothurnata* or Marlowe, the marvellous lad of Kent, the Villon of England, who wrote it, as I have surmised, in the summer of 1590, when he was working under the orders of Thomas Kyd's unknown Lord, most likely, Edward de Vere, the Earl of Oxford, the Lord Chamberlain of England.

Notes

1   Felix E. Schelling, *Elizabethan Playwrights* (New York 1925) 88.
2   See Henry Hitch Adams, *English Domestic or Homiletic Tragedy* (New York 1943).
3   Prologue, by a Friend, to George Lillo's *Arden of Feversham; An Historical Tragedy*, in *Lillo's Dramatic Works*, ed. Thomas Davies (second edition, improved: London 1810) II, 174.
4   *Transcript of the Stationers' Company's Register*, ed. Edward Arber, II, 607.
5   Copies of the first quarto are in the Bodleian Library and the Dyce Collection of South Kensington, London; reprinted as a Tudor Facsimile Text in 1911.
6   Records of the Court of the Stationers' Company, eds. W. W. Greg and E. Boswell, 44.
7   The only copy of the second quarto extant belonged to the library of Dukes of Devonshire before the Huntington Library of California could afford it for its rarities. Its variations from the first quarto were minutely noted by Karl Warnke and Ludwig Proescholdt in *Arden of Feversham. Revised and Edited with Introduction and Notes* (Halle 1888).
8   Q3 is found in the Bodleian Library and the British Museum.
9   Jacob's edition was an octavo, printed at Faversham by Stephen Doorne. Cp Charles Edward Donne, *An Essay on the Tragedy of Arden of Feversham* (London 1873).
10 *Edinburgh Review*, LXXI, 471.
11 Bullen, ed. *Arden of Feversham, a Tragedy*; reprinted from the edition of 1592 (London 1887). Cp N. Delius, *Arden of Feversham, Ein Shakspere zugeschriebenes Drama* (Elberfeld 1885). Also Eva Turner Clark, *Hidden Allusions in Shakespeare's Plays* (New York 1931; reprinted with elaborate notes by Ruth Loyd Miller, Jennings, La. 1974) 252-297. Mrs Miller suggested "A Stylistic Computer Study Would Identify the Author of *Arden* "(297).
12 Swinburne, *A Study of Shakespeare* (London 1880) 136.
13 J. Chilton, *The History of Arden of Feversham. A Tragic Fact of 1550.* (London 1804). A. F. Hopkinson, ed. *Arden of Feversham*, With Introduction and Notes (London 1907); Play Sources, ed. Anon. The Original Stories on Which Were Founded the Tragedies of 'Arden of Feversham', & 'A Warning for Fair

Women', to Which Is Added Thomas Kyd's Pamphlet, 'The Murder of John Brewen' (London 1913). -

14   E. K. Chambers, *The Elizabethan Stage* (Oxford 1923) II, 93.

15   Schelling, *op. cit.* 46. J. A. Symonds, *Shakspere's Predecessors in the English Drama* (London 1884) 332.

16   Fleay, *Biographical Chronicle of the English Drama* (London 1891) II, 28. See Bronson Feldman, "Thomas Watson, Dramatist", *The Bard* 1(1977)132-6.

17   Crawford, "The Authorship of 'Arden of Feversham'", *Shakespeare Jahrbuch*, XXXIX, 74-86; also in *Collectanea*, First Series (Stratford on Avon 1906) 101-130. F. S. Boas, ed., *Works of Thomas Kyd* (Oxford 1901) liv-lx.

18   *Arden of Feversham*, III, vi, 17-19, in *The Shakespeare Apocrypha*, ed. C. F. Tucker Brooke (Oxford 1929). Perhaps the best modernised text of *Arden* is the edition of Ronald Bayne (London 1897).

19   *Solyman and Perseda*, I, iv, 74, in Kyd's *Works*, ed. Boas.

20   *Arden*, 5.1, 308-9.

21   Solyman, II, i, 49-50.

22   Boas, *op. cit.*, lxxxix-xc.

23   Boas, *Christopher Marlowe* (Oxford 1940) 199. In the *Works of Kyd* Boas read the letter to Puckering erroneously, and made Marlowe and Kyd collaborators for the unknown Lord of their players for "iij" years instead of "vi" as the original document plainly states.

24   *Solyman*, I, iii, 211; *Arden*, 4.4, 54. In *The Bard* (loc. cit. 131 f.) I have given reasons for identifying Watson as the writer of *Solyman*.

25   Boas, *Marlowe*, 200.

26   See Crawford, *op. cit.*, 115, for a succinct description of the parallels.

27   *Arden*, V, Epilogue, 14-18. The "naked" manner of *Arden* presents Marlovian art, precisely as we see it in *The Massacre at Paris*, both, I assume, penned at the command of Marlowe's Lord.

28   H. B. Charlton and R. D. Waller, eds., *Edward II* (London 1933) 17-18.

29   *Arden*, II, i, 49-54; *The Jew of Malta*, 4.1, 7-8. According to my chronology, the latter play was composed in 1589.

30   Verses from Watson's *Tears* are in the Rawlinson MS (British Museum). The passage quoted is from Sonnet 43, paralleled by *Arden*, II, ii, 16.

31   Arden, 4.2, 6-8. If I am right in relating this "mystical mist" verse to Marlowe, the lines that follow become queerly prophetic of his murder: "Twere pitty but his scull were opened to make more Chimny roome."

32   Chambers, *The Elizabethan Stage*, II, 112. John Adams, formerly the top comedian of the Sussex company, was conscripted into the Queen's troop in 1583.

33   Feldman, *op. cit.* 141.

34   For references to summer weather in *Arden*, see I, 58; II, ii, 102-5.

35   Cp Henry Eths, ed., *Original Letters, Illustrative of English History*, 2d Series (London 1827) III, 185.

36 *Arden*, I, 556; III, v, 159. Cp notes in Bayne edition.
37 Alexander Dyce, ed., *Dramatic and Poetical Works of Robert Greene* (London 1861) 22.
38 *Arden*, I, 446-7, 523.
39 *Ibid.*, 5.1, 7.
40 *Ibid.*, I, 589-590.
41 *Ibid.*, III, vi, 30. The reader may remember Robert Greene's use of Aesop alleged by Henry Chettle in *Greene's Groatsworth of Wit* (1592).
42 *Arden*, III, i, 70.
43 Mark Eccles, *Christopher Marlowe in London* (Harvard 1934) 61f. Dr Eccles found a record of Orrell's indictment for breaking into the home of Aaron Holland, the owner of the Red Bull playhouse, and attacking Holland and his wife so savagely they were afraid they would die (*idem*).
44 *Arden*, III, ii, 19-20; II, ii, 116.
45 Eccles, *op. cit.*, 57. One of the minor characters involved in the crime of Arden was named Bradshaw. The dramatist changed the name of another shady character in the story from William Blackburn to Clarke, none can tell why.
46 Eccles, *op. cit.* 49-50.
47 *Arden*, 5.1, 21 *et seq.*
48 Eccles, *op. cit.*, 10. Tucker Brooke, *op. cit.* xiii, remarked that 1590 is the earliest year to which "the actual writing of the play (*Arden*) can easily be referred"; but advanced no reasons for choosing this date.
49 Allardyce Nicoll, *Early Eighteenth Century Drama* (Cambridge 1925) 71n.
50 Thomas Davies, ed. *Lillo's Dramatic Works*, II, 37. Lillo sentimentally softened the character of Alice Arden; and he kept a unity of scenes at Faversham.
51 John Genest, *Some Account of the English Stage* (London 1832) IV, 553-5; VI, 602.
52 Symonds, *op. cit.*, 332. Henry Tyrrell (*The Doubtful Plays of Shakespeare*, London 1851) harmonised with Symonds.
53 Oliphant, *Shakespeare and His Fellow Dramatists* (New York 1929) I, 28 1-2; Boas, *Marlowe* 200.
54 Ward, *History of English Dramatic Literature to the Death of Queen Anne* (London 1899) II, 218. I am unacquainted with the position on authorship taken by Laurette Brumus and Loleh Bellon in their recent translation, *Arden de Faversham, Drame en 5 Actes* (Paris 1957).
55 *Arden*, 5.1, 26 1-2.
56 *Ibid.*, II, ii, 102-5.

Chapter 12–A Tyrant's Vein

As the chief defender of Christendom against the onslaughts of Islam the absolute monarchy of Spain commanded the respect of all faithful Europeans. For its services at war with the slave-hunting navies of the Turks and the Barbary pirates, if for nothing else, the Spanish autocracy deserved the glory cast on it by Lope de Vega, Cervantes, Tirso de Molina, El Greco, Velasquez and Calderón, and the rest of its masters of painting and poetry. The national dignity they expressed had its roots, I imagine, in the tragic conscience developed by the people in their centuries of struggle with the Moors and the Jews, struggle that ended in the triumph of Christianity, destruction of great alien civilisation, and the permanent penury of Spain. Their conscience secured a brief era of justification and grandeur – no matter how grotesque the grandeur – when the struggle was transferred to the theatre of the Mediterranean Sea.

The golden age of the Spanish drama seems to have evolved from the conflict in the nation's hearts between the sense of guilt for what they had done to their country and the sense of pride for what they contributed to the continent. Spanish literary genius never solved the riddles that absorbed it during the battles of the Crescent and the Cross. But fiction does not mainly aim at the solution of problems: its purpose primarily is to console people beautifully for their failure to solve them. And the solaces of literature increased the pride of Spaniards in their quixotic victories. All Christendom felt the suffering in Spanish pride and experienced a terror and pity in its presence that no humour could overwhelm. If other nations laughed at the vanity of the Spaniards, and portrayed them satirically on the stage, especially the arrogance of their warriors, the laughter ordinarily carried with it quavers and overtones of envy or reverence. It was only when the ramparts of Europe no longer needed watching by the soldiers of Spain, to prevent the barbaric incursions of Africa and Asia, that the light of her arms and arts paled down.

Spanish culture paid a heavy price for its victories over the Moslem menace. After long years of strife and truce with it, Spain unconsciously came to imitate certain Turkish manners and practices. These took more or less amusing forms in rhetoric and styles of court behaviour and diplomacy. The pomps of the sultans and their satraps, the gorgeous solemnities of language, and the dumbshows of despotism and servility that constituted good conduct at the Sublime Porte, in the radiance of the Solimans and Amuraths, found grave mimicries at the court of Madrid. So we see the heroes of Calderón's dramas unable to distinguish between genuine nobility, the greatness of personality, and the distinction of public artifice. Fondly they introduce themselves with ceremonious enumeration of their titles. The Spanish ideal in speech and art was the bizarre, sublimity in torment, with all voluptuous impulses cruelly restrained and transformed to the ecstasy of the *auto de fé* – the feat of faith, self-sacrifice with megalomania, in courtesy, piety, sport or war. On the stage the Spaniards thinned and lengthened their figures just as El Greco distorted his saints, "to make celestial bodies – appear large, however small they are, like we see lights when we see them from a distance" (1). Nothing that attracted the contemplation of the grandee and hidalgo could be considered small. And the small could always aggrandise itself by emphasis of deformity, by dwarfish stunts of buffoon or tragedian. The very beggars of Spain boasted of having aristocratic blood.

The "Most Catholic" King Philip II maintained in his own region a state curiously resembling the Turkish government. Not only did he employ assassins to get rid of dangerous critics of his regime. He was suspected of poisoning his own kin in order to preserve his will supreme. He kept the souls of his officers, like the Ottoman lords their women, locked indoors. The officers, like the Moslem women, were rewarded for their loyalty with luxuries. Philip's absolutism covered a multitude of barely united provinces, each practically autonomous under the dictatorship of viceroys and governors. Like the tyrants of the Orient he let the folk pursue their old usage, with different provincial customs and laws, different modes of taxes and currency, even war flags of various colours. Like the sultans, emperor Philip refused to encourage the collaboration of his subjects, to promote their commerce and industry. And as their exchange declined, their means of communication were neglected, the national roads deserted, left without light, and the conversation that inspires and circulates literature faded away. Writing at the capital city, of course, went on in the conventional ways.

But the unconscious mimicry of Turkish techniques had an infinitely less funny effect on Spanish morality, on the national code of honour. The ferocity and frigidity with which the Solimans and Amuraths treated the "infidels" of their empire, the rebels against their religion, had their counterparts in the Philippic empire. The Christian autocrat was no less murderous and merciless to men, women and children who would not bow down before his Roman Catholic categories and dogmas. The horrors performed by the Spanish champions of the Papacy and their Holy Office of inquisition on the heretics in their power wrung from desperate fighters for liberty in religion the cry "Better the Turk than the Pope!" (2). The Catholics triumphantly took this outburst as proof that the Protestants were enemies of Christendom. The cry however was a response of torture to the policy of Philip and his Hapsburg cousin, the Kaiser of the Holy Roman Empire, Ferdinand II, who vowed that he "would rather make his dominion a desert than rule over Protestants" (3). Ferdinand too had learnt many lessons, obliviously, from the wrestlings of his Austria with the Moslem menace.

For the absolute royalists there could be no compromise with the preachers of free conscience in theology. Philip and his kindred knew that popular freedom in matters of church was bound to extend itself to freedom of decision in matters of state. They had always before their eyes the republic of the Protestants in Switzerland. The enthusiasm of Calvinists for congregational self-rule provoked the autocrats to greater violence against all critics of the Roman sanctions of their state. The English experiment under the boy Edward VI and his uncles of the Seymour family, to combine central political power with reform of the state religion in favour of

Calvinist destiny doctrine, left no doubt in the minds of the continental dynasts that their government and the new orthodoxy could only make peace over one or the other's corpse.

They saw burgess upstarts climbing to influence in England, pushing over the heads of old Catholic nobility, turning the court of Edward into rings of intrigue which threatened to pull the land into a pit of civil war. The nine-days queendom of Jane Grey, which proclaimed the heirs of the Tudor crown to be bastards, convinced the Hapsburgs and the Valois monarchs that their own crowns would be flung to dirt if Protestants were permitted to gather strength, the requisite political strength. When Mary Tudor married King Philip and restored the Church of Rome to ritual authority in England, the absolutists breathed easier. But Mary could not give back to the Roman creed the economic might that her father had stripped away for the Tudor crown. Her own absolutism depended on the fidelity of courtiers, both ardent Catholics and renegade Calvinists, who profited from his expropriation of monasteries, convents, hospitals, chantries and other riches of the church. Racking and burning heretics were poor compensation to Mary and Philip for the Catholic loss. He left England with the determination to keep the Protestants of his continental and colonial lands from ever making a mockery of his crown and creed. Rather than see them challenging his sovereignty he would make his reign one of perpetual terror.

Philip went to the Netherlands, whose overlordship he enjoyed by right of inheritance from the dukedom of Burgundy, and saw the little country overrun by Calvinists, Lutherans, Anabaptists, and every variety of rebellion against the religion he upheld. Here and there the inquisitors serving the Vicar in the Vatican had the force to commit heretics to chains and the stake, but in general the Catholic nobles of the Low Countries allowed the insurgent sects to run riot so long as they restricted themselves to speech and press. Those nobles loved their ancient feudal privileges and were hostile to the single supremacy of the Roman priesthood as they were to the concentration of political power in the hands of their Spanish king. Philip left the Low Countries with the resolution to back up the inquisitor with the best troops his American silver mines could buy.

* * * * *

In 1559, in the treaty of Château Cambresis, Philip of Hapsburg reached an agreement with Henry VII of Valois for a secret war against their common enemy (4).

The alliance of the Roman-resolute dynasts threw a chill across the Christmas revelries of the new Protestant queen of England. For centuries the foreign policy of the English had run contrary to French interest and found aid and comfort in the policy of Spain, which William Cecil liked to call "Burgundian". The pact of marriage between King Philip and Princess Elizabeth of France, arranged at Château Cambresis, appeared to spell ruin for English prosperity and peace. Elizabeth Tudor and her councillors watched the wedding festivities in Paris with emotions that must have left a trace in literature. The Protestant playwrights of London surely felt a vocation to answer the challenge of the French and Spanish kings.

On 6 February 1559, a gentleman named Schifanoya wrote to Vivaldino, the ambassador of Mantua with King Philip in Brussels, reporting events in London. Among these he mentioned: "There are still many frivolous foolish people who daily invent plays in taverns deriding the religion, and by placards posted at the corners of streets, they invite people to the taverns, to see these representations, taking money from their audience" (5).

When the arm of divine providence seemed to manifest itself on 31 June 1559, in the accidental death of King Henry, at the height of his rejoicing in a tournament, the vocation would have sounded irresistible. Count Gabriel Montgomery, the Scottish commander of the King's bodyguards, inflicted the fatal wound by what is designated nowadays a Freudian error of his spear. Instead of lowering it according to the tournament rules, he raised his lance suddenly and struck the King in one eye. Horror-stricken at his mistake, Montgomery went down on his knees to the Queenmother Catherine de'Medici, but she never forgave him. I believe that she perceived in the brave and devout soldier a Caledonian conscience, which had been severely strained by having recently been ordered to observe the execution of certain Huguenot heretics. She forced Montgomery to quit the royal court, and in his banishment he became a commander of Huguenot troops. King Henry died of his brain wound on 10 July. His sixteen-year-old daughter-in-law, Mary Stuart of Scotland, stood by his deathbed with her husband, poor Francis II, who at fifteen had no desire to be sovereign of France: "O God," he cried, "how can I live if my father dies!"

On 8 September 1559, Queen Elizabeth held her official mourning ritual for the unfortunate King Henry. Among her minor annoyances at this time was the obstinacy of Sebastian Westcott, Master of the Choristers at Paul's Cathedral, who refused obedience to the royal reform of the Church. The first famous production of the Elizabethan theatre, *Cambises, King of Persia*, was, in my judgement, a response to the triumphal insolence and tragedy of the tyrant of France.

A Lamentable Tragedy, Mixed Full of Pleasant Mirth, Containing the Life of Cambises, King of Persia, written by Thomas Preston, was registered in the London Stationers guild book in 1569-70 by the printer John Ailde. Scholars long supposed that Preston wrote the play in the late autumn of 1559, because of a reference in the past tense to the Catholic prelate Bishop Edmund Bonner, who died in September 1569. Yet the same passage also refers to King Cambises in the past tense, although he does not die until the next scene.

What a king was he that hath used such tyranny,
He was akin to Bishop Bonner, I think verily,
For both their delights was to shed blood,
But never intended to do any good (6).

It appears likely that Preston interpolated these lines on the eve of his play's publication, when Bonner's death was news fit for sharpening a moral on state cruelty. Investigators now believe that the farcical tragedy must have been composed several years before it was printed. Customarily the theatrical companies of the time guarded their manuscripts jealously until the stage had exhausted all profit from them. The popularity of Preston's work would have kept it from the press for years. It might have been produced as early as the Christmas of 1560, or the following January, for in this holiday season Elizabeth and her court were entertained with a play called *Huff, Snuff and Ruff* names which acridly remind us of the three ruffian soldiers in *Cambises*, Huf, Snuf and Ruf (7).

The death of the Persian autocrat in the play invokes the memory of the tragic fate of Henry II of France, when that monarch displayed his prowess at the tournament in honour of the approaching marriage of his princess Elizabeth and the despot of Spain. The tournament took place at the foot of the Bastille prison, where the Protestant leader Anne Dubourg waited for martyrdom. A broken lance wielded by Gabriel Montgomery, the King's guard from Scotland, mortally hurt Henry above his right eye, as I have already noted, and he left his beloved Catherine de'Medici a widow on 10 July (8). From the oblivion of Montgomery's own brain sprang this deed, which led to his development to valiant leadership of French heretics in war. He died a hero of insurrection against Valois rule. At the moment when his lance pierced Henry's head his Scottish heart may have already been beating unaware in sympathy with the faith of John Knox and Anne Dubourg. At all events, there is a strong probability that some vision of the French monarch's misfortune raced in Thomas Preston's mind when he had Cambises come on the stage in the final scene to describe how he had been accidentally struck to death:

> As I on horseback up did leap my sword from scabbard shot,
> And ran me thus into the side, as you right well may see (9).

It is conceivable that the poet got the story of his despot's takingoff from the Latin translation of Herodotus by Lorenzo Valla. More likely, he used Richard Taverner's *Garden of Wisdom* (1539), founded on the *Apophthegmata* of Erasmus, a standard text of wise saws and classic history instances. No matter what source Preston used, it would seem most suitable soon after the summer of 1559, when news of the French tyrant's end would give the last episode of *Cambises* its keenest dramatic poignancy in English Protestant eyes. It would be absurd to argue that Preston's protagonist was meant as an image of Catherine de Medici's husband. Cambises clearly stands for tyranny in general, as the English patriot of the period understood it.

A patriotic playwright under the last of the Tudors could not write about tyranny without conjuring up in the souls of his hearers the idea of Philip of Spain. To a poet who abhorred the spirit of Bishop Bonner, the Spaniard's "Most Catholic" Majesty was the terror of the world. Preston must have been a compassionate witness, if not an active penman, of the comedies in derision of King Philip which were staged in London immediately after the death of his English wife, Bonner's fanatic queen. "Bloody Mary", as the enthusiasts for Bloody Bess always called her, and her dear Cardinal Pole had lain scarcely two months in the grave, when the Venetian Paolo Tiepolo reported to his senate how the English capital went wild over these farces directed at Romanist royalty. "The demonstrations and performances of plays by the London populace in the hostels and taverns," he said, were "so vituperative and abominable that it was marvellous they should so long have been tolerated, for they brought upon the stage all personages whom they wished to revile, however exalted their station, and among the rest, in one play, they represented King Philip, the late Queen of England, and Cardinal Pole, reasoning together about such things as they imagined might have been said by them in the matter of religion" (10).

Elizabeth herself seems to have indulged at least once in the mood of these Protestant plays. In January 1559 she was entertained by a masque entitled *Papists* (11). The Spanish ambassador, Conde de Feria, protested to her about the common theatre polemics against his King. He wrote to Philip in April: "She was very emphatic in saying that she wished to punish severely certain persons who had represented some comedies in which your Majesty was aped" (12). De Feria had a firm suspicion, who was responsible for the eruption of these plays. "I knew," he told Philip, "that a member of her Council had given the arguments to construct these comedies; which is true, for Cecil gave them, as indeed she partly admitted to me" (13). None of the comedies that Sir William Cecil, the Principal Secretary of State (meaning secret-keeper), was accused of instigating on the Philippic church and state survived. The Spanish embassy complained no more about them after the spring of 1559. In May Queen Bess warned her people that she would "permit none to be played wherein either matters of religion or of the governance of the estate of the common weal shall be handled or treated, being no meet matters to be written or treated upon, but by men of authority, learning and wisdom, nor to be handled before any audience, but of grave and discreet persons" (14). Still it is plausible that the dramatic propaganda against the despotism of Spain and the Papacy continued in a less downright outspoken shape. Meanwhile the common people clung to the conviction that virtually all actors of the realm were fellows of the "Popery" persuasion.

As the literal drama declined the literary drama improved. When Thomas Preston pictured Cambises inheriting his crown from the great Cyrus, and declaring war on the people of Egypt who resisted his brutal government, the gallery wits and the groundlings could have discerned in his Persian features the heir of Francis I hounding the Huguenots, or the son of Charles V persecuting the Netherlands. At the same time the Oriental fiction expanded their imaginations almost to global proportions and fortified the power to generalise thought. There is humour but not contempt in Shakespeare's parody of "King Cambises' vein" in the First Part of *Henry IV* (2.4), where Falstaff mimes the tyrant's mixture of wine and rant, and the treatment of his queen's tears. Preston's ludicrous tragedy marked a milestone in the education of English dramatists, on the road from sermons and journalism to art.

The Epilogue of *Cambises* seems to indicate that Preston made it at the request of a person or persons whom he was bound to oblige.

"Quod Thomas Preston" to his gentle auditors:

> According to our duty we have not refused,
> But to our best intent exprest everything:
> We trust none is offended for this our doing.

Perhaps the play did give offence with its spectacles of butchery mingled with bawdry. (It compels recall of Hamlet's remark about the Lord Chamberlain of Denmark whom historians have deemed an image of William Cecil: "He's for a jig or a tale of bawdry, else he sleeps.") The monotonous rhythm of *Cambises*, its infinite fustian, would have irritated any mind cosmopolitan enough to endure its mayhem of history. During the Yuletide revels of 1559 the Queen was vexed by one of the dramas performed at court. London gossip stated, "The players played such matter that they were commanded to leave off" (15). We have no record of the title of that matter. It may well have been *Huff, Snuff and Ruff*. If the players acted the atrocities of *Cambises* in such a way that the courtiers would be harassed by sights of the scaffold death of Dubourg on 23 December, we can understand why the show was stopped. Henry II had sworn that he would see the adversary of the physical extirpation of heresy burned with his own eyes (16). Such a king presented the British Protestants of 1559 with a superb modern instance of the lesson of *Cambises*.

The marriage of the Spanish tyrant and the Princess of France was solemnised in the night of Henry's last hour. Philip returned to Madrid and never left his gloomy kingdom again. From his enormous palace he conducted the imperial enterprises that were plotted at Chateau Cambresis, to put a bloody period to the efforts of the folks who wanted independence from the Papacy, from all authority remote, gold-robed and irrevocable. With the gold and silver that torrented into Philip's chests from the bowels of Mexico and Peru he financed whole armies and individual assassins for this crusade within Christendom. His main allies in the campaign were the men who governed France under Francis II, the Duke of Guise and his brother, the Cardinal of Lorraine. The French people looked up to Guise because he had commanded the battle in which the English invaders lost the city of Calais. That victory exalted him in their eyes almost to the station of their saint Joan of Lorraine, whose life's dream had been the liberation of her country from the empire of the English "Goddams". But Guise and the Cardinal proved powerless to heal the economic maladies of France and the measures they took for financial reform raised a host of hungry thousands against them. Naturally, in affairs concerning Mammon not God, they could expect no help from King Philip, to whom the impoverishment of the French meant their eventual subordination to Spain.

Thomas Preston's name is not connected with any play but *Cambises, King of Persia*. It occurs at the end of a couple of ballads published about 1570, when the first edition of his tragedy came from John Ailde's press. One of them dealt with the same imperial motive as the play: it was quaintly titled *A Gillyflower Gentle or Sweet Marygold wherein the fruits of tyranny you may behold*. It is difficult to believe that these three booklets form the complete works poetical of Preston. An attractive suggestion has been offered, that he wrote *The History of the Two Valiant Knights, Sir Clyomon, Knight of the Golden Shield, Son to the Kings of Denmark, and Clamydes, the White Knight, Son to the King of Suavia*, which Thomas Creede printed in 1599, "As it hath been sundry times acted by her Majesty's Players" (17). This fustian romance sounds exactly like the sort of play Preston might have written after quitting political themes, "matters of religion or of the governance of the estate of the common weal". The clown or vice in the play, Subtle Shift, is plainly shaped in the image of the famous vice of *Cambises*, Ambidexter, to whom he humorously refers. *Cambises* was reprinted with minor changes in or shortly after 1584, when Edward Allde succeeded to his father's trade. The Thomas Preston who dwelt in the theatrical district of Bishopsgate, and married Margaret Clarke there on 18 October 1576 was perhaps our playwright, still active in the popular playhouses (18). I wonder if the idea of composing a tragedy on the fate of Cambises came from a politician's pun on Cambresis?

Notes

1   El Greco, quoted by Thomas Craven, *Men of Art* (1931) 300.

2   John Lothrop Motley, *The Rise of the Dutch Republic* (1880) ii, 563. Motley quotes the slogan as "Liever Turx dan Paus", and translates it, "Rather Turkish than Popish", but Paus means Pope. The Dutch word for Popish is *Paapsch*.

3   Victor von Klarwill, ed., *Queen Elizabeth and Some Foreigners* (1928) 23.

4   Jules Michelet, *Modern History* (1900) 101. *Cambridge Modern History*, ii, 296f.

5   *Calendar of State Papers Venetian, 1558-1580*, 27.

6   *Cambises, King of Persia* (c. 1584), lines 1147-50.

7   E. K. Chambers, *The Elizabethan Stage* (1923) iv, 79.

8   *Cambridge Modern History, loc. cit.*

9   *Cambises,* 1166-67.

10 *Calendar of State Papers and Manuscripts, Relating to English Affairs, Existing in the Archives and Collections of Venice* (1890) vii, 80-1.

11 Chambers, *op. cit.* iv, 77.

12 *Calendar of Letters and State Papers Relating to English Affairs, Preserved Principally in the Archives of Simancas* (1892) 1, 62.

13 *Idem.*

14 John Payne Collier, *History of English Dramatic Poetry* (1831) i, 166.

15 *The Diary of Henry Machyn* (1848) 221.

16 *Cambridge Modern History, loc. cit.*

17 G. L. Kittredge, "Notes on Elizabethan Plays", *Journal of Germanic Philology* (1898-99) ii, 8.

18 *Registers of St. Helen's, Bishopsgate* (1904) 116. The parish records of 17 March 1580 and 23 November 1585, note the burial of Elizabeth and Mary Preston, respectively; perhaps the dramatist's daughters.

(I first suggested that William Cecil was the mastermind behind Preston's play and other stage propaganda in "King Cambises' Vein", *Notes & Queries*, 3 March 1951, vol. 196, pp. 98-100.)

Chapter 13–Thomas Watson, Dramatist

I

Among the mysteries that abound in the world of Tudor drama there are few so tantalising as the question of the place occupied by Thomas Watson (1557?-1592) in the story of that world. The mystery seems to become deeper with each addition to our knowledge of Watson. It was to be expected that research would yield us the picture of a far more complex personality than the singer of sweet sobs whom Edward Arber drew as "our English Petrarch." (1) We have assimilated the fact that Watson had the spirit to produce, beside the *Passionate Centurie of Loue* and *The Tears of Fancie,* sarcasms for Gabriel Harvey, the Cambridge pedant, "in the company of diuers Gentlemen one night at supper at the Nags head in *Cheape.*" (2) Less concilable with the picture of the scholar-lyricist generally conjured up by students of Watson from the days of Anthony à Wood (3) to our own is the revelation of "the froth of witty Tom Watson's jests" given by the unknown author of *Vlisses vpon Ajax* (1596): "I heard them in *Paris* fourteen years ago; besides what balductum play is not full of them?" (4) It is hard to imagine the poet of the *Passionate Centurie* as a scatalogic wit in the vein of Sir John Harington, the more famous forerunner of Thomas Crapper the sanitary engineer. The discovery of Sir William Cornwallis's remark about the "twenty fictions and knaveryes in a play" which Watson habitually manufactured – "his daily practyse and his living" (5) – does not make it easier.

By the findings of Professor Mark Eccles, published in a volume that might with justice have been titled *Thomas Watson in London* (1934), our information concerning the man who appears to have been Christopher Marlowe's most intimate friend is certainly enriched. We are enriched and simultaneously embarrassed. For the image Professor Eccies evokes of "the wise man" of St. Helen's parish, Bishopsgate, sporting gently with the superstitions of his neighbours about Popery and Spain, mystifies more than all the prior portrayals of Watson. Since the publication of *Christopher Marlowe in London* no researcher has come from the scrutiny of Watson's works and biographic vestiges (in Arber's phrase) "like a diver returning from the deep," with any gem to illuminate these discreet facts. Apparently, we are as powerless in 1950 as Arber was in 1870 to ascertain the true position of Watson in "the Story of English Mind."

Starting from the hypothesis that a poor hypothesis is better than none, I have ventured a series of conjectures that may provide future historians of the Tudor stage with the framework for all the facts they collect about Watson. The facts in our possession are now strung with the utmost rigour of logic in the lapidary design I present here.

At the beginning of the sequence is set the testimony of Francis Meres that Watson belonged with Marlowe, Peele, Kyd and Shakespeare among "our best for Tragedie."(6) Since none of his tragedies have survived or rather come down to us under his name, we have to guess what sort of plays they were. It is safe to assume that they were products of a rare erudition, a profound acquaintance with the drama *cothurnata* of Athens, Rome, Italy and France. Our poet first emerged in print with a Latin version of Sophocles' *Antigone* (1581). In his *Hekatompathia or Passionate Centurie of Loue* (1582) allusions occur to five, possibly six, other plays by Sophocles: *Trachiniae* (compare poems xxxviii, xciii), *Electra* (compare lxiii), *Ajax Flagellifer* (lxxxii), *Oedipus Rex* (xxxv), *Oedipus Coloneus* (xciii), perhaps *Philoctetes* (see lxviii). The poet also mentions how "Haemon choase to die / To follow his Antigone" (xxx). And of course Watson was familiar with Seneca, to whose *Hippolytus* and *Oedipus* he refers in the poems lxxxiv and xxxv respectively. He imitated the Roman dramatist in one sonnet, ii. It would not surprise us, therefore, to find him devoutly emulating Sophocles and Seneca in tragedies of his own.

Anthony a Wood states that Watson came of "gentle" stock. There is no evidence of kinship between him and the Th. Watson who was employed as a stage carpenter at Cambridge University in

1571 (7). More likely, the poet came from the kin of the Watson who served Lord John Lumley, lover of the Muses and plastic arts, as a chaplain, and probably shared the warm loyalty of his Lordship to the old Catholic faith (8). According to Wood, the poet matriculated at Oxford, where he studied "romance". He left the university without a degree about 1572 in order to pursue the liberal arts in France and Italy, and for reasons less ostensible.

He went to Europe at the time when the Protestants of the Netherlands were winning their first victories against Spain. Watson was a witness of the war. He remembered as late as 1590 how the Iberian,

> a dreadfull Lyon in his pride
> descended downe the *Pyrenaean* mount,
> And roaring through the pastures farre and wide,
> deour'd whole *Belgian* heards of chief account. (9)

Whatever he thought of King Philip as a political power, Watson manifestly felt sympathy for the Spaniard's religious convictions when he travelled on the continent. He dedicated his first book, his translation of *Antigone* to the King's namesake, the Catholic Earl of Arundel. In Latin verses preluding the drama he described how he had long ago dreamed of gaining Lord Philip Howard's patronage ("*dicar tuus esse Poeta*") (10). For nearly six years, a lustrum and a half, he told the Earl, he journeyed in the realms of Romance outside of Spain. And after a residence in Paris, he entered the college of English Catholics in Douai to study languages and law. He left the school in October 1576, and returned in the following May, overtly absorbed in jurisprudence.

In November 1576 the Spanish army, not far from Douai, horrified both Catholic and Protestant Christendom by its rapine in Antwerp. The English envoy in that metropolis, Dr Thomas Wilson, the friend of Nicholas Udall and author of *The Art of Rhetorique*, employed as a courier this year a certain John Watson, who may have been a kinsman of our dramatist (11). In July 1577 Don John of

Austria and his Spanish legions swooped down on Namur and frightened hosts of Belgian catholics into alliance with the protestant Prince William of Orange. The latter's soldiers were thus able to march triumphantly through Belgium and arrived at Douai. Watson quit the town in August, before the protestant troops advanced to drive the English collegians away. "Often my studies were obstructed by wars," he chanted to Arundel. "Still I fled from camps, save those of Phoebus." (12).

Watson returned to England. Perhaps he came home to attend the funeral of Elizabeth, the wife of John Watson, gentleman, who was buried at St Helen's church in Bishopsgate on 5 May, 1578. Her connexion – if any existed – with Queen Elizabeth's agent, John Watson, remains obscure. The poet made his residence in her parish and won golden opinions for his wisdom there. If Elizabeth Watson was his mother, as I surmise, we can understand why he wanted to make his home by St Helen's Yard. And the allurements of James Burbage's Theatre and the nearby Curtain doubtless helped to keep him in Bishopsgate.

On the fringe of Bishopsgate, in the mansion known as Jasper Fisher's Folly, dwelt the poetic, play-loving Earl of Oxford, to whom Watson later dedicated his *Passionate Centurie*. Lord Edward de Vere had clandestinely become a Catholic and maintained a torrid friendship with the family circle of the Earl of Arundel. Oxford's passion for Romance culture carried him to ludicrous and sometimes dangerous extremes. But in 1578 he basked in the eyelight of Queen Elizabeth, whom even his spiritual divorce from her Lord Treasurer's daughter could not seriously vex. The Earl's ardour for the Italianate gave it wings of wildfire among the scholars and playwrights who clustered round his largesse. He acted as patron for George Baker, the physician whose pastime was translating Spanish rarities. Gabriel Harvey declared in rhapsodic Latin that Oxford once meditated sending him to France and Italy (13). From the Preface to Watson's Latin translation of the *Antigone* by Sophocles, dedicated to Philip Howard, 20th Earl of Arundel, we learn that Watson had spent seven and a half years on the Continent. In addition, there are commendatory verses signed "E.K., Gentleman" preceding Anthony Munday's *Mirror of Mutability*, a work dedicated to Oxford. Plausible is the identification of Edward Knight with the E. K. who enjoyed the friendship of Harvey and Edmund Spenser, and supplied the notes to *The Shepheardes Calendar* in 1579. [One or more lines of Feldman's original typescript were dropped when the type was set to print this article in *The Bard* (1977), so something is unfortunately missing here. W.H.] We know from Harvey's correspondence with Spenser that these scholars and poets were fond of visiting the playhouses, to "laugh their bellies full for pence," or to see popular chivalric novels of the period staged.

It was with a romantic tragedy of chivalry, I imagine, that Thomas Watson began his career as a dramatist. We may behold the ruins of that tragedy, after several companies of players had worked their professional havoc on it, in the anonymous drama called *Soliman and Perseda*. There is no date on the titlepage of the extant edition of this play; it was registered by Edward White in November 1592, not long after Watson's death. The prime source of *The Tragedye of Soliman and Perseda*, Jacques Yver's anthology of tales *Printemps d'Iver*, appeared in 1572, the year when Watson is believed to have started his tour of France. The romance itself enjoyed a wide circulation in England when Henry Wotton's version was published, in 1578, in his *Courtlie Controuersie of Cupids Cautels*. In 1578 Watson returned to London, and the next year, in my belief, saw the composition of the original version of *Soliman and Perseda*. It must have been written before the onset of theatrical propaganda against Spain which was signalled by the expulsion of the ambassador Bernardino de Mendoza in January 1584. The play is remarkable for the extraordinary sympathy with Spanish cavaliers that its author displays, while serenely postulating the superiority of English men of war.

Representatives of both nations are shown at a tournament in Rhodes:

The fiery Spaniard bearing in his face
The empresse of a noble warriour...

And English Archers, hardy men at armes,
Eclipped Lyons of the Western worlde. (14)

The Spanish knight thus had received his accolade, we are informed, in a battle with German rutters on an unnamed field (1.3). English listeners to the lines, however, might have instantly recalled the "Almain rutters with their horsemen's staves" who were active as mercenaries in the Netherland wars (15). In the summer of 1579 the rutters (Reiter) of Prince Hans Casimir of the Palatinate, fighting under the banner of Orange but financed by Lord Burghley's office, had disgraced themselves in encounters with the Spanish troops (16). The ridiculous knight of the play, Basilisco, contrary to the impression of his nationality we get from his name, is really "a Rutter born in Germanie." He is pictured as a veteran of battles in Belgia, and cheerfully confesses an atrocity he performed there to feed his "Frize-land horse" in a season of drouth. He slaughtered the male children of the region, says he, "That the mothers teares might releeve the pearched earth" (1.3). "The men died, the women wept, and the grass grewe." Later playwrights would have made this miles gloriosus an Iberian sooner than a German. Some actors apparently made an effort to give the character a stamp of Spain; otherwise it is difficult to explain why Love refers to him as "The fond Bragardo" (1.6), or why Piston should greet him with a "Basolus manus" (4.2) There is no hint of derision however in the scene of the tournament where the knight from Spain exults:

The golden Fleece is that we cry upon,
And Iaques, Iaques is the Spaniards choice.

As strange as the praise of Spanish knighthood may have rung in contemporary English ears, stranger still must have sounded the dramatist's admiration for the Mahometan prince Soliman, whom he portrayed as the most courteous and kindest of kings. Only in the plays of Watson's dear friend Marlowe do we find an equal critique of English monarchy in their time. The portrait of the Sultan

Soliman constantly recalls John Lyly's ideal figure of the pagan king Alexander in his first comedy, *Campaspe*, which was possibly composed in 1580. Indeed, the moral of Lyly's play could not be better defined than in these noble lines spoken by Soliman (4.1):

> What should he doe with crowne and Emperie,
> That cannot gouerne priuate fond affections?

How close Lyly stood to Watson at the time when I conceive that *Soliman and Perseda* was first produced may be discerned from the letter of commendation the former wrote for the *Passionate Centurie of Love*. Lyly perused Watson's love poems before they were sent to the press.

My final fragment of evidence to date the original production of the tragedy is the fact that early in 1580 there existed a play with a title that fits it well. In February the actors of Henry Stanley, Earl of Derby, performed at Court *The history of the Soldan and the Duke of ---*. The last name was left unfinished by the clerk of the Revels accounts (17). If he had written Rhodes there would have been scarcely an iota of doubt that the "history" was our romance of *Soliman and Eratus*, whom the Sultan appointed lord of Rhodes.

Soliman and Perseda is usually claimed for Thomas Kyd, on the ground of its style, so eloquently like the rhetoric of *The Spanish Tragedy*, considered Kyd's masterpiece, and because it seems to be an elaboration of the play within that play. The argument would be formidable if we could be sure that Kyd was in truth the author of *The Spanish Tragedy*. But the glory that Kyd has been crowned with posthumously for the sake of that anonymous drama rests on nothing more substantial than the word of Thomas Heywood, who spoke of Kyd as its creator in his *Apology for Actors* (1612), eighteen years after Kyd's death. Although Heywood is not customarily upheld as an accurate historian, his word on the authorship of the Tragedy has gone unchallenged for centuries. I am convinced that he reported the truth as he knew it, the histrionic tradition that Kyd was the writer of the most popular play of the age. But there are writers and writers. In justice we can speak of Kyd's ability as playwright only on the basis of the single drama issued under his signature, the wretched translation *Cornelia*, printed in 1594.

Thomas Kyd was by trade a scrivener. He might have been employed to copy the stage versions of the anonymous plays which now pass under his name. In view of Thomas Nashe's satiric reference to him in the notorious preface to Robert Greene's *Menaphon* (1589), we are inclined to think that Kyd left his father's trade of noverint, and busied himself "with the endeavours of art," trying to make a living as a playwright. Nashe laughed at his ignorance, contending that he could scarcely Latinize his "neck-verse" if he had been sentenced to hang and pleaded for the benefit of clerics. While Kyd's advocates and editors do not go so far as Nashe in criticism of his learning, they candidly exhibit his multitudinous blunders in Latin, Italian, and French. The play he signed his own, *Cornelia*, proves he was unable to translate French with any respectable degree of fidelity. "Nor was he sufficiently conversant with classical mythology and history." (18) Yet the charge of insufficient knowledge of the classics would seem to be enough to damn any candidate for the authorship of *The Spanish Tragedy*.

The play of *Soliman and Perseda* introduced in *The Spanish Tragedy* is prologued by Hieronimo with the remark that he wrote it when he was a student in Toledo. Frederick Boas fancied that Kyd may have composed a drama on the subject at some university, but adds, "this is a very doubtful assumption." (19) Kyd's formal education appears to have been confined to Richard Mulcaster's academy for the Merchant Taylors' boys. Excellent as that school's curriculum was, it could not enable a graduate to fulfil the project of Hieronimo's drama. When Edward. White, the publisher of *Soliman and Perseda*, issued *The Spanish Tragedy* (likewise without a date), he included a note (4.4) saying that the play within the play was originally intended to be recited in French, Latin, Italian, and Greek. Hieronimo confirms the statement in alluding to "our sundry languages" (ibid.). Such a project would have been a labour after Thomas Watson's own heart. Aut Watson, aut diabolus! I am confident he wrote at least the initial version of the Tragedy, when memories of his alma mater Oxford and the college at Douai were refreshed in his mind, late in 1580, about the time he used to lodge in Westminster with "one Mr. Beale a preacher & his acquaintance in Oxforde before"(20).

Fear and preference for imperial Spain were rife in Westminster in those days. When Watson dwelt there he met a crazy woman who proclaimed herself the child of King Philip; and the poet humoured her fantasy (21). The Earl of Oxford indulged in dreams of his admission to Spanish aristocracy hardly less mad (22), but escaped the accusation of craziness under the cloudy reputation of a drunkard. His companions of the cup, Lord Henry Howard, Charles Arundel, and Philip Howard, Earl of Arundel, disdained to conceal their enthusiasm over the victories of Spanish arms, at least in the invasion of Portugal. In April 1580 the French statesman Mauvissiere de Castelnau wrote to Queen Elizabeth that his royal mistress Catherine de' Medici favoured a united effort of France and England to prevent Philip's conquest of Portugal. But the Portuguese tragedy had to be enacted to its cruel conclusion at Alcantara without an English interlude. On 26 August the Duke of Alva crushed the arms of the young King of Portugal, Antonio, and the throne of England experienced percussions of rumours about a coming Spanish fleet, and an invasion by united troops of Philip and the Pope (23).

The Spanish Tragedy displays a consideration of Spain and her autocrat which is not satisfactorily explained by Christian charity. The drama was certainly revised often before Edward White obtained his licence to print it in 1592, one month before he registered his copy of *Soliman and Perseda*. Yet the *Tragedy* is still sultry with the political temperature of the circle of the Earls of Arundel, Oxford, and Derby in the epoch of Alva's victory at Alcantara. The ghost of Andrea as Prologue opens the play with a reference to "the late conflict with Portingale". The carnage is described at length in Act 1, scene 2 (lines 22-84). Other scholars after J. Schick have recognised the "conflict" in the battle fought on 26 August, 1580, but none followed him in taking earnestly the adjective "late" as a clue to the play's chronology. Some are tempted to adopt a suggestion of Ben Jonson's Induction to *Bartholomew Fayre* (1614) and set the date of the *Tragedy* in 1584. That was a year of uncommon butchery by Philip's legions in the Low Countries, and there were not many intellects in England that could have listened with gravity to the nameless King of Spain in the *Tragedy* declaiming, "We pleasure more in kindness than in warres" (1.5). We hear no hint of irony in the King's speech to the defeated Portuguese:

> Yet shalt thou know that Spain is honourable
> Our peace will grow the stronger for these warres. (1.2)

There is not a word to show that the dramatist was not in sympathy with the conquerors of Portugal. The ruler of that country is depicted as a vassal, a Viceroy, who had betrayed his master of Madrid.

It is curious that the Viceroy confesses his treason in a verse form (1.3) that Watson toyed with twice in *Hekatompathia* (xli, lxiv), "a somewhat tedious or too much affected continuation of that figure in Rhethorique, whiche of the Grekes is called *palilogia* or *anadiplosis,* of the *Latines Reduplicatio.*" (24) Another trick of poetry executed by the poet of the *Tragedy* and the poet of the *Passionate Centurie of Loue* is the weaving of phrases from various classic authors into a single lyric (3.4; Quatorzain lxxxix). More direct echoes of Watson's sonnets have been heard in the second act of *The Spanish Tragedy* (2.1, lines 3-6, 9-10). One likeness between the play and one of Watson's poems has apparently gone unobserved. The famous verse "O eies! No eies, but fountaines fraught with teares" (3.2) reverberates in the line "Mine eies, now eies no more, but seas of teares" from a song by Watson printed in *The Phoenix Nest* (1593) and *Englands Helicon* (1602) (25). Not on such parallels, however, do I rely for the conviction that Watson was the creator of Hieronimo.

The art and content of the drama designate Watson as its prime mover. As I see it, the *Tragedy* was aimed as moral criticism of the

"deadly sin" of pride, particularly the pride of Spain; the play deliv-
ers a Sophoclean lesson in *hybris* or, as the Tudor poets quaintly
name it, *surquedry*, The dramatist showed the Spanish empire was
drunk with tribute and the triumphs of its warriors. He presents
Duke Cyprian of Castile extolling his King in the words of the Roman poem of Claudian (1.1): "O much beloved of God, heaven battles for you, and the peoples of the world combined submit on bent
knees." (26) In the rapture of the Spaniards over their gilded
achievements they fail to realise that from this pinnacle there is nowhere to go but down. And the horrors of the domestic crime and
punishment in the play foreshadow the greater horrors of the fall of
the house of Spanish royalty. The moral is driven home by various
devices. There is the tragic irony of the King's boast of his power
over Portugal (3.4):

> As we now are, so sometimes were these,
> Kings and commanders of the westerne Indies.

An explicit rebuke of Iberian arrogance is Hieronimo's "pompous
jest" or masque of two legendary English knights who once captured kings of Portugal, followed by Duke John of Gaunt, who took
the King of Castile prisoner. The patriotic morality of the poet
brought his art to the verge of the naive in this scene of the Con-
quistadores being entertained by history of their kingdom's disgrace.
The King is pleased by the spectacle and solemnly counsels his Portuguese victims to take it as consolation.

> Portingale may daine to beare our yoake,
> When it by little England hath been yoakt.

But the Ambassador points out the actual teaching of the
"jest" (1.5):

> Spaine may not insult for her successe,
> Since English warriours likewise conquered Spaine,

And made them bow their knees to Albion.

The poet's faith in the ability of English soldiers to defeat the terrible Spanish *tercios* blurts through the lips of the Portuguese humbled at the throne of Madrid. Yet his pathos for the fate of Spain never permits the utterance of a single "philippic" line, such as you get from John Lyly in his *Midas*. For the ethical purpose of *The Spanish Tragedy* the artist deranged history and punished the insolence of Spain by bereaving its dynasty in the play of the prince, "the whole succeeding hope" (4.4). The dramatist may have had in mind the mysterious death of Philip's first heir, Don Carlos, in 1568. In Schiller's tragedy *Don Carlos* the prince's death is likewise treated as if it meant the breakdown of Spain's esperance.

In the summer of 1580 English courtiers were more excited by imperial French amours than by Spanish arms. The dynastic heir of France, the Duke of Anjou, courted the Queen to a degree of warmth that kindled Sir Philip Sidney into daring to read where poor John Stubbe had rushed in and lost his right hand. Sidney's antagonism to the French alliance was aggravated by his severest critic, the Earl of Oxford, who was fervidly for it. The Howards and Arundels, devoted as they were to the policy of Spain, imitated King Philip's sport with Catherine de' Medici, and pretended to Elizabeth that they were all "strong advocates of the marriage" with Catholic France (27). If the author of *The Spanish Tragedy* was Thomas Watson, we should expect to find in the play an allusion to the Anjou affair. Our expectation is fulfilled in these lines, proposing a union of Castile and Portugal by a wedding of their dynastic heirs:

Aduise thy King to make this marriage vp,
For strengthening of our late confirmed league;
I know no better meanes to make vs freends ...
Yong virgins must be ruled by their freends.
The Prince is amiable and loues her well;
If she neglect him and forgoe his loue,
She both will wrong her owne estate and ours.

If Elizabeth ever heard this admonition, she must have been grimly amused by the comment on the government of virgins. Yet she was deeply tempted by the project of the Valois 'league', despite its sinister attendant, the Holy League of the Guise ring.

It is hardly conceivable that her Majesty would have missed her people's favourite play. In my opinion, she heard *The Spanish Tragedy* on 1 January, 1581, when, according to the cryptic Revels record, the actors of the Earl of Derby performed for the Court *The Storie of ----.* (28) The name that perplexed the clerk was, I feel sure, Hieronimo. From the histrionic servants of Derby *The Story of Hieronimo* passed into the property of the actors who served Derby's son, Ferdinando, Lord Strange. These men earned their supreme plaudits with *The Spanish Tragedy.* In *Bartholomew Fayre* Jonson refers to the drama (which he had revised and extended) by the name of *Ieronimo.*

The companion piece of *The Tragedy* known as *The First Part of Ieronimo* seems to have been revived together with it in February 1592, by Lord Strange's company (29). Few scholars regard *Ieronimo* as worthy of Kyd. In its present form it is certainly not Watson's work. Its posture toward Spain is far less compassionate than the viewpoint of *The Spanish Tragedy.* When its Marshal Ieronimo expresses alacrity to serve his King in the extortion of tribute from Portugal, the heroine, Belimperia, cries (1.2):

> Trybute? Alas, that Spaine cannot of peace forbeare
> A little coin, the Indies being so neere.

She appeals to her soldier lover,

> O deere *Andrea,* pray, lets haue no wars.
> First let them pay the souldiers that were maimde
> In the last battaile, ere more wretches fall,
> Or walke on stilts to timeless Funerall.

The pacific appeal could have come from Watson's pen (copied for the prompter by Kyd). But whoever wrote the play was no friend of the Howards and Arundels then. It breathes a hot hostility to the Spanish lust for dominion, the majesty which the Earl of Arundel ecstatically lauded, according to a letter Mendoza sent his master in Madrid on 1 March, 1582. One evening, Mendoza reported, the Earl sat at dinner with Sir Francis Drake, who vaunted himself "the man to wage war on Your Majesty. At this Arundel said that a like he could have no sense of shame, to imagine such a thing of the greatest monarch there had been on earth, who was strong enough to make war on all the princes of the world." (30)

By this time, it is true, Watson had taken a stand in opposition to the Earl of Arundel's politics. He had become a close friend of Thomas Walsingham, Marlowe's comrade, the courier and cousin of Sir Francis Walsingham, the Principal Secretary of State, whom the Catholics (and occasionally the Queen) detested as the champion of heretics. It is possible that the dramatist altered his *Hieronimo*, after its premier triumph, into a tragedy in two parts, making it a kind of farewell warning to Lord Philip Howard and his group. One can fancy the poet at work on his study of *surquedry*, murmuring to himself, in Hieronimo's unforgettable phrase on setting the stage for his own little play, "Ile fit you".

At the end of *The First Part of Ieronimo* there is mute testimony of the poet's haste in writing the play. Two Spanish officers named Philippo and Cassimero come on the stage and are left without a word in the extant text. Perhaps they were designed to mimic the King of Spain or his *caballeros* and Duke Casimir or his rutters, whose campaign in the Low Countries had squandered English funds. There appears to be a vicious jibe on the chief of the Dutch forces in the following gloat of Ieronimo, comparing the flesh of his son's adversaries to Sevillian fruit (3.1):

His sword so fals vpon the Portugales,
As he would slise them out like Orenges,
And squeeze their blouds out.

That Watson was capable of the pun, we comprehend from the glimpse of his dirty wit offered in *Vlisses Vpon Ajax*. But I prefer to regard the verse as the handiwork of Tom Kyd, translating Watson's rather academic art into the vulgate, so to speak. One of the few established facts of Kyd's biography is a record of his arrest in 1593 on the suspicion that he was the writer of "lewd and mutinous libels" against the Dutch which were fixed to the wall of their churchyard in London (31). A gentleman of Watson's attainments would have to be soaked in sack to perpetrate the joke on Orange for the mob of apprentices in the playhouses who hated the industrious Dutch. Watson knew how it felt to be a foreigner. It is likely that he was the Thomas Watson, "yeoman", who was reported in June 1581 among the "strangers" in St Helen's parish, Bishopsgate, "who did not go to church." (32)

II

During Christmas 1580 the fantastic Earl of Oxford exploded the Court peace with a scandal that had a decisive effect on Watson's career. Oxford charged Lord Henry Howard, Charles Arundel, and their kinsman Francis Southwell, with conspiracy against the state. He disclosed their political services to Rome, notably the hiding of Jesuits, who entered England at the risk of their necks. Confessing that he had been swayed to fidelity to the Vatican and sheltered "massing priests" himself, the Earl denied that he was ever acquainted with a Papist plot to overthrow Elizabeth until this time. He appealed to the French ambassador, Castelnau, to tell her what he knew about the Howard group's protection of Jesuits. But his sole witness declined to imperil them: "They and their friends," he wrote to Paris, "have always been in favour of the (Anjou) marriage and the French alliance... The Earl of Oxford," he added, "thus found himself alone in his evidence and accusations. He has lost credit and honour and has been abandoned by all his friends and all the ladies of the Court." The ambassador wondered if he did not secretly belong to "the Spanish faction." (1)

The Spanish ambassador described the event to Philip, and how he had concealed the "very Catholic" Lord Howard and his companions from violent enemies. They were arrested, but nothing could be proved against them. Lord Harry, testified Mendoza, was profoundly loyal to Philip: "To touch on the greatness of the affection with which he occupies himself in the service of Your Majesty is impossible." (2)

Shortly after, Charles Arundel fled to the continent and occupied himself at Paris with a plot to crown Mary Stuart Queen of England. The Earl of Arundel kept his name clear of conspiracy and treason. He indicated the direction of his heart, however, on 22 January, 1581, when he rode as challenger in a tournament against the Earl of Oxford. On the side of Oxford, encountering Sir William Drury, rode none other than Sir Philip Sidney, who had quarreled with Oxford so cordially more than a twelvemonth before – over possession of a tennis court and the question of the Valois league (3). Arundel went down to defeat in the contest. In March he had the sour satisfaction of watching the victor drop to infamy when Anne Vavasor, a lady of her Majesty's bedchamber, and a tender friend of Charles Arundel, gave birth to a boy at Court and pointed out Oxford as the father. Elizabeth locked the unlucky Earl in the Tower and he stayed there till June.

In the next month John Wolfe registered Watson's Latin translation of Sophocles, dedicated to the Earl of Arundel. Four allegorical poems entitled *Pompae* accompanied the *Antigone*, also dedicated to the Earl. We do not know what Philip Howard said or did about the offering, or the poet's selection of obedience to the sovereign as the main ethical motive of the Greek play. *"Quam sit malum publico Magistratus edicto non parere, Antigonae exemplum docet."* (4)

At the time of Oxford's misfortune Watson appears to have been in Paris. The German jurist and poet Stephen Broelmann of Cologne wrote Latin verses for him which were prefixed to the *Antigone*, urging the publication of his work; they were addressed to the French capital. Possibly the jurist was a relative of Elizabeth Broylman, the cutler's widow, "born in Douchland", who lived near Watson's lodging in Westminster (5). According to George Peele, the lays of love Watson published in his *Hekatompathia*, and dedicated to Oxford, followed fast his sad *Antigone* (6). He probably read them to Thomas Walsingham in Paris, for that gentleman is presented in the poet's elegy on Sir Francis Walsingham complimenting Watson on his songs thus:

> "Thy tunes haue often pleas'd mine eare of yore,
> When milk-white swans did flocke to hear thee sing,
> Where *Seine* in Paris makes a double shore." (7)

What was the poet doing in France? Carrying messages for the Queen's Secretary and spy-master, I suppose. Sir Francis had already employed a scholar-playwright, the late George Gascoigne, as a courier to Paris (8).

Not long after Oxford emerged from the Tower, he "willinglie voutchsafed the acceptance" of Watson's *Passionate Centurie of Loue,* "and at conuenient leisures fauorable perused it." (9) Gabriel Cawood licensed the book on 31 March. 1582, Cawood was the publisher of Lyly's novels celebrating the courtly philosophy and language dear to the Earl of Oxford, patron of a Latin translation of Castiglione's *Courtier.* In pedestrian Euphuism Lyly wrote a prefatory letter on Watson's sonnets, commending them to the public as genuine love-songs. Lyly and Peele were not the only theatrical men who advertised the *Centurie.* Thomas Acheley and Matthew Roydon, more obscure writers for the stage, also produced commendatory poems for Watson. And so did George Bucke, who eventually became Master of the Revels.

In the happy companionship of these men, perhaps Watson wrote the romantic comedy called the *Historie of Loue and Fortune,* which the Earl of Derby's servants acted for the Queen in December 1582. This is doubtless the play, printed for Edward White in 1589, under the title of *The Rare Triumphes of Loue and Fortune,* "wherein are manye fine Conceites with great delight."

Sir Edmund Chambers perceived one link between *Love and Fortune* and *Soliman and Perseda* (10). The subtitle of the tragedy in quarto is "Loues constancy, Fortunes inconstancy, and Deaths Triumphs", which immediately reminds us of the comedy. According to my theory, they were both staged by Derby's men. It is strange that no critic has claimed *Love and Fortune* for Kyd. It has much in common with the dramas credited to him. It commences in Senecan style with a Fury, Tisiphone, broaching debate among the Roman gods. They are set at odds disputing which is the superior goddess, Fortuna or Venus, and these entertain the Olympians with pompous masques of their accomplishments, shows of Troilus and Cressida, Alexander, Pompey, Caesar, Hero and Leander. The rival goddesses are then invited to test their powers on a prince and his love in the nameless land of the play; and so the romance of Hermione (*sic*) and his Fidelia is enacted. We note the same incongruous comparison of a gallant young lover with old blind Oedipus that Watson made in *Hekatompathia* (11). A light echo of *The Spanish Tragedy* occurs in the scene (3) where Bomelio calls on the Furies Alecto and Tisiphone, and the infernal judge Rhadamanth, to curse his tormentors. Reminiscent of *Vlisses Vpon Ajax* and its smear for "witty Tom Watson" are the excremental humor of the clown Lentulo (4) and Romelio's angry obscenity in the same act. The linguistic talent of the anonymous playwright is put to comic use in the passages where Bomelio counterfeits a foreign physician, uttering broken Italian and French. We are poignantly reminded of Watson's friend Marlowe and his *Doctor Faustus* in the scene of prince Hermione's burning of the "vile blasphemous" books of his father, the magician Bomelio. Addressing his gentle auditors, Hermione earnestly exhorts them: "Abhor this study, for it will confound you all." (12) The play concludes with Fortune's prayer, "God save her Majesty that keeps us all in peace," which indicates a date of production prior to January 1584, when the Queen expelled the ambassador of Spain; at any rate, prior to June 1585, when Holland sent twelve deputies to London to make a treaty of war with her. Incidentally, there was a Captain Thomas Watson fighting for the Low Countries at this time (13).

October 1584 witnessed the movement of the Earl of Leycester for an association of Englishmen to destroy all plotters against the

Queen's life (14). Leycester launched it after the murder of the Prince of Orange had shown how high fanatic assassins could reach. In March 1585 Parliament agreed on a law containing the substance of the association's vow. Perhaps in allusion to this act, the weird compliment to "sacred *Cynthias* friend" was inserted among the speeches of Death in *Soliman and Perseda*:

> For holy fates haue grauen it in their tables
> That *Death* shall die, if he attempts her end,
> Whose life is heauens delight, and *Cynthias* friend.

I suspect that this interpolation came from Kyd, in the precise spirit of his "Verses of Praise and Joy" over the frustration of the Babington intrigue in 1586 (15).

The atmosphere of England in that year was fevered by the arming of regiments to join Leycester's expedition in the Netherlands. Watson apparently was not pleased by the manoeuvres of Mayors in London; he endeavoured to forget the tumults of the military in Lethean melody and Romanesque literature. He dashed off in doggerel "A gratification vnto Mr. John Case, for his learned Booke, lately made in the prayes of Musick," a poem admitting his pacifism, dated 1586.

> Let Eris then delight in warrs,
> Let Enuy barke against the starts,
> Let Folly sayle which way thee please:
> With him I wish my dayes to spende
> Whose quill hath stood fayre Musicks friend,
> Chief friend to peace, chief port of ease.
>   q.ᵈ Tho. Watson. (16)

Students of *The Passionate Centurie* will recall the poet's expression of his pleasure in the somnolent lyrics of Luca Marenzio and other Italian tunes.

On 6 September, 1585, Watson married Anne Swift at the church of St Antholin. With her brother and Kit Marlowe he became involved in a tenebrous feud that brought both poets within the shadow of the gallows. In 1586 Watson's paraphrase in Latin of *The Rape of Helen* by Coluthus appeared in modest print. He dedicated it to Henry Percy, the Earl of Northumberland, a man extravagantly fond of books like those the hero of *Love and Fortune* burnt. Marlowe's adaptation of Watson's work in English rime, said to have been made in 1587, is lost. The time when Marlowe entered Northumberland's charming circle is unclear. In the spring of 1587 the Privy Council employed Marlowe "in matters touching the benefitt of his Countrie": matters quite murky. One outcome of his enigmatic activity was the rumour that he had determined to travel "beyond the seas to Reames," where the English fugitives from the Douai college had established their school (17). Marlowe and Watson had plenty of common interests, including the same adversaries in their art.

The Lord Admiral's men, headed by Edward Alleyn, acted *Tamburlaine the Great* in 1587, and the response of the theatre crowds to Marlowe's colossal muse made Robert Greene virid with envy. He ventured to ape it in *Alphonsus, King of Arragon,* and failed. In the preface to his novel *Perimedes the Blacksmith* (registered on 29 March 1588) he complained that Marlowe and a fellow playwright had insulted him on the stage. "Lately," Greene wrote, "two Gentlemen Poets made two madmen of Rome," *i.e.,* two London comedians, beat his Horatian motto, *Omne tulit punctum,* out of paper bucklers, in a sort of brutal mockery or pun. To this charade on Greene's points they added ridicule – "for that I could not make my verses iet vpon the stage in tragical buskins, euery word filling the mouth like the faburden of Bo-Bell, daring God out of heauen with that Atheist *Tamburlan,* or blaspheming with the mad preest of the sonne." (18) The consensus of scholars holds that "the mad priest of the sun" was the protagonist of a tragedy no longer extant, *The Lyfe and Death of Heliogabilus,* licensed for printing in June 1594. I suggest that Tom Watson was the writer of this tragedy of imperial

Rome. His usually tranquil temperament kept him out of the glare of playhouse and tavern publicity, just as Marlowe's perfervid nature thrust him into it. Greene carried on a kind of feud with Marlowe, striving to surpass the popularity of *Doctor Faustus* with his patriotic *Friar Bacon*. If he had recognized a competitor in Watson, he would have waxed fluently clever about him. One nearly regrets that our hero was indeed more a gentleman than a poet.

In the winter of 1587, according to Kyd, he entered the service of the unknown Lord to whom he referred in his pathetic letter to Sir John Puckering of autumn 1592 (19). The opinion prevails that he was already the distinguished creator of *The Spanish Tragedy*, although no contemporary allusions connect them or clarify his repute. We know more about the glory acquired by little Richard Burbage, who seems to have risen to theatrical stardom in the role of Hieronimo. The *Verses of Praise and Joy* by F. K. which the printer registered on 21 September, 1586, are destitute of beauty and rudimentary in skill. They mimic verbal tricks used in the *Tragedy*, combining "hope" and "hap" in one line, and repeating the play's affirmation, "Time is the author both of truth and right." More important is the quest for identification of the nobleman whom Kyd served for nearly six years, at least as a calligrapher, including some kind of collaboration with Christopher Marlowe: "some occasion of or wrytinge in one chamber twoe yeares synce" (in the autumn of 1591 or earlier season).

"My first acquaintance wth this Marlowe," Kyd informed his inquisitor Puckering, "rose vpon his bearing name to serve my Lo: although his L[p] never knewe his service, but in writing for his plaiers, ffor never cold my L. endure his name or sight, when he had heard of his conditions, nor wold indeed the forme of devyne praiers vsed duelie in his L[ps] house, haue quadred wth such reprobates." (20)

Scholars have attempted to find "his Lordship" in the Earl of Derby or his son Lord Strange, or the Earl of Sussex, to whose Countess Kyd dedicated his *Cornelia*. But Sussex was Governor of Portsmouth during the period when Kyd and Marlowe wrote for the unnamed patron's players; and there is nothing in Marlowe's life to link him to the house of Derby. Moreover, scholars have been too quick to suppose that "his Lordship's house" must mean his home. And a peculiar presbyopia has steadily steered them away from the singular Elizabethan courtier who was most closely connected with the theatrical world, most intimate with dramatists. We have the authority of Edmund Spenser for singling out Edward de Vere, Earl of Oxford, as the fittest for the role of Marlowe's master and Kyd's Lord. In January 1589 Spenser had the satisfaction of delivering the first cantos of *The Faerie Queene* to the press. He preluded the volume with a series of sonnets to outstanding courtiers, and to "the Earle of Oxenford, Lord high Chamberlayne of England," he appealed for defence of his epic against envious tongues. Spenser appealed to de Vere

> for the love which thou doest beare
> To th' Heliconian imps, and they to thee;
> They unto thee, and thou to them, most deare.

The "Heliconian imps" (the phrase is, I suggest, Oxford's own) were of course poets, and in those days that word signified almost always playwrights. Even Spenser, under the influence of the innyard theatres and others of London, ventured to compose nine comedies in the spirit of Ariosto. There is no need to review here the patronage of Oxford for such writers as Lyly, Mundy, and Robert Greene, whose extolments of the Earl are inscribed on dedication pages. It is necessary to call attention to the fact that Oxford maintained a magnificent residence for unknown persons in the mansion that was once the goldsmith Jasper Fisher's Folly, outside Bishopsgate, where the next door was that of messuages belonging to the brothers Edward and John Alleyn. Tall Ned went from stage training in the Earl of Worcester's company to stardom with Strange's and afterwards the Lord Admiral's men, especially in Marlowe's tragedies (21). Marlowe resided in Norton Folgate, a short walk from the playhouses of Shoreditch northward and from Ox-

ford's house of luxury and obscure labour southward. The Earl
lived in the latter only as a lord of literature; his ordinary residence
was in Oxford House by London Stone in Candlewick Street.

The Bishopsgate mansion, in my opinion, served for the office
that the Earl held for Elizabeth. On 26 June, 1586, the Queen had
granted him, under privy seal warrant, one thousand pounds a year
from the secret service fund of his father-in-law's Treasury, for
work never defined (22). Whatever the nature of the Earl's employment, he derived very little pride from it. He begged Burghley to get
him a more honourable post, in a letter his father-in-law did not
deem worthy to preserve. The Lord Treasurer, however, kept his
reply, dated 15 December, 1587: "You seem to infer that the lack of
your preferment cometh of me, for that you could never hear of any
way prepared for your preferment. My Lord, for a direct answer, I
affirm for a truth – and it is to be well proved – that your Lordship
mistaketh my power." (23) Colonel B. R. Ward surmised that the
Queen had resolved to engage Oxford's genius in "exploitation of
the now famous Elizabethan historical dramas" for purposes of
propaganda in the Anglo-Spanish war (24). Three days before she
gave Oxford his secret service payment, the Star Chamber decreed
the restriction of all printing in England to the presses of London,
Cambridge and Oxford, and the stern supervision of those presses
by the Stationers Company. No similar decree was ever issued for
the English theatre, but we know how the London magistrates demonstrated a zeal which academic minds have mistakenly classified as
Puritan in religio-political control of the stage companies. Among
the measures for this control was the decision to allow only John
Charlwood to print the players' announcement bills. The Stationers
Company gave Charlwood this licence on 30 October, 1587, less
than a month before the Queen summoned her chief warriors to a
council to select the tactics of resistance to invaders expected from
Spain. Following Colonel Ward, I believe that we have in Oxford's
appointment the explanation for the outbreak on the London stages
in the summer of 1586 of what might be called "Philippic" plays.
On 20 July, 1586, Hieronimo Lippomano, the ambassador of Ven-

ice to Madrid wrote to his Senate about King Philip's fury against the English theatre:

> "But what has enraged him more than all else, and has caused him to show a resentment such as he has never before displayed in all his life, is the account of the maskerades and comedies which the Queen of England orders to be acted at his expense." (25)

To the tempests of patriotism excited by these "maskerades and comedies" were added, perhaps at the instigation of Burghley and Walsingham, plays of propaganda against the captive Queen of Scots: "in divers plays and comedies in public," King James VI learnt from his envoys in the English capital, "they have brought your mother in a rope to the Queen of England in derision, whereof we mind to complain." (26) This report was sent to Scotland in January 1587. It was on 10 January that Philip Henslowe, future father-in-law of Edward Alleyn, turned his mind from the business of a pawnbroker to finish the commercial arrangements for erecting the Rose theatre. Histrionic enterprise fevered other brains in England which had never before felt the inspiration of the comic or tragic muses. Even Burghley's son Thomas Cecil experimented with patronage of a troupe of players, which left one solitary record of activity at Norwich, also in January 1587 (27).

Among the features of the Earl of Oxford's occupation which made it nastily distasteful to him was the insistence by Burghley that his obscene friends with the inkhorn should be prepared to serve the state as couriers, political reporters, spies. I cannot imagine any other reason for Thomas Watson's intimacy with Thomas Walsingham in Paris. That is what the pilots of the government had in mind when they appointed Anthony Mundy "Messenger of her Majesty's Chamber". Presumably it was what the Privy Council meant when they informed the Cambridge University dons "that in all his actions" Christopher Marlowe "had behaved him selfe orderlie and discreetly, whereby he had done her majestie good service ... it was not her Majestie's pleasure that anie one employed as he had

been in matters touching the benefitt of his Countrie should be defamed by those who are ignorant in the affaires he went
about." (28) Remember, Burghley was Chancellor of the University
when this message went to Cambridge on 29 June, 1587. A letter to
Burghley from Utrecht dated 2 October, 1587, mentions "Mr Morley" as one of his messengers (29).

On 6 February, 1588, the Stationers Register noted the arrival at
the press of Thomas Kyd's translation of Torquato Tasso's *Padre de
Famiglia*, which he called *The Householder's Philosophy*. Admirers of
Kyd are compelled to admit, his version is "crowded with blunders,
and fully deserves Nashe's sneer in the prefatory epistle to *Menaphon*
at the 'home-born mediocritie' of the translator." (30) This sarcasm
of Nashe, printed in front of Robert Greene's romance *Menaphon*,
which the printer registered on 23 August, 1589, merits our micros-
copy, because it is not only the main excuse for crediting Kyd with
the composition of the earliest version of *Hamlet*; it is used to justify
his nomination as author of *The Spanish Tragedy*. "It is a common
practise now a daies," Nashe begins, "amongst a sort of shifting
companions, that runne through euery art and thriue by none to
leaue the trade of *Nouerint*, whereto they were borne, and busie
themselues with the indeuors of art, that could scarcelie latinise
their neck-verse if they should haue neede." We recognise that
Nashe's barbs here have been aimed at but one man, "Thomas, son
of Francis Kidd, Citizen and Writer of the Courte Letter of London," *i.e.* scribe of legal documents often beginning "*Nouerint uni-
versi*". "Yet English Seneca read by candlelight," Nashe continues,
"yeeldes manie good sentences as '*bloud is a beggar*' and so forth: and
if you intreate him faire in a frostie morning, he will affoord you
whole *Hamlets*, I should say hand-fulls of tragical speeches. But o
griefe! *tempus edax rerum*; what's that will last alwaies? The sea ex-
haled by droppes will in continuance be drie, and Seneca let bloud
line by line, and page by page, at length must needes die to our
stage." Usually the collegiate cranium accepts the words "English
Seneca" as a reference to some British translation of the Roman
dramatist, and every known version of his Latin plays in English has

been scoured in search of any expression resembling "Blood is a beggar." It seems, however, to me more reasonable to suppose that English Seneca must have been a live poet, not a book, a man who could be approached on a frosty morning with a request for some products of his prolific artistry, a man of some renown for his eloquence in tragedy. The English master of tragic poetry had already surpassed the best rhetoric of Seneca with a play called *Hamlet*. His verses were echoed and emulated by innumerable men of the pen. And Nashe comically laments that their constant drawing on the well of his marvels apparently exhausted it. "Which makes his famisht followers to imitate the Kidde in *Aesop*, who enamored with the Foxes newfangles, forsooke all hopes of life to leape into a new occupation; and these men renowncing all possibilities of credit or estimation, to intermeddle with Italian translations: wherein how poorelie they haue plodded (as those that are neither prouenzall men nor are able to distinguish of Articles) let all indifferent Gentlemen that haue trauailed in that tongue discerne by their twopenie pamphlets: and no meruaile though their home-born mediocritie be such in this matter." At this point there can be no question, who was the target of Nashe's laughter, and what had provoked it? "For what can be hoped of those that thrust *Elisium* into hell, and haue not learned, as long as they haue liued in the spheares, the iust measure of the Horizon without an hexameter. Sufficeth them to bodge vp a blanke verse with ifs and ands ..."

Professor Boas was able to detect in *The Spanish Tragedy* the influence of Watson's *Passionate Centurie*, whose sonnet 47 was clearly adapted for the play (2.1). "Sonnet 21 possibly inspired *Soliman and Perseda*," (4.1), he observed. But he felt confident that, when Nashe talks about "thrusting Elysium into hell", he had in view *The Spanish Tragedy* (1.1) where the "faire Elizian greene" is pictured as a region beyond Acheron, the dwelling place of Pluto and Proserpina – manifestly not Hell. Nashe's allusion to measuring "the Horizon" with the help of hexameters, Boas took as an attack on the *Tragedy's* use of Vergil's epic to picture details of the netherworld of death. The picture contains no vision of any horizon. There may, however, be a mockery of the *Tragedy* in the derision of blank verse patched up with ifs and ands. For 2.1 presents Lorenzo shouting at Pedringano, "What, Villaine, ifs and ands?" And if that joke of Nashe does attack the *Tragedy*, then it can stand as evidence that he believed Thomas Kyd wrote *Hieronimo*. But he might have been mocking an effort by Kyd to imitate the *Tragedy*.

Toward the end of his preface to *Menaphon* Nashe warns the fellows whom he satirised in it to pray for refreshment of their master's magic. This time he is not called "English Seneca." "Yet let subjects, for all their insolence, dedicate a *de profundis* every morning to the preservation of their *Caesar*, lest their increasing indignities return them ere long their juggling to mediocrity, and they bewail in weeping blanks the wane of their monarchy."

Between the Autumn of 1587, when Kyd went to work for his concealed Lord, and February 1588, when his translation of Tasso was ready for publication, the "Caesar" of blank-verse bards in London underwent a crisis that promised the decline of his kingdom. The only record from the Earl of Oxford in this interval that I am acquainted with is "A view of frank pledge", a document of land economy, in which Oxford granted one Matthew Ellison on 23 September, 1587, a portion of waste land in his manor of Hedingham Upland (31).We know that in this period the Earl manned and armed a ship he named *Edward Bonaventure* in the hope of commanding her crew in a battle with the Armada sailing from Spain. It must have been in connexion with this naval interest that Burghley informed him: "How often I have propounded way to prefer your services. But why these could not take place, I must not particularly set down in writing, lest either I discover the hinderers or offend yourself, in showing the allegations to impeach your Lordship from such preferments." (32) This information is dated 15 December, 1587; the Lord Treasurer wrote it with burning remembrance of "my poor daughter's affliction, whom her husband had in the afternoon [of 4 May, 1587] so troubled with words of reproach of me to her – as though I had no care of him as I had to please others ... she spent all the evening in dolour and weeping." (33) The poor Countess Anne Cecil de Vere gave birth to her fourth daughter, Susan, on 26 May, but did not live more than a month after the child's first birthday. On 12 September, 1587, her little girl Frances was buried near Burghley's rural retreat of Pymmes. We can imagine Oxford's tragic wife – "like Niobe, all tears" – in the weeks that followed the funeral, until 5 June, 1588, when she herself died of a fever in the Queen's palace at Greenwich, while her husband apparently hunted for Spanish vessels in the Channel. He had not time for artificial drama; the sufferings of his wife alone would have silenced his muse. Soon after the funeral of his wife in Westminster Abbey, he sold both Oxford Court in Candlewick Street and the house of 'Folly' in Bishopsgate. He retained however a residence near his beloved theatres, "a messuage or tenement called the Gate House, with its appurtenances and a garden commonly known as the Great Garden... situated in the parish of St Bartolph without Aldgate, London." (34)

The story of Tom Watson is almost utterly overwhelmed by darkness all this time. Probably he was the T. W. who supplied verses approving George Whetstone's *Heptameron of Civil Discourses*, which the printer registered on 11 January, 1582. That book is said to have inspired Shakespeare to write *Measure for Measure*. On 7 May, 1582, the Stationers Company licensed Christopher Ockland's *Eirenarkia*, which got the privilege of public reading in schools. To its broadcasting Watson contributed a brief Latin applause. Several years later Watson published a little treatise on memory training, *Compendium Memoriae Localis*, dedicated to an obscure gentleman named Henry Noel. In 1585 he dedicated his elegiac *Amyntas* to Henry "Nowell". Humbly Watson warned readers that his work could not be compared with the treatise on memory discipline written by Giordano Bruno, "the mystical and deeply learned *Sigillis* of the Nolan."

In the same year that saw publication of Greene's *Menaphon*, 1589, he also dashed off a trivial pamphlet entitled *Ciceronis Amor*. It carried an advertisement "Ad Lectorem", six lines of Latin, from Watson's pen. The little notice must have made Greene feel that Watson's catholic generous nature did not share Marlowe's antipathy toward him. So he was glad to include in Nashe's preface to *Menaphon* the two lines about Watson, "whose *Amintas*, and translated *Antigone*, may march in equipage of honour with any of our ancient Poets."

In the summer of 1589 a ruffian William Bradley appealed to law for "security of peace" against the printer Hugo Swift, believed to be a brother of Anne, Watson's wife, John Allen, and Thomas Watson, we know not why. The sheriff of Middlesex received an order to summon them to Westminster Hall on 25 November. But on 18 September Bradley found himself exchanging sword strokes near the Curtain theatre with Christopher Marlowe. Watson arrived and interrupted the fray. Bradley turned his weapon on him with hotter zest. Watson drove his blade into his antagonist's chest and killed him. Constable Stephen Wild came to bring Watson, "gentleman", and Marlowe, "yeoman", before Sir Owen Hopton, Lieutenant of the Tower, who lived in Norton Folgate, a few steps from Marlowe's room. From Hopton's house the fighting poets went to Newgate prison. The coroner's jury decided that Watson had slain in self-defence, just as he claimed. On 3 December the two playwrights came before the justices of Old Bailey, including Sir Roger Manwood from Marlowe's home county, Kent. They cleared the younger dramatist of responsibility for Bradley's death, but Watson had to remain behind Newgate bars until 10 February, when he received the Queen's pardon (35).

Early in April 1590 Sir Francis Walsingham, the expert on espionage, died in torment from his diseases at his home in Seething Lane. Watson composed a Latin elegy addressed to Thomas Walsingham, his patron, but dedicated to Lady Frances Sidney, Sir Philip's widow, the master-spy's daughter. Hardly was the corpse cold when "all his papers and books, both public and private, were seized and carried away," Robert Beale, his brother-in-law declared, "perhaps by those who would be loth to be used so themselves." (36)

Watson diverted his wits from his sorrows by means of favourite music. In 1590 Thomas Este printed *Superius. The first sett of Italian madrigalls Englished, not to the sense of the originall dittie, but after the affec-tion of the Noate.* By Thomas Watson, Gentleman. He enriched the book with "two excellent Madrigalls of Master William Byrd, com-posed after the Italian vaine at the request of the said Thomas Wat-son." And he added a Latin poem in praise of Luca Marenzio and his sleep tunes. He dedicated *Superius* to Robert Devereux, Earl of Essex, "Noble pupil of Mars, sweet child of the Muses," and thus obliquely told his readers about "the endeavors" of the Earl in lit-erature: "your verses often to be sung to an Aonian lyre." (37) Mas-ter Byrd must have been familiar with Watson from the days when they both served the Earl of Oxford, whom Byrd delighted with galliards and marches which were surely performed in plays.

Dated about 1590 is a romantic play in manuscript called *The Dead Man's Fortune*, evidently an actor's copy, for Richard Burbage, Robert Lee, and Darlowe (probably Richard Darloe, player, of St Botolph's parish, Aldgate, where Lee too lived) are named in it. The characters form a medley of Greek and Italian names, including one Laertes, a lover. The play most likely belonged to Lord Strange's servants or the Admiral's, and I suspect it was a frolic of Tom Wat-son's wit, one of those offshoots William Cornwallis, who em-ployed the poet as a family tutor, remembered when he declared, Watson "could devise twenty fictions and knaveries in a play, which was his daily practice and his living." (38)

1590, according to Tucker Brooke, is the earliest year to which the writing of the anonymous tragedy *Arden of Feversham* can be re-ferred comfortably. The indefatigable Fleay ascribed *Arden* to Kyd on the basis of three parallels with *The Spanish Tragedy.* These did not include the glaring likeness of the villains in *Arden*, Black Will and Shakebag, to Pedringano and Serberine in the *Tragedy.* Charles Craw-ford exhibited numerous striking resemblances between *Arden* and *Soliman and Perseda.* Boas agreed that in the cadence and diction of many passages, and in the combination of lyrically elaborate verse-structure with colloquial directness of dialogue, *Arden* recalls "the manner of Kyd." (39) Yet Marlowe was the author of *Arden,* in the judgment of Boas. Kyd, he argued, "so far as we can judge, was not given to repetition. Marlowe, on the other hand, was a frequent borrower, and he might readily have adapted Kyd's lines to his own use, especially at a time when they were in close contact." (40) Substituting Watson for Kyd in this sentence, I support Boas's argument. Of course, the most plausible reason for crediting Marlowe with the tragedy of bourgeois marriage is the evidence of the writer's familiarity with Kentish landscapes.

The author of *Arden of Feversham* took remarkable liberties with his material, the chronicle of Holinshed. Perhaps he did this following the instruction of a patron to renovate the old play *Murderous Michael,* acted at Court by the Earl of Sussex's men on 3 March, 1579; that lost tragedy is commonly considered the source of *Arden.* Holinshed depicted Black Will, the partner of the murderess Alice Arden, as a grim fearless killer. In the play he turns out a ludicrous braggart, shaped in the image of Basilisco of *Soliman and Perseda.* Incidentally, the description of Dick Reed in *Arden* as "the raylingest knaue in christendome" (4.4) echoes an allusion to Basilisco – "the braginest knaue in Christendom" *(Soliman and Perseda,* 1.3).

Black Will and George Shakebag are presented as denizens of Marlowe's shire. "Two Ruffer Ruffins neuer liued in Kent." But they are heartily at home in London's wickedest streets. They strongly resemble two men who played evil roles in the life of Marlowe and Watson, also named Will and George. We have already met the murderous Will Bradley. This Will had a comrade, wrynecked George Orrell, a professional soldier, mentioned in a state record of the Earl of Essex's last demonstration as "a most desperate rakehell as lives." (41) He seems to have been more courageous brute than braggart, and could have said with Shakebag: "I cannot paint my valour out with words" (2.2), or sneered like him at warnings of ghosts and hell, "Nay then lets go sleepe, when buges and feares / Shall kill our courages with their fancies worke."

In the summer of 1589 Watson's brother-in-law, Hugo Swift, requested protection of the law against George Orrell, who had menaced him with death. The Court of the Queen's Bench overlooked the relation of that appeal with Will Bradley's petition against Swift and Watson *ob metum mortis*. He was probably the Bradley who assaulted one Robert Wood with a cudgel in the autumn of 1588, so that Wood's friends despaired of his life. The victim had denounced Bradley on the day of the attack as a worthless fellow, a bully (42). The likeness between this Will and his cudgel and Black Will in *Arden*, with his boasts of assault and battery, is manifest "In Temes streete a brewers carte was lyke to haue runne ouer me: I made no more ado, but went to the clark and cult all the natches of his tales and beat them about his head ... I haue broken a Sariants head with his own mace" (5.1). The spitting image of the bully whose doleful days Tom Watson abridged! One of the minor characters in *Arden*, by the way, is named Bradshaw, a petty accomplice in the main crime. The playwright changed the name of another shady person of the story from William Blackburn to Clarke: we cannot tell why. Perhaps he viewed the suggestion of William Bradley's name so close to the names of Bradshaw and Black Will as excessive cruelty to the dead? The rakehell Orrell, we ought to note, lived to win honour for gallantry during the Irish wars.

Among the minor figures of *Arden of Feversham* I detect another contemporary portrait, a caricature of Robert Greene. A poor gentleman named Greene joined the plotters against the actual Master Arden. The poet went to peculiar lengths to make his name infamous. The original Greene was christened John; the playwright changed it to Richard. Robert Green was well known in London as a companion of criminals, in particular one Cutting Ball. Richard Greene makes his first appearance in the play after Alice Arden has declared,

In London many alehouse Ruffins keepe,
Which, as I heare, will murther men for gould.

Richard Greene promises to free her from husbanage, to "hyre some Cutter to cut (Arden) short." This Greene is supposed to be a citizen of Faversham; but the play reports that he has known Black Will in London for twelve years (5.1). Despite his pleasure in consorting with cut-throats, Richard, like the literary Robert, is "religious", a man of "great douation" (1, 589). Thus Marlowe might have avenged himself for Robin Greene's reference to "that Atheist *Tamburlan.*" Also noteworthy is the fondness of the two Greenes for the fables of Aesop. In *Never Too Late,* and the imitation of Greene called *Groatsworth of Wit,* probably perpetrated by Henry Chettle, actors are taunted with odious comparisons of their profession with the pride of Aesop's crow. In *Arden* the cutters Will and Shakebag are lessoned by Richard Greene with one of Aesop's tales (3.6). The Greene of the drama is a coward; he does not participate in the final stabbing scene; and the last we see of him is when he trembles in fear of arrest and pleads with the stronger spirited Alice, "But cleaue to vs as we will stick to you." If the author of *Arden* had made him a man of letters, the etching from life would have been unmistakable.

The Epilogue describes the play as bare of ornament: "no filed points are foisted in / To make it gratious to the eare or eye." Yet the speeding pen of the playwright found occasion to "foist" in references to Tisiphone, Hydra, Endymion, and "raving Hercules". Moreover, he set the absurd servant Michael to making love with the elegant phrase from Watson's sonnets in *The Teares of Fancie:* "Let my passions penetrate." (43)

Tom Nashe preserved a memory of Watson jesting about Gabriel Harvey at a supper in the Nag's Head Inn. We wonder if this inn was the same as "the Nages head, the 18 pence ordinarye," at which Arden of Feversham ate supper when he visited London (2.2). Harvey is said to have provoked Watson's joke by his hexameter lampoon of 1580 on "The Mirror of Tuscanism," the Earl of Oxford. Presumably Watson's irony did not come to the scholar's ears, or we might have been regaled with some heavy darts of wit about him such as Harvey shot at Greene and Nashe. The Earl of Oxford had sold his Bishopsgate mansion, Fisher's Folly, to William Cornwalls, who hired Watson to teach his children Latin. That may have been the way in which Anne Cornwallis began her beautiful collection of courtiers' poetry, including some of Oxford's finest. One of his extant poems, his solitary sonnet, appears to have been mixed with Watson's work, and came to be published as the last lyric in his posthumous *Tears*.

On 26 September 1592, "Thomas Watson, gent. was buried" at the church of St Bartholomew the Less. A few months before, Edward White obtained licence to print *Arden of Feversham,* which he sold in his shop at "the little north door" in Paul's Churchyard. A month later Abel Jeffes and White wrangled for ownership of *The Spanish Tragedy.* In November White arranged to publish *Soliman and Perseda.* He and Jeffes were called to the court of the Stationers Company, which resolved, on 18 December, 1592, that "Edward White and Abel Ieffes haue eche of them offended. Viz Edw White in hauinge printed the spanish tragedie belonging to Abel Jeffes / and Abel Ieffes in hauing printed the tragedie of Arden of kent belonginge to Edw White." The two editions were ordered confiscated and forfeited to "thuse of the poore of the companye." (44)

I have tried to prove that the two or three plays on which the artistic reputation of Thomas Kyd is said to rest, together with *The First Part of Jeronimo* and *The Rare Triumphs of Love and Fortune,* were essentially the compositions of a man of superior learning, a poet skilled in classical and Romance literatures, a spirit of quiet and sequestered life, writing plays for pelf but an earnest workman, capable of violence only in self-defence, a fellow of robust humour without malice, having indeed a genius for long friendship, an artist and a lover of the arts. Who else but the poet extolled by Thomas Heywood in these words:

> Tom Watson ... wrote
> Able to make Apollo's self to dote
> Upon his Muse. (45)

Postscript

Most of this article I made while enjoying a Harrison Fellowship in Tudor and Stuart stage productions at the University ot Pennsylvania in 1951. Since then I have heard of a doctoral dissertation on

Thomas Watson as Latinist, done at the University of California, but could not even get a glimpse of it. And Arthur Freeman's *Thomas Kyd: Facts and Problems* has been issued by the Oxford Clarendon Press in 1967. I have refrained from reading his book, in the hope that my article would be printed, and provide students with the opportunity of comparison of our two arguments which is bound to be educational and entertaining.

Notes

I

1   Arber, ed. *Thomas Watson: Poems* (English Reprints, 1870) 17.
2   Nashe, *Haue with you to Saffron-Walden,* in *Works,* ed. McKerrow (London 1910) III, 126.
3   Wood, *Athenae Oxonienses,* ed. Bliss (London 1813) I, 601.
4   Quoted by E. K. Chambers, *The Elizabethan Stage* (1913) III, 506.
5   *Ibid.*
6   Meres, *Palladis Tamia: Wits Treasury* (1598) fol. 283A.
7   *Malone Society Collections* (1923) II, ii.167.
8   John Strype, *Annals of the Reformation* (1731) III, 345.
9   Watson, *Meliboeus,* in Arber, *op. cit.,* 155.
10 Arber, *op. cit.,* 6.
11 *Relations Politiques des Pays Bas et l'Angleterre, sous le Règne de Philippe II,* ed. Lettenhove (1900) IX, 62, 252, 328.
12 Arber, *op. cit. supra.*
13 Harvey, *Gratulationes Valdinenses* (1578) in *Works,* ed. Grosart, I, xxxix.
14 *Soliman and Perseda* (1.2), in *The Works of Thomas Kyd,* ed. Boas (Clarendon Press, 1901).
15 Cf. Marlowe, *Doctor Faustus,* I, i.
16 J. L. Motley, *The Rise of the Dutch Republic* (New York 1880) 111, 384, 389.
17 Chambers, *op. cit.,* IV, 157. See Arthur Acheson, *Shakespeare, Chapman, & Sir Thomas More* (London: Bernard Quaritch 1931) 195.
18 Alexander Witherspoon, *The Influence of Robert Garnier on Elizabethan Drama* (1924) 94. Cf. Boas, *op. cit.,* xviii-xix.
19 Boas, *op. cit.,* lvi.
20 Mark Eccies, *Christopher Marlowe in London* (1934) 146.
21 *Ibid.* 151.
22 B. M. Ward, *The Seventeenth Earl of Oxford* (1928) 99.
23 Calendar of State Papers, Domestic Series, cxl, 665.

24 Arber, *op. cit.*, 77.
25 *Ibid.* 15.
26 Claudian, *De Tertio Consulatu Honorii*, 96-98
27 Ambassador Castelnau, quoted in *Philip Howard, First Earl of Arundel*, ed. Pollen and MacMahon (Catholic Record Society 1919) 29.
28 Chambers, *op. cit.*, IV, 157.
29 *Henslowe's Diary*, ed. Greg (A. H. Bullen, 1904) 150, 154. *Jeronimo* was published by Thomas Pavier in 1605, anonymously.
30 *Philip Howard*, 31.
31 Boas, *op. cit.*, lxvii ff.
32 *Returns of Aliens Dwelling in the City and Suburbs of London from the Reign of Henry VIII to that of James I*, ed. Kirk (1900) II, 220.

II

1   Pollen and McMahon, *op. cit.*, 29.
2   *Ibid.*, 30.
3   Fulke Greville, *The Life of the Renowned Sir Philip Sidney*, ed. Nowell-Smith (1907), 63.
4   Watson, *Poems*, ed. Arber, 7.
5   *Returns of Aliens...* III, 397.
6   Arber, *op. cit.*, 36.
7   *Ibid.*, 157.
8   "The Journey of Sir Francis Walsingham," ed. Martin, in *Camden Miscellany* (1870) VI, 29.
9   Arber, *op. cit.*, 25.
10 *The Elizabethan Stage*, IV, 28.
11 Quatorzain xxxv; *Love and Fortune*, in Dodsley's *Old English Plays*, ed. Carew Hazlitt, VI, 166.
12 Dodsley, *op. cit.*, 219. The idea of Bomelio doubtless came from the astrologer and magician Dr Elis Bomelius who was imprisoned early in 1570 for practising medicine without a licence and other perilous labours (Thomas Wright, *Queen Elizabeth and Her Times*, 1838, I, 361). He published an *Almanac and Prognostications* in 1567 and 1568, and arranged to leave England in April 1570.
13 Calendar of State Papers, Foreign Series, xx, 25.
14 Sidney Lee, (ed.) *Dictionary of National Biography* xvii, *s.v.*, "Elizabeth."
15 Boas, (ed.) *Works of Thomas Kyd*, 340-1.
16 British Museum: Rawlinson MS. Poet. 148; Arber, *op. cit.*, 11. John Case's *Apologia Musices* is known only in the 1588 edition.
17 *Acts of the Privy Council*, ed. Dasent, xv, 141. On 16 April, 1595, Richard Jones registered *Raptus Helenae*, "Helen's Rape by the Athenian Duke Theseus."
18 *The Lyfe and Death of Heliogabilus* was registered in June 1594. Greene, *Complete*

Works, ed. Grosart (1886) VII, 7, 8.

19 Boas made an error in transcribing Kyd's letter: he read the number of Kyd's years in the service of his Lord as iij instead of vj.: T. W. Baldwin, 'On the Chronology of Thomas Kyd's Plays,' *Modern Language Notes*, XL, 1925, 343f. Tucker Brooke upheld Baldwin's correction in his edition of the *Works of Christopher Marlowe*, Dial Press 1930.

20 Boas, *op. cit.*, cviii-cix

21 G. F. Warner, *Catalogue of the Manuscripts & Muniments of Alleyn's College of God's Gift at Dulwich* (1881) 251, 252. See Eccles *op.cit.* 65 and Gwynneth Bowen, *The Shakespearean Authorship Review*, no. 29, Summer 1974, 4-8.

22 Ward, *op. cit.*, 257.

23 British Museum: Lansdowne MS. 103:38.

24 Colonel Bernard Rowland Ward, 'Shakespeare and Elizabethan War Propaganda,' *Royal Engineers Journal*, Dec. 1928, reprinted in Looney, *"Shakespeare" Identified*, ed. Ruth Loyd Miller, 1975, II, 469-482.

25 Calendar of State Papers: Venetian, viii. 182 (1581-91).

26 Robert S. Rait & Annie Cameron, (eds.) *King James's Secret: Negotiations between Elizabeth and James VI relating to the Execution of Mary Queen of Scots, from the Warrender Papers* (London 1927) 171.

27 John Tucker Murray, *English Dramatic Companies* (1910) II, 80.

28 Acts of the Privy Council, xv. 141. See John Bakeless, *The Tragical History of Christopher Marlowe* (1942) I, 77.

29 Calendar of State Papers: Domestic Series, Eliz. Add. 1580-1625, 217.

30 Boas, *op. cit.*, xx. We may suspect that it was this translation from the Italian that prompted Francis Meres to put Kyd on a plane with Tasso in his *Wits Treasury*: Absurd as that piece of pedantry may seem, we must admit there is method in Meres' madness when he ranks Watson ahead of Kyd and Shakespeare among Britain's chief dramatists.

31 Calendar of State Papers: Domestic Series (1587) cciii. 50.

32 British Museum: Lansdowne MS. 103:38.

33 Letter to Walsingham, 5 May, in Calendar of State Papers: Domestic Series (1587) cci. 3.

34 Gwynneth Bowen, *The Shakespearean Authorship Review*, no. 28, Summer 1973, 3, 6, where she corrects a mistake of Rowland Ward concerning Oxford's Covent Garden in *The Mystery of "Mr. W. H."* (1923) 29.

35 Eccles, *op. cit.*, 8ff.

36 Yelverton MS. clxii, quoted by Conyers Read, *Mr Secretary Walsingham*, 1925, 1, 431.

37 E. Tenison, *Elizabethan England* (Leamington: The Author, 1930-39) VIII, 299. Watson's transmutations of the Italian to English have been reprinted in A. Obertello's *Madrigali italiani in Inghilterra* (1949) 259ff. Arber repeats the Latin of the poem to Luca Marenzio (*Watson: Poems*, 12), which may be Englished

for the sake of these lines: "The sweet power of your music stabs me; so may I often die, for in your song is life. When you sing, I dream it is the music of the spheres, the harmony of the Muses."

38 Quoted in *Athenaeum,* 23 August 1890, 256.

39 C. F. Tucker Brooke, *The Life of Marlowe* (1930) xiii. Frederick Gard Fleay, *Biographical Chronicle of the English Drama* (1891) II, 28. Charles Crawford, *Collect Collectanea* (1906) 101-130. Boas, *op. cit.,* xc.

40 Boas, *Christopher Marlowe* (1940) 199.

41 Eccies, *op. cit.,* 61.

42 *Ibid.,* 49, 57.

43 Watson, *Poems,* 200. Cf. *Arden of Feversham,* II, ii.

44 *Records of the Court of the Stationers' Company,* ed. Greg and Boswell (1930), 44. Thomas Heywood, *Hierarchy of the Blessed Angels* (1635).

45 Thomas Heywood, *Hierarchy of Blessed Angels.*

Appendix I–Oxford's Sole Acrostic

Let me commend for scholars' attention the pair of quatrains published in *Brittons Bowre of Delights* (1591) signed "Finis. Trentame." Nicholas Breton protested that he had nothing to do with the composition or collection of the volume. The name Trentame plainly identifies the writer, or the subject, of the rimes, Elizabeth Trentham, the royal Maid of Honor, who married Edward de Vere shortly after the *Bower of Delights* came from Richard Jones's press. The poem is the only acrostic that could be credited to the Earl of Oxford.

> Time made a stay when highest powers wrought,
> Regard of loue where vertue had her grace,
> Excellence rare of euerie beautie sought,
> Notes of the heart where honour had her place,
> Tried by the touch of most approued truth,
> A worthie Saint to serue a heauenly Queene,
> More faire then she that was the fame of youth,
> Except but one, the like was neuer seene.

The reservation phrase in the final line is just what might have been expected from the playful "madcap" Earl of Oxford.

Note: This is excerpted from "The Secret Verses of Edward de Vere", the article which Dr. Feldman recently prepared and submitted to *Studies in Philology* in an attempt to expand the collection of De Vere poems issued by Stephen May in that journal.

Appendix II
The Rape of Antwerp in a Tudor Play

Since the chronology of many Elizabethan plays remains a mystery, lighted here and there by brilliant guesswork, it is impossible to say with certitude when the Spanish wars in the Netherlands were first reflected in the English drama.

Some version of the popular tragedy named *Alarum for London, or The Siege of Antwerp*, which was finally printed in 1602, may have been current on the London stage shortly after November 1576, when the event it portrays horrified Europe. The twelfth scene of the play exhibits the plot of a lost tragedy named *Timoclea at the Siege of Thebes* (doubtless inspired by Plutarch's life of Alexander) which was performed at the court in February 1574. *The Siege of Thebes* could have been fresh in the memory of the author of *The Siege of Antwerp* when he wrote the scene; or perhaps he went directly to Plutarch for his material.

There is a passage in John Northbrooke's tract against *Dicing, Dauncing, Vain Playes, or Enterludes* (registered in December 1577) which leads one to believe the enthusiasts of the theatre in London at the time Northbrooke preached were still being thrilled by scenes of the massacre at Antwerp. He accused the city players of instructing their listeners "howe to murther, howe to poyson, howe to disobey and rebel against princes, to consume treasures prodigally, to mooue to lustes, to ransacke and spoyle cities and townes..." (1) This sounds as if the Rev. Northbrooke had gone to an inn-yard himself to witness a production of *The Siege of Antwerp*. At all events, the Tudor poets for decades drew profitable lessons from the tragedy. There was at least one ballad on the catastrophe, composed by Rafe Norris, "A Warning to London by the Fall of Antwerp". (2)

On May 29, 1600, James Roberts applied for a license to print the *Alarum for London*. The grant was made, "provided that yt be not printed without further Aucthoritie" than the Wardens of the Stationers' guild possessed. (3) If Roberts ever fulfilled this condition, there is no record of it; the *Alarum* was actually published in 1602 by William Ferbrand, with the press emblem of Edward Allde. The play was announced as the property of the Lord Chamberlain's company, to which Richard Burbage and William Shakespeare belonged, but no scholar has attempted to distribute the roles of the *Alarum* among the Chamberlain's men. The hands of Lodge, Marlowe, and even Shakespeare have been glimpsed in the tragedy, but with our present-day knowledge of the Elizabethan theatre it is futile to speculate on the identity of the writer, or writers. I myself think Thomas Kyd the writer of this play, because it is pungently thick with reminders of his *Jeronimo*.

The figure of Time as Epilogue declares the purpose of the play:

> To rubbe the memory
> Of actions long since cast behinde —

Specifically, the memory of the Spanish rape of Antwerp in 1576, at a time when the economic capital of Europe lay obedient at the feet of Philip II, and spurned every proposal for the creation of a municipal army to guard its wealth. The rape was the work of mercenaries, Spaniards, Italians, and Germans, who had been long without their wages, and were goaded to madness by the sight of Antwerp's riches and fat ease. Don Sancho de Avila was the ringleader of the attack, but the play brands the Duke of Alva as the chief culprit. The fact is that Alva had quit the Netherlands three years before. But the unknown dramatist wished him to be regarded as the Herod of the Low-Country innocents,

> Whose guiltless bloud hath dyed poor Belgiaes cheeks,
> And chang'd her like a drunken Bacchanall. (Scene 5)

Not King Philip, but his prime general bears the blame. Alva comes on the stage disguised as a corpse, carried in a coffin "upon a horse (i.e., hearse) covered with black: soldiers after, trayling their Pykes." His first words, uttered from the hearse, are a bogeyman's threat, to "fright these Bouzing Belgians" who think he is dead (Scene 2).

The pursy burghers of Antwerp are shown disdaining the appeals for employment of professional soldiers in the city's defence. The Prince of Orange's offer to protect Antwerp from all enemies is rejected. The burghers insist on strict neutrality in the war between King Philip,

> That great Prince,
> And our kinde friend the Co-vnited States.

Cornelius van Ende, the leader of the German mercenaries in the Spanish army, is gratified by the thrifty citizens' refusal to hire troops to defend the tempting town:

> Their myserie shall bring their miserie.
> …Now (Antwerp) comes the Spaniards holly-day .(4)

What ensues is horror with worse horrors at its heels. Davila shoots a virgin he had loved, and orders her father to be stabbed, thus setting an example to his men of remorseless fury against the people who had prospered so long in the shadow of Spanish arms. Two factors of London merchants are tortured, hoisted on ropes, in order to wring ransom out of their English friends. (5) Meekly the governor of the English merchants in Antwerp protests to the Duke of Alva, in the name of

> Englands league with Spaine. King Phillips word,
> Past to our gratious Mistris…
> But if now
> Your Highness hath commission to breake
> The holie contract which your King hath made,
> We must be patient and abide the worst.

He repudiates any suspicion of sympathy with the Orange revolt.

> We are not here great Lord, to ioyne with them
> In any bold confederacie of warre,

But for the trafficke, which all nations else,
(As well as England) have within this place. (6)

But the bogey Alva will not listen to any other sound "in our warres musicke" except the ringing of gold, for ransoms or bribes (Scene 11). The thought of Antwerp's resistance spurs him to rave.

One Spaniards bloud, I value better worth
Then many hundreds of these drunken Dutch.

Yet he tries to rescue young Count Egmont from slaughter because he has manifested a "high spirit even in the face of death." As he moves to protect the youth, angry Spaniards strike and wound the Duke, but he persists in his gallantry. (7) The memory of this generous deed is soon blotted out by the most excruciating scene in the tragedy, which has no historical or literary source known to us. Scene 10 opens with "Lenchy and Martin, two little children running," chased by Spaniards yelling, "Fuora villiaco, sa, sa, sa ,sa!" The father, old blind Harman, and his wife appear, and in their presence the children are knifed. Then the crying mother is killed, and, as the scene concludes, Harman falls to the ground. We are left in the dark as to whether he has fainted or died.

There is a hero in the tragedy, the only hero in the history of the Tudor theatre who is undeniably Dutch. He is named Lieutenant Vaughan – a name that sounds more Welsh than Dutch – but he is glorified as a son of Brabant. The lieutenant is customarily called "Stump," because he is lame. He bravely gathers a handful of men to fight the Spaniards, although the burghers of Antwerp have despised him as useless. In aristocratic language he bitterly exposes their measuring of human worth by money:

An object base mechanicke set aworke;
A swettie Cobler, whose best Industrie,
Is but to cloute a Shoe, shall haue his fee;
But let a Soldier, who has let his bloud,

Is lam'd, diseas'd, or any way distrest,
Appeal for succour, then you looke a sconce
As if you knew him not; respecting more
An Ostler, or some drudge that rakes your kennels,
Than one that fighteth for the common wealth. (8)

The lieutenant is outraged into taking up arms by Spaniards who are brutally searching a woman for jewelry. "It is inhumaine," cries Stump, "to abuse a woman"; and he draws a sword in her defence. He manages to beat the scoundrels off, accomplishes other feats of warlike mercy, and at last, fatally wounded, dies with a happy soul, proud that his steel was "never drawn but in a rightful cause."

Now I have it on my brest,
The Honourable congisance of death....
Antwerpe farewell, if thou haue done me wrong,
This latest gasp, sends pardon from my tung.

A flourish of trumpets is sounded over the body of this son of the Netherlands, who so faithfully exemplifies the ideal of the Christian warrior upheld by his countryman Erasmus. With him dies another brave champion of Antwerp, and Davila pays tribute to both:

There never lived two more Heroycke spirits;
That for their Country haue deseru'd as much
To be renouned; as ever Curtious was,
Or Romaine Decius, or the two valiant Cocles.

There is no character in Gascoigne's *Spoyle of Antwerpe* who corresponds with Lieutenant Vaughan. Whether the author of the *Alarum for London* derived him from other stories of the Spanish atrocity, or invented him simply as a model veteran of British calibre, the tragedy lives in our recollection because of the vitality of its portrait of "Stump." The rest of the play is mere dumbshow and noise, signifying propaganda on the perils of a metropolis that neglects its professional soldiers, an ever-popular theme on the Tudor stage.

Notes

1   Quoted by E.K. Chambers in *The Elizabethan Stage*, IV, 150. On the court play *Timoclea*, see Chambers, *op.cit.*, IV, 90.

2   *Old Ballads*, ed. J. P. Collier, 89-92.

3   *A Transcript of the Registers of the Company of Stationers of London*, ed. Edward Arber, II, 160.

4   Scene 3. Gascoigne names Charles Fugger as the chief of the German mercenaries of Spain (*Works*, ed Cunliffe, II, 586ff).

5   *Alarum for London*, Scenes 8, 9.

6   *Ibid.*, Scene 7.

7   Scenes 5,7. According to Gascoigne (*Works*, II, 589), the deed was really done by Colonel Alonzo Verdugo.

8   Scene 4.

9   Scene 15.

Index

A

The Abridgement of the Histories of Trogus Pom-peius, translated by Arthur Golding, 100
Absolute monarchy, doctrine of, 187
Acheley, Thomas, 312
Acheson, Arthur, *Shakespeare, Chapman, and Thomas More* by, 45
Adams, John, 272
Adams, Joseph Quincy, *Shakespearian Play-houses* by, 8
Addenbroke, John 40
Admiral's company of players, 11,46
Adonis and Cytherea, 52
Alarum for London or The Siege of Antwerp, 238,335
Alcantara, 304
Allde, Edward, 336
Allde, Elizabeth, 270
Allde, John, 289
Allen, Cardinal William, 207,223,228
Allen, Percy, *The Life Story of Edward de Vere as "William Shakespeare"* by, 55,135
Allen, Sir Francis, 238
Allen, John, 234
Alleyn, Edward, 39,45,65,115,194,2021227,241,315,317
In Shakespearean roles, 116
Alleyn, John, 46,65,115,194,317
All's Well That Ends Well, 7,77
Alva, Duke of, 101,304
Ambidexter, 294
American Imago, 98
Amores by Ovid, 274
Amoretti by Edmund Spenser, 164
Angell, Pauline K., 141
Anjou, Duke of, 190,231
Anthropophagi, 95, 107
Antigone by Sophocles, Watson's Latin ver-sion of 297
The Antipodes by Richard Brome, 76
Antiquities of Warwickshire by Dugdale, 74
Antony and Cleopatra, 180
Antwerp, 220, 335

fall of to Spain, 184
siege of, 112
Arcadia by Sir Philip Sidney, 118
Archbishop Parker scholarships, Marlowe and 183
Arden, Alice, 271,280
Arden, Mary, 27
Arden of Feversham, 240,269,325
Ardens of Warwickshire, 27
Aretino, 140
Ariosto, 209
Aristotle, 57
Armada, 215,223
Armin, Robert, 8
Arnold, Matthew, 23
The Art of English Poesy, 48
on the Earl of Oxford as a secret writer, 126
Arundel, Charles, 106,108,123,157,189,304,310
and the Throckmorton plot, 109
Arundel, Philip Howard, earl of, 189,298,311
As You Like It, 256,262
Touchstone and William in, 159
Ashton, John, 243
Aubrey, John, 28,61,255
on the Earl of Oxford, 77
Austin Friars, 251
Avisa, 162
Aylmer, John, 187
Azores, 165

B

Babcock's *Genesis of Shakespeare Idolatry*, 16
Babington, Anthony, 195,203
Bacon, Anthony, 238
Bacon, Delia, 20
Bacon, Sir Francis, 167
Baines, Richard, 250,253,259,270
Baiazet, 202
Bakeless, John, 275
Baker, Dr. George, 299
The Practice of the New and Old Physic by, 172

"Ballad of the Life and Death of Doctor Faustus the Conjuror," 218
Ballard, Father John, 195,203
Baldwin, T.W., 8
Bancroft, Richard, 218
Barabas, 225,234
Barbara, 95
  Desdemona's mother's maid, 112
Barbary, 95
Barnes, Barnabe, 163
Baron Hunsdon, George Carey, 11
Barrell, Charles Wisner, 15,68,142,181
Bartholomew, 42
Bartholomew Fair, by Ben Jonson, 305
Barton-on-the-heath, 50
The Basic Writings of Sigmund Freud, 134
Basilisco, 273,301
Bazzi, alias Sodoma, 140
Beale, Robert, 244,304,324
Beeston, Christopher, 63
Beeston, William, 62
Beggar, in Induction to *The Shrew*, 40
Bergler, Dr. Edmund, 239
Bertie, Peregrine, Lord Willoughby, 116
Bethlehem, 21
Betterton, Thomas, 62
Bianca, and Anne Vavasor, 123
Bilson, Bishop Thomas, 187
Bilton, manor of, 66,143
"The Birthplace" by Henry James, 19,133
Bishop of Worcester, 62
Bishopsgate, 46,115,294,299
  as first London residence of Will Shakspere, 47
Blackfriars, 12
Blackfriars theatre, 186
Black Will, 273,276
Blunt, Christopher, 190
Blunt, Edward, 191
  dedication of "Hero and Leander" to Sir Thomas Walsingham by, 262
Boar, as Oxford's nickname, 121
Boar's Head, 13,46,65
Boas, Frederick S., 272,280,303
  Shakespeare and the Universities by, 45
Bologna, 106
Bonn, 219

Bonner, Bishop Edmund, 289
Boswell, James, 30
  on the Stratford Jubilee, 19
Bottom, Nick, 35,72,159,181
Brabant, 103
Brabantio, 106
  and Sir William Cecil, 102
  Senator and Othello's father-in-law, 83
Bradley, William, 234,240,254,277,324,326
Brandes, Georg, 27,58
  on *Hamlet*, 133
  on Shakespeare's life, 18
Breton, Nicholas, 334
Breviary of Britain by Thomas Twyne, dedicated to Oxford, 102
Brewen, Alice, 274
Brewen, John, 274
Bridewell, where Kyd was tortured, 252
A Brief and True Report of the New-found Land of America by Thomas Harriot, 250
Brief Discourse on the Spanish State by Edward Daunce, 127
Brill, 113,185
Britons Bower of Delights, 334
Broelmann, Stephen, 311
Brome, Richard, *The Antipodes* by, 76
Brooke, Tucker, 275,325
Brooke, William, Lord Cobham, 15
Brown, Robert, 46,65
Brussels, surrender of to Spain, 184
Buck, Sir George, 77,312
Buckhurst, Lord, 212
Bulbec, Viscount, Oxford's early title and crest, 66,142
Bull, Eleanor, 253
Bullen, A.H. 211,271,279
Burbage, Cuthbert, and rights to the Globe, 76
Burbage, Heming, and Condell, 27
Burbage, James, 11,64
Burbage, Richard, 36,39,43,45,73,316,336
Burbage family, 47
Burghley, Lord, 7,49,52,101 *See also* Cecil, Sir William.
  on France and Holland, 184
Byrd, William, 52,325

C

Cadiz, 165
Caesar, 81,106
Calais, 165
Calderon, plays of, 285
Callender, Sir Geoffrey, 79
Calymath, 225
Cambises, 292
Cambises, King of Persia, 289,294
  Epilogue of, 292
Cambridge University, 45,66
  Corpus Christi College of, 183
Camden, William, 205,243
Campaspe by John Lyly, 302
Cannibalism, 108
Canterbury, 183
Card of Fancy by Robert Greene, dedicated
  to Oxford, 124
Carey, George, Baron Hunsdon, 11
Carey, Henry, Lord Hunsdon, 12
Case, John, 314
Casimir, Prince Hans of the Palatinate,
  218,301
Cassio, Michael, 84,94,107
  and Bianca, 123
  as a Florentine, 85
  as Sidney, 119
  promotion of, 85
  Shakespeare's conception of, 86
Castelnau, French ambassador, 310
Castle Hedingham, reflected in the Son-
  nets, 152
Castration, terror of in *Othello,* 95
Catholic League, 228
Catlyn, Maliverny, 69,207
Caviar, 82
Cawood, Gabriel, 312
Cecil, Anne, Countess of Oxford,
  53,114,130
  and Desdemona, 102
  and Sidney, 119
  Burghley's daughter and Oxford's wife,
  102
  death of, 7,126
  "Notes by an ill-used Wife" and, 105
  to her husband, 109

Cecil, Diana, 75
Cecil, Robert, Lord Cranborne,
  15,49,73,128,165,221,245,254
  as master of Robert Poley, 259
Cecil, Thomas, 78,114
Cecil, Sir William, Lord Burghley,
  7,49,52,101,110,114,139,189,195,204,213,
  228,244,288,292,319
  and Brabantio, 102
  as Polonius, 82
  as provider for Oxford's children, 123
  death of, 166
Chamberlain's men, 11
Chambers, Sir Edmund, 275,312
  on Armin, 10
  The Elizabethan Stage by, 10,45
  Shakespeare: Facts and Problems by, 44
Chandos, Baron William, 10
Chandos, Mary, 11
Chapel Royal, 106
Chapman, George, 160,163
  as rival poet of the Sonnets, 151
Chappuys, Gabriel, translator of *Hecatommithi,*
  111
Chateau Cambresis, treaty of, 288,293
Cheapside, 69
Chettle, Henry, 43,328
Children of the Chapel, 186
"Choice of Valentines" by Thomas Nashe,
  dedicated to Southampton, 162
Cholmley, Richard, 250,254,260
Christ, 21
Christ's Tears Over Jerusalem by Thomas Nashe,
  12
Christianity, Othello's, 94
Christopher Marlowe in London by Mark Eccles,
  297
Chronicles of England, Scotland, and Ireland by
  Holinshed, 271
Cicero, 106
Ciceronis Amor: Tullie's Love by Robert Greene,
  238
Cinthio, Giraldi, Hecatommithi by,111
Civilization and Its Discontents by Sigmund
  Freud, 132
Clark, Eva Turner, 271
  Hidden Allusions in Shakespeare's Plays by, 135

Clarke, Margaret, 294
Clayton, John, and Shakspere, 40,69
Cleopatra, 95
Cleopatra's Clown, Armin as, 8
Clinton, Henry, earl of Lincoln, 13
"Clonnico del Mondo Snuffe," Armin's
  pen name, 11
"Clunnyco de Curtanio Snuffe," 8
Cobham, Henry Brooke, Baron, 261
Colchester Castle, 62
Colchester prison, 62
Coleridge, Samuel Taylor, 22,58,83
  on *Othello*, 88
Collier, John Payne, 8,36
Coluthus, 208
Comedy as "a kind of history," 54
The Comedy of Errors, 6,54,137,159
Constable, Henry, 233
Contarini, Giovanni, *History of the war be-*
  tween Turkey and Venice by, 111
Cope, Sir Walter, 73
Corambis, in the first quarto of *Hamlet*,
  166
Coriolanus, 16
Cornelia by Thomas Kyd, 303,316
Cornwallis, Anne, 328
Cornwallis, Sir William, 46,194,296,325
Corpus Christi College of Cambridge
  University, 46,183
Cotton, George, 260
The Courtier by Castiglione, 312
Cowell, John, 187
Cranbourne, Lord, 73. See also Cecil,
  Robert.
Crawford, Charles, 272
Creagh, Richard, Archbishop of Armagh,
  191
Cressida, 95
Croft, Sir James, 213,221
Cross Keys Inn, 12
Cumberland, Richard, 31
Cunningham, Francis, 211
Curtail, 276
Curtain theatre, 8,11,46,64,69,299
  the Lord Chamberlain's players and, 11
Cymbeline, 121
Cyprus, 85,93,123,292

D

Dame Kitely, 129
Danter, John, 141
Daphne and Apollo,52
Dark Lady of the Sonnets, 7,27,173
Daunce, Edward, *Brief Discourse on the Span-*
  ish State, 127
Davenant, William, 44
Davies, Archdeacon Richard, 38
Davies, John, of Hereford, 8
Davila, 103
Da Vinci, Leonardo, 140
Davison, William, 115
The Dead Man's Fortune, 325
Dee, Dr. John, 243
Defense of Military Profession by Goeffrey
  Gates, dedicated to Oxford, 105
De Feria,Conde, Spanish Ambassador,
  291
Del Bosco, Martin, 224
Demblon, Celestin, 78
De Medici, Catherine, 228,289
Deptford, 253
Derby, Henry Stanley, earl of, players of,
  302,305
Derby, William Stanley, earl of, 76,78
De Rebus Burgundicis by P. Heuterus, 51
Desdemona, 84,86,130
  and Anne Cecil de Vere, 102
  and Cassio,89
  and Emilia, 93
Des Trappes, 206
De Vega, Antonio, 216
De Vere, Anne Cecil, death of, 71. *See also*
  Cecil, Anne, Countess of Oxford.
De Vere, Bridget, 75
De Vere, Edward, earl of Oxford, 6. *See*
  also Oxford, earl of.
De Vere, Elizabeth, 76
De Vere, Henry, eighteenth earl of Ox-
  ford, 75
De Vere, Margery, Countess, Oxford's
  mother, 169
De Vere, Susan, Countess of Montgom-
  ery, 75,77
Devereux, Penelope, and Sidney, 119

Devonshire, earl of, 119
Dickens, Charles, 56
Dictionary of National Biography, 8
Dido, Queen of Carthage, 46,256
Dixie, Wolstan, 185
Doctor Faustus, 218,247,257,273,313
Don Carlos by Schiller, 307
Don John of Austria, 298
Douai, 298
Drake, Sir Francis, 114,215,224,230,309
Drury, Sir William, 311
DuBellay, Jean, 229
Dubourg, Anne, 290
Dugdale, Gilbert, 11
Dugdale, William, 74
Duke Cyprian of Castile, 306
Duke John of Gaunt, 306
Duke of Alva, 336
Duke of Anjou, 307
Duke of Norfolk, 102
Duke Philip of Burgundy, 50
Dumas, Alexandre, 30
Duttons, and Oxford's men, 13

E

Earl of Derby's players, 39
Earl of Leicester, 45 *See also* Leicester, Robert Dudley, earl of.
Earl of Oxford, purchase of Fisher's Folly by, 46
Earl of Oxford's company of players in Warwickshire, 45
Earl of Sheffield's players, 65
Earl of Worcester's players, 65,317
Early Shakespeare by A. Bronson Feldman, 6
Eastcheap, 65
Eccles, Mark, 296
Edinburgh Review, 271
Edward the Second, 237,247,273
Edward VI, 286
Egmont, Count, 338
Egypt, 95
Elba, 219
Eld, George, 143
El Greco, 285
Elizabeth, Queen, 101,103 *See also* Queen

Elizabeth.
Elizabethan Lords Chamberlain, Chambers on, 12
The Elizabethan Stage by E.K. Chambers, 10,45
Elsinore, 82
Emden, 222
Emerson, Ralph Waldo, 22
Emilia, 87,93
Empedocles, 248
Englands Helicon, 305
English Dramatic Companies by John Tucker Murray,11
English foreign policy, Conyers Read on, 184
Erasmus, 291,339
Essex, Robert Devereux, earl of, 114,129,154,165,189,211,214,233,238, 240,245,254,259,325
beheading of, 167,173
in Ireland, 167
Euphues his Censure to Philautus by Robert Greene, 214
Evans, Henry, 186
and the Children of Her Majesty's Chapel, 46
Every Man in his Humor by Ben Jonson, 129
The Execution of Justice by Lord Burghley, 204

F

The Faery Queen by Edmund Spenser, 164,317
Fair Em, The Miller's Daughter of Manchester, 124
Falstaff, 31
Family romance and the Stratford cult, 28
Farmer, John, 52
Feldman's view of *Othello* and that of Theodore Reik compared, 98-99
Ferbrand, William, 10,336
Ferdinand II, 286
Feuillerat, Albert, 7,176
Fiennes, Henry, earl of Lincoln, as "suborned informer" of Sonnet CXXV, 168
Finch, John, 176

First Folio of 1623, 34,39,75
Fisher's Folly, 46,65,115,299,317
Fitlen, Jack, 274
Fitton, Anne, 54
Fitton, Mary, 28,54,174
Fleay, Frederick, 272
Fleet Jail, 166
Fleetwood, William, 191
Flanders, 103
Flushing, 113,185, 189
Fontescue, Thomas, *The Forest* translated by, 197
Foole Upon Foole by Robert Armin, 10
Ford, John, 278
Forest of Arden, 66
Forest of Essex, 161
The Forest, Thomas Fontescue's translation of Mexia's Silva de varia lecciones, 197
Fort, J.A., *A Time-Scheme for Shakespeare's Sonnets* by, 146
Fortune theatre, 8
Fotheringhay, 204
"A Fourfold Meditation" and William Hall, 143
France, Anatole, 57
Francis II, 289
Franklin, 280
Freud, Sigmund, 6,25,58,77,181
   Civilization and Its Discontents by, 132
   The Interpretation of Dreams by, 149
   on Oxford as Shakespeare, 132
Freud's "secular distortion" and the Stratford cult, 29
Friar Bacon by Robert Greene, 316
Frizer, Ingram, 192,253,261
Furness, Howard, 17,56,81

G

Gager, William, Meleager by, 45
Garden of Wisdom by Richard Taverner, 290
Garnett, Father Henry, 139
Garrick, David, 25,32
   and the Stratford Jubilee of 1769, 18
Gascoigne, George, 312,339
   on Rowland York, 105
Gates, Geoffrey, *Defense of Military Profession* by, dedicated to Oxford, 105

Gazellus, 209
Genesis, 72
Genesis of Shakespeare Idolatry, 16
George Scanderbeg, 13
Gheeraerts, Marcus, 175
"Gentle Master William," Nashe's name for Oxford, 68
Gianibelli, Federigo, 184,220
Gilbert, Sir Humphrey, 105
Globe Theatre, 10
   property rights in, 76
Glorious Revolution, 31
Godes Peace and the Queenes by Norreys Jephson O'Conor, 13
Goethe, 58
Golding, Arthur, 100,122,172
   Oxford's uncle and translator of Ovid's *Metamorphoses*, 52
Gorboduc, 212
"Gorgon" by Gabriel Harvey, 255
Greece, Plato's, 140
Greene, Reverend Joseph, 74
Greene, Richard, in *Arden of Feversham*, 241,276
Greene, Robert, 43,64,69,194,213,229,276,315,327
   Card of Fancy by, dedicated to Oxford, 124
   Ciceronis Amor: Tullie's Love by, 238
   Comical History of Alphonsus, King of Aragon by, 216
   Farewell to Folly by, 124
   Friar Bacon by, 222
   Menaphon by, 235,276
   on Marlowe, 217
   on secret poets, 125
   Perimedes the Blacksmith by, 217
Greene's Groatsworth of Wit, 43,64,69
Greet in Gloucestershire, 50
Greenwich Palace, 184
Gregory XIV, 243
Grey, Lady Jane, 188,287
Grosart, Alexander, *The Works of Robert Armin* by, 20
Guilpin, Everard, *Skialetheia* by, 11
Guise, Henry Balafre, Duke of, 228,293
   portrayed by Marlowe, 230

H

Hackney, 10,12,15,143
Hall, William, as Mr. W.H., 143
Halliwell-Phillipps, James, 17,38,59
Hamlet, 7,68,81,159,162,321
  Ernest Jones on, 78,133
  Freud on, 132
  Hamlet's father's ghost, 82
  Will Shakspere as, 69
Hammon, Edward, 128
Handkerchief, Othello's mother's, 94,96
Harbone, William, ambassador to Constantinople, 197
Harrington, Sir John, 111,296
Harriot, Thomas, 250,275
Harris, Frank, on Othello, 94
  on the Dark Lady, 174
  The Man Shakespeare by, 18
Hart, Joan, 44,64
Harvey, Gabriel,
  6,66,142,162,222,255,296,299,328
  "Gorgon" by, 194,255
  "The Mirror of Tuscanism" by, 111
Harvey, Richard, 255
Harwich, 126
Hathaway, Anne, 25,37,62,67
Hatton, Sir Christopher, 107,118,187,204
Haywood, Mrs. Eliza, 279
Hekatompathia by Thomas Watson, 274
  echoes of in *The Spanish Tragedy*, 305
Helen of Troy, 221
Helliott, Nicholas, 245
Heminges, John, 39
Henri III, 228
Henry IV, 292
  part two, 39,95
Henry V, 171
Henry VI, 39,137,144,247
  part three, 43
Henry VII of Valois, 288
Henry VIII, 196
Henslowe, Philip, 42,208,234,245
Heraclitus, 248
Herbert, Philip, earl of Montgomery, 75
Herbert, William, earl of Pembroke, 75
Heretics of the Stratford cult, 33

"Hero and Leander" by Christopher Marlowe, 247,256
Herodotus, 290
Heuterus, P., *De Rebus Burgundicis* by, 51
Heywood, Thomas, 329
  Apology for Actors by, 302
  on *The Jew of Malta*, 225
Hidden Allusions in Shakespeare's Plays by
  Eva Turner Clark, 135,271
Hieronimo, 306,316
Hill, Nicholas, 172
Historia von D. Johann Fausten, 218
Historie of Love and Fortune, 312
History of Agamemnon and Ulysses, 47,186
History of Error, 54
The History of George Scanderbeg, 194
History of the Life and Reign of Richard III by
  Sir George Buck, 77
The History of Murderous Michael, 271
The History of the Two Valiant Knights, attributed to Thomas Preston, 294
Hoffman, Calvin, *The Murder of the Man Who Was Shakespeare* by, 182
Holinshed, Raphael, 240,271
Hog Lane, 234
Hohenlohe, Count, 117
Holmes, Oliver Wendell, 18
Holywell Priory, 231
Hopton, Sir Owen, 245,324
Horace, 155
Horneby, Thomas, 40
Hotman, Francois, *De Furoribus Gallicis* by, 230
Hotman, Jean, 233
Hotson, Leslie, 40
The Householder's Philosophy by Thomas Kyd, 320
Howard, Charles, later Lord Admiral, 194
Howard, Lord Henry, later earl of Northampton,
  77,104,106,139,157,189,245,261,304,310
  charge of pederasty against Oxford by, 149
Howard, Philip, earl of Arundel, author of "A Fourfold Meditation," 143
Howard, Thomas, Duke of Norfolk, 244

Huff, Snuff, and Ruff, 290
Huguenots, 101,209,228,231,289
Humphrey, Rowland, 234
Hunsdon, George Carey, Baron, 11
Hunsdon, Lord, 101
Huss, John, 209

I

Iago, 32,84,87,107,129
  and the promotion of Michael Cassio, 85
  as a cuckold, 87
  Rowland York as model for, 120
Ides of March, 81
India, 95
Induction to *The Taming of the Shrew,* 35
Innocent IX, 243
Instructions for the Wars, 229
The Interpretation of Dreams by Sigmund
    Freud, 149
Io and Zeus, 52
Ireland, 81,167
Irving, Washington, 18,20,22
  Tales of a Traveller by, 37
Islam, 198
Iscariot, Judas, 122
Is Shakespeare Dead? By Mark Twain, 135
Italy, 140
  Oxford in, 103,152
Ithamore, 227
Ive, Paul, 229
  The Practice of Fortification by, 211

J

Jack and the beanstalk, 26
Jacob, Edward, 269
James, Henry,25,30,135
  on the "Divine William," 19
  "The Birthplace" by, 19,133
Jeffes, Abel, 270,329
Jekels, Dr. Ludwig, 91
Jeronimo, 37,238
Jersey, Oxford's application for governor-
    ship of, 165
The Jew of Malta by Christopher Marlowe,
    111,222,224,227,233,246,254,257
Jews, Christians and, 227
Job, 70

Johnson, Samuel, 44
Jones, Ernest, 77,168,172
  on *Hamlet,* 78,133
Jones, Richard, 46,65,207,334
Jones, Rose, 143
Jonson, Ben, 7,61,63,160,255
  Bartholomew Fair by, 305
  Every Man in his Humor by, 129
  Sejanus by, 167
Joyce, James, 24
Jubilee of 1769 at Stratford, 18
Judas, 122
Julius Caesar, 31,81,201

K

Kempe, William, 14
  Nine Days Wonder by, 54
King Henri III, 103,228
King Henry VI, part three, 39
King James Stuart, 195,245,253,258
  and release of Southampton from the
    Tower, 167
  coronation of in the Sonnets, 167
  on Walsingham as a Machiavel, 207
King Lear, 7,96,107,128,165,179
King Lear's Fool, Armin as, 8
King of Denmark, 82
King Philip II of Spain,
    183,203,216,228,285,287,291,336
  attacked in plays, 318
King Sigismund, 209
King's Place, Hackney, 7,12,144
King's players, 63
Kitchen, Richard, 234
Kitely, 129
Knight, Joseph, 8
Knox, John, 188,290
Knyvet, Sir Thomas, 120,139,152,161,175
  Uncle of Anne Vavasor, 109-110
Kyd, Thomas,
    220,242,251,269,272,275,281,302,316,
    320

L

Lacy, John, 63
Laertes, 32
LaHarpe and French criticism of Shake-

speare, 32
Lambert, Edward, 50
Lancaster, 237
Last Will and Testament of Will
    Shakspere, 26
A Late Murder of the Son Upon the Mother,
    278
Latin Ode in praise of Oxford by Gabriel
    Harvey, 66
Lee,Sir Henry, 127,176
Lee, Sir Sidney, 47,59
    on Shakspere's love of litigations, 40
Lefranc, Abel, 78
Leicester, Robert Dudley, earl of,
    45,64,107,119,126,188,212,215,313
    and Oxford, 114
    as instigator of Rowland York, 110
    death of, 224
    marriage of, 114
Leicester's Commonwealth, 110,176,189
Leicester's players, 69
Lelius, 70
Lent, 82
Lenten entertainment in *Hamlet*, 82
Leslie, John, Bishop of Ross, 189
Libels on Oxford by Lord Henry Howard
    and Charles Arundel, 106
Lidgate the Bookman, 39
Lieutenant Vaughan, 338
The Life and Death of Heliogabalus, 217
A Life of William Shakespeare by Sir Sidney
    Lee, 40
*The Life Story of Edward de Vere as "William
    Shakespeare"* by Percy Allen, 55,135
Lillies That Fester by William Poel, 279
Lillo, George, 279
Lincoln, earl of, 13
Lonicer, Philip, *Chronicorum Tureicorum* by,
    111
Looney, John Thomas, 77
    and Freud, 181
    author of *Shakespeare Identified*, 135
Lord Admiral's players, 8,69,202,218,317
Lord Chamberlain, evidence for Oxford as
    the, 135
    uses of, 15
Lord Chamberlain's players,

6,10,116,138,336
    at the Curtain in 1599,11
Lord Chandos's players, 10
Lord Cobham, William Brooke, 15
Lord Cranborne, 15 *See also* Cecil, Robert.
Lord Great Chamberlain of England,
    Oxford as, 6,12,167
Lord Hunsdon, Henry Carey as the
    first,12
"Lord Oxford as Supervising Patron of
    Shakespeare's Theatrical Company"
    by Charles Wisner   Barrell, 15
Lord St. John, letter of to the Earl of Rut-
    land, 102
Lord Strange's players, 38,45,317
    in Stratford on Avon, 39
    played *Henry VI* at the Rose, 42
Love's Labour's Lost, 73,123,255,258
Lucan, 201
*Lucan's first book of the famous Civil War
    betwixt Pompey and Caesar*, Marlowe's
    translation of, 185
Lucentio the Florentine, 34
Lucy, Sir Thomas, 25,37,40
Lumley, Lord John, 52,298
Lyly, John, 12,176,186,194,312
    Campaspe, by 302
    Commendatory letter for Watson's *Pas-
        sionate Centurie* by, 302
    Midas by, 186,207,307
    Oxford's secretary, and the Children of
        Her Majesty's Chapel, 46

M

Macaulay, Thomas, 83
Macbeth, 31,57,132
Machiavelli, 228
Maecenas, 155
Malone Society Collections, Chambers on the
    Elizabethan Lords Chamberlain in, 12
Malvolio, 31
The Man Shakespeare by Frank Harris, on
    Othello, 94
Manners, Bridget, on Southampton, 157
Manners, Roger, 204
Manningham, John, 36
Manwood, Sir Roger, 235,240,246,276

Manwaring, 276
March 15,81
March 17,81
Marenzio, Luca, 325
Markham, Gervase, 163
Marlowe, Christopher,
    43,46,48,63,78,111,116,182,273,301,30
    9,313,315
  awarded Master of Arts degree, 212
  "Hero and Leander" by, 235
  The Massacre at Paris by, 230,238
  on the Apostle Paul, 188
  Tamburlaine by, 194
  The Tragedy of Dido, Queen of Carthage by,
    185
  translator of Lucan, 185
Marlowe, Thomas, 269
Marston, John, 160
  The Malcontent by, 39
  Scourge of Villainy by, 11
Marvell, Andrew, 150
Marxist view of Shakespeare, 23
Mary, Queen of Scots,
    102,189,195,203,205,244,311
  attacked in plays, 319
The Massacre at Paris, 230,238
Maunder, Henry, 252
Mauretania, 95
Measure for Measure, 7,16,24,77,132,197,323
Medici, Catherine de, government of in
    France, 101
Mehring, Franz, as defender of the original
    Marxist view of Shakespeare, 23
Meleager by William Gager, 45
Mendenhall, Dr. Thomas Corwin, 182
Mendoza, Bernardino de, Spanish ambas-
    sador, 300
  on English forces in the Netherlands,
    113
Menaphon by Robert Greene, 235,276,320
Menin, Josse van, 184
The Merchant of Venice,
    21,40,111,121,154,225
  Freud on, 132
Merchant Taylors' School, 303
Meres, Francis, 6,8,72,158,256,297
Metamorphoses by Ovid, 52

Midas by John Lyly, 186,207,307
A Midsummer Night's Dream,
    35,75,128,159,181
Milton, John, on Shakespeare, 32
Minola, Katherine and Bianca, 34
"The Mirror of Tuscanism" by Gabriel
    Harvey, 111,328
Mitchell, S. Weir, 56
Modern Language Notes, 8
Mondragon, 103
Montaigne, on the authorship of plays
    attributed to Terence, 70
Montaigne's *Essays*, 107
Montgomery, Count Gabriel, 288
Montgomery, earl of, 75
Montgomery, James, 30
The Monthly Magazine; or British Register, 44
"Moors" in England, Roman Catholics as,
    101
Morgan, Thomas, 189,192
Mortimer, 237
Mosbie, 274
Mr. W.H., William Hall as, 143
Mulcaster, Richard, 303
Munday, Anthony, 34,48
  Mirror of Mutability by, 300
Munday, Christopher, 48
Mundy, John, set a poem by Oxford to
    music, 170
The Murder of the Man Who Was Shakespeare
    by Calvin Hoffman, 182
Murray, John Tucker, *English Dramatic
    Companies* by, 11
Mycetes, 188
The Mystery of Mr. W.H. by B.R. Ward, 144

                        N

Nag's Head Inn, 296,328
Naps, John, 50
Nashe, Thomas,
    43,68,159,163,195,210,216,250,276,30
    3,328
  "Choice of Valentines" by, 162
  Christ's Tears Over Jerusalem by, 12
  "Epistle Dedicatorie" to *Strange News* by,
    68
  lost Latin elegy on Marlowe by, 256

Pierce Penniless by, 42
prefatory epistle to Greene's *Menaphon*
  by, 235,320
Strange News by, 141
Nasi, Joseph, 226
Navigations by Nicholas Nicholay, 209
Naxos, 226
Needham, Francis, 212
Netherlands, Spain in the, 101,112
New Place, Stratford, 74
Newgate Prison, 234,278,324
Nicholay, Nicholas, *Navigations* by, 209
Nichols, Allen, 245
Nine Days Wonder by Will Kempe, 54
Noel, Henry, dedicatee of works by Watson, 323
Norfolk, Thomas Howard, Duke of, 102,244
Norris, Edward, 117
Norris, John, 113
Norris, Rafe, ballad by, 335
Norris, Sir John, 230
North Sea, 152
Northbrooke, John, 335
Northampton, Henry Howard, earl of, 77,245
Northumberland, Henry Percy, earl of, 315
Norton Folgate, 46,231

O

Ockland, Christopher, 323
O'Conor, Norreys Jephson, *Godes Peace and the Queenes* by, 13,168
Oedipus complex, and the Stratford cult, 27
Old Knowell, 129
Oliphant, E.H. 280
Ophelia, 166
Orange, Prince William of, 188,298
Orlando Furioso, by Ariosto, 111,209
Orlando Innamorata, 111
Orrell, George, 240,260,277,326
Orthodoxy, Shakespearean, 33
Osborne, Francis, *Traditional Memoirs of the Reigns of Queen Elizabeth and King James I* by, 77

Ostend, 185,221
Otelle, old French for a kind of spear, 127
Othello, 7,57,162
  and Oxford's bragging, 103
  as a study of jealousy, 83
  Biblical imagery in, 12
  Frank Harris on, 94
  Inspiration for writing, 123
  sources of plot of, 111
  theatrical metaphors in, 115
Othello, and Iago as two parts of a single personality, 92
  and the military life, 85
Othello's father, 96
Othello's father-in-law, 83
Othello's mother, 94,96
Outline of Psychoanalysis by Sigmund Freud, 134
Ouvry, Frederic, 8
Ovid, *Amores* by, 274
  Marlowe's translation of, 185
Ovid's *Metamorphoses*, 52
Oxford, Anne Cecil de Vere, Countess of, 53. *See also* Cecil, Anne.
Oxford, Edward de Vere, seventeenth earl of, 6,12,64,100,113,186,242,281,299,307,311,328
  an acrostic by, 334
  and attempt to put Hastings on the throne, 168
  and Fisher's Folly, 193
  and his father's death, 122
  and his wife, 109
  and the boy players of, 47
  and the tennis court quarrel with Sidney, 118
  and *Willobie his Avisa*, 141
  and Will Shakspere, 69
  annual grant to, 116
  as patron, 6,246
  Boar as nickname of, 121
  death of, 73
  praised in *The Art of English* Poesie, 49
  reputation of, 134
  rumor of the death of in 1591, 72
  Spenser's dedicatory sonnet to, 317

Turk as nickname of, 121
Oxford, Elizabeth Trentham de Vere,
    Countess of, 144,334
Oxford, Henry de Vere, eighteenth earl of,
    75,138
Oxford House by London Stone, 318
Oxford portrait as Hampton Court Por-
    trait of Shakespeare, 113
Oxford stages entertainment for Queen
    Elizabeth in Warwickshire, 68
Oxford's birth date, 67
Oxford's bragging and *Othello,* 103
Oxford's coat of arms, star in and the
    sonnets, 150
Oxford's companies of players, 46,65, 69,
    194
Oxford's lameness, 120
Oxford's marital troubles, 103
Oxford's travels, 103
Oxford University, 45

P

Padua, 35,106
Paracelsus, Oxford and, 107
Padre de Famiglia by Tasso, translated by
    Thomas Kyd, 320
Paget, Charles, 189
Papists, 291
Palladis Tamia by Francis Meres, 158
Paris, 109,296
Passionate Centurie of Love by Thomas Wat-
    son, 296
    echoes of in *The Spanish Tragedy,* 305
The Passionate Pilgrim, 177
Patroclus, Southampton as, 155
Peele, George, 43,185,214,230,312
    "Polyhymnia" by echoes *Othello,* 127
    sister Isabel of, 67
Pembroke, earl of, 75
Pembroke, Henry Herbert, earl of, 206
    the company of players of, 237
Pembroke, Mary Herbert, Countess of,
    246
Penry, John, 253
Pericles, 6
Perimedes the Blacksmith by Robert Greene,
    217

*Personal Clues in Shakespeare Poems and Son-
    nets* by Gerald H. Rendall, 135
Persons, Robert, 259
Petruchio of Verona, 34
Peyton, Sir John, Lieutenant of the Tower,
    13,168
Phelippes, Thomas, 205
Philip, King of Spain, and Pope Sixtus V,
    112
Phillips, Gerald, 142
Phillips, Sir Richard, 44,64
The Phoenix Nest, 305
Phrenology, 57
Pilia-Borza, 228,233,274
    Nicholas Skeres and, 257
Pistol, 95
Plutarch, life of Alexander by, 335
Poel, William, 279
Poet, associations of the term among
    Elizabethan aristocrats, 70
Pole, Cardinal, 291
Poley, Robert,
    190,192,195,203,205,215,234,245,253,
    257
    and the Scottish court, 259
Polonius, 7,32,166
    acting the part of Caesar, 82
Poole, John, 235
Pope, Alexander, on the Stratford creed,
    24
Pope Sixtus V, 184,228
    And King Philip of Spain, 112
Portugal, 305
The Practice of Fortification by Paul Ive, 211
The Practice of the New and Old Physic by Dr.
    George Baker, 172
Preston, Thomas, 289
    ballads attributed to, 294
Prince Hal, 95
Prince of Darkness, Oxford charged with
    conjuring 106
Prince of Orange, 337
    murder of the, 314
Prince of Parma, 184,223
    in *Doctor Faustus,* 219
Proctor, John, *The Fall of the Late Arian* by,
    243

Publications of the Modern Language Association, 141
Puckering, Sir John, 275,316
Puritan government of the City of London, 14

Q

Queen Elizabeth,
    101,173,183,195,204,216,288,299,307
annual grant to Oxford of, 116
as a target of assassins, 188
company of players of, 193
death of, 166
on plays, 292
reaction of to Anne Vavasor's giving
    birth, 108
visit to Warwickshire of, 68
Queen Mary of Scotland, 102
Queen Mary Tudor, 291
Queen Titania, 181
Quips Upon Questions, 8,15

R

Ralegh, Sir Walter,
    110,173,221,238,250,258,275
History of the World by, 215
on Oxford's character, 152
Ramekins Castle, 113,185
Ramus, Peter, 231
The Rape of Lucrece, 72,136,140
dedication of, 150
Raptus Helenae, 208
Ratsey's Ghost, 73
Read, Conyers, on English foreign policy,
    184
Reik, Theodore, 98
Reik's view of *Othello* and Feldman's compared, 98-99
Relics, Stratfordian, 18
Religious worship of popular image of
    Shakespeare, 16
Rendall, Gerald, H. 78
The Restorer of the French Estate, 229
The Return from Parnassus, 210
Rheims, 211
Rhetoric, opposition to in the Sonnets,
    160

Rhine, 219
Ribner, Irving, 51
Rich, Lady Penelope, 233
Richard II, 62
Richard III, 132
Richardson, John, 177
Robertson, John M., 22,59
Roderigo, 87,95,107,116
Roman Catholics, 101
Rome, 95
Romeo, 170
Romeo and Juliet,
    7,11,127,141,159,176,180,225
the Nurse in, 173
The Rose Theatre, 8,11,14208,245
Rowe, Nicholas, biographer of Shakspere,
    38,62,69
Rowse, A.L., 262
Roxburghe Collection, 279
Roydon, Matthew, 191,253,312
Rudolph, Holy Roman Emperor, 196
Russia, 176
Rutland, earl of, 78,102

S

Sachs, Hanns, 63,74,79
on Freud's analysis of Shakespeare, 132
on Freud's rejection of the Stratford
    myth, 24
Sackville, Thomas, Lord Buckhurst, 212
Sadler, Hamnet and Judith, 62
Sagittary Inn, 84, 120
Sanders, Nicholas, 231
Sandys, William, 57
Saunders, Matthew, dedicatee of "A Fourfold Meditation," 144
Scheldt river, 184
Schenck, Martin, 219
Schick, J. 304
Scipio, 70
The Scourge of Folly by John Davies of Hereford, 8
Scourge of Villainy by John Marston, 11
Scythians, 96,107
Second Part of Tarlton's Jests, 10
Sejanus by Ben Jonson, 168
Senate, Venetian, 84

orders Othello home, 93
Seneca, Watson and, 297
The Seven Deadly Sins, 39
The Seventeenth Earl of Oxford by B.M.
    Ward, 12,52,135
Seymour family, 286
Shakebag, 276
Shakespeare and the Universities by F.S.
    Boas, 45
Shakespeare authorship claimants, 151
Shakespeare, Chapman, and Thomas More by
    Arthur Acheson, 45
Shakespeare, Edmund, 67
Shakespeare Facts and Problems by E.K.
    Chambers, 44
Shakespeare Fellowship Quarterly, 142
Shakespeare Identified by J. Thomas
    Looney, 135
Shakespeare Improved by Hazelton Spencer,
    32
The Shakespeare Industry by Brown and
    Fearon, 17
Shakespeare orthodoxy, 33
Shake-speare's Sonnets, 7,143
Shakespeare's Theater by Ashley H.
    Thorndike, 12
Shakespearian Playhouses by Joseph Quincy
    Adams, 8
Shakspere, John, 50,62,74
Shakspere, Thomas, 62
Shakspere, Walter, 62
Shakspere, William, 37
  death of, 74
  hanged in 1248, 62
Sharpe, Ella Freeman, 179
Sheffield's players, 45
The Shepherd's Calendar by Edmund
    Spenser, 66,164,276
"Shepherd Tonie," the lyrics of, 48
Shoreditch, 64
Shrewsbury, earl of, 228
Sidney, Lady Frances, 324
Sidney, Sir Philip,
    105,107,114,116,169,189,307,311
  and Anne Cecil, 119
  and Oxford, 111
  and the tennis court quarrel with Ox-
    ford, 118
  Arcadia by, 118
  as model for Michael Cassio, 119
  death of, 117
  funeral for, 206
  response to *Leicester's Commonwealth* by,
    111
Sidney, Sir Robert, 72
Sincler, John, 39,41
Singer, John, 8
Sinklo, 39
Sitwell, Edith, 222
Skeres, Nicholas, 191,233,253,255,257
Skialetheia By Guilpin, 11
Sluys, English defense of, 213
Sly, Christopher or Kit, 34
  modeled on Will Shakspere, 39
Smirnov, A. and his Russian Communist
    view of Shakespeare, 23
Smith, J.M., 44
Smithfield, 64
Sodomy, 107
Soliman, 301
Soliman and Perseda, 272,300,312,325
Sonnet CVI, praise of Spenser's *Faery Queen*
    in, 164
Sonnets, Shakespeare's, 76
  as less personal than Shakespeare's plays,
    179
Southampton, Henry Wriothesley, earl of,
    72,136,140,154
  as a soldier, 165
  release of from the Tower by King James,
    167
Southwark, 208
Southwell, Francis, 107,310
Southwell, Robert, An Humble Supplica-
    tion to Her Majesty by, 205
Spain, as defender of Christendom, 284
  in the Netherlands, 112,183
Spanish Armada, 126
Spanish drama, golden age of, 284
Spanish Inquisition, 286
The Spanish Masquerado by Robert Greenne,
    229
The Spanish Tragedy,
    37,46,115,203,227,238,270,302,308,325

echoes of *Hekatompathia* in, 305
Spencer, Hazelton, 22
Shakespeare Improved by, 32
Spenser, Edmund, 66,142,164,276,300,317
  dedicatory sonnet to the earl of Oxford
    by, 164
  "Tears of the Muses" by, 71
Spoyle of Antwerp by George Gascoigne,
    339
Stafford, Sir Edward, 188,213
Stafford, William, 206
Stanley, Ferdinando, Lord Strange, death
    of, 128
Stanley, William, earl of Derby, 76,128,207
  See also Derby.
Steele, Richard, 31
St. John, Lord, 67,102
St. Patrick's Day, 81
Stoke Newington, 12,138
Stow, John, 215
  Survey of London by, 46
Strachey, James, translator of Freud, 134
Strange, Lord, the players of, 124,308
Stratford, 66
Stratford cult, 16
  the id and, 25
Stringer, Philip, 136
Stuart, King James, 73,192
Stuart, Mary, Queen of Scots, 289 *See also*
    Queen of Scots.
Stubbe, John, 307
"Stump," the nickname of Lieutenant
    Vaughan, 338
Sturmius, John, 112
Style of the sonnets compared with that of
    contemporaries, 160
Subtle Shift, 294
Sudeley Castle, 11
Sultan Amurath, 196
Survey of London by John Stow, 46
Sussex, Thomas Radcliffe, earl of, 101
  the players of, 272
Swift, Anne, wife of Thomas Watson, 234,
    315
Swift, Hugo, 234,240,277,324,326
Swinburne, Algernon, 271,280
Symonds, John Addington, 280

Symons, John, and the earl of Oxford's
    players, 45

T

Talbot, Thomas Nashe on, 42
Tallis, Thomas, and the "Willow song"
    Desdemona heard, 112
Tamburlaine the Great,
    188,194,197,202,208,211,214,216,224,
    227,255,273
The Taming of a Shrew, 34
The Taming of the Shrew,
    34,39,47,55,116,137,159
  date of composition of the Induction to,
    42,53
Tarlton, Richard, 193,203,224
Taverner, Richard, *Garden of Wisdom* by,
    290
Tears of Fancy, 274,296
"Tears of the Muses" by Edmund
    Spenser, 71,142,164
The Tempest, 24,63,132
Tenor by John Mundy, 170
Tercentenary Festival of Shakespeare at
    Stratford, 17
Terence, 70
The Theatre, James Burbage's,
    11,47,64,231
Thorndike, Ashley H., *Shakespeare's Theater*
    by, 12
Thorpe, Thomas, 143
Throckmorton plot, Charles Arundel and
    the, 109
Tiepolo, Paolo, 291
Timoclea at the Siege of Thebes, 335
Timon of Athens, 16,22,40
Titania, 72
Titus Andronicus, 137,247
Touchstone, 15,257
  Armin as, 8
The Tragedy of Dido, Queen of Carthage, 185
Trentham, Elizabeth, Countess of Oxford,
    13,71,144,334
The Troublesome Reign of King John, 214
*The True Difference Between Christian Subjec-
    tion and Unchristian Rebellion* by Bilson,
    187

True Discourse on the Poisoning of Thomas Caldwell by Gilbert Dugdale, 11
"Truth" in the sonnets as a pun, 147
Tudor, Queen Mary, 287
Turk, Queen Elizabeth's nickname for Oxford, 121
Turkey, 196
Turkey and Spain, 285
Turkish Affairs by Andrew Cambine, 196
Turks, 86,103
Twain, Mark, 22
  Is Shakespeare Dead? By, 135
  on the fabrication of Shakespeare biographies, 18
Twelfth Night, 36
Twyne, Thomas, *The Breviary of Britain* by, dedicated to Oxford, 102
The Two Gentlemen of Verona, 137
Tyrone, 167
Tyrrel, Anthony, 205
Tyrrell, Charles, 169

U

Udall, Nicholas, 298
Ulisses upon Ajax, 296,310
Ulysses, by James Joyce, the treatment of Shakespeare in, 29
Unton, Sir Henry, 244
Urry, Dr. William, researches of into Marlowe's family, 262

V

Valdes, 103
Valla, Lorenzo, 290
Vandermast, Jacques, 223
Van Ende, Cornelius, 337
Variorum edition of Shakespeare's works, 17,81
Vaughan, Lieutenant, 338
Vaughan, William, 253
  The Golden Grove by, 255
Vavasor, Anne, 7,55,66,108,111,114,139,152,157,175,311
Vavasor, Thomas, 176
Venice, 106
  Oxford in, 103

rulers of 83
the Duke of, 85
Venus and Adonis, 7,72,136,138,145,147,155
Venus and Cyprus, 86
Vere, Edward de, earl of Oxford, 64 *See also* De Vere and Oxford.
Vere, Elizabeth, and Southampton, 139
  Oxford's daughter and Derby's wife, 128
Vere, Sir Edward, 176
Vere, Sir Francis, 128,165,213
  Oxford's cousin, 115
Vere, Sir Horace, 128,165
Vernon, Elizabeth, and Southampton, 158,162,166
Verses of Praise and Joy, 316
Viscount Bulbec, the crest of Oxford as, 66,142
Voltaire and French criticism of Shakespeare, 32
Vox Graculi or Jack Dawes Prognostication, 65

W

Walsingham, Audrey, wife of Sir Thomas, 258
Walsingham, Sir Francis, 107,109,113,116,124,189,197,203,205, 212,309,319
  death of, 243
Walsingham, Sir Thomas, 190,203,215,252,262,296,309
  dedicatee of Marlowe's "Hero and Leander," 191
  with Watson in Paris, 312
Ward, Adolphus W., 180
Ward, B.M., *The Seventeenth Earl of Oxford* by, 6,12,52,135
Ward, Colonel B.R., 318
  The Mystery of Mr. W.H. by, 144
Ward, Reverend John, Vicar of Stratford, 74
Wardmote Book, 271
A Warning for Fair Women, 278
Warwick, earl of, 104
Warwickshire, 35
  Queen Elizabeth's visit to, 68

Watson, Elizabeth, 299
Watson, John, 299
Watson, Thomas,
    37,46,190,193,208,217,234,238,240,25
    4,274,278
  Amyntas by, 323
  Compendium
  Memoriae Localis by, 323
  death of, 246
  Latin elegy on Sir Francis Walsingham
    by, 321
  Madrigals Englished by, 325
  Nashe on, 324
  The Tears of Fancy by, 141
The Weakest Goeth to the Wall, 13
Webbe, William, 6
Webster, John, 278
"Were I a King" by Oxford, 169
Wertham, Frederick, 168
Westcott, Sebastian, 289
Westminster Abbey, burial place of Anne
    Cecil de Vere, Countess of Oxford,
    127
Whately, Anne, of Temple Grafton, 26,68
Whetstone, George, *The English Mirror* by,
    197
  Heptameron of Civil Discourses by, 323
  on Sidney's death, 117
  Promos and Cassandra by, 197
White, Edward, 269,279,329
Whitman, Walt, 22,79
Whittington, Dick, and his cat, 26
Whyte, Roland, 72
Wild, Stephen, 324
William of Orange, Prince, 299
Williams, Sir Roger, 213,230
"William Wit, Wit's Will, or Will's Wit;
    Choose you Whether," 71
"Willie" in *The Shepherd's Calendar*, 66
Willobie his Avisa, 140,151
  And the earl of Oxford, 141
Willoughby, Peregrine Bertie, Lord,
    116,225,230
Wilmcote, 50
Wilson, Dr. Thomas, 298
Wincot, 36,50
Winwood, Sir Ralph, 232

Wit's Treasury by Francis Meres, 8
Wittenberg, 219
Wivenhoe, Essex, 152
Wolf, John, 185
  Printer of Watson's Latin *Antigone*, 311
Wood, Robert, 240,277
Woodleff, Drew, 254
Worcester, Bishop of, 62
Worcester, earl of, the players of,
    13,45,115,194
Wordsworth, William, 83
The Works of Robert Armin, Actor, by Alex-
    ander Grosart, 10
Wotton, Sir Henry, 261,300
Wright, John, 222
Wright, Thomas, history of Essex by, 77
Wriothesley, Henry, earl of Southampton,
    136. *See also* Southampton.

                    Y

Yarington, Robert, 278
York, Edward, 110
  brother of Rowland and servant of the
    earl of Leicester, 105
York, Rowland, 107,110,115,207
  as model for Iago, 104,120
  betrays Zutphen to Spain, 120
The Yorkshire Tragedy, 278
Young, Henry, 251
Yver, Jacques, *Printemps d'Iver* by, 300

                    Z

Zenocrate, 202,209
Ziegler, Wilbur, 182
Zutphen, Rowland York's betrayal of to
    Spain, 120